Robert W. Ottman

North Texas State University

ELEMENTARY HARMONY

Theory and Practice

THIRD EDITION

Prentice-Hall, Inc., Englewood Cliffs, New Jersey 07632

Library of Congress Cataloging in Publication Data

Ottman, Robert W.
Elementary harmony.

Includes index.
1. Harmony. I. Title.
MT50.0924 1983 781.3 82-20541
ISBN 0-13-257436-5

Editorial/production supervision and interior design: Peter Roberts
Manufacturing buyer: Raymond Keating

Printed in the United States of America

10 9 8 7 6 5 4 3 2

ISBN 0-13-257436-5

Prentice-Hall International, Inc., *London*
Prentice-Hall of Australia Pty. Limited, *Sydney*
Editora Prentice-Hall do Brasil, Ltda, *Rio de Janeiro*
Prentice-Hall Canada Inc., *Toronto*
Prentice-Hall of India Private Limited, *New Delhi*
Prentice-Hall of Japan, Inc., *Tokyo*
Prentice-Hall of Southeast Asia Pte. Ltd., *Singapore*
Whitehall Books Limited, *Wellington, New Zealand*

Contents

Preface

Elementary Harmony: Theory and Practice and its companion volume, *Advanced Harmony: Theory and Practice,* together with their accompanying workbooks, are designed to meet the needs of college music courses in basic music theory. These include not only studies in analysis and written harmony, but also a complete course of instruction in ear training and keyboard harmony. Studies in sight singing are correlated throughout with the author's *Music for Sight Singing,* second edition (Prentice-Hall, Inc., 1967) and *More Music for Sight Singing* (Prentice-Hall, Inc., 1981). The subject matter of each chapter and its application to each of these areas of instruction are so presented that they can be taught successfully either in the correlated class (all areas in one class), or in several classes, each devoted to one or more of these areas.

The present third edition of *Elementary Harmony* maintains the format and general pedagogical procedures that have characterized the usefulness of the text's previous editions. Users of these earlier editions will find a number of features new to the present edition:

(1) Opportunity for students to work in analysis of music scores beginning in the opening chapters, through preliminary studies of nonharmonic tones and seventh chords along with the principal studies of triads.

(2) Extensive revisions, with additional materials, in the areas of melody (including the medieval modes), nonharmonic tones and harmonic sequence.

(3) Expansion of the course in keyboard harmony through studies preparatory to keyboard harmonization of melodies by the use of "lead sheet" or "fake book" symbols, as commonly used in music education and in popular music.

(4) Inclusion of examples from music scores for analysis, in addition to references to outside sources.

(5) A complete survey of all secondary dominant chords.

(6) Separate articles, included within chapters, of peripheral theoretical and historical interest to the subject matter of the chapter and of comparisons with pre-seventeenth century and post-nineteenth century music styles.

The pedagogical and musical effectiveness of these texts is a result of many years of experimentation and use in the theory classes of North Texas State University. Many thanks are due to the thousands of undergraduate students and to the many graduate theory students and teaching fellows whose reactions have helped shape the format and contents of the texts. Particular thanks for professional criticism are due to colleagues including Gene Cho, Paul Dworak, William Gardner, Joàn Groom-Thronton, Rosemary Killam, Frank Mainous, Alan Richardson and Benito Rivera. A special note of thanks is due to Peter Roberts of Prentice-Hall, Inc. for his invaluable assistance both in editing the manuscript and in managing the intricacies of the publication of the texts throughout the period of their production.

ROBERT W. OTTMAN

CHAPTER 1

Starting at the Beginning: The Fundamentals of Music Theory

For many college-level students, most of this chapter will constitute a review of basic materials already learned from previous musical experiences. More detailed study of most of this material, including drills and assignments, can be found in each of two texts designed to precede Elementary Harmony. *They are 1)* Rudiments of Music, *(Prentice-Hall, Inc., 1970) and 2)* Programmed Rudiments of Music, *(Prentice-Hall, Inc., 1979), both by Robert W. Ottman and Frank D. Mainous.*

When we hear a given music sound, we can react to it in four different ways simultaneously: 1) by perceiving how high or how low it is (*pitch*); 2) how long it is held (*duration*); 3) what is its quality (that is, is the sound that of a piano, an oboe, a voice, etc.—*timbre*); and 4) how loud or how soft it is (*intensity*). But since we seldom listen to a single sound, we are also interested in how pitches are grouped, how durations are grouped, and how these are combined with timbres and intensities to create a musical composition. To accomplish this, we must first know the symbols used to represent the four parameters of musical sound in the preceding list, how they are placed on paper, and how to interpret them.

The material of this chapter covers elementary considerations in the areas of pitch and duration. The timbre of a musical sound is a function of acoustics (see Appendix 3, *Elementary Acoustics*). Terms indicating intensity and other aspects of music performance, such as tempo, can be found in the Appendix of each of the Rudiments texts listed at the head of this chapter, as well as in general music dictionaries and dictionaries of musical terms.

For the student of harmony, it is particularly important that he be knowledgeable in keys, key signatures, and scale spellings to the extent that he can do the following with absolute accuracy and without hesitation:

1. Name both the major and minor key for any given key signature.
2. State the number of sharps or flats in the signature of a given key, and spell these accidentals in their correct order on the staff.
3. Spell any major scale and the three forms of any minor scale, ascending and descending.

4. Sing a major scale and each of the three forms of the minor scale on "la," or sing any of these scales in any key with letter names when the name of the key is given.

Pitch

1. Pitch Names. Pitches are named with the first seven letters of the alphabet, A B C D E F G.

2. Staff The staff (plural, *staves*) consists of five lines and four spaces.

3. G Clef 𝄞. When placed on the staff, the line encircled by the lower loop of the clef sign is designated G. This clef sign is commonly used to designate the second line as G, and in this position it is known as a *treble clef.*

4. F Clef 𝄢. When placed on the staff, the line between the dots is designated F. This clef commonly designates the fourth line as F, and in this position it is known as a *bass clef.*

5.[1] *Staff Spellings.* Adjacent lines and spaces use adjacent pitch names from the alphabet.

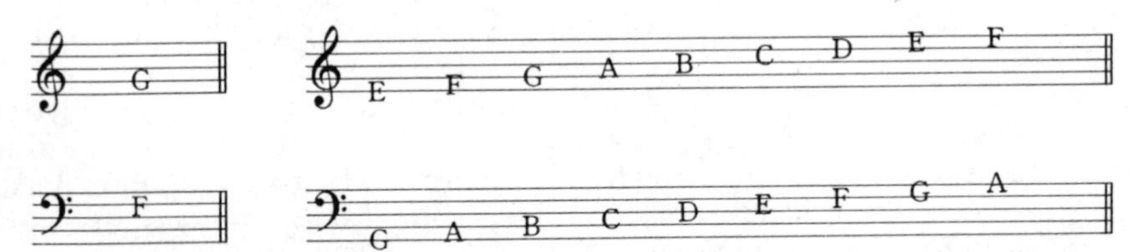

6. Ledger (Leger) Lines and Spaces. Ledger lines are short lines written above or below the staff for the purpose of extending the staff. Spaces between ledger lines are ledger spaces.

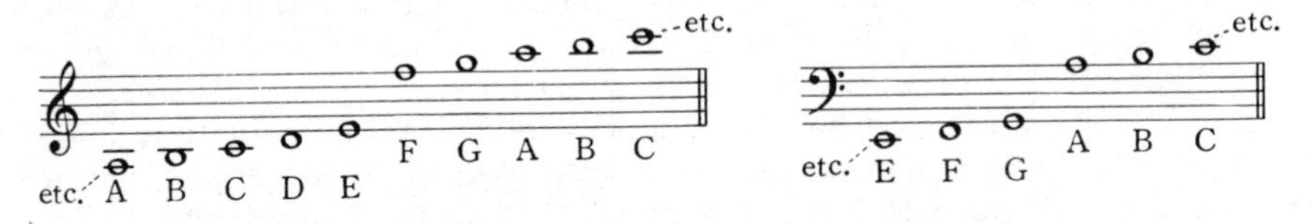

7. Great Staff (Grand Staff). The treble and bass clefs joined together constitute the great staff.

[1]The C clefs and their staff spellings are presented in Chapter 7.

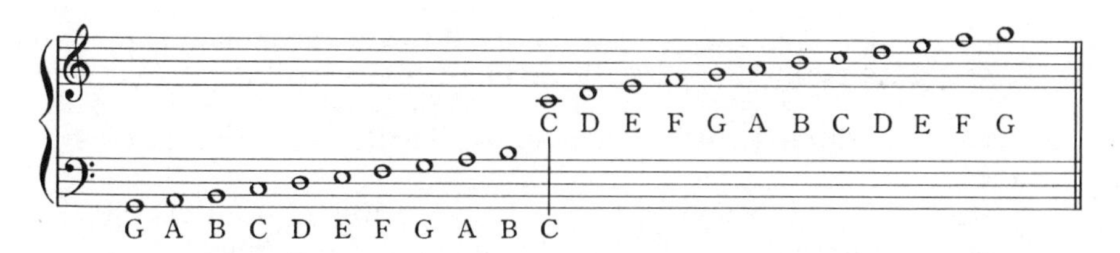

8. Half Steps and Whole Steps. Two pitches from the musical alphabet or from the piano keyboard as close together as possible constitute a half step. In the musical alphabet, E–F and B–C are half steps, since no pitch sound is found between them. Other adjacent pairs of letter names are whole steps (two half steps). On the keyboard, any two adjacent keys sound a half step.

9. Accidentals (Chromatics).

A *sharp* (♯) raises the pitch of a tone one half step. (C is one half step higher than C.)

A *flat* (♭) lowers the pitch of a tone one half step.

A *double sharp* (𝄪) raises the pitch of a tone a whole step.

A *double flat* (♭♭) lowers the pitch of a tone a whole step.

A *natural* (♮) cancels out a previously used accidental.

The relative pitch relationships of the accidentals are

(low) 𝄫 ♭ ♮ ♯ 𝄪 (high)

10. The Keyboard. Names of the keys on the piano can be seen in the figure below.

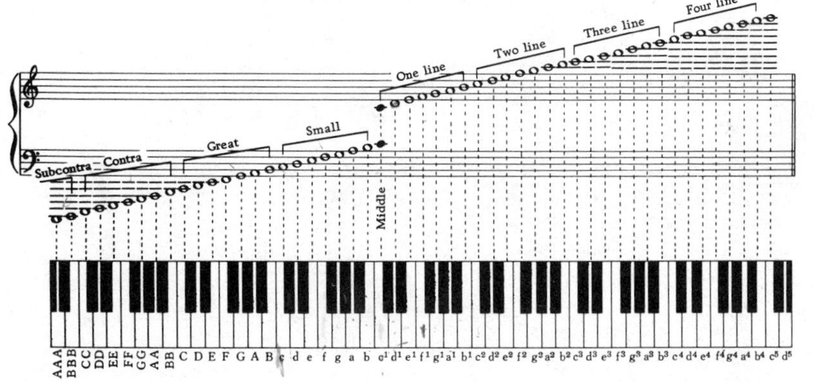

11. Octave Registers. This is a system in which identical pitch names in various octave positions may be differentiated from each other. Middle C is designated c^1 (read "one-line C"). Each pitch is designated in the figure above. (For other systems of pitch differentiation, see "Pitch names" in *Harvard Dictionary of Music.*)

12. Scales. A scale is a series of pitches using, in order, the seven letter names of the musical alphabet, beginning on any one letter.

Major Scale. A series of eight tones (8 being the pitch-name repetition of 1) in which the relationship between successive tones is as follows (1 = whole step, ½ = half step):

Scale tones	1		2		3		4		5		6		7		8
Step size		1		1		½		1		1		1		½	

Using C on the keyboard as 1, the major scale makes use of the white keys exclusively.

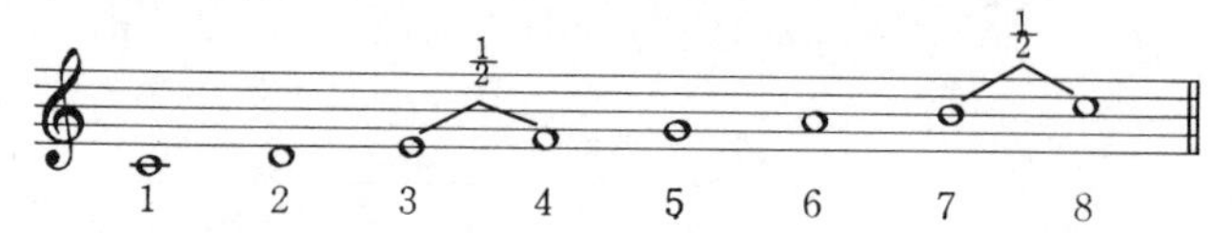

When beginning the major scale on any other letter name, it is necessary to add accidentals to maintain the relationship of half steps and whole steps.

Minor Scales. A series of eight tones in which the relationship between successive tones differs from that of the major scale. There are three forms of minor scales.

a) Pure (natural) Minor Scale. The relationship between successive tones is as follows:

Scale tones	1		2		3		4		5		6		7		8
Step size		1		½		1		1		½		1		1	

The following are examples of the pure minor scale starting on A, requiring no accidentals, and on G, requiring two flats.

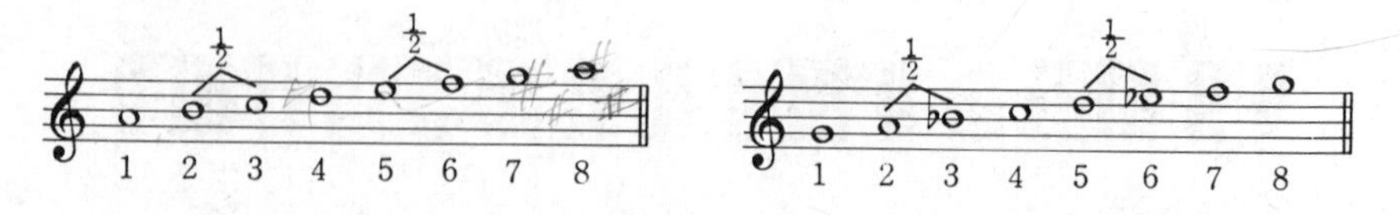

b) Harmonic Minor Scale. The harmonic form of the minor scale is similar to the pure form, with the seventh scale degree raised one half step. This results in a distance of 1 ½ steps between 6 and 7 and a half step between 7 and 8.

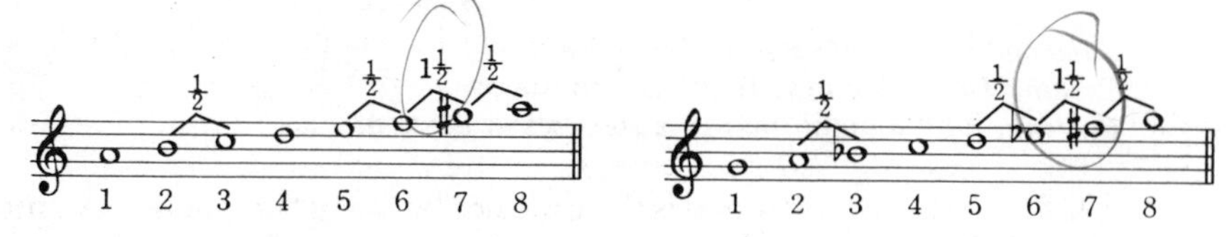

c) Melodic Minor Scale. Ascending only, the melodic form of the minor scale is similar to the pure form with the sixth and seventh degrees each raised one half step.

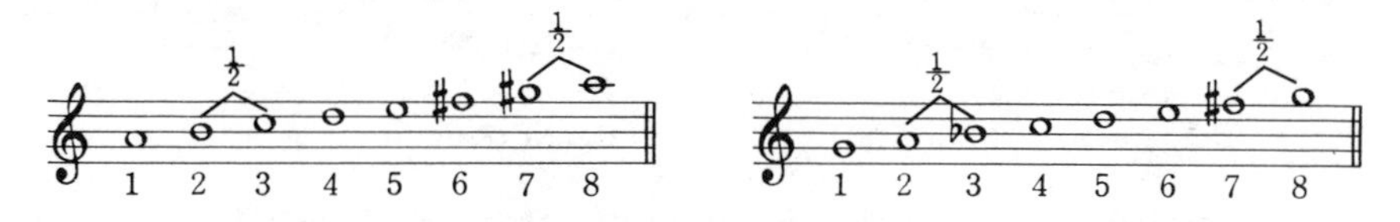

The descending form of the melodic minor scale is identical to that of the pure minor scale.

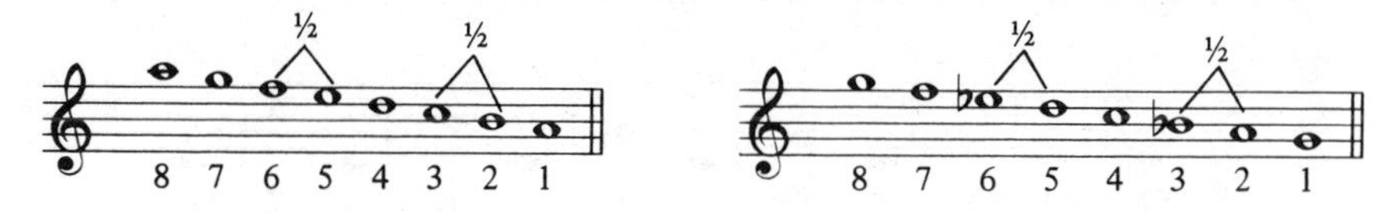

Chromatic Scale. A scale consisting exclusively of half steps.

C C♯ D D♯ E F F♯ G G♯ A A♯ B C	ascending
C B B♭ A A♭ G G♭ F E E♭ D D♭ C	descending

13. Scale Degree Names

Scale degree	*Name: major key*	*Scale degree*	*Name: minor key*
1	Tonic	1	Tonic
2	Supertonic	2	Supertonic
3	Mediant	3	Mediant
4	Subdominant	4	Subdominant
5	Dominant	5	Dominant
6	Submediant	6	Submediant
7	Leading tone	♯6	Raised submediant
		7	Subtonic
		♯7	Leading tone

(♯6 and ♯7 mean raised sixth scale step and raised seventh scale step.)

The following are the meanings of the scale degree names:

Tonic: The tone that identifies the key
Dominant: The tone next in importance to the tonic, located a fifth[2] above the tonic
Subdominant: The tone a fifth[2] below the tonic
Mediant: The tone halfway between tonic and dominant
Submediant: The tone halfway between tonic and subdominant

[2]See section 14 immediately following.

Supertonic: The tone a step above the tonic
Leading Tone: The tone that leads to the tonic
Subtonic: The tone, in minor, a step below the tonic

14. Intervals. An interval is the distance between two pitches. An interval is identified by the number of letter names it encompasses. For example, from C up to E is a third because three letter names (C, D, and E) are encompassed.

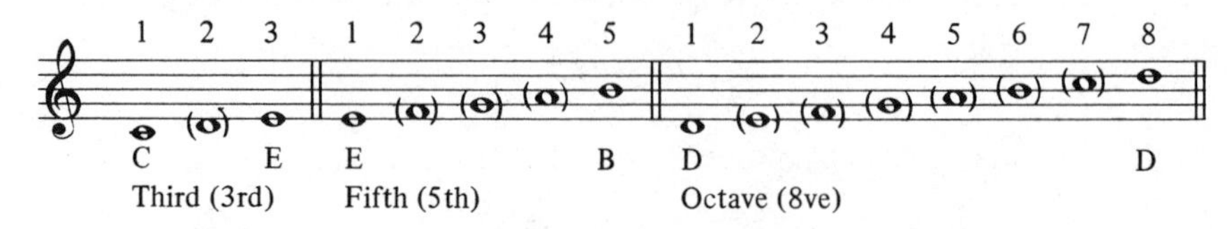

Interval names are also qualified by the terms *major* (M), *minor* (m), *diminished* (d), and *augmented* (A).

Ascending major and perfect intervals may be calculated by considering the lower note of the interval as the tonic of a major scale.

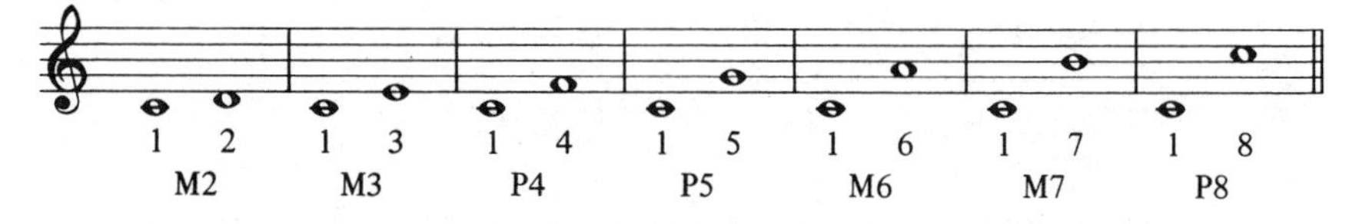

Minor intervals are one half step smaller than major intervals.

Diminished intervals are one half step smaller than minor or perfect intervals.

Augmented intervals are one half step larger than major or perfect intervals.

The diminished fifth (d5) and the augmented fourth (A4) are also identified by the term *tritone* (see Chapter 12).

In addition, there are two other intervals, the *perfect prime* (PP), no distance between pitches, and the *augmented prime* (AP), a half step in which both pitches use the same letter name.

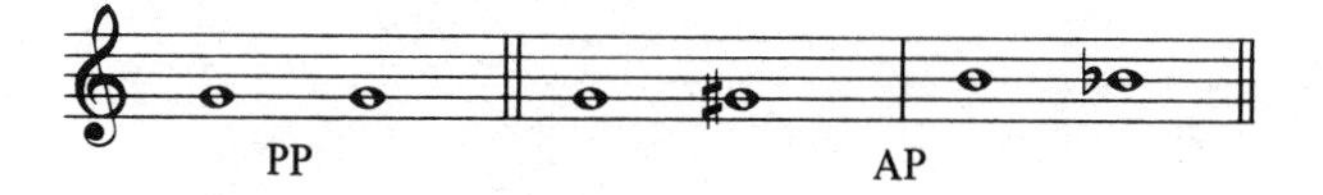

Intervals are *harmonic intervals* when the two pitches are sounded simultaneously, and *melodic intervals* when the two pitches are sounded successively.

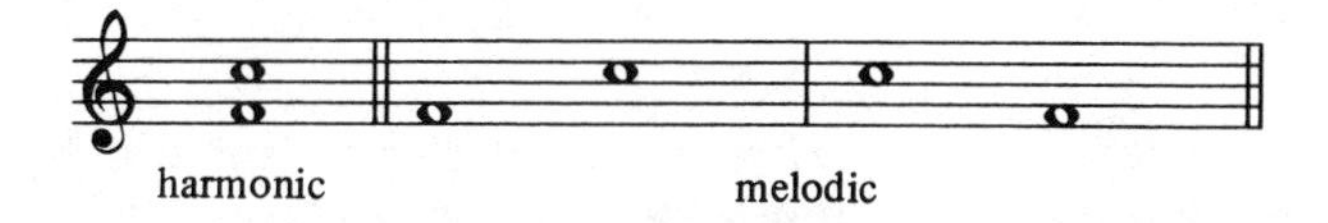

15. Inversion of Intervals. Simple intervals (an octave or less) may be inverted by placing the lower note one octave higher, or the higher note one octave lower. In this process, major intervals invert to minor intervals, and minor intervals invert to major intervals. Perfect intervals remain perfect, hence their name. Diminished intervals invert to augmented intervals, and vice versa.

In this illustration only major, minor, and perfect intervals are shown Other simple intervals invert in the same way.

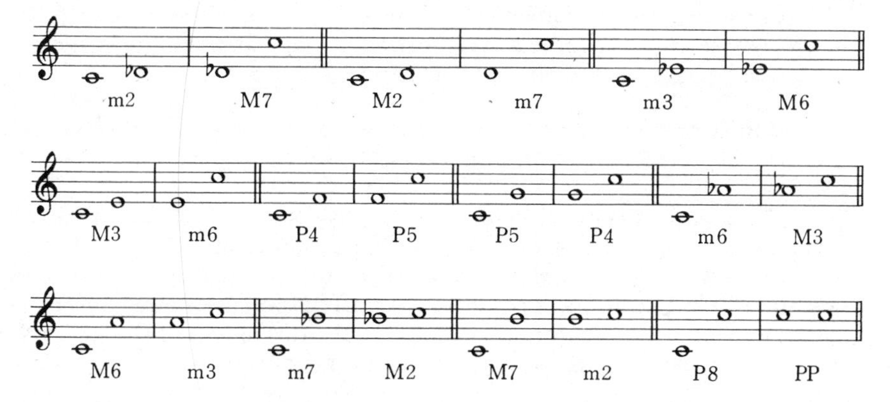

The sum of the two intervals in inversion is always 9: For example, 2 + 7 = 9, 4 + 5 = 9, and so on, even though the movement of the transposed pitch is an octave (8). The reason for this apparent discrepancy is that one pitch is counted twice when the number of the original interval is added to the number of its inversion.

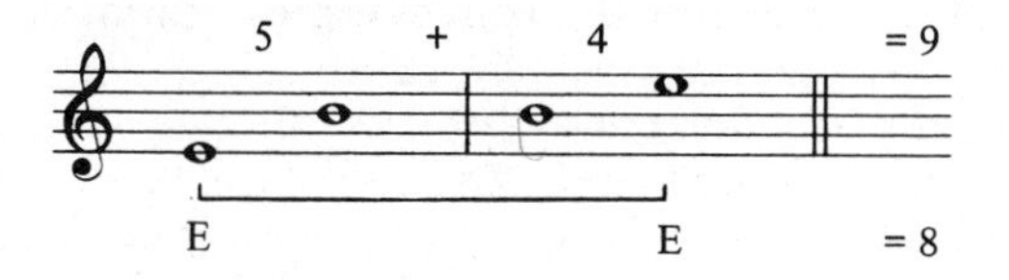

16. Compound Intervals. Intervals larger than an octave are known as compound intervals. Except when the distinction is necessary, a compound interval is usually referred to by the name of its simple form: for example, the tenth is the compound form of the third, but is often referred to as a third.

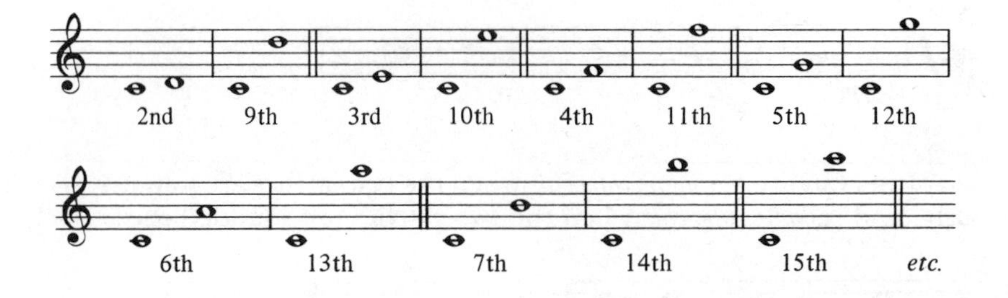

17. Consonance and Dissonance. These terms are used to subjectively evaluate the pleasantness (consonance) or unpleasantness (dissonance) of two or more tones sounding simultaneously or in close proximity. By commonly accepted definition, consonances in the Baroque, Classical, and Romantic periods of composition are the octave, perfect fifth, and the major and minor thirds, and the inversions of these (except for the perfect fourth—discussed in Chapter 9). All other intervals are dissonant by definition, though many of them hardly seem to be so in their musical context.

A chord containing only the "consonant" intervals is considered a consonant chord. If it contains any other interval, the chord is dissonant.

Intervals are sometimes listed linearly in order of consonance and dissonance, where any given interval is more consonant than the one after it, or more dissonant than the one before it on the line.

Most consonant | | | | | | | | | | | Most dissonant
P8 P5 P4 M3 m6 m3 M6 M2 m7 m2 M7 Tritone

Music of the twentieth century generally disregards any distinction between consonance and dissonance, except perhaps on a relative basis.

18. Key and Key Signature. A key signature is a grouping of those accidentals found in the scale and placed on the staff immediately after the clef sign. For example, from the E major scale shown in the discussion of the major scale, the four sharps may be extracted and placed on the staff.

These accidentals ordinarily need not appear thereafter in the musical composition. For minor key signatures, accidentals from the pure minor scale are used. The pure minor scale on C♯ also has four sharps.

In music of the seventeenth to nineteenth centuries, the key signature is commonly used to identify the tonic note of the scale used at the beginning and end of the composition. Thus a signature of four sharps will indicate to the performer that the tonic note is either E of the E major scale, or C♯ of the C♯ minor scale.

A given piece is said to be in a certain *key,* the name of which is identical with the letter name of the tonic note of the scale. These are the key signatures, together with their tonic notes and names.

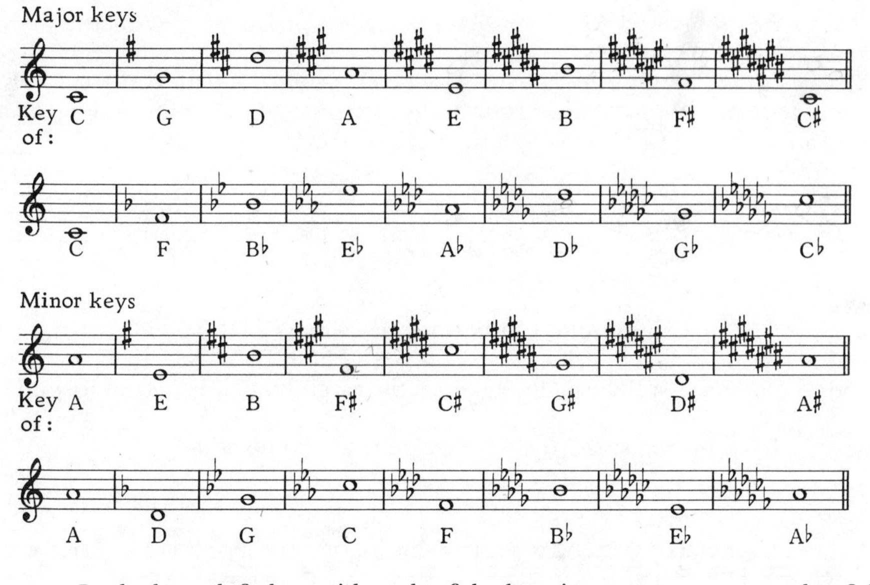

In the bass clef, the accidentals of the key signature are arranged as follows:

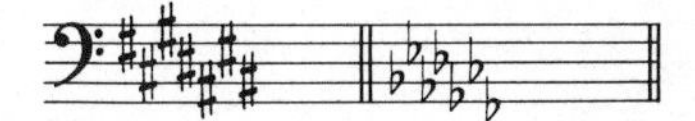

Relative keys. Two keys, each using the same key signature, are known as relative keys; for example, G major (1 sharp) and E minor (1 sharp).

Parallel keys. Two keys, each using the same letter name for tonic note, are known as parallel keys; e.g., G major and G minor.

19. Circle of Fifths. Keys whose tonic notes are located at the interval of a perfect fifth (or its inversion, the perfect fourth) from each other will show one accidental difference in their key signatures. Upon this principle, all keys may be shown in a circle of fifths.

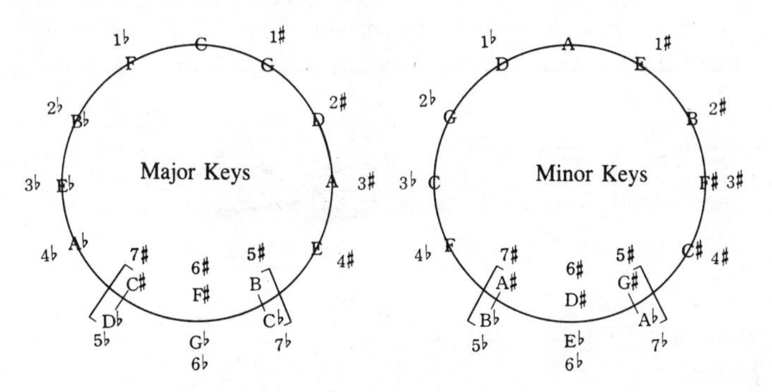

Key names within brackets are *enharmonic* keys, indicating that a single pitch is spelled two different ways. For example, C♯ and D♭ are the same pitch and use the same key on the piano keyboard.

20. Scales and Keys. With so much emphasis placed on the learning of scales in music lessons, one might be led to believe that music is derived from scales. Just the opposite is true. The scale is simply a pattern formed by the arrangement in alphabetical order of the pitches used in a composition. An obvious example is the Christmas hymn, *Joy to the World.*

The first eight notes of the tune encompass all the pitch names, and are in descending alphabetical order: D C♯ B A G F♯ E D. This is the descending form of the D major scale, usually stated in the ascending alphabetical form: D E F♯ G A B C♯ D.

In most tunes, the scale structure is not so obvious.

Here the same D scale tones are present, but in a more random order. Note that the Mozart example neither begins nor ends on D. Why then is this scale a D scale? Because all the notes seem to gravitate to the single pitch D. Note the strength of the first D you hear, and notice how the last note "wants" to continue on to D (as it does in the sonata). A pitch with this quality of stability and finality is called the *tonic,* and functions as the first note of a scale. It is usually found at or near the beginning of a composition, and more often than not it is also the last pitch. Music from which the scale is derived is said to be in the key of the tonic note. In the preceding two cases, it is the key of D.

Whether the scale is major or minor depends on the arrangement of whole and half steps, as described in section 12 of this chapter. The scales of the two previous pieces are major, while the following scale is minor.

Not all scales are major or minor.

The note F in this folk song possesses the quality of tonic, but the scale is not major or minor. The configuration of scale steps shows it to be one of the modal scales, in this case, the Mixolydian. See *Music For Sight Singing,* page 173, or *More Music For Sight Singing,* page 248 for further information about modal scales.

A key signature is nothing more than the accidentals of the scale placed at the beginning of a composition. It does not determine the key, it merely reports the accidentals used, although for convenience we commonly do use the key signature to identify the key. A key signature of two flats, for example, usually indicates B♭ major or G minor, but in the preceding English folk song it indicates F Mixolydian.

See Chapter 14 to find further information on modal scales and Chapter 6 for reasons for the use of accidentals in minor scales.

21. Chord. A chord is a group of different notes, usually three or more, sounded either simultaneously (*block chord*), or successively (*broken chord*). Chords in pre-twentieth century music are ordinarily spelled in thirds, such as C E G or D F♯ A C.

22. Triad. The simplest type of chord is the triad, a three-note chord built in thirds. It may be constructed above any letter name of the music alphabet simply by selecting the third and fifth letter names above the given letter name. For example, choosing A, we construct the triad A C E; choosing G, we construct the triad G B D. When arranged in thirds, as these are, the lowest note is known as the *root,* above which are the *third* and *fifth.*

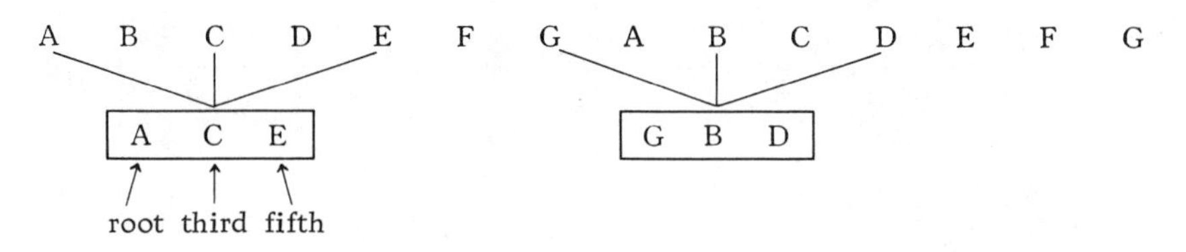

There are four types of triads, each distinguished by the quality of the intervals contained therein:

1. A *major triad* consists of a major third and a perfect fifth above its root, or of a major third and a minor third from the root upwards.
2. A *minor triad* consists of a minor third and perfect fifth above its root, or of a minor third and a major third from the root upwards.
3. A *diminished triad* consists of a minor third and a diminished fifth above its root, or of two minor thirds from the root upwards.
4. An *augmented triad* consists of a major third and an augmented fifth above its root, or of two major thirds from the root upwards.

Constructing triads above each of the seven letter names of the musical alphabet will produce three different types of triads, major, minor, or diminished, according to the arrangement of thirds within the triad.

A	C	E	minor triad
B	D	F	diminished triad
C	E	G	major triad
D	F	A	minor triad
E	G	B	minor triad
F	A	C	major triad
G	B	D	major triad

23. The Triad in a Key. Triads can be built above each note of any major or minor scale. When used in a key, the number of the scale step serving as the root of the triad may also be an identifying number for the triad. It is usually expressed as a roman numeral.

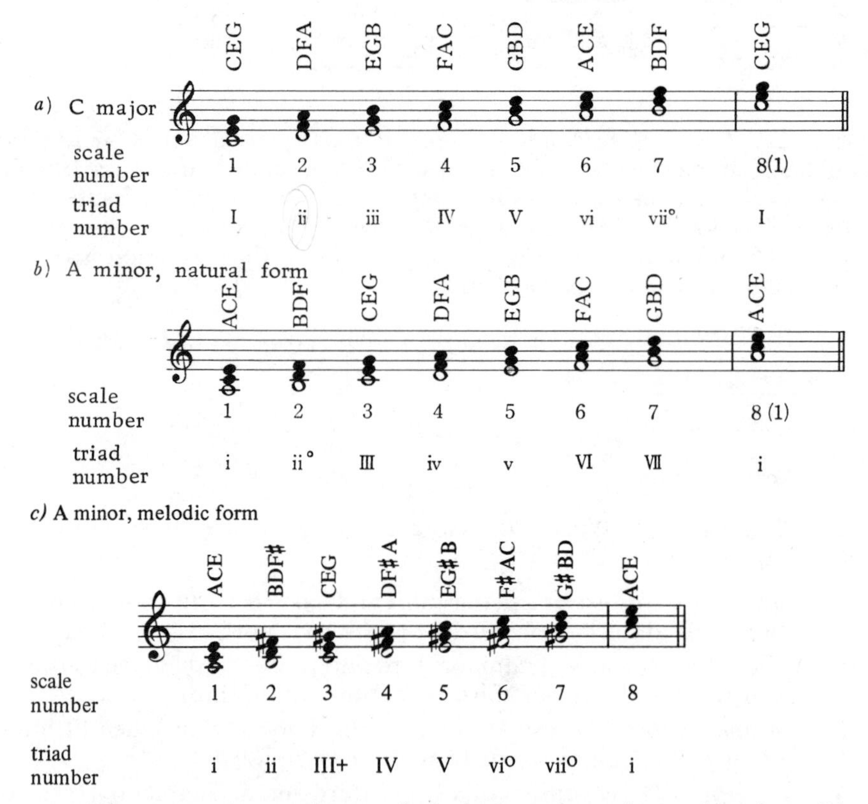

The roman numeral not only designates the scale step location of the root of the triad, but also indicates triad construction:

Large numeral = major triad (I in C major = C E G)
Small numeral = minor triad (ii in C major = D F A)

Small numeral with small° = diminished triad (vii° in C major = B D F)
Large numeral with + = augmented triad (III+ in A minor = C E G♯)

Thus, for example, IV indicates a major triad built on the fourth scale degree, while iv indicates a minor triad built on the fourth scale degree.

A triad in a key may also be designated by the name of the scale step on which it is built; for example: I = tonic triad, V = dominant triad.

24. Chords Larger Than a Triad. These are also built in thirds, and are identified by the interval between the root and the final note in the series of thirds. In the following examples built on C, all such possibilities are shown. Adding one more third above the thirteenth repeats the root C.

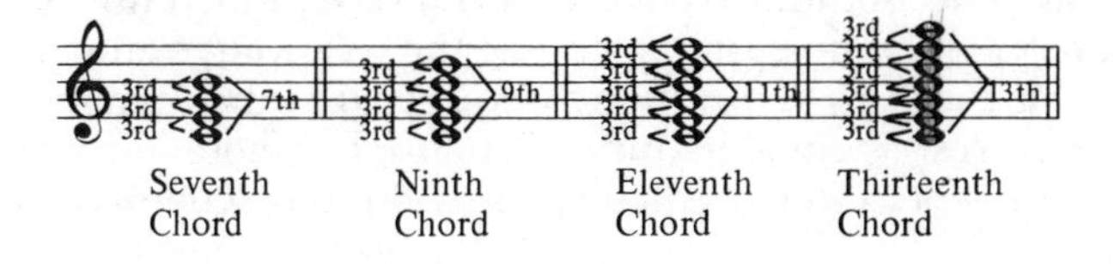

Seventh Chord | Ninth Chord | Eleventh Chord | Thirteenth Chord

As with triads, various qualities (major, minor, and so on) of the thirds will be found, although normally not all possibilities are used. The ninth, eleventh, and thirteenth chords are rarely found in any other than root position.

25. Inversion of Chords. Any triad or chord is said to be in inversion when some member other than the root is the lowest note.

In a *first inversion* the third is the lowest note.
In a *second inversion* the fifth is the lowest note.
In a *third inversion* the seventh is the lowest note.

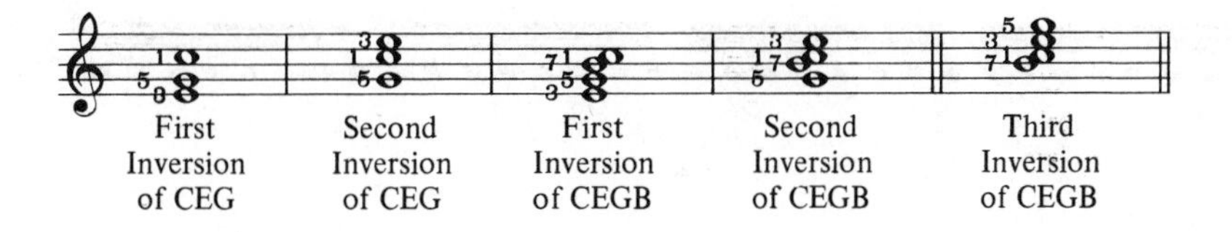

First Inversion of CEG | Second Inversion of CEG | First Inversion of CEGB | Second Inversion of CEGB | Third Inversion of CEGB

Duration

26. Notes and Rests. Durations of pitch or silence may be indicated by characteristic note-shapes or rest signs. (British names are given in parentheses.)

Note	Rest
Double Whole Note (Breve)	Double Whole Rest
Whole Note (Semibreve)	Whole Rest
Half Note (Minim)	Half Rest
Quarter Note (Crotchet)	Quarter Rest or

Eighth Note (Quaver)		Eighth Rest	
Sixteenth Note (Semiquaver)		Sixteenth Rest	
Thirty-Second Note (Demisemiquaver)		Thirty-Second Rest	
Sixty-Fourth Note (Hemisemidemiquaver)		Sixty-Fourth Rest	

The whole rest is also used to indicate a complete measure rest regardless of the number of beats in the measure.

These note-shapes do not indicate actual duration of time until combined with a tempo indication and a time signature (see the following example). They do indicate relative relationships of duration as expressed by their names. For example, a whole note (or rest) is equal in duration to two half notes (or rests) or to four quarter notes. Any note value is equal in duration to two notes of the next smaller value.

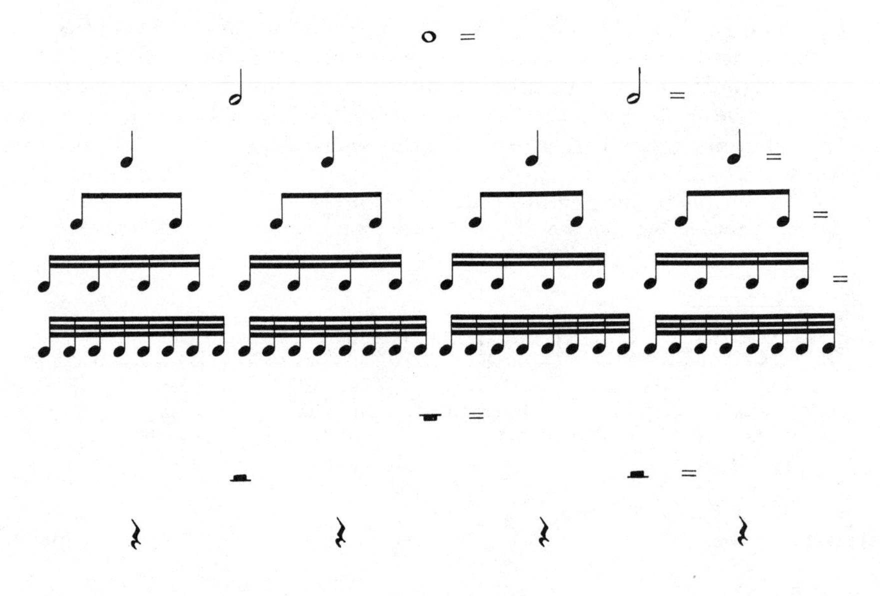

27. Beat. A beat is a unit of musical time. It can be represented visibly by the movement of a conductor's hand, or audibly by the ticking sound of a metronome. A beat may be represented on the staff by any note value indicated above. (See also "dot" in section 31 and "time signature" in section 34.)

28. Bar. This is a vertical line appearing on the staff (sometimes called a "bar line").

29. Double Bar. Two vertical lines on the staff at the close of a composition or a major division of a composition are called a double bar.

30. Measure. A measure is the space between two bars (bar lines), or between the clef sign and the first bar. Usually each measure represents a fixed number of beats, as indicated by the time signature (see section 34, below). The word "bar" is often used to mean "measure."

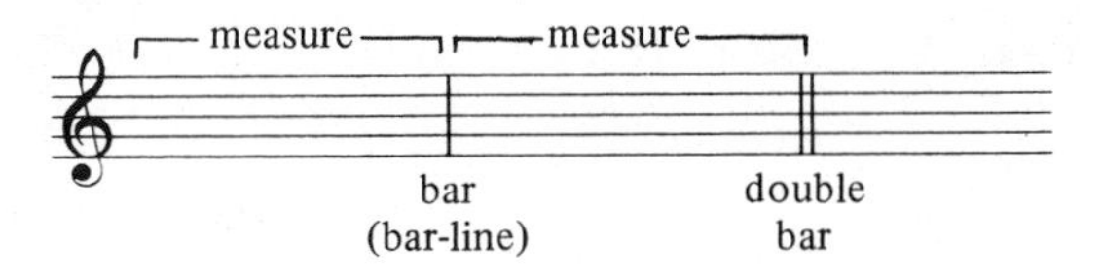

31. Dot. A dot appearing after a note or rest, for example ♩., increases the value of the note by one half: ♩. = ♩ + ♪. A dotted note or rest is equal in value to three notes of the next smaller value: 𝅗𝅥. = ♩ ♩ ♩, ♩. = ♪ ♪ ♪, ♪. = 𝅘𝅥𝅯 𝅘𝅥𝅯 𝅘𝅥𝅯, 𝄼. = 𝄽 𝄽 𝄽.
Any dotted note can be used to represent the beat.

32. Tie. A curved line joining two successive notes of identical pitch is a tie. The two tied notes sound as one note. ♩‿♩ = 𝅗𝅥

33. Tempo. Tempo is the rate of speed of a composition. It may be expressed at the beginning of a composition or during a composition by musical terms such as *allegro* or *adagio* or by a metronome marking such as ♩ = 60 M. M. (M. M. is Maelzel's Metronome). "60" on the metronome indicates one tick per second. The marking ♩ = 60 means that the duration of each quarter note will be one second.

34. Time Signature. The time signature consists of two arabic numerals, arranged vertically, found at the beginning of a musical composition following the clef and the key signature.

In its simplest definition, the upper number of the time signature states the number of beats to be found in each measure, while the lower number indicates which of the possible note values will receive one beat.

$\frac{2}{4}$ indicates that there are two beats in a measure, and that a quarter note receives one beat.

$\frac{3}{4}$ indicates that there are three beats in a measure, and that a quarter note receives one beat.

Very often, certain time signatures in certain situations will convey other meanings. In a slow tempo, $\frac{6}{8}$ may be interpreted as above, but in a fast tempo it invariably indicates two beats in a measure with a ♩. note receiving one beat (two ♩. = six ♪ notes). In any case, the upper number always indicates how many of the note values expressed by the lower number will be found in one measure. Clarification of this situation will be found in Chapter 3.

Although the time signature can be made up of many combinations of two numbers, the following are the combinations most often used.

Upper number:	2,3,4,6,9,12
Lower number:	2,4,8,16

The sign **C** (often called *common time*) is a substitute for $\frac{4}{4}$.
The sign **¢** (often called *cut time* or *alla breve*) is a substitute for $\frac{2}{2}$.

Elementary Notation

35. The Single Note. A note is drawn with one, two, or three parts:

o head ♩← stem ♪← flag

An ascending stem is found on the right side of the head: 𝅗𝅥.

A descending stem is found on the left side of the head: 𝅗𝅥.

36. Notes on the Staff. *a*) When writing notes for a single part (one voice or one instrument) on the staff, place descending stems on notes found on the middle line or above, and ascending stems on notes below the middle line.

When the note on the middle line is the highest note of the measure, it is often found with an ascending stem.

b) When writing for two parts on a single staff, notes for the upper part use ascending stems and notes for the lower part use descending stems, regardless of their location on the staff.

c) To indicate two parts performing the same pitch on a single staff (unisons), use a single note head with both ascending and descending stems. For two whole notes in unison, use two overlapping whole notes.

37. Notes Using Ledger Lines or Spaces. Above the staff, do not write ledger lines above the highest note. Below the staff, do not write ledger lines below the lowest note.

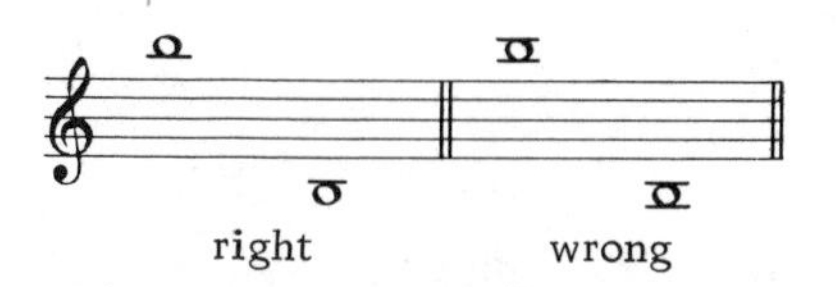

38. Dotted Notes. When the note head is on a space, the dot is found in the same space. When the note is on the line, the dot is usually found in the space above, though it is sometimes in the space below.

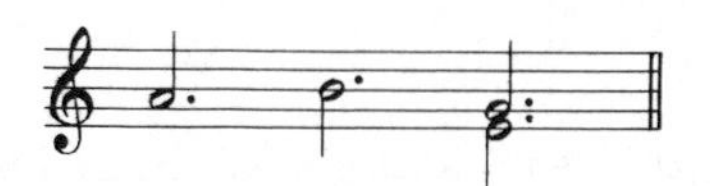

39. Vertical Arrangement of Notes. All notes sounding simultaneously must be written so that a line drawn through the note heads will be perpendicular to the lines of the staff.

40. Horizontal Arrangment of Notes. Space between notes should be in proportion to their time values.

41. Placement of Accidentals. An accidental before a note is placed on the same line or space as the note head.

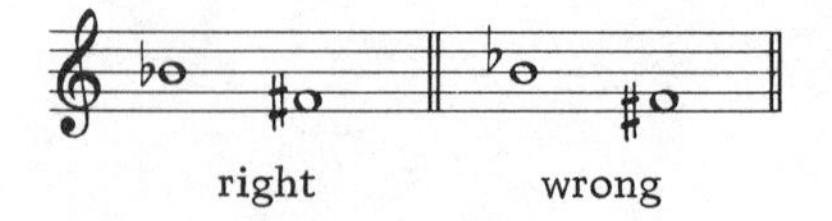

The effect of an accidental lasts until the following bar line, unless it is cancelled by a natural sign or unless the note is tied into the following measure or measures.

42. Beams. Notes employing flags may be grouped together with beams.

instead of

Notes ordinarily should be beamed in terms of beat units. indicates a beat unit.

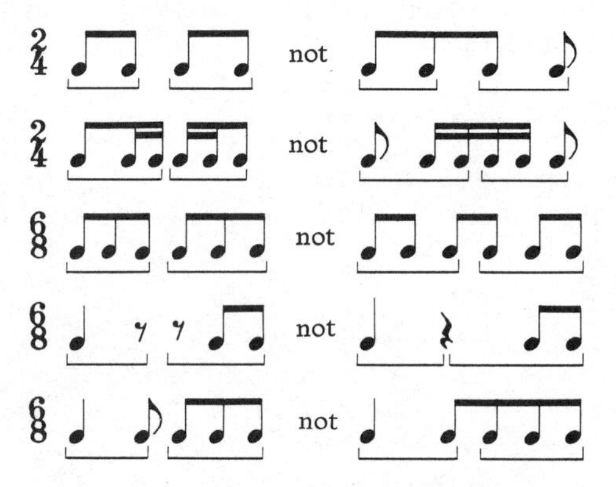

When a group of beamed notes is placed on the staff, use a stem direction that is correct for a majority of the notes in the group.

In most vocal music, beams are used only when two or more notes are found on a single syllable.

Santa Lucia

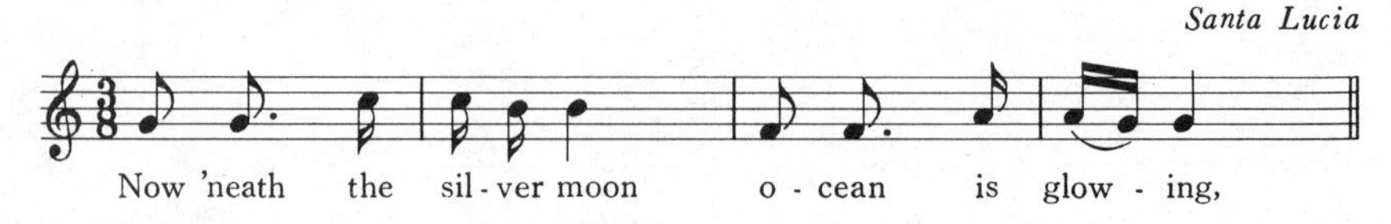

The curved line connecting two or more notes of different pitch is known as a *slur*.

CHAPTER 2

Tonic and Dominant

Be sure to review Chapter 1, Fundamentals of Music Theory, before beginning this chapter. Chapter 3, *Rhythm and Meter,* may be studied concurrently with this chapter.

Theory and Analysis

What is Music Theory?

Music is universal. It exists in some form in every part of the world inhabited by man. Its existence for thousands of years is proven by references in mankind's earliest writings, pictures, and artifacts. During all this time, and in all these places, music has developed in a multitude of different ways, each expressing the local culture and historical era of its creators. The seemingly endless diversity of human music is illustrated by a brief list of musical forms: symphony, aboriginal folk song, military march, rock and roll, liturgical mass, electronic music, and music of the Orient, to name only a few.

All these diverse musical styles have one characteristic in common: they use sound characterized by its qualities of pitch, duration, intensity, and timbre as their basic raw material. What makes each of these diverse compositional styles unique is the way in which these raw materials of sound are organized. The creation of music, whether by professional or amateur, is a result of the creator's choices from the materials of sound and by the methods he adopts to organize those materials of pitch, rhythm, and so on, into a musical composition.

The study of music theory is, in the broadest sense, the study of how man has organized sound to make music, regardless of its geographical or historical origins.

Although a complete study of music theory would be a task of great magnitude, the task has been simplified somewhat by the fact that, throughout music history, the principles of organizing musical sound in a given historical period and in a given geographical area are often similar, making it convenient for the scholar to concentrate on one such period and/or area at a time. The elementary aspects of our present study will focus on music composed in Western Europe and the areas under its influence, such as the Americas, between the years 1600 and 1900, although constant comparative reference will be made to both older and newer styles. The era chosen encompasses the Baroque, Classic, and Romantic periods of music history, and includes most of the best-known names in the present day concert repertoire, ranging from the forerunners of J. S. Bach through Haydn, Mozart, Beethoven, Chopin, and concluding with Brahms and Wagner at the end of the nineteenth century.

It was during this period that harmony was the predominant characteristic in music. The use of harmony by composers forms a continuous thread throughout these three centuries, in contrast to both the emphasis on contrapuntal technique before c. 1600, and to the many novel features of twentieth century music.

Harmony, in its broadest definition, is the relationship between two or more tones sounding either simultaneously or in close proximity. When treated as a specific area of study, harmony can be defined as the study of chords—their formations, successions, and relationships to each other, and also their relationships to the remaining factors in music composition, namely, melody, rhythm, and form.

We will begin with two music excerpts to demonstrate what is perhaps the most significant harmonic relationship in music.

The Cadence

Fig. 2.1

Bach, *Herz und Mund und That und Leben* (Cantata No. 147), "Jesu Joy of Man's Desiring"

Fig. 2.2 Mozart, Sonata in A Major for Piano, K.[1] 545

These excerpts (Figures 2.1 and 2.2) from two well-known works in the music literature serve to point out a universal characteristic of music composition, the *cadence.* After listening to them, sing the melody line of each with or without the piano. As you arrive at the final note you should feel satisfied that you have come to a good stopping place, and that there is no absolute necessity for continuing further.

It is this sensation of arriving at a stopping palce that indicates a *cadence.* You may have noticed another stopping place in these examples, for instance, at the end of measure four in each excerpt. But in those cases, the cadences seem incomplete, and you should feel the necessity that the music continue after this temporary pause. Poetry also exhibits these same traits. In this stanza from an American folk ballad, note the two temporary pauses, and the final stop at the end.

> When the curtains of night
> Are pinned back by the stars, (*pause*)
> And the beautiful moon sweeps the sky, (*pause*)
> I'll remember you, love, in my prayers. (*final stop*)

As you read the poem, or sing the tunes above, the function of the cadence is clear: to mark a pause, complete or incomplete, in the poetic or musical thought being expressed. In this way cadences make it possible for poetry or music to be a true structure, rather than just a nonstop flow of words or pitches. See article "The Universality of the Cadence" at the end of this chapter.

The Cadence in Relation to Form

The structure of a piece of music is known as its *form.*[2] The terminology of music form is used to describe all aspects of the musical structure, from the smallest unit

[1] K., abbreviation for Ludwig von Köchel, who in 1862 made a chronological list of Mozart's works. Mozart did not number his own compositions.

[2] The major presentation of Form begins in Chapter 6.

of pitch or rhythm to the complete composition. In our examples, a cadence appears at the end of each four-measure grouping and marks the end of a "form," which in this case is a *phrase.* The two phrases together, one with a temporary cadence and the other with a full stop, comprise a form known as a *period,* as shown in Figure 2.3, the melody line of the preceding Bach example (Figure 2.1).

Fig. 2.3

The Mozart example (Figure 2.2 and its melody line in Figure 2.4) is only slightly more complex than the Bach, showing small melodic units called *motives,* which in their variegated repetitions combine to form the four-measure phrase and the eight-measure period.

Fig. 2.4

In Figure 2.4, motive 2a is like motive 2, but in a scale step pattern. At the asterisk, the E is decorative, which leaves C♯–D as the motive.

In both of these musical examples, as indeed throughout most music literature, it is the cadence that defines these formal structures, marking the end of one structure and, if the music continues, the beginning of another. The cadence thus forms a goal for the music material that precedes it.

Goals can be temporary, as in measure four of both the Mozart and Bach example, or final, as in measure eight of both. The final goal of a melodic line is commonly the tonic note of the key, as both examples show. The same rule is true of a harmony, where the ultimate goal of a progression of chords is almost invariably the tonic triad.

In listening to a composition, it is this feeling of reaching the goal, the tonic, that imparts to it a sense of key. Thus the feeling of the tonic resides in the sound of the music itself. By looking at the musical score the tonic can be identified by pitch name, which is then designated as the name of the key. In listening to the Bach example (Figure 2.1), we recognize that the final melody note and the final bass note are tonic. By looking at the score and seeing that both notes are G, we know that G represents finality and that therefore the music is in the key of G. Find the key of the Mozart example (Figure 2.2) by using the same method.

Harmony at the Cadence

In harmony, a cadence is usually defined as the progression of the last two chords of a formal structure. These are commonly built on the dominant and tonic notes of a key, and are referred to as the V and I triads, respectively. In C major these are G B D (V) and C E G (I). The roots of these triads are at the interval of a fifth or at its inversion, the fourth, as shown in Figure 2.5. (Review Inversion of Intervals, Chapter 1, section 15.)

RETROGRADE (BACKWARDS)
ELISION (SKIP)

Fig. 2.5

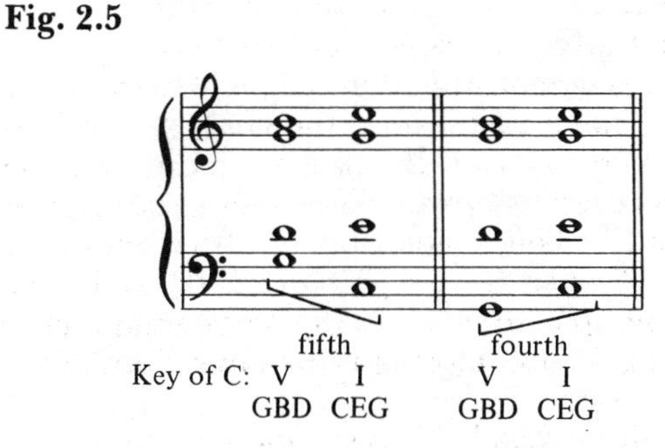

The final cadences of Figures 2.1 and 2.2 both show chords with this relationship. The additional note in these V chords creates a V^7 chord in each case, but no change in analysis is required, as Figure 2.6 shows us.

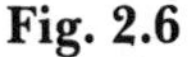

Fig. 2.6

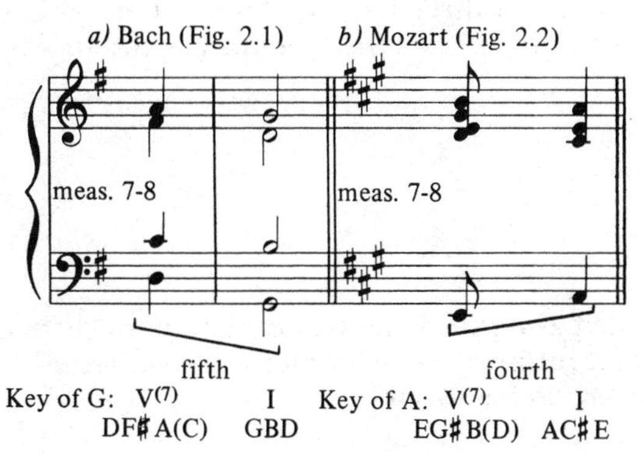

A cadence also exists at the end of measure four in Figures 2.1 and 2.2, but this time with the chords reversed: I–V. At points such as these it is obvious both that the music pauses and that it must continue. A cadence that indicates a pause but that has no feeling of finality is known as a *half cadence* (sometimes called a *progressive cadence,* indicating the necessity of continuation).

Fig. 2.7

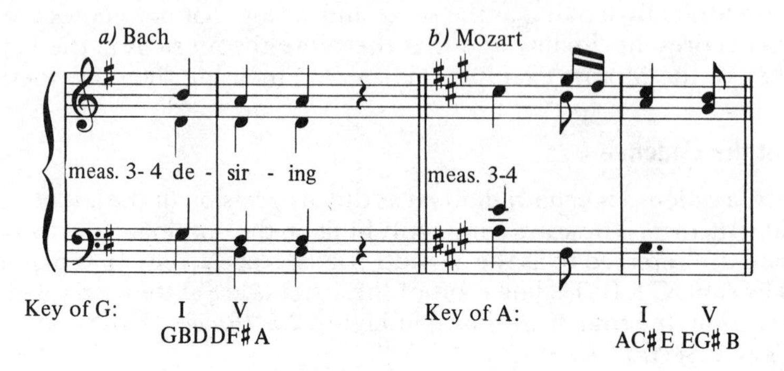

In Figure 2.7b, the root of the I triad is not in the bass, but this inversion (review Chapter 1, section 25) does not affect the concept of cadence.

Root relationship by perfect fifth, as demonstrated in cadential harmony, is probably the most important single element delineating the character of harmonic music. Chord movements based on roots a fifth apart are more common than others, and the most common key relationships are based on this interval, as in the circle of fifths (Chapter 1, section 19). This relationship by fifth is one of the chief characteristics of the whole body of music from c.1600 to c.1900, and is the principal reason for identifying this time span in music as the "common practice period," meaning that this common usage causes most music compositions of the period to bear striking resemblances to one another.

Our study will now move on to a more detailed investigation of the two triads making up the cadence, and of tonic–dominant relationships, as seen both in cadences and in harmonic progressions leading up to the cadence.

Spelling the Major Triad

To review, the major triad consists of three tones and is constructed in thirds: a major third plus a minor third, figuring from the root up. The distance from root to fifth is a perfect fifth.

Fig. 2.8.

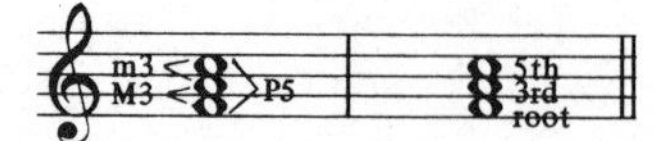

Major triads can be spelled using any letter name, diatonic or chromatic, as a root. As a basis for present and future work in harmony, it is necessary to be able to spell any major triad quickly and accurately.

Method 1. Major triads may be spelled by interval. If you can already spell intervals with facility, as described in Chapter 1, section 14, you can spell any major triad simply by spelling a major third and a perfect fifth above any given pitch name designated as the root of a triad. Another approach is to spell a major third above the root, and a minor third above the third of the triad.

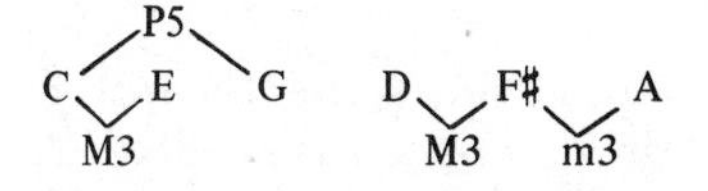

Method 2. Students lacking facility in spelling intervals will find the following method convenient until such facility is developed.

There are seven basic triad spellings, using each of the seven letter names of the musical alphabet as root. These are ACE, BDF, CEG, DFA, EGB, FAC, GBD. Three are already major, three are minor, and one is diminished. In the diagrams below, the arrow indicates the letter name or names to be raised one half step to convert the basic triad spelling to a major triad spelling. For example, to convert the basic triad D F A, raise F to F♯ to get the major triad D F♯ A.

Group I (*major*)			Group II (*minor*)			Group III (*diminished*)		
C	E	G	D	F	A	B	D	F
F	A	C	E	G	B			
G	B	D	A	C	E			
-	-	-	-	↑	-	-	↑	↑

Group I. Triads in Group I will always be major when each member carries no accidental or when each carries the same accidental, as indicated by the symbol - - -.

C	E	G,	C♯	E♯	G♯,	C𝄪	E𝄪	G𝄪,	C♭	E♭	G♭,	C𝄫	E𝄫	G𝄫
-	-	-	-	-	-	-	-	-	-	-	-	-	-	-

Assignment 2.1. Spell major triads on *a)* F, F♯, F𝄪, F♭, F𝄫; *b)* G, G♯, G𝄪, G♭, G𝄫.

Group II. Triads in Group II will be major when the third carries an accidental one half step higher than the root and the fifth (- ↑ -).

A	C♯	E,	A♯	C𝄪	E♯,	A♭	C	E♭,	A𝄫	C♭	E𝄫
-	↑	-	-	↑	-	-	↑	-	-	↑	-

Assignment 2.2. Spell major triads on *a)* D, D♯, D♭, D𝄫; *b)* E, E♯, E♭, E𝄫

Group III. This single triad on the pitch name B is major when the third and fifth carry an accidental one half step higher than the root (- ↑ ↑).

B	D♯	F♯,	B♯	D𝄪	F𝄪,	B♭	D	F,	B𝄫	D♭	F♭
-	↑	↑	-	↑	↑	-	↑	↑	-	↑	↑

Assignment 2.3. Without reference to the above, spell major triads on B, B♯, B♭, B♭♭.

Assignment 2.4. Spell major triads when the root, the third, or the fifth is given. Use either method of triad spelling.

a) Spell with letter names the major triad when each of the following is the root: C, F, E, G♭, E♭, A♯, B♭, F♯, D♭, B.

b) Spell the major triad when each of the following is the third: B, E♯, F♯, C, D, G♯, A♭, D♭, A♭♭, F. (Example: A is the third, so triad is spelled FAC)

c) Spell the major triad when each of the following is the fifth: D, C♯, E♭, B♯, A, F, F♯, D♭, E♭♭, F♭. (Example: A♭ is the fifth, so triad is spelled D♭ F A♭)

See article "The Difficult Major Triad Spelling" at the end of this chapter.

Spelling Tonic and Dominant Triads

Cadences in music are most often comprised of tonic and dominant harmonies, and these cadences are known as *authentic* cadences (to be studied in more detail in Chapter 4). The tonic chord is almost always a triad. The dominant harmony mav be built on the fifth scale step (V) as a triad, (Fig. 2.9), or as a V^7 chord, as shown in the final cadence of Figure 2.1, and to be studied in detail later.

Fig. 2.9 S. Scheidt, *O Jesulein Süss*

Both the tonic and dominant triads in a major key are major triads. The root of the tonic triad is the first scale step of the key, while the root of the dominant triad is the fifth scale step of the key. Also note that the fifth of the tonic triad and the root of the dominant triad are the same letter names. In Figure 2.10, arabic numbers refer to scale steps while roman numerals refer to chord roots.

Fig. 2.10

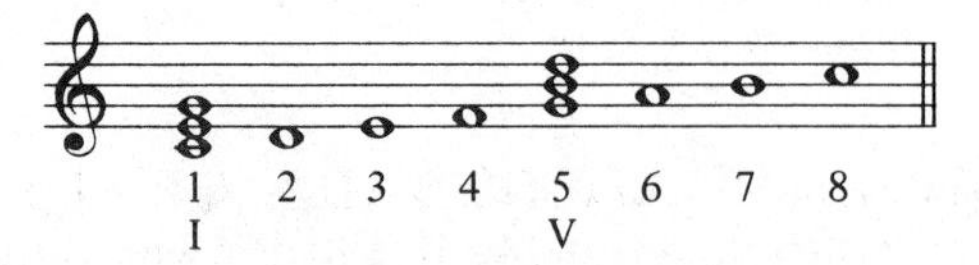

Assignment 2.5. Spell the tonic triad in each major key. Using the circle of fifths (see Chapter 1, section 19) start in C major and spell each tonic triad in turn around the circle. (C major tonic triad is C E G; G major tonic triad is G B D; D major tonic triad is D F♯ A, and so on.)

Assignment 2.6. Spell the dominant triad in each major key, using the circle of fifths as above. (C major, dominant triad is G B D; G major dominant triad D F♯ A, and so on.)

Intervals in the Major Triad

The major triad contains a number of intervals, which can be found by extracting and combining any two notes from the three-note triad.

1 up to 3	Major Third (M3)	3 down to 1
3 up to 5	Minor Third (m3)	5 down to 3
5 up to 1	Perfect Fourth (P4)	1 down to 5
1 up to 5	Perfect Fifth (P5)	5 down to 1
3 up to 1	Minor Sixth (m6)	1 down to 3
5 up to 3	Major Sixth (M6)	3 down to 5
1 up to 1		1 down to 1
3 up to 3	Perfect Octave (P8)	3 down to 3
5 up to 5		5 down to 5

Fig. 2.11

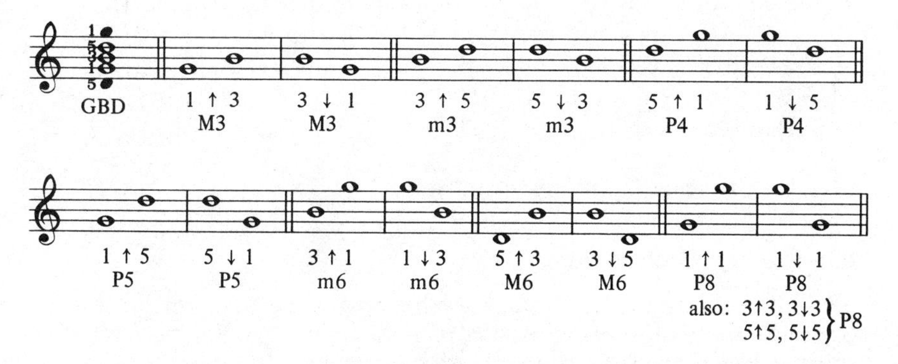

The numbers 1, 3, and 5 in the preceding example refer to the root, third, and fifth of the triad and not to scale step numbers, although of course they are identical for the tonic triad. When the major triad is found as a V triad (or any numbered triad) its members can still be numbered 1, 3, and 5, and its intervals deduced in the same manner.

Fig. 2.12

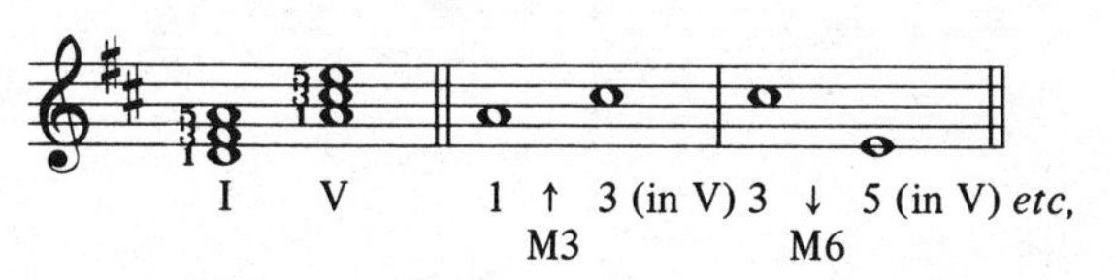

Assignment 2.7. Based on a given major triad, spell each of the intervals in the preceding table of intervals. For example, for the D major triad (D F♯ A) write

M3	D up to F♯	M6	A up to F♯
m3	F♯ up to A	m6	F♯ up to D
P4	A up to D	P8	D up to D
P5	D up to A		F♯ up to F♯
			A up to A

Do the same with the following triads, or others as assigned: G, F, B♭, E♭, A, B, F♯, C♭, D♯, D♭.

Assignment 2.8. Spell each of the intervals in the table of intervals from a given letter name. For example, when G is given:

M3 up from G is B	(M3 = 1 ↑ 3; when G is 1, B is 3)
M3 down from G is E♭	(M3 = 3 ↓ 1; when G is 3, E♭ is 1)
m3 up from G is B♭	(m3 = 3 ↑ 5; when G is 3, B♭ is 5)
m3 down from G is E	(m3 = 5 ↓ 3; when G is 5, E is 3)
P4 up from G is C	(P4 = 5 ↑ 1; when G is 5, C is 1)
P4 down from G is D	(P4 = 1 ↓ 5; when G is 1, D is 5)
P5 up from G is D	(P5 = 1 ↑ 5; when G is 1, D is 5)
P5 down from G is C	(P5 = 5 ↓ 1; when G is 5, C is 1)
m6 up from G is E♭	(m6 = 3 ↑ 1; when G is 3, E♭ is 1)
m6 down from G is B	(m6 = 1 ↓ 3; when G is 1, B is 3)
M6 up from G is E	(M6 = 5 ↑ 3; when G is 5, E is 3)
M6 down from G is B♭	(M6 = 5 ↓ 3; when G is 3, B♭ is 5)
P8 up from G is G	(P8 = 1 ↑ 1; when G is 1, G is 1)

Do the same from any given note.

Intervals in Melodic Writing

The intervals studied thus far, together with scale steps (major and minor seconds) are those most often used in melodic writing. In Figure 2.13, all intervals a third or larger are from the tonic triad of the key. In Figure 2.14, intervals from both the tonic and dominant triads may be found.

Fig. 2.13 Skips in tonic triad only

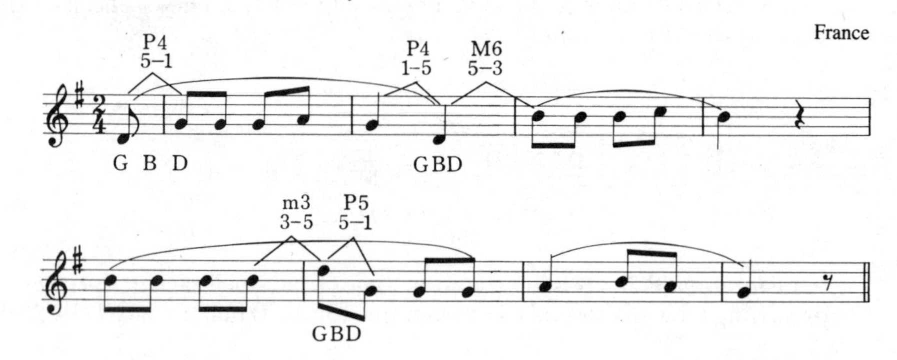

Fig. 2.14 Skips in tonic and dominant triads

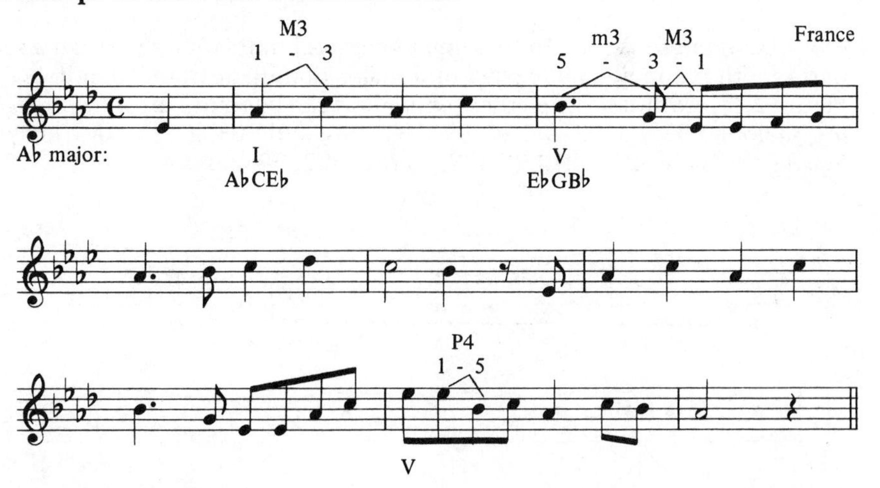

Assignment 2.9. In these melodies each interval larger than a second is part of a major tonic triad. Identify each, as in Figure 2.13. Additional melodies for analysis can be found in the author's other publications, *Music for Sight Singing*[3] (melodies numbered 1, 3–22, 34–44, and 58–73), and *More Music for Sight Singing*[4] (melodies numbered 266, 267, 268, 270, 272, 280, 283, 295, 296, 308, 310, 311, and 320).

[3]Robert W. Ottman, *Music for Sight Singing*, 2nd ed. (Englewood Cliffs, N.J.: Prentice-Hall, Inc., 1967).

[4]Robert W. Ottman, *More Music for Sight Singing*, (Englewood Cliffs, N.J.: Prentice-Hall, Inc., 1981).

Assignment 2.10. In these melodies, each interval larger than a second is part of either a major tonic triad or a major dominant triad. Identify each as in Figure 2.14. Additional melodies for analysis can be found in *Music for Sight Singing,* melodies 82–86, 92–95, 97–99, 105, 106, and 108, and *More Music for Sight Singing,* melodies 271, 273, 274, 279, 282, 322, 398, and 455.

Application

Written Materials

Writing Major Triads and Intervals

Assignment 2.11. Write the major triads on the staff. Using the circle of fifths, write the tonic (I) triad of the key, followed by the dominant (V) triad. Here are the first three keys on the sharp side of the circle of fifths. Do the same for all keys.

Fig. 2.15

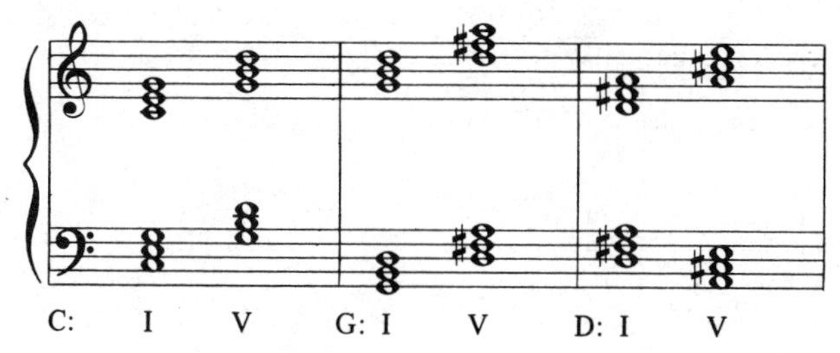

(Note: The root of the V triad may be at the interval of a perfect fifth above or a perfect fourth below the root of the I triad. Review Chapter 1, section 15, Inversion of Intervals.)

Assignment 2.12. Write intervals on the staff. From the given triad, place each interval listed here on the staff, in both ascending and descending form:

M3, m3, P4, P5, m6, M6, P8

Here are the first of these from the D major triad:

Fig. 2.16

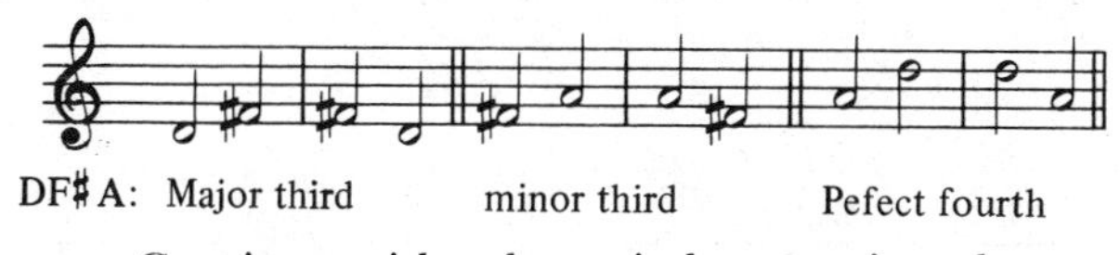

Continue with other triads, as assigned.

Assignment 2.13. Fill in the second note of the interval according to the direction given for each interval.

Ear Training and Music Reading

Singing the Major Triad

Exercise 2.1. Singing the C major triad.

a) Sing the first five notes of the C major scale. Then, starting with 1, sing only the notes 1, 3, and 5.

Fig. 2.17

b) Starting on 5, sing the descending scale, followed by 5, 3, and 1 only.

Fig. 2.18

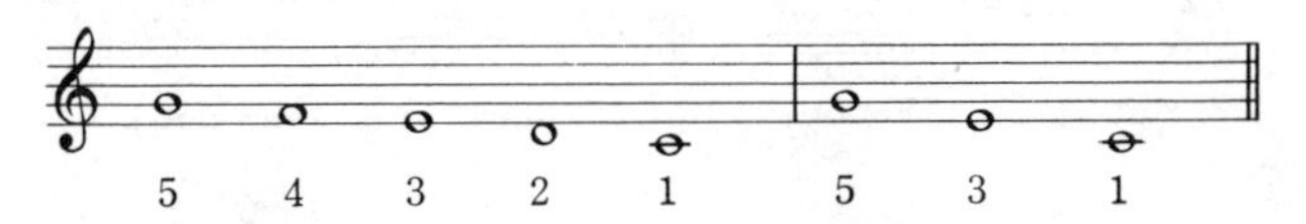

c) Sing the C major triad ascending and descending.

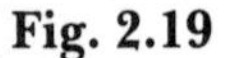

Fig. 2.19

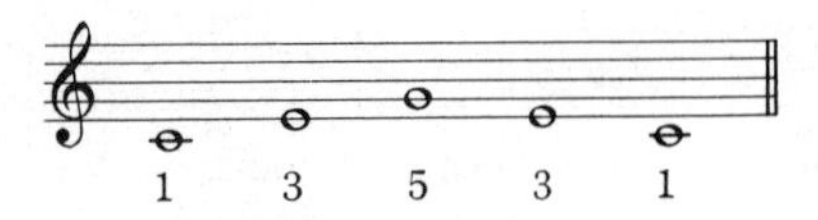

Exercise 2.2. *a*) Singing any major triad. Listen to major triads played at the piano. After each triad is sounded, sing the pattern 1–3–5–3–1.

b) Listen to the triad. Sing the root only.

Fig. 2.20

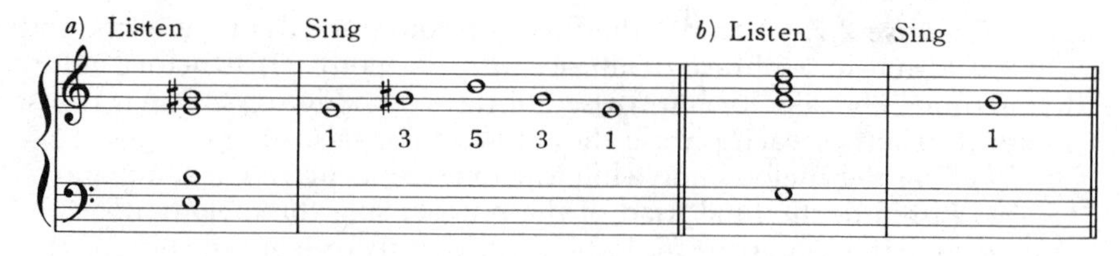

Exercise 2.3. Singing any major triad from its root. Play or listen to any given pitch. Call this pitch 1. Sing a major triad from this pitch.

Fig. 2.21

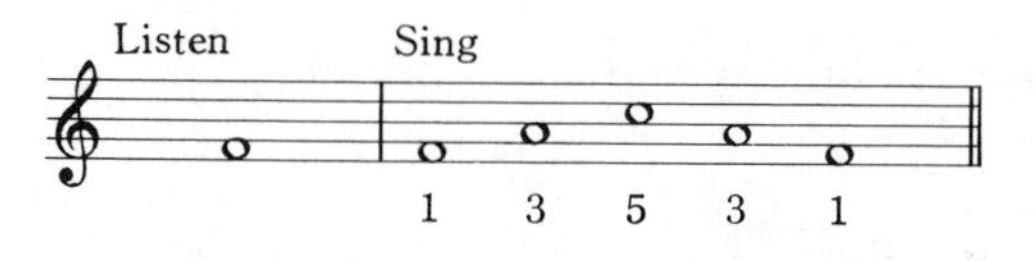

Exercise 2.4. Singing any major triad from its fifth. Play or listen to any given pitch. Call this pitch 5. Sing the triad pattern 5–3–1–3–5.

Fig. 2.22

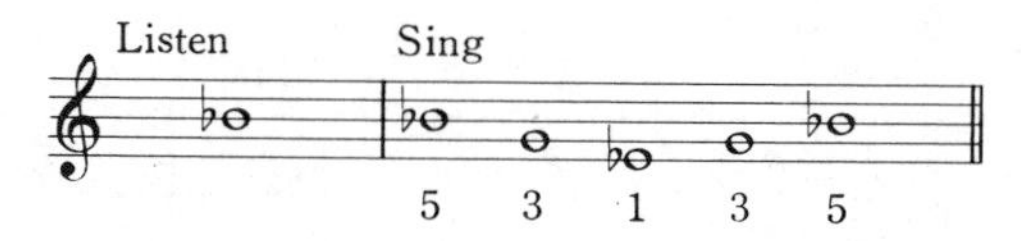

Exercise 2.5. Singing any major triad from its third. Play or listen to any given pitch. Call this pitch 3. Sing the triad pattern 3–1–3–5–3.

Fig. 2.23

Exercise 2.6. Repeat exercises 2.3, 2.4, and 2.5. Instead of singing numbers, sing with letter names when the name of the first pitch is given. (When letter name includes an accidental, sing repeated note, as in "D flat.")

Fig. 2.24

Identifying Members of the Major Triad

Exercise 2.7. Identify the final soprano (melody) note in the cadence.

a) Listen to a phrase of music, with harmony. (Instructor: phrases from hymn tunes, chorales, or improvised phrases as in Figure 2.25 may be used. The final two triads of each phrase should be major triads.)

b) Sing the melody line while the exercise is played at the piano.

c) Listen to the final triad of the phrase; sing the melody note.

d) Sing the triad pattern, 1–3–5, and identify the soprano note as 1, 3, or 5 by singing the soprano note with a number or by reciting the number of the soprano note.

Fig. 2.25

Step *a*) Listen

Step *b*) Sing the soprano line as step *a* is repeated.

Exercise 2.8. Follow directions for Exercise 2.7, but at *b*) sing the melody line without the piano. This will help develop your musical memory, a skill necessary in taking melodic dictation, which begins in Chapter 6.

Exercise 2.9. Identify the soprano note of a single triad. Listen to a single triad and identify the soprano note as 1, 3, or 5.

a) by singing the soprano note with its correct number, *or*

b) by reciting the correct number of the soprano note, *or*

c) by writing the correct number of the soprano note.

With continued practice, sing, recite, or write the correct number immediately after hearing the triad.

Exercise 2.10. Spell the major triad when the letter name of the soprano note is known. The letter name of the soprano note will be given. Identify the soprano note by number and then spell the triad. Example: F♯ is given as the soprano note. Listen to the triad. If the soprano note is identified as the third of the triad, the triad is spelled D F♯ A.

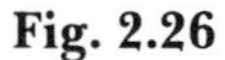
Fig. 2.26

Self-Help in Ear Training

Upon completion of Exercise 2.18 (playing the major triad at the keyboard), students working in pairs can practice Exercises 2.9 and 2.10 outside the classroom. One student will play a triad while the other proceeds with either of the two exercises. After approximately ten triads have been played and identified or spelled, the students should change places. Both students will derive much valuable practice in both keyboard harmony and ear training.

Singing Intervals

Exercise 2.11. Singing intervals from major triads by number.

a) Sing a major triad from a given pitch, using the numbers 1–3–5–3–1. Then sing two-note combinations (intervals) from this triad, as directed: 1 up to 3, 3 up to 5, 1 up to 5, 3 down to 1, 5 down to 3, 5 down to 1.

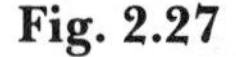
Fig. 2.27

b) Sing the triad with additional upper or lower tones, as many above and below the given triad as lie in a comfortable singing range. For example, for the E♭ major triad below, 1 above the triad and 5 and 3 below the triad are in a comfortable singing range.

Fig. 2.28

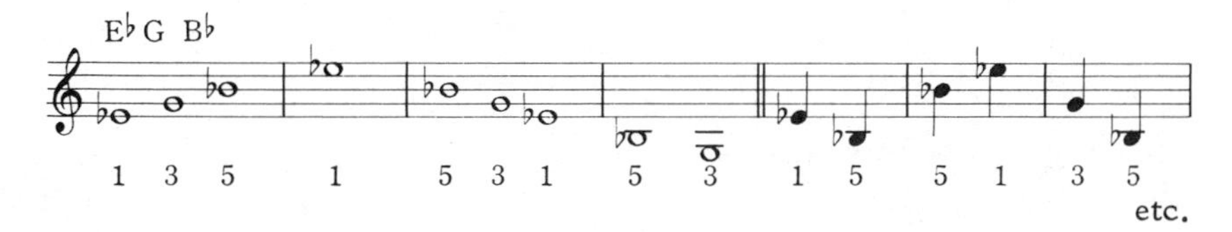

Exercise 2.12. Sing a given interval with triad numbers from a given pitch. For example, when asked to sing 3 up to 5, first sing aloud the major triad pattern 3–1–3–5–3. Then sing 3 up to 5. With practice you should be able to discontinue singing the triad aloud, singing only the interval.

Identifying Intervals

Exercise 2.13. Identify melodic or harmonic intervals aurally. (Review Chapter 1, section 14.)

a) You will hear a triad at the piano.
b) You will hear an interval (melodic or harmonic) from that triad.
c) Sing the interval on *la.*
d) Sing the complete triad, using 1–3–5–3–1.
e) Sing the interval again, using correct numbers. Example:

Fig. 2.29 (Melodic Interval)

Fig. 2.30 (Harmonic interval: sing lower note of interval first)

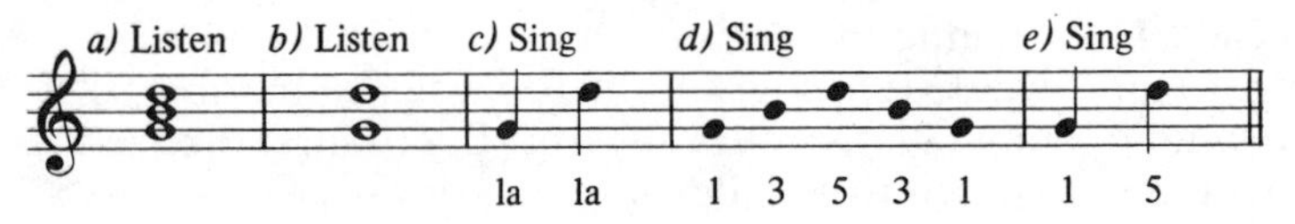

With continued practice, eliminate steps *a, c,* and *d.*

Exercise 2.14. Identify intervals aurally by writing number relationships. Follow the procedure for Exercise 2.13. For the problem given in Figure 2.29 or 2.30, write the answer 1 up to 5, or 1 /\ 5, or 1 ↑ 5.

Exercise 2.15. Identify intervals aurally by naming the interval. Follow the procedure for Exercise 2.13. For the problem in Figure 2.29, state or write the answer: perfect fifth, or P5.

Exercise 2.16. Sing interval when name of interval is given and one note of interval is played at the piano. Sing the triad on 1–3–5–3–1 first if necessary. Example: Sing a minor sixth down from G. First, think interval numbers–a minor sixth down is 1 down to 3.

Fig. 2.31

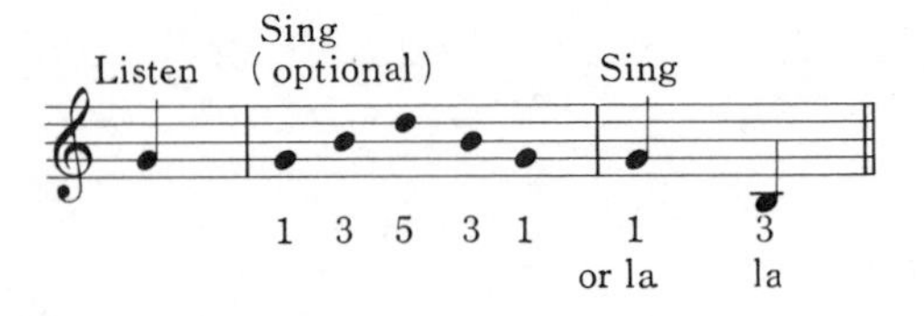

Exercise 2.17. Write intervals on the staff from dictation. The first note of the interval will be given; place this on the staff. Listen to the interval, then write:

a) the numbers of the interval
b) the name of the interval
c) the triad spelling
d) the second note of the interval. Example:

Fig. 2.32

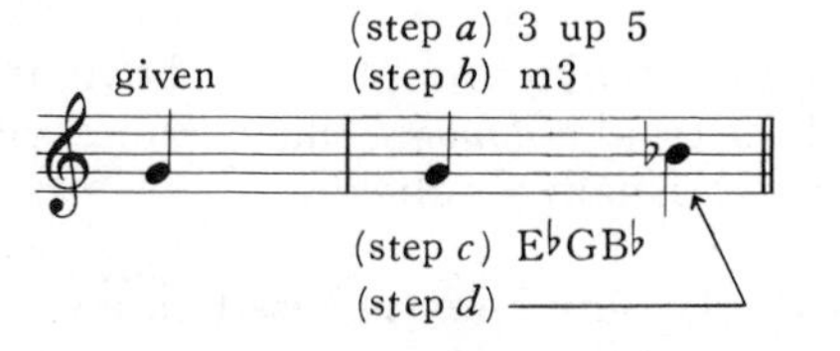

After sufficient practice, continue drill by omitting steps *a* and *c*.

Self-Help Procedure for Intervals

Upon completion of Exercises 2.19 and 2.20 (playing intervals at the keyboard), students working in pairs can aid each other in mastering Exercises 2.13–2.17. One student will play the interval while the other student identifies the interval.

Keyboard Harmony

Playing the Major Triad and Intervals

You will find these keyboard exercises easy to do even if you have no prior keyboard facility, assuming that you know the names of the keys on the piano (review Chapter 1, section 10). Play each example carefully, making sure you are covering the correct keys before sounding the notes. Practice until you can play triads or intervals quickly and accurately. This facility is absolutely necessary if you are to acquire keyboard skills required in later chapters.

Exercise 2.18. Play a major triad with its root in the bass. Play each major triad spelling as listed in Groups I, II, and III on page 25. Play each spelling in each of three soprano positions: root, third, and fifth in soprano. Follow these steps initially. After sufficient practice, use step *e* only.

a) Spell the triad
b) Find the root of the triad in the left hand. Do not play.
c) Place the little finger of the right hand on the given soprano note. Do not play.
d) Find the other two notes of the triad immediately below the soprano note, using the right hand. Do not play.
e) Play all four notes of the triad simultaneously.

Example: D major triad with its third in the soprano.

Fig. 2.33

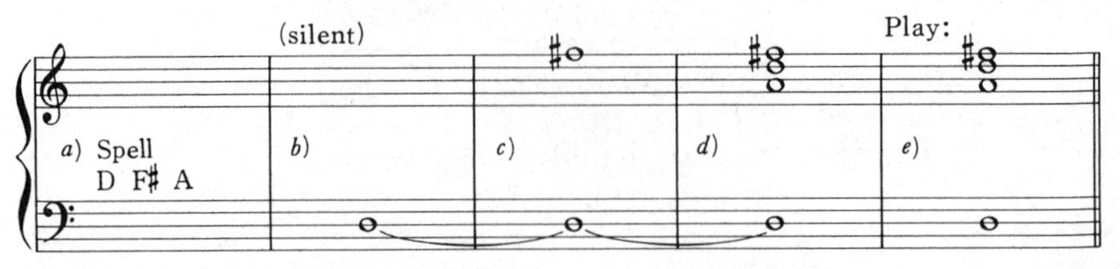

The triad is commonly played and written in four parts, as above. In adding the extra note, one of the members of the triad is *doubled,* that is, there will be two of that member. The root of the triad is usually doubled.

Exercise 2.19. At the keyboard, play any interval based on a given triad.

Procedure	*Example*
a) Listen to directions.	*a*) Play 5 up to 1 in the A♭ major triad, or play an ascending perfect fourth in the A♭ major triad.
b) Spell the triad.	*b*) A♭ C E♭
c) Spell the interval.	*c*) 5 up to 1 is E♭ up to A♭, or, a perfect fourth up is E♭ up to A♭.
d) Play the interval.	*d*) or

Exercise 2.20. Play any interval, ascending or descending, from a given pitch. Play the intervals in Assignment 2.12 (page 31), and others as assigned.

Pitch Notation from Earliest Times

We know that music existed in ancient times from sources such as pictures, artifacts, and literary works (Psalm 150 from the Bible, for example). However, because there was no music notation in those times we will never know exactly how ancient music sounded.

The earliest known notation is that of pre–Christian Greece, in which letters of the alphabet were used to represent pitches. Because very little of this notation survives, we know only a little about the sound of their music, depsite the fact that the Greeks were prolific in writing about music.

The beginnings of our present notation date back to approximately the eighth century A.D., when the object of notation was to indicate pitch levels and directions in singing the chants of the church service. This was done with signs, called *neumes,* placed directly over the words of the chant. The result was a vague indication of the movement of the melody—helpful, probably, only to someone already acquainted with the melody.

Neumes, circa eighth century

It occurred to someone in the tenth century that pitch could be indicated by drawing a line indicating a certain pitch (usually F) and placing neumes on, above, and below it. Staves with more lines followed, with four and five-line staves appearing in the thirteenth century. By that time, neumes had evolved into note shapes more readily recognizable as precursors of our present notation. Notation was all black until the fifteenth century, when white notation appeared with the black to form a system that was used until approximately 1600. (See "Rhythm Notation," on page 62.)

One-line staff, circa 10th century

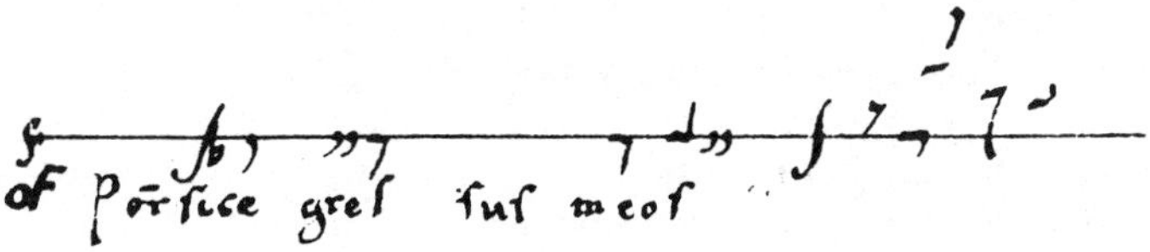

Two-line staff, circa 11th century

Four-line staff, circa 13th century

Five-line staff with white notation, 16th century

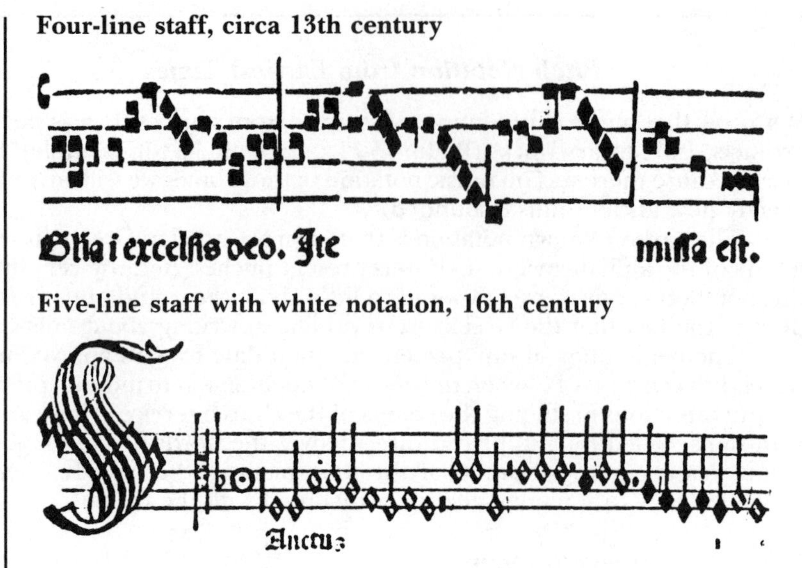

Clef signs developed from the need to designate the pitch names of the lines and spaces of the staff. The earliest clefs were representations of the letter names needed. These changed over the centuries to the forms used today.

Clefs

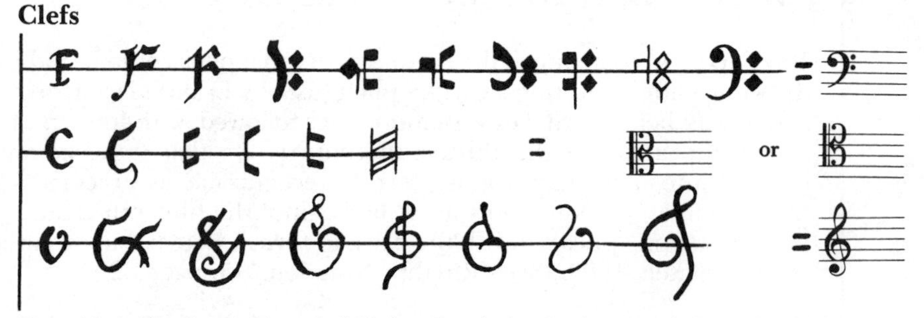

From *Music Notation: A Manual of Modern Practice* by Gardner Read, Second Edition (Taplinger/Crescendo, 1979). © 1969 by Crescendo Publishing Company. Reprinted by permission.

From 1600 up to the present century, notation has undergone few developments. Contemporary composers express new ideas with a variety of notational devices, including conventional notation displayed in unconventional ways, new notational symbols accompanied by their own written directions, and graphic representations of the sounds the composer wishes to have produced.

The wide variety of these notational devices, too numerous to be shown here, will be considered in *Advanced Harmony, Theory and Practice,* Third edition. Further information can also be found in these texts: Reginald Smith Brindle, *The New Music* (London: Oxford University Press, 1975), and Kurt Stone, *Music Notation in the Twentieth Century* ((New York: W. W. Norton & Co., 1980).

The Universality of the Cadence

The use of cadences is a typical feature of all music, regardless of historical period or geographical area. There must always be places in any piece of music where the melody or the ensemble reaches a temporary or concluding resting point. How this is accomplished varies widely in differing times and places, as is demonstrated in the few but diverse examples that follow.

In contrast to these examples, most of the cadences of the common practice period reflect some type of tonic-dominant relationship, with V-I as a final cadence used almost exclusively.

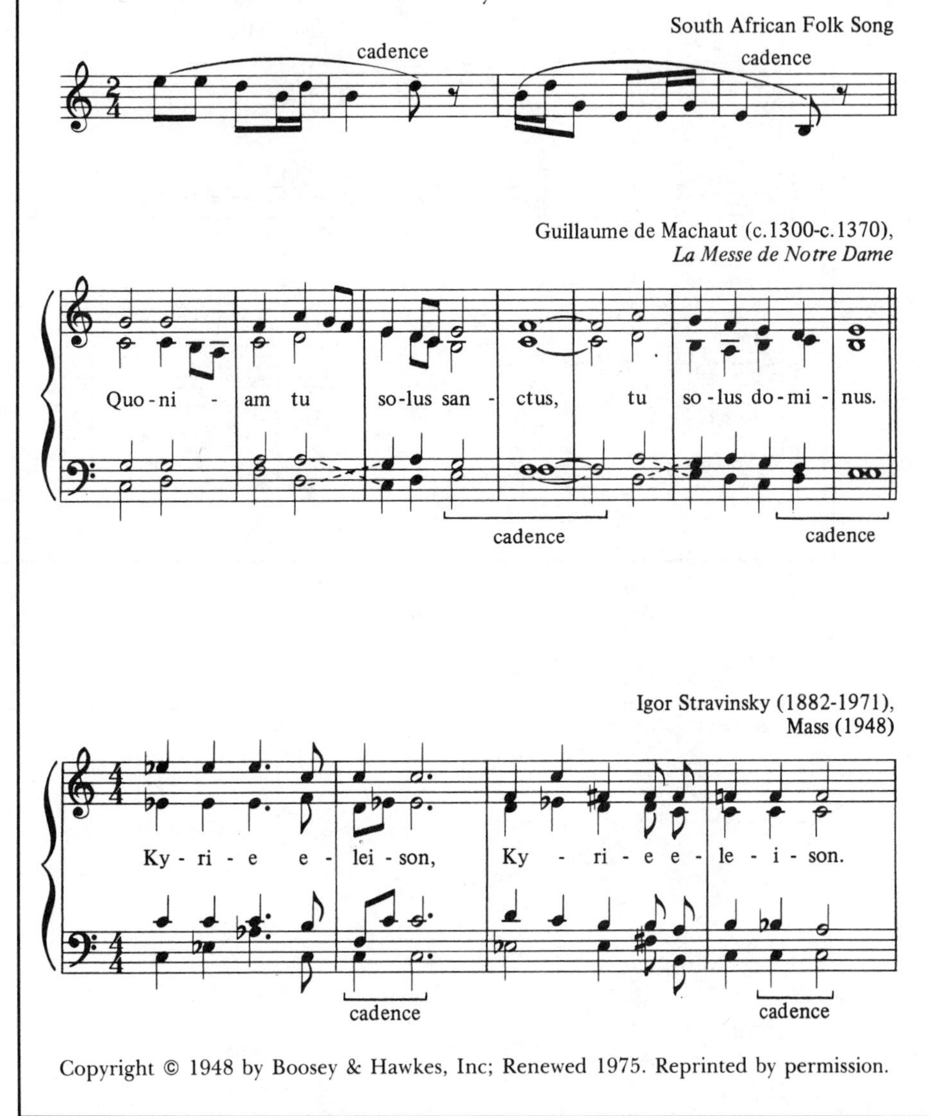

The "Difficult" Major Triad Spellings

When spelling tonic and dominant triads, you have probably noticed that not all possible major triad spellings are used, especially those with double sharps or double flats. All major triad spellings are useful and will be encountered regularly as your knowledge of harmony expands. Here are two examples: (1) F♭ A♭ C♭, used as the enharmonic of E G♯ B and as the triad built on the lowered sixth scale step (F♭) in the key of A♭ major; (2) D♯ F𝄪 A♯, used as the dominant triad in G♯ minor.

CHAPTER 3

Meter and Rhythm

This chapter may be studied concurrently with Chapter 2, after reviewing sections 26–34 in Chapter 1.

The material of this chapter properly belongs in the study of music fundamentals covered in a similar manner in Rudiments of Music *(Prentice-Hall, Inc., 1970) by Robert W. Ottman and Frank D. Mainous, and in the same authors'* Programmed Rudiments of Music *(Prentice-Hall, Inc., 1979). Students who have completed either of these texts or comparable material from other sources may wish to use this chapter as a review or go on to Chapter 4.*

Theory and Analysis

Since music exists in time, a given pitch must sound for a given length of time until it is replaced by another pitch or by a rest, the duration of which may be longer or shorter. The different note values indicate lengths of time relative to each other (for example, a half note equals two quarter notes), but they do not specify the temporal length of the sounds they represent. These durations need to be measured before they can be set down on paper to become part of the music score.

The Beat

The standard of measurement in musical time is the *beat.* Fortunately, the beat is easily recognizable by almost every person. If, in listening to music, you make a regular series of taps with your finger or with your foot, you are making beats. Each tap is measuring a small unit of time, and if the taps are regular each tap, or beat, measures the same amount of time. When representing the sound of music on paper, any note value may be chosen to represent a beat, as when a quarter note equals one beat.

Composers specify the time value of the beat by using temporal directions at the beginning of a composition. Among others, the word *allegro,* meaning *fast,* indicates a beat of short duration, whereas *adagio,* meaning *slow,* indicates a beat of longer duration. These tempo indications are not specific, and can lead to a range of interpretations. More specific are metronome markings, where M.M. 60 means one tick of the metronome per second, M.M. 120 means two ticks per second, and so forth. When assigned to a note value, such as ♩= 60 or ♪= 100 an exact duration for the beat is obtained.

In Figure 3.1, two excerpts from the same work show contrasting assignments of beat duration. In *a,* the duration of the beat, a half note, is slightly more than one second, as indicated by the marking 𝅗𝅥= 54, while in *b* the duration of the quarter note beat is less than one half second, indicated by ♩= 144.

Fig. 3.1

Exercise 3.1. Listening for beats. The instructor will play several melodies or other music examples in a variety of tempos. With your right hand, make taps of equal time durations, conforming to your feeling for the beat in the music.

Grouping of Beats

As you listen, you will note that beats tend to group themselves with one beat assuming more importance than the following beats. In most music the more important, or stronger, beat recurs regularly, marking off groups of 2, 3, or 4 beats.

Exercise 3.2. Listening for beat groupings. Listen to music examples, as in Exercise 3.1. When you have located the strong beat, count aloud 1-2 or 1-2-3, depending on the emphasis. (It is often difficult to recognize four-beat groupings since the first and third beats are both stronger beats, the third only a little less so. Four-beat groupings can easily be confused with two two-beat groupings.)

Fig. 3.2

```
>       >       >
|   |   |   |   |   |
1   2   1   2   1   2

>           >
|   |   |   |   |   |
1   2   3   1   2   3          ( > = accent)

>               >
|   |   |   |   |   |   |   |
1   2   3   4   1   2   3   4
```

Varieties of the Beat

Two varieties of the beat exist. These can best be illustrated by listening to two different folk songs, Figures 3.3 and 3.5. In each folk song, the beats are in groups of two, but the nature of the beat differs in each of the two songs.

Fig. 3.3

Listen to the melody in Figure 3.3. Note that each beat in this melody can be divided into two parts. This can be demonstrated by tapping the beats in the right hand and, with the left hand, making two taps for each beat in the right hand.

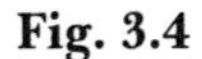

Fig. 3.4

```
             1       2       1       2
right hand   |       |       |       |

left hand    |   |   |   |   |   |   |   |
```

Fig. 3.5

Listen to the melody in Figure 3.5. Note that each beat in this melody can be divided into three parts. This can be demonstrated by tapping the beats in the right hand and, with the left hand, making three taps for each beat in the right hand.

Fig. 3.6

	1			2			1			2		
right hand	|			|			|			|		
left hand	|	|	|	|	|	|	|	|	|	|	|	|

The above procedure is known as dividing the beat. A beat that can be divided into two parts is known as a *simple* beat, a division often called "background of two." A beat that can be divided into three parts is known as a *compound* beat, often called "background of three."

Exercise 3.3. Listen to music examples played by your instructor: *a*) determine whether the background of the beat is simple or compound, and determine whether the beats are in groupings of two or three. Diagram your pattern of beats and divisions as in Figures 3.4 and 3.6.

Meter

The meter of a piece of music is the basic scheme of beat groupings used; most music has a meter of two, three, or four beats per measure. Meter is not to be confused with rhythm. The term "rhythm" indicates the pattern of longer and shorter note values used; the sum total of the note or rest values in each measure will be equal to the number of beats per measure.

Fig. 3.7

The Time Signature

It is the function of the time signature (meter signature) to indicate

1) the beat groupings,
2) the simple or compound divisions of the beat, and
3) the notation to be used.

The numerator of the time signature fulfills the first two of these functions, while the denominator fulfills the third. Although all time signatures look alike, in that they consist of one number placed over another, those for simple time are interpreted differently from those for compound time.

Simple Time. Music in which the beat is divisible into two parts is said to be in *simple time.* Let us assume that we have heard some music, and determined the beat grouping and beat division to be | | / | | | | . To determine the time signature, we first assign to the beat a note value that can be divided into two parts. Any undotted noted will do (♩ = ♫, 𝅗𝅥 = ♩ ♩, etc.). The quarter note is most commonly used to represent the simple beat. Using the quarter note, our diagram appears as 1 ♩ 2 ♩ / | | | | , and by showing the division of each beat, 1 ♩ ♫ 2 ♩ ♫ we have notated one complete beat grouping, comparable to one measure of music. This information can be compressed into a device known as a *time signature.*

Beats: 1 ♩ 2 ♩

Note value: (♩) = $\frac{1}{4} + \frac{1}{4} = \frac{2}{4}$ (or, $2 \times \frac{1}{4} = \frac{2}{4}$)

Or, for example, we can assign the eighth note as the beat note in a three-beat grouping:

Beats 1 ♪ 2 ♪ 3 ♪

Note value (♪) = $\frac{1}{8} + \frac{1}{8} + \frac{1}{8} = \frac{3}{8}$ (or, $3 \times \frac{1}{8} = \frac{3}{8}$)

TABLE 3.1 SIMPLE TIME SIGNATURES

Beat note	*2 beats per measure (Duple)*	*3 beats per measure (Triple)*	*4 beats per measure (Quadruple)*
𝅝 ($\frac{1}{1}$)	$\frac{2}{1}$	$\frac{3}{1}$	$\frac{4}{1}$
𝅗𝅥 ($\frac{1}{2}$)	$\frac{2}{2}$ or ¢	$\frac{3}{2}$	$\frac{4}{2}$
♩ ($\frac{1}{4}$)	$\frac{2}{4}$	$\frac{3}{4}$	$\frac{4}{4}$ or C
♪ ($\frac{1}{8}$)	$\frac{2}{8}$	$\frac{3}{8}$	$\frac{4}{8}$
𝅘𝅥𝅯 ($\frac{1}{16}$)	$\frac{2}{16}$	$\frac{3}{16}$	$\frac{4}{16}$
𝅘𝅥𝅰 ($\frac{1}{32}$)	$\frac{2}{32}$	$\frac{3}{32}$	$\frac{4}{32}$

Table 3.1 shows the derivation of the simple time signatures. Here, instead of adding together each of the beat notes, we have multiplied the number of beat notes by the beat value ($\frac{1}{4} + \frac{1}{4} = \frac{2}{4}$, or $2 \times \frac{1}{4} = \frac{2}{4}$).

Observe from Table 3.1 that in simple time, the numerators of time signatures are 2, 3, and 4.

2—duple simple time (meter)
3—triple simple time
4—quadruple simple time

A complete explanation of $\frac{2}{4}$, for example, is that the numerator 2 indicates duple simple time, where *duple* means two beats per measure and *simple* means two divisions for each beat. The denominator 4 indicates that the quarter note represents the beat, and it is divisible into two eighth notes.

Fig. 3.8

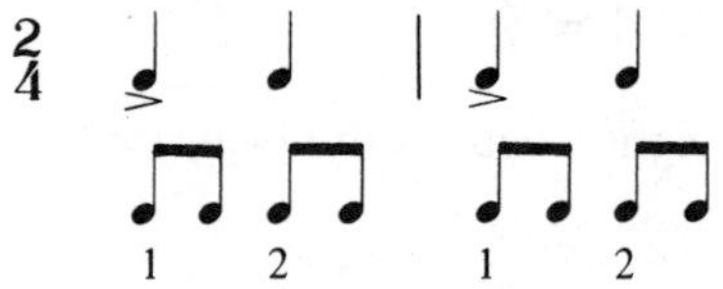

$\frac{2}{4}$

1 2 1 2

Exercise 3.4. Explain verbally, or by diagram as in Figure 3.8, the meaning of the following time signatures.

$\frac{3}{4}$, $\frac{4}{4}$, $\frac{2}{8}$, $\frac{3}{2}$, $\frac{3}{8}$, $\frac{4}{16}$, $\frac{4}{2}$

It should be carefully noted that the properties of beat grouping and beat divisions exist within the music itself, whereas the time signature only reports this information and places it in abbreviated form for easy reference at the beginning of the music. It is particularly important to keep this concept in mind when studying compound time signatures where beat groupings and beat divisions produce a signature that must be interpreted differently from the simple time signature.

Compound Time. Music in which the beat is a compound beat is said to be in *compound time.* We shall follow the same procedure as that used for simple time, but our results will be somewhat different.

1. Let us assume from listening that the beat grouping and the beat divisions are 1 2 .

2. Assign a note value for the beat. Any dotted note value will do. Choosing a ♩. as the beat, the pattern appears as 1 2

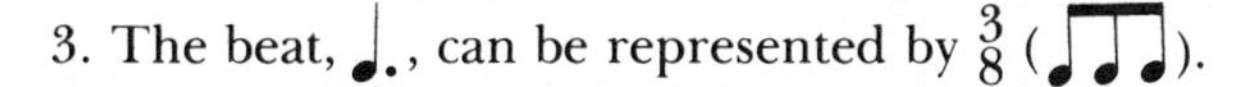

3. The beat, ♩., can be represented by $\frac{3}{8}$ (♪♪♪).

4. Adding together two beats, $\frac{3}{8} + \frac{3}{8}$, produces the time signature $\frac{6}{8}$; or 2 (beats) $\times \frac{3}{8} = \frac{6}{8}$.

Follow the same procedure to express any compound meter, for example, a three-beat grouping using a 𝅗𝅥. as the beat note.

1. The beat, 𝅗𝅥., can be represented by $\frac{3}{4}$ (♩ ♩ ♩).

2. Adding three beats, $\frac{3}{4} + \frac{3}{4} + \frac{3}{4}$, produces the time signature $\frac{9}{4}$; or 3 (beats) $\times \frac{3}{4} = \frac{9}{4}$.

It is obvious that compound time signatures do not indicate the number of beats per measure and the note value receiving one beat as conveniently as do the simple time signatures. Actually, the upper number of the compound signature indicates the number of *beat divisions* per measure, while the lower number states the *note value* that represents the beat division.

To verify this, listen again to Figure 3.5. Figure 3.9 is an analysis of its first two measures.

Fig. 3.9

TABLE 3.2 COMPOUND TIME SIGNATURES

Beat note	*2 beats per measure (Duple)*	*3 beats per measure (Triple)*	*4 beats per measure (Quadruple)*
𝅝. $(\frac{3}{2})$	$\frac{6}{2}$	$\frac{9}{2}$	$\frac{12}{2}$
𝅗𝅥. $(\frac{3}{4})$	$\frac{6}{4}$	$\frac{9}{4}$	$\frac{12}{4}$
♩. $(\frac{3}{8})$	$\frac{6}{8}$	$\frac{9}{8}$	$\frac{12}{8}$
♪. $(\frac{3}{16})$	$\frac{6}{16}$	$\frac{9}{16}$	$\frac{12}{16}$
𝅘𝅥𝅯. $(\frac{3}{32})$	$\frac{6}{32}$	$\frac{9}{32}$	$\frac{12}{32}$

Table 3.2 shows the derivations of compound time signatures, obtained by multiplying the beat grouping by the fractional value of the note assigned to receive one beat.

Observe from Table 3.2 that in compound time the numerators of the time signatures are 6, 9, and 12.

6 = duple compound time
9 = triple compound time
12 = quadruple compound time

A complete explanation of $\frac{6}{8}$, for example, is that the numerator 6 denotes duple compound time, where *duple* means two beats per measure and *compound* means three divisions for each beat. The denominator 8 indicates that the eighth note represents a beat division, three of which equal the beat note, a dotted quarter note.

Fig. 3.10

Exercise 3.5. Explain verbally, or by diagram as in Figure 3.10, the meaning of the following time signatures.

$\frac{6}{4}$, $\frac{9}{8}$, $\frac{12}{8}$, $\frac{6}{16}$, $\frac{12}{4}$, $\frac{9}{2}$,

A Simplified System of Time Signatures

A few twentieth century composers, and a few textbooks, have attempted to introduce a simplified system of signatures, in which the numerator is always the actual number of beats per measure and the denominator always shows the actual note value receiving one beat.

Examples:

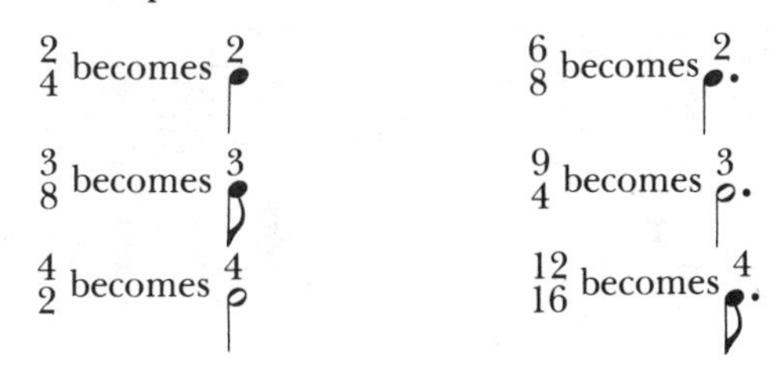

Fig. 3.11

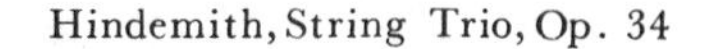

Other Interpretations of Time Signatures

In any time signature the upper number always indicates how many of the note values expressed by the lower number will be found in one measure. While interpretations of time signatures such as those just presented are generally useful, there are occasions when a very fast or a very slow tempo requires a different interpretation.

1. Numerator of 4. In a fast tempo, there may actually be two beats per measure. In fast $\frac{4}{4}$ meter, for example, the beat may be felt as a half note rather than as the quarter note. The beat is frequently identified by a metronome marking (e.g., $\frac{4}{4}$, 𝅗𝅥 = 120), the direction *alla breve,* or by substituting either of the signatures ¢ or $\frac{2}{2}$, in which the half note equals one beat (Fig. 3.12a)

In a few instances, ¢ is used with markings for a slow tempo, indicating as slow a "2" feeling as possible without becoming "4." For examples of this, see Schubert songs, *Ihr Bild* (¢ Langsam), *Die Taubenpost* (¢ Ziemlich langsam), and *Der Wanderer* (¢ Sehr langsam), all in Volume 1 of the *Collected Songs of Schubert.*

Where only a tempo marking is indicated, as in Figure 3.12b, the decision as to whether the measure contains two or four beats can, in many cases, only be the result of personal judgment. In this case, two beats per measure seems to be the best judgment. Subjective evaluations are also frequently the bases for the interpretation of other time signatures in the remaining paragraphs of this discussion.

Fig. 3.12

2. *Numerator of 3.* In a fast tempo, there may actually be one beat per measure. In a fast $\frac{3}{4}$, the beat may be a 𝅗𝅥. , with three beat divisions of quarter notes. Thus the effect is that of compound time, one beat per measure.

Fig. 3.13

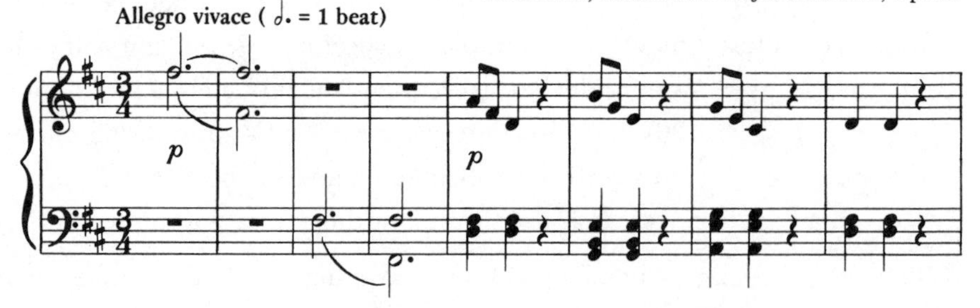

3. *Numerator of 2, 3, or 4.* In a very slow tempo, the division of the note value indicated in the denominator may become the beat note. In the slow $\frac{4}{4}$ in Figure 3.14, the eighth note is the beat, with eight beats per measure.

4. *Numerator of 6, 9, or 12.* In a very slow tempo, the division of the beat note may receive the beat. In this case the denominator of the signature indicates

the note receiving one beat. The effect of compound time is maintained by the stress given to the first beat in each group of three beats:

6/8 ♪ ♪ ♪ ♪ ♪ ♪
1 2 3 4 5 6

Fig. 3.14

Fig. 3.15

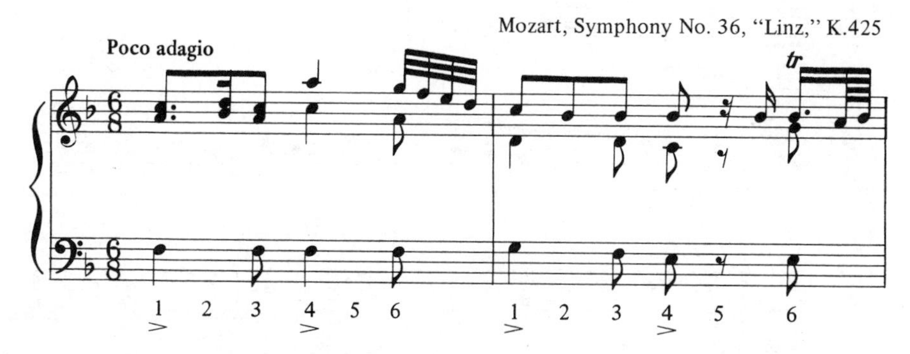

Terminology Variant

The term *simple time* sometimes refers only to those time signatures with a numerator of 2 or 3. Compound time then refers to multiples of 2 or 3 such as $\frac{4}{4}$ $(\frac{2}{4} + \frac{2}{4})$ or $\frac{6}{8}$ $(\frac{3}{8} + \frac{3}{8})$.

Application

Written Materials

Identifying Meters

Assignment 3.1. Place a correct time signature before each musical example. The first measure of an example may be incomplete, in which case the last measure is also incomplete; the two partial measures equal one complete measure in time value. In a few cases, more than one correct signature is possible.

Assignment 3.2. Find examples of time signatures in music scores, particularly those other than the commonly used $\frac{2}{4}$, $\frac{3}{4}$, $\frac{4}{4}$, and $\frac{6}{8}$. Copy out one or two measures of the music, including the time signature; indicate source of music including composer, title, publisher, and page number.

Rhythmic Transcription

Now that you have studied the derivation of time signatures, it should be obvious to you that any two or more signatures with identical numerators designate the same meter.

If, for example, you hear music that you can identify as being in duple compound time, you can assume that the numerator of the time signature is 6, but it would be absolutely impossible to tell which of the possible denominators the composer had used. It could be any of them, as the denominator affects only the notation to be used. The same music with like numerators but with differing denominators will sound identical when the tempo of the beat note is equal in each, as shown in Figure 3.16.

Fig. 3.16

Assignment 3.3. Rewrite each of these melodies using the time signatures indicated.

a) in $\frac{4}{2}$ and $\frac{4}{8}$

Ear Training and Music Reading

Music Reading

Music reading refers to the ability to understand a piece of music at first sight, much as one does when reading a book, and to perform it. In one sense, music reading is nothing more than the interpretation of music notation as a set of directions: what fingers to use in what place, what key to push, and other similar mechanical procedures. When followed correctly, these directions will help the music reader produce the sounds indicated in the music score.

A more sophisticated music reader can hear the music mentally, and knows what it sounds like before actually playing it. In such a case, manipulation of keys, strings, and the like only confirms what he or she already knows.

We will study music reading as it is understood in this latter sense. This skill is developed through *sight singing*. Because no mechanical manipulation is possible in singing, a sight singing performance gives the singer a clear indication of whether or not the sound indicated by the music notation is being comprehended mentally.

In reading a melodic line, the performer is required to read notation symbols that indicate both rhythm and pitch simultaneously. We will begin our study of music reading by concentrating first on the reading of rhythm. Pitch will be dealt with in a subsequent chapter.

The Conductor's Beat

Use of the conductor's beats of 2, 3 and 4 will facilitate the development of rhythmic reading ability. Each of these conductor's beats is characterized by a preparatory upbeat, followed by a downbeat on the first beat of the measure. The upbeat is the preparation for the following downbeat; the downbeat drops in a straight line and describes a small bounce at the instant the first beat occurs. After the downbeat, each of the conductor's beats follows a different course.

Fig. 3.17

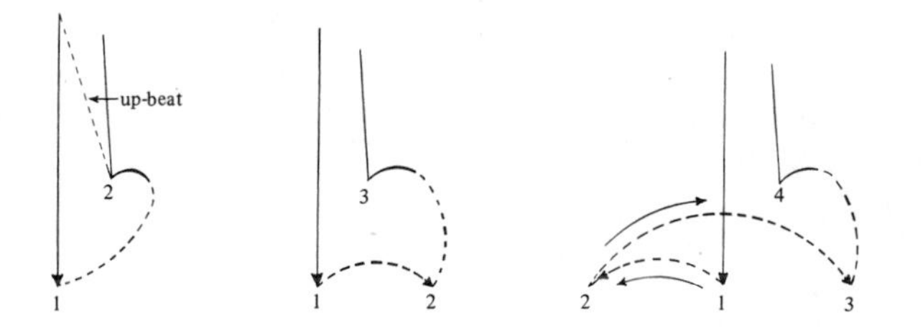

At the completion of one measure, the last beat of the measure is the upbeat of the next measure.

Exercise 3.6. Practice each of the conductor's beats before a mirror and with a metronome. Set the metronome at a slow rate at first (about M.M. 50). These movements must become completely automatic, so that when you read rhythm or sing at sight, your attention can be devoted to the musical notation.

Exercise 3.7. Add simple background to each of these conductor's beats by tapping twice with the left hand to each beat of the right hand. In doing so, you are conducting duple simple, triple simple, and quadruple simple times. Follow all directions given in Exercise 3.6.

Exercise 3.8. Practice the conductor's beats (2, 3 and 4), adding a compound background by tapping three times with the left hand to each beat in the right hand. In doing so, you are conducting duple compound, triple compound, and quadruple compound times. Follow other directions given in Exercise 3.6.

When a time signature requires special interpretation because of tempo, the following conductor's beats are used.

1. Fast tempo ($\frac{3}{8}$, $\frac{3}{4}$, etc.) The conductor's beat is one beat per measure. Make either a succession of downbeats, or a circle with a hand accent at the bottom of the circle.

(All "one" beats occur at the same point in front of the body.)

2. Slow Tempo. Make a hand movement for each of the beat divisions by simply dividing the beat into each of the 2, 3, and 4 basic conductor's beats.

Exercise 3.9. Continue to practice, using beat patterns shown in Figures 3.18 and 3.19.

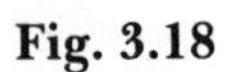

Fig. 3.18

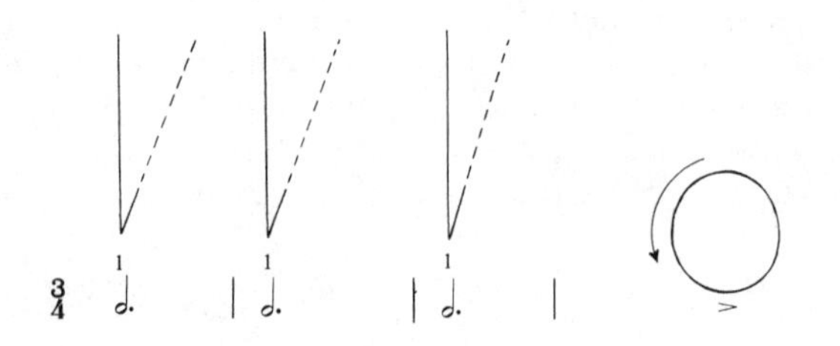

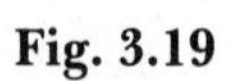

Fig. 3.19

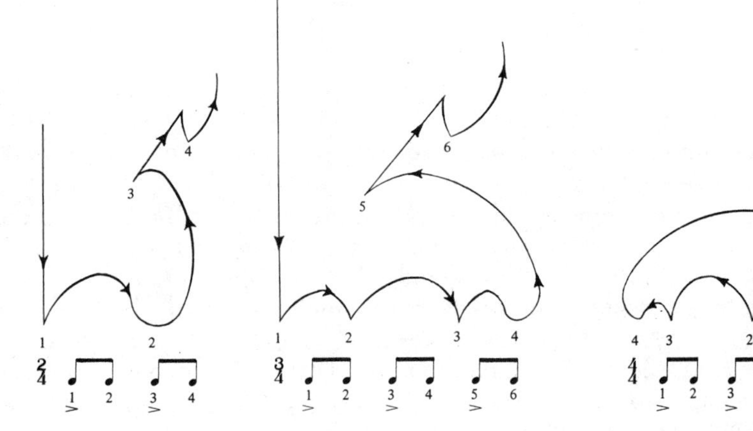

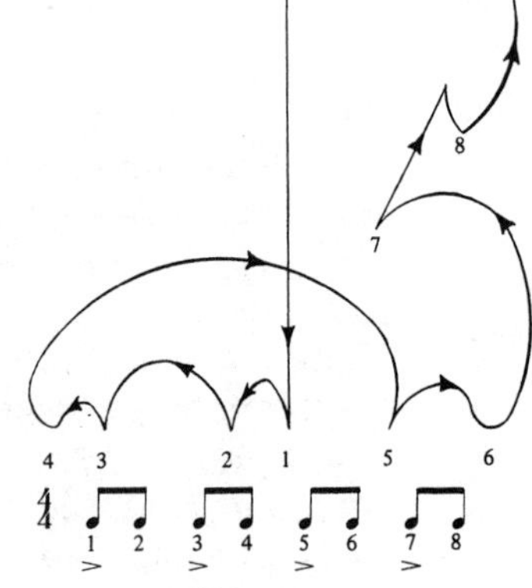

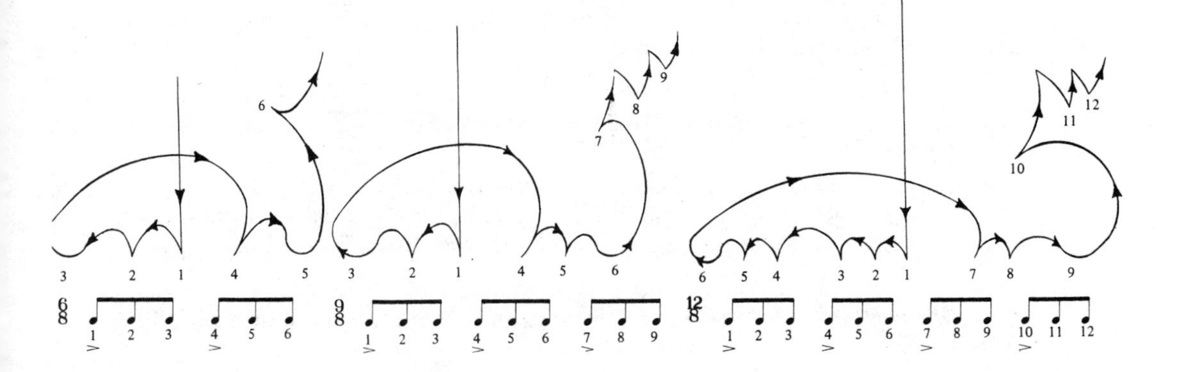

Rhythmic Reading

Rhythmic reading is more precise when rhythmic syllables are used. Of all of the systems in use presently, two appear to be in particular favor and are acceptable for our purposes. In both of these systems, when the note falls on the beat speak the number of that beat. When the note is longer than a beat, hold the number for the duration of the note value.

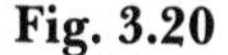
Fig. 3.20

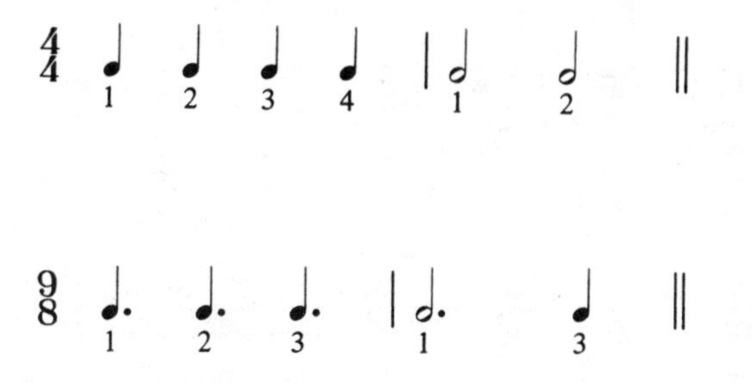

In the first system, all note values smaller than the beat use the syllable *ta.*[1] In the second system, syllables differ for simple and compound time. In simple time, the division of the beat is *te,* pronounced *tay,* and smaller units are *ta,* (pronounced *tah*). In compound time, the second and third divisions of the beat are *la* and *lee,* while still smaller divisions are *ta.*

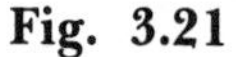
Fig. 3.21

[1]Syllables other than *ta* may be used to read durations shorter than the beat, if desired. Rhythmic reading is more precise, and therefore more likely to be accurate, if the rhythmic syllable begins with an explosive consonant.

Here are some examples:

Fig. 3.22

At this point in our study, rhythmic reading will include only the beat value, notes longer than the beat value, the division of the beat value (two in simple time, three in compound time), and comparable rests. Before reading, make the following preparations:

1. Review the meaning of the time signature.
2. Choose the appropriate conductor's beat.
3. Start the conductor's beat and background at least one measure before beginning to read.

Try to read each piece of music through without stopping. If you make an error, do not stop to correct it, but keep going. The conductor's downbeat always coincides with a bar-line in the music, and it will help you keep your place. At the end of the piece, go back to review the reasons for any errors you made and reread those places to correct the errors.

Exercise 3.10. Rhythmic reading in simple time. Ample material will be found in the following sources.

Music for Sight Singing: All melodies in Chapters 1, 3, and 6, and all melodies in simple time from Chapters 5 and 8. Read the rhythm only of these melodies, disregarding the pitch element of the notation.

More Music for Sight Singing: Specific rhythmic reading drills are found on pages 1–17, Examples 1–19, 32–44, 53–74, and 90–101. Melodies in simple time in Examples 266–394 contain the same rhythmic problems.

Exercise 3.11. Rhythmic reading in compound time. Use the following sources:

Music for Sight Singing: All melodies in Chapters 2, 4, and 7, and all melodies in compound time in Chapters 5 and 8.

More Music for Sight Singing: Pages 1–17, Examples 20–31, 45–52, 75–89, and 101–113. Melodies in compound time in Examples 266–394 contain the same rhythmic problems.

Rhythmic Dictation

This is the converse of rhythmic reading. In rhythmic reading the rhythmic symbols are converted into sound. In rhythmic dictation, the rhythmic sounds are converted into notation. At this point, rhythmic dictation will contain the same problems as studied in rhythmic reading.

Exercise 3.12. Rhythmic dictation, simple time. Follow this procedure in taking rhythmic dictation:

a) The time signature will be announced. Write this on your paper.

b) At the given signal, make the proper conductor's beat and tap the background.

c) Listen to the melody played, while conducting.

d) Sing back the melody, aloud or silently as directed, still using the conductor's beat. (Hearing and singing a melody helps you to remember more of the exercise than if you hear and recite abstract durations alone.)

e) Write rhythmic notation on your paper. Had Figure 3.23a been dictated, your solution should be like Figure 3.23b.

Fig. 3.23.

Use your conductor's beat and background taps 1) to determine on what beat or part of beat the note occurs; 2) to determine how long the note is held; and 3) to detemine how and where the beat is divided.

Here are some examples of this procedure from Figure 3.23:

1. The first note is on the third conductor's beat.
2. The note after the first bar line is on the down beat and lasts for two conductor's beats.
3. The dotted quarter note lasts for three background taps (each tap = ♪). On the following note, one tap = ♪.

4. Notes in the last full measure are the same as the six background taps, meaning that they are six eighth notes.

Self-Help Procedures

In listening to a melody being dictated, it is of utmost importance that the student *memorize* the melody as soon as possible, since it is impossible to write on paper that which cannot be recalled to mind. The ability to remember the sounds heard will be equally important in later studies, such as melodic and harmonic dictation.

Students working in pairs can be of great assistance to each other in training melodic memory or rhythmic dictation outside regular classroom time. These procedures may be followed.

Memory. Using sources in Exercises 3.10 and 3.11, student A chooses a melody. From this melody he plays one to four measures. Student B immediately sings the phrase back. If there is an error or if it is incomplete, the procedure is repeated until a correct response is achieved. Continued practice will reduce the number of hearings necessary to achieve a correct response. When the number of playings is reduced to one, extend the length of the melody.

Dictation. Using sources in Exercises 3.10 and 3.11, student A chooses a melody and announces the time signature. Student B makes the appropriate condutor's beat, with background. Student A plays one phrase, which student B sings back using rhythmic syllables. Repeat playing and singing until phrase is sung back correctly. Then write the rhythmic notation only on paper. Aim to reduce the number of hearings necessary and to extend the amount of material heard at one time.

History of Rhythmic Notation

In the history of the notation of rhythm, the time signature made its appearance at a comparatively late date. One reason for this is that music prior to the seventeenth century did not make use of bar lines, and another is that a note value did not come to indicate a specific division (such as 𝅗𝅥 = ♩ ♩) until about the same time.

The earliest notation, as found in the religious chants of the eighth and ninth centuries, represented pitch only. How the rhythmic element of this plain chant notation was interperted is still not entirely clear.

The first measurable rhythmic notation was produced in the thirteenth century. In this system, the duration of each note depended upon what note value or values followed it. The system, called *mensural notation* and developed by Franco of Cologne around 1280, was used to represent the rhythmic modes—a series of six rhythm patterns, each representing the triple division in which the music of the time was composed.

Observe in the figure that the *longa* (▀▌) equals a quarter note at some times and a dotted quarter note at others, depending on its context. The same principle holds true for the *breve* (■). This music needed no time signatures. Its symbols were often combined into groups called *ligatures,* such as ▀▄, ▐, or ▄▀▄. An example of ligatures can be seen in the article, "Pitch Notation," on page 39.

Mensural Notation

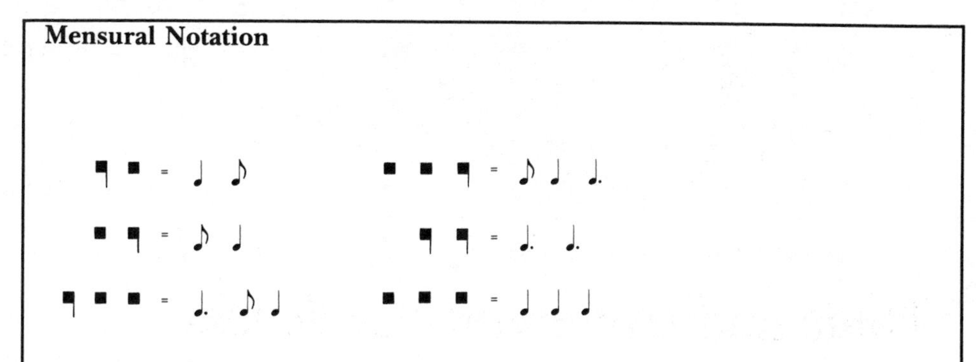

In about 1320, Phillipe de Vitry, in his treatise *Ars Nova* (*The New Art*), recognized duple rhythm (note values divisible by two) as well as triple rhythm. Also at this time, white notation was gradually replacing much of the black notation. To indicate division of note values into two or three, a system of *mensural signatures* was devised around 1450. But in this system, as opposed to the mensural notation just discussed, the actual value of a given note was still determined by its relation to its preceding or following note.

(See the example in the article "*Pitch Notation,*" on page 39)

Signature	Divisions	Modern Notation, if 𝅜 = 𝅗𝅥 or 𝅗𝅥.
C	𝅜 = ◇ ◇, ◇ = ◊ ◊	𝅗𝅥 = ♩ ♩, ♩ = ♫
○	𝅜 = ◇ ◇ ◇, ◇ = ◊ ◊	𝅗𝅥. = ♩ ♩ ♩, ♩ = ♫
C·	𝅜 = ◇ ◇, ◇ = ◊ ◊ ◊	𝅗𝅥. = ♩. ♩., ♩. = ♪♪♪
⊙	𝅜 = ◇ ◇ ◇, ◇ = ◊ ◊ ◊	𝅗𝅥.‿♩. = ♩. ♩. ♩., ♩. = ♪♪♪

Of these, the signature **C** still remains, indicating duple division at all levels, and now used to indicate $\frac{4}{4}$ meter. Another mensural signature, **¢**, indicated that all notes following it were to be taken twice as fast as before. Known as "cut time," or "alla breve" (the symbol 𝅜 in the above table), it is still used today to indicate $\frac{2}{2}$ meter. The signatures we use today had developed by the early seventeenth century, and they have remained virtually unchanged since that time.

CHAPTER 4

Tonic and Dominant: Cadences

Theory and Analysis

In Chapter 2 we investigated the nature of the cadence from a harmonic point of view: that is, as the use of two successive harmonies to mark the end of a musical idea. The complete musical idea, therefore, was a succession of chords leading up to and including the cadence and forming a phrase, as Figures 2.1, 2.2, and 4.2 demonstrate. The most common cadences are those that include dominant and tonic harmony. Most of the remaining cadences incorporate subdominant and tonic harmony and are described in Chapter 8.

Cadences Incorporating Dominant Harmony

1. *Perfect Authentic* This cadence is the progression V–I, or V^7–I, in which the root of each chord is in the bass voice and the tonic tone is in the soprano of the final tonic chord. The soprano line connecting the two chords usually proceeds from leading tone to tonic (7–1) or supertonic to tonic (2–1).

Fig. 4.1

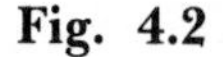

Fig. 4.2

Fig. 4.3

2. *Imperfect Authentic Cadence.* This cadence is the progression V–I, in which the soprano of the final tonic triad is the third or the fifth, or, in which one of the triads is found in inversion (see Chapter 9). Soprano lines commonly used are 2–3, 5–5 and 5 down to 3.

Fig. 4.4

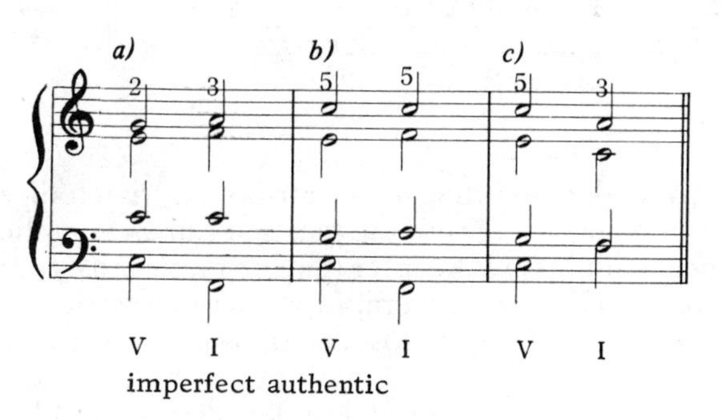

Fig. 4.5

Fig. 4.6

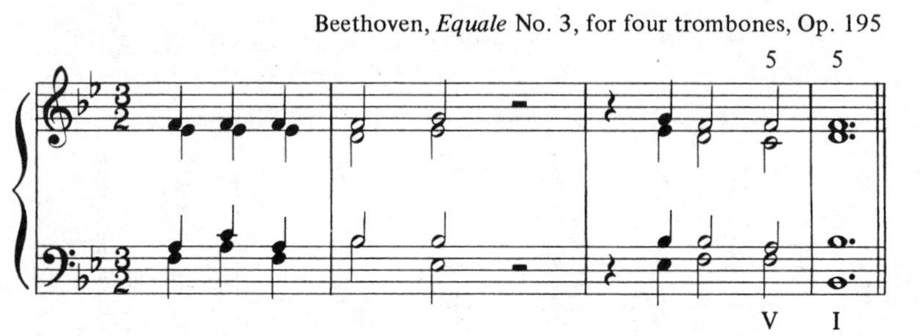

Fig. 4.7

3. Half Cadence. Any cadence ending on a chord other than tonic is a half cadence, the most common being I–V. From the fact that cadences ending on V lack the stability of cadences ending on I, we infer that the music must continue to a cadence with more stability. There are several soprano movements: 1–7, 1–2, 3–2, 5–5, and by various skips. By far the most common is the 3–2.

[1]This number refers to the number of the chorale in the collected editions of J. S. Bach's chorales, such as *The 371 Chorales of Johann Sebastian Bach,* edited, with English texts, by Frank D. Mainous and Robert W. Ottman (New York: Holt, Rinehart & Winston, Inc., 1966). These chorales will be used extensively for illustration and analysis in this text.

Fig. 4.8

Fig. 4.9

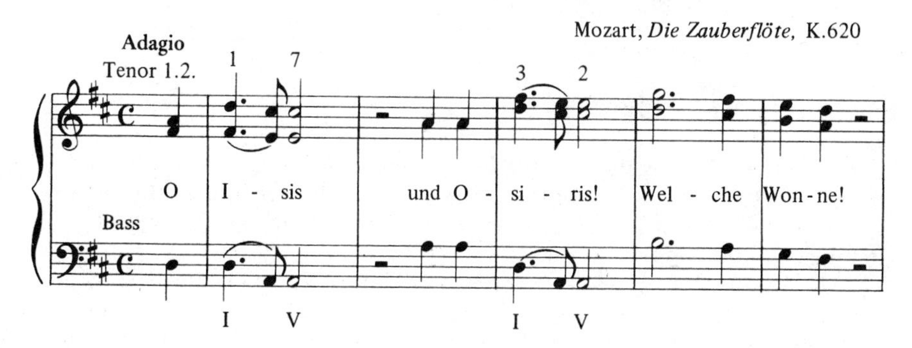

Fig. 4.10

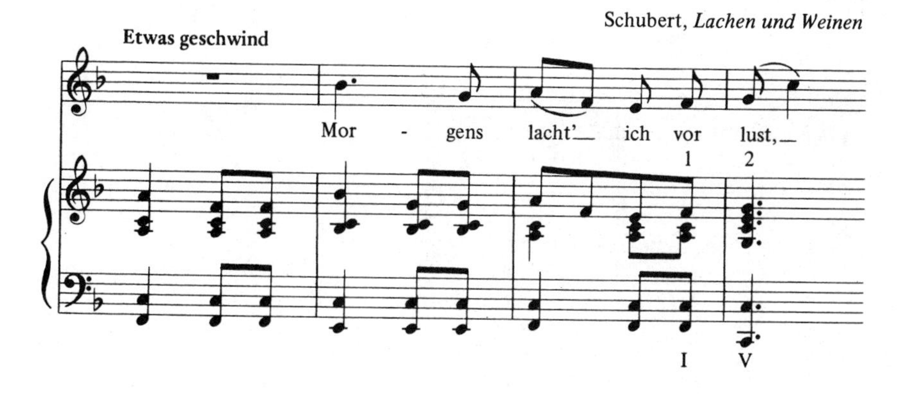

Assignment 4.1. Identify each of these cadences as either perfect authentic, imperfect authentic, or half, and describe the soprano line in each. Assume that each key signature is the signature for a major key.

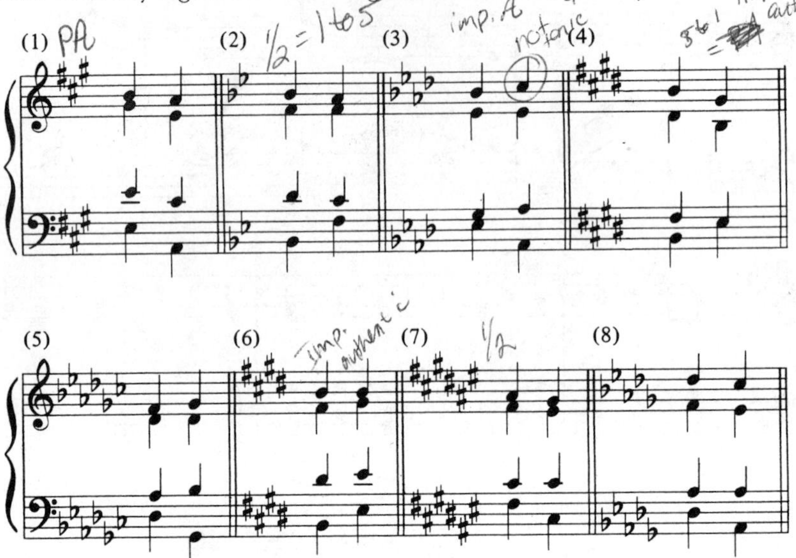

Cadences Using the V⁷ Chord

Reference has already been made in Chapter 2 (Figure 2.6 and its preceding paragraph) to the presence of the seventh in a cadence. In actual practice, cadences composed without a dissonance such as the seventh are not common, except in music of the utmost simplicity.

A note at the interval of the seventh above the *root* of the V sonority, whether or not the root is in the bass voice, is a very common use of dissonance. Spelled on the dominant of C major, the chord is G B D F (Figure 4.11a). Note also that the seventh is a minor third above the fifth of the triad, and (2) that the seventh of the

Fig. 4.11

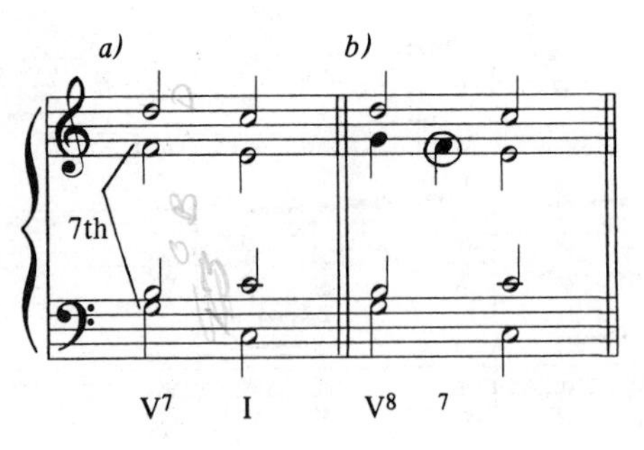

V^7 is the fourth scale step of the key (F in C major). The seventh is also commonly found as part of a melodic movement downward by step, a dissonance known as a *passing tone* (Figure 4.11b).

Fig. 4.12

Fig. 4.13

The theory behind the seventh chord and its part-writing techniques will be found in Chapter 17, following the study of the nonharmonic tone, the principles of which govern the creation and use of the seventh chord. However, because the dominant seventh chord will appear so frequently in the music examples offered here for illustrative purposes, it is prudent to learn the basic construction of the chord at this time. This can be done simply by adding the interval of the minor seventh to the V triad, as described in the preceding paragraph.

Assignment 4.2. Spell the dominant seventh chord in each major key.

The V^7 Chord in the Melodic Line

Intervals from the V^7 chord are often incorporated into the melodic line. In Figure 4.14a, the entire V^7 is outlined: in b we see the interval 7 down to 3.

Fig. 4.14

The intervals in the list below are from the dominant seventh chord and are those in which the seventh of the chord is involved. The underlined intervals are those most commonly used in melodic writing.

1 up to 7	minor seventh	7 down to 1
3 up to 7	diminished fifth	7 down to 3
5 up to 7	minor third	7 down to 5
7 up to 1	major second	1 down to 7
7 up to 3	augmented fourth	3 down to 7
7 up to 5	major sixth	5 down to 7

Fig. 4.15

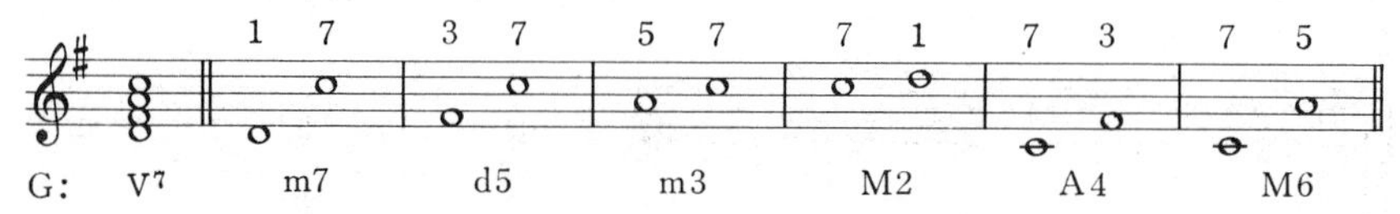

The diminished fifth and the augmented fourth are each also known as a *tritone*. The tritone is discussed further in Chapter 12.

Assignment 4.3. Spell each of the intervals in Figure 4.15 based on the dominant seventh chord of any major key.

Cadences Including Nonharmonic Tones and Inversions

Other dissonances, with or without the seventh, can also be incorporated into the texture of a cadence. They can be observed by first spelling the V and I triads, and then locating those notes that are not part of these spellings. In the next example, the V^7 is extended for two measures and contains, other than the seventh of the V^7, six nonharmonic tones, all of which are circled.

Fig. 4.16

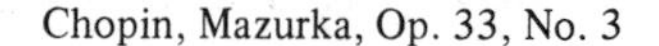

Either chord of a cadence may be found with a note other than its root in the bass (inversion). Figure 4.17 shows the tonic triad in first inversion (third in the bass) and Figure 4.18 shows the V^7 in second inversion (fifth in the bass). Nonharmonic tones in each cadence are circled.

Fig. 4.17

Fig. 4.18

Cadences for One or Two Voices

Cadences for one voice can usually be identified by the scale step numbers of the melody at the point of the cadence. Figure 4.19, in B♭ major, shows two cadences: 3–2 (D–C) implies I (B♭ D F)–V (F A C), whereas the final cadence 2–1 (C–B♭) implies V–I. In two voices, enough of the harmony is present to imply the remaining notes. In Figure 4.20 the 7-1 line in the upper voice and the triad roots D–G in the lower voice make the perfect authentic cadence clear.

Fig. 4.19

Fig. 4.20

Assignment 4.4. Locate and identify by name and by chord numbers each cadence in these examples. Circle any notes that are not members of the chords indicated.

(3)
Brahms, *Wiegenlied,* Op. 49, No. 4
Zart bewegt
p
Mor - gern früh, wenn Gott will, wirst du wie - der ge - deckt.
p

(4)
Tchaikovski, Symphony No. 6
Andante cantabile
Horn
pp
Strings

Bach, Fugue in C Major
(5)

tr

Application

Written Materials

Principles of Part-Writing

Should we wish to write the two successive chords of the cadence, or any succession of chords, it might seem only necessary to string one chord after another. But this process would ignore another important and necessary element: the melodic aspect of each of the voice lines (see the article "Voice Lines in Harmony").

In the simple hymn shown in Figure 4.21, each triad is identified by its spelling (a process that constitutes an analysis of the hymn's *vertical* structures), but at the same time the music consists of four voice lines. Together these represent the *horizontal* aspect of the musical phrase. The tune in the soprano (highest voice line) is obviously a melody, but the alto, tenor, and bass lines are also melody lines. If you sing the notes of the alto line (treble clef, the notes with stems downward), you are singing a melodic line. The same is true of the tenor and bass lines.

Fig. 4.21

To achieve good melodic writing in all voices during the succession of harmonies, we use a technique known as *part-writing*. Part-writing principles indicate 1) how to distribute the various members of the chord among the number of voices in the composition (four voices in Figure 4.1; three voices in Figure 2.1, and so on), and 2) how to move each note in a given voice from chord to chord. Placing individual notes of a given triad in one voice part or another at random

Fig. 4.22

will not produce good melodic lines, except perhaps accidentally. If we were to rewrite Figure 4.21 using the same melody, the same bass line and the same chords, but filling in the remaining chord tones in the alto and tenor voices at random, an arrangement such as that of Figure 4.22 might result.

As this "arrangement" is played at the piano, try to sing the alto line. It is difficult because the alto part is a poor melodic line. Now compare the alto line of Figure 4.22 with that of the original, as shown in Figure 4.23, noting how much easier it is to sing the original alto line. The same comparison can be made between the two tenor lines.

Fig. 4.23

This and succeeding chapters will present procedures for part-writing. For convenience, they are codified as a set of rules (see the article "Rules? Why Rules?" on page 97). These will aid you in connecting chords so that each voice is smooth and singable, and will help to prevent such poor voice lines as those seen in Figure 4.22.

An Alternate Presentation of Part-Writing Procedures

For those classes where it is desirable to present all the diatonic triads and their connections early in the course of study, this procedure is recommended:

1. Chapter 1, section 23, presents all the diatonic triads in both major and minor keys.

2. Appendix 1 "The Essentials of Part-Writing," lists all the basic part-writing procedures, providing the necessary information for the connection of any diatonic triads and their inversions in any pairing. Each entry in the list includes a page number reference to the initial presentation of the procedure, discussion and illustration of its use, and written assignments.

3. Exercises in the part-writing of triads (soprano and bass given, with no nonharmonic tones or seventh chords) may be found in the following locations:

Repeated triads (roots in bass)	Chapter 4	Assignment 4.7
Tonic and Dominant triads (roots in bass a fifth apart)	Chapter 4 Chapter 5	Assignments 4.8–4.13 Assignments 5.8–5.11
Subdominant triad (roots in bass a second apart)	Chapter 8	Assignments 8.10, 8.11
First Inversions and Cadential Six-four Chord	Chapter 9	Assignments 9.3–9.7

Leading Tone triad	Chapter 12	Assignments 12.5–12.7
Supertonic triad	Chapter 13	Assignment 13.3 (1–7, 10)
Submediant and Mediant triads	Chapter 15	Assignment 15.8 (1–4)
The Minor Dominant and the Major Subtonic triads in minor keys; Six-four chords	Chapter 16	Assignments 16.3–16.5 Assignment 16.6 (1–4)

Writing a Single Triad

For the first part-writing project, we will place on the staff a single major triad, with its root in the bass. Simple as this might seem, it serves to introduce several procedures necessary for the development of part-writing skill.

Our triad will be written in four voices: soprano, alto, tenor, and bass, conforming to the four ranges of the human voice. When the treble and bass staves are used, the soprano and alto voices appear on the treble staff and the tenor and bass voices appear on the bass staff. Observe the stem directions: soprano, stem up; alto, stem down; tenor, stem up; bass, stem down (Figure 4.24a). When two voices on the same staff are the same note, the note carries both stem up and stem down (Figure 4.24b), or, if the note is a whole note, the two whole notes are interlocked (Figure 4.24c).

Fig. 4.24

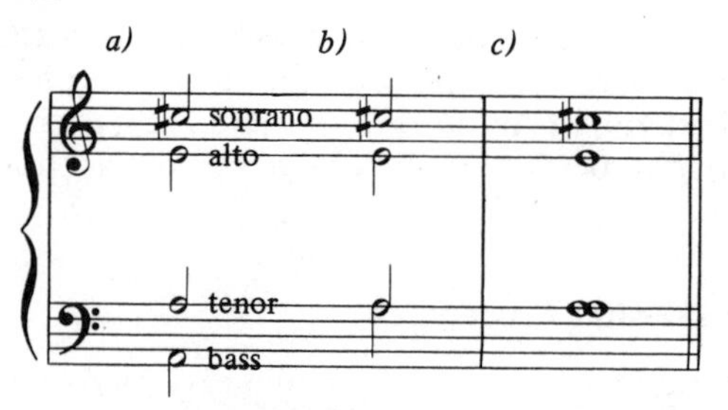

However, when the two identical pitches are the alto and tenor voices, each must remain on its own staff (Figure 4.25).

Fig. 4.25

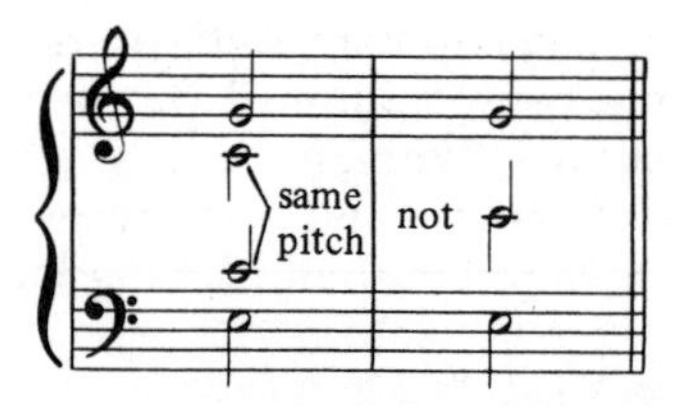

In part-writing the single triad, four factors must be taken into consideration: 1) voice range, 2) doubling, 3) triad position, and 4) distance between voices.

1. Range. Each of the four voices should, as a rule, be written in the normal singing range of that voice.

Fig. 4.26

Voices ordinarily should be kept within the ranges outlined by the whole notes. Pitches outside of these ranges are possible but should be used only sparingly and within the limits of the black notes.

2. *Doubling.* Since four notes will be used, one note of the triad must be doubled, that is, two voices will have to use the same letter name, either in unison or in an octave relationship. A general rule for doubling in most triads is to double that tone which is strongest and most stable in the key. These tones are the tonic, the dominant, and the subdominant. In the case of tonic and dominant triads, the root will ordinarily be doubled. (Fig. 4.27).

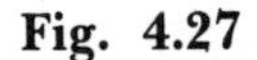
Fig. 4.27

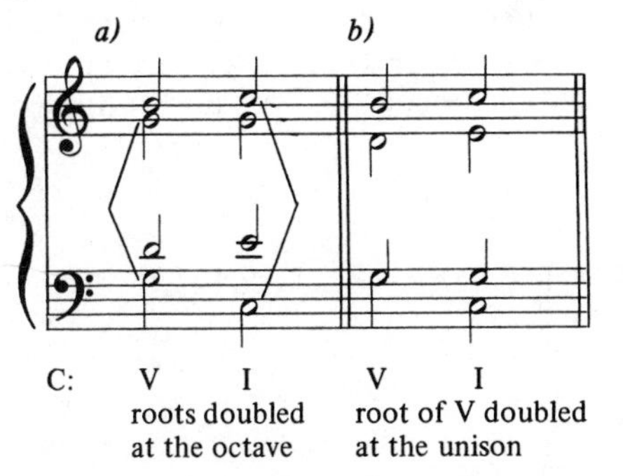

Other doublings are not necessarily "wrong." There are circumstances in which doubling the third or the fifth of the triad is desirable, as will be shown in later chapters. However, doublings should not be chosen haphazardly. If there is no particular reason to double the third or the fifth in a major triad, doubling the root is preferable.

Listen to the triad in Figure 4.28, which is written with three different doublings. Notice how the doubled third or the doubled fifth tends to stand out, and to some degree overpowers the sonority, whereas the triad with the doubled root

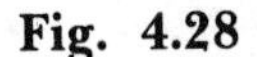
Fig. 4.28

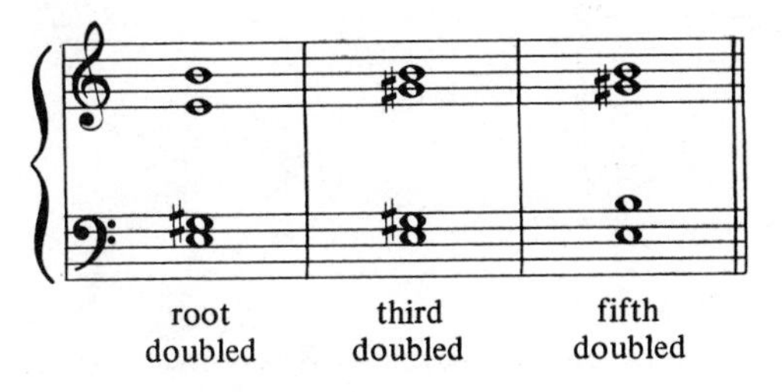

seems to have a better balance. This may seem like a small point, but achieving success in the creation of any art form depends upon such attention to detail.

3. *Position.* Triads may appear in either of two positions, open or close. In *open position*[2] the distance between the soprano and tenor is an octave or more; in *close position,* the distance between the soprano and tenor is less than an octave. In either position, any interval may appear between tenor and bass.

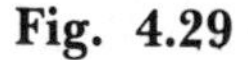

Fig. 4.29

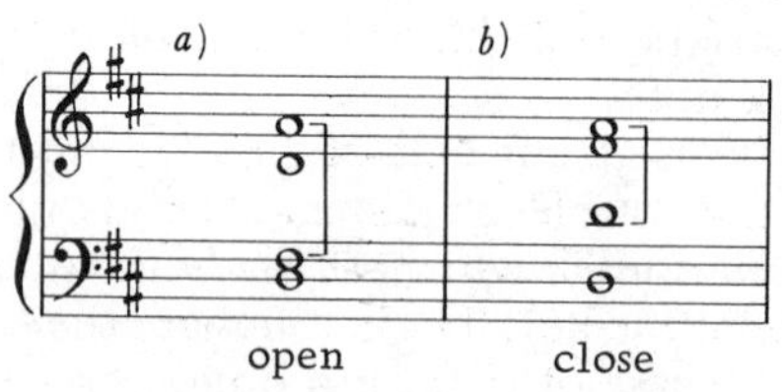

Note also that in open position another note of the triad could be inserted between the tenor and the soprano, while in close position, the three upper voices are as close together as possible.

4. *Distance between voices.* The distance between any two adjacent voices (for example, soprano and alto) usually does not exceed an octave, except that an interval larger than an octave may appear between the bass and tenor voices.

Fig. 4.30

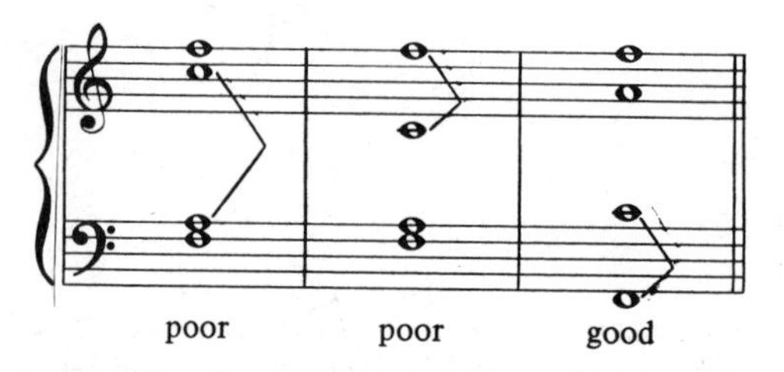

For the present, voices should not be crossed; that is, the tenor should not be higher than the alto, the alto should not be higher than the soprano, and so forth.

Assignment 4.5. Fill in the inner voices of each triad in both close position and open position, in that order. At present use two roots, one third and one fifth; keep voices in correct pitch range. Here is an example.

Fig. 4.31

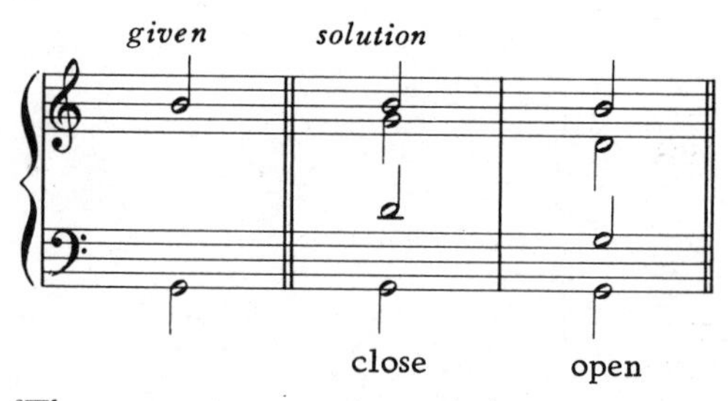

[2]The terms *open structure* and *close structure* are commonly used synonymously with *open position* and *close position.*

The given note on the bass staff is always the root of a major triad.

Assignment 4.6. Write each of the following triads on the staff in both close and open position. The bass will carry the root of the triad in all cases. Observe doubling and voice range instructions. The number after the triad indicates the soprano note to be used. **Example: G♭**(3).

G (3), D (5), E (3), C♯ (5), D♭ (1), B (1), C♭ (1), D♯ (5), A♭ (3), F♯ (3).

Fig. 4.32

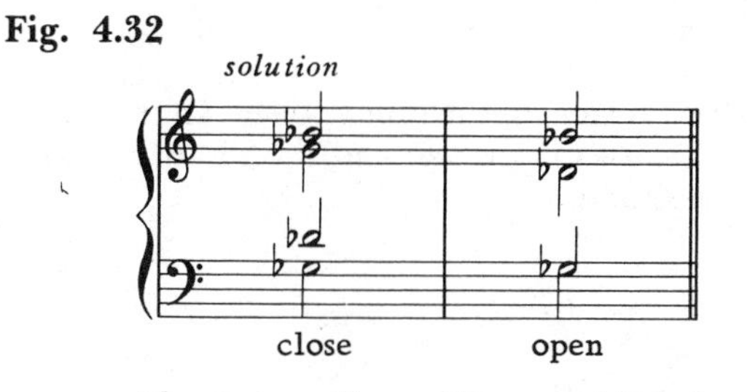

The Connection of Repeated Triads

Part-Writing Rule No. 1. When two triads, each with the same spelling and each with its root in the bass, are used in succession with differing soprano notes:

a) each may be written in the same position by moving the three upper voices in similar motion;

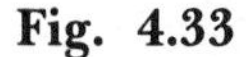
Fig. 4.33

b) each may be in a different position; when changing position, two voices, the bass and one other, remain stationary while the other two voices exchange tones.

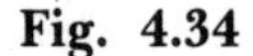
Fig. 4.34

Several factors determine which method will be used.

1) The necessity of keeping voices in a good register. In the example, continuing close position (*a*) places both tenor and alto in excessively high ranges. Changing the position (*b*) corrects this situation.

Fig. 4.35

2. Avoidance of large leaps (fifth or larger) in the inner voices. In the example, maintaining the same position (*a*) causes large leaps in the tenor and alto. Changing the position (*b*) corrects this situation.

Fig. 4.36

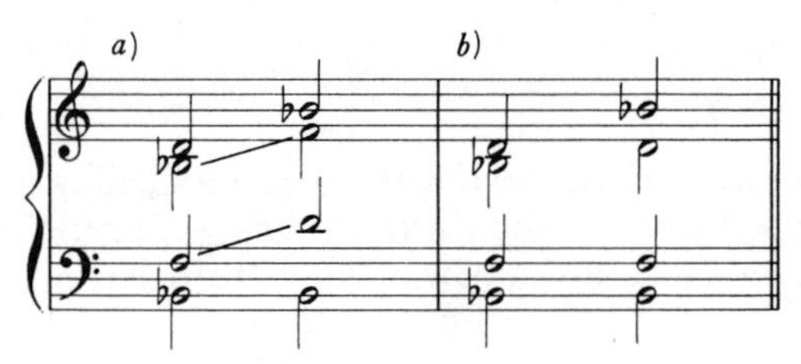

3. The necessity to maintain correct voice distribution (two roots, one third and one fifth). Maintaining the same position (Figure 4.37 *a*) makes it impossible to keep the correct chord distribution. Changing the position (*b*) corrects this situation.

Often either solution is correct. In Figure 4.38, changing position (*a*) is correct; maintaining the same position (*b*) is also correct.

Fig. 4.37

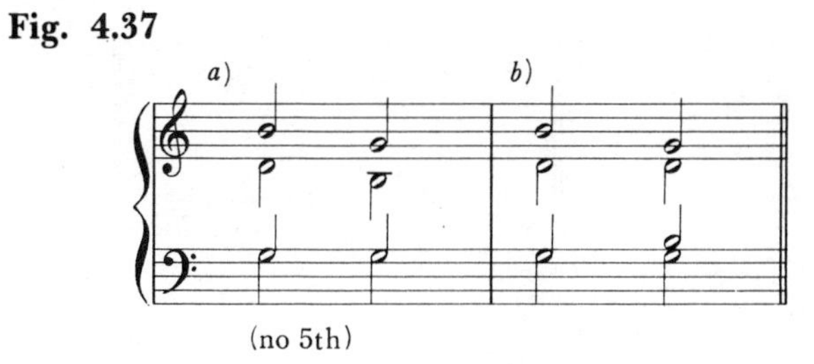

Fig. 4.38

Assignment 4.7. Write each pair of repeated triads using whichever method is more appropriate. Each bass note is the root of a triad.

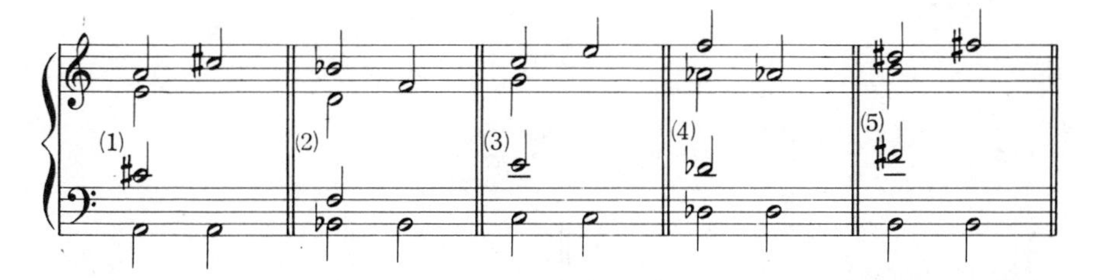

Writing the Authentic Cadence

In the various forms of the authentic cadence, the roots are always separated by the interval of a fifth, or its inversion, the fourth. In speaking of root movement by fifth, root movement by fourth is always implied, so that only the term "root movement by fifth" is necessary to convey both meanings. The following procedures, while useful in connecting any two triads whose *roots in the bass* are a fifth apart, are here applied to the writing of the authentic cadence.

We will identify these procedures as Part-Writing Rule No. 2, and as there are four different ways of connecting a pair of triads with this root movement, we will designate them as 2A, 2B, 2C, and 2D.

Part-Writing Rule 2A. Triads with roots in the bass a fifth apart. In a progression of two triads whose roots in the bass line are a fifth apart, hold the common tone in one voice from one triad to the next, and move the other two voices stepwise.

Fig. 4.39

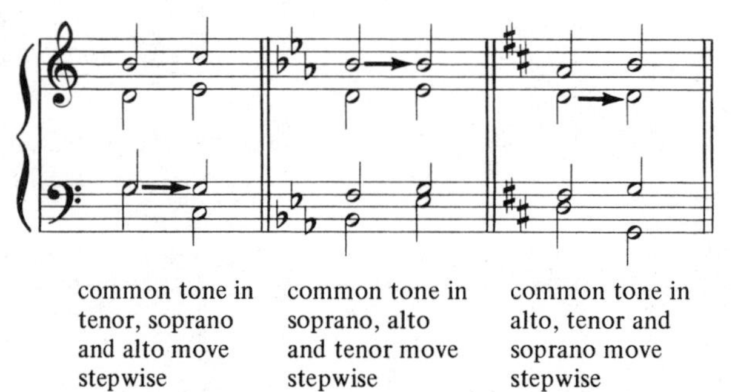

common tone in tenor, soprano and alto move stepwise | common tone in soprano, alto and tenor move stepwise | common tone in alto, tenor and soprano move stepwise

For examples from the music literature showing use of this procedure, see Figures 4.2, 4.5, 4.6, and 4.8 earlier in this chapter.

Assignment 4.8. Writing authentic cadences. Fill in alto and tenor voices, using Rule 2A. Remember that each individual triad should conform to the procedures given for writing single triads. Identify each cadence as authentic perfect, authentic imperfect, or authentic half.

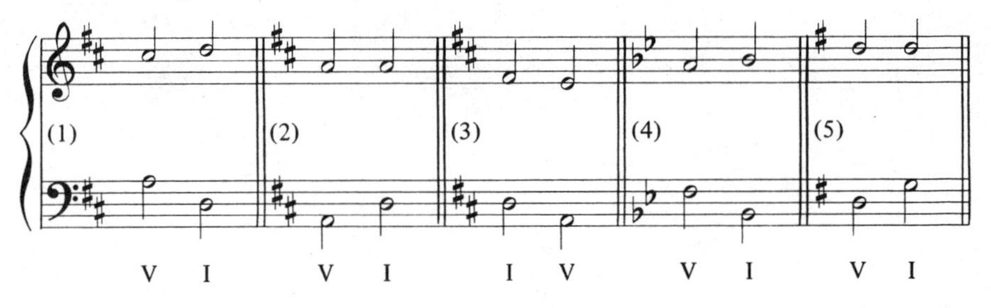

Assignment 4.9. Writing authentic cadences where only the bass line is given. Supply a soprano note, and then part-write the cadence, as in Assignment 4.8.

Assignment 4.10. Writing authentic cadences where only the soprano is given. Follow these steps:

1. Identify the key.
2. Identify the scale step numbers of the soprano line, and determine what cadence it will accommodate. For example, if the soprano line is 7–1, the cadence will be perfect authentic.
3. Write the bass line, and add alto and tenor voices.

It is occasionally impossible to hold the common tone when writing two triads that have their roots in the bass a fifth apart, and therefore another procedure is necessary.

Part-Writing Rule 2B. Triads with roots in the bass a fifth apart. When it is impossible to hold the common tone, move the three upper voices in similar motion to the nearest tones of the next triad.

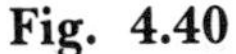
Fig. 4.40

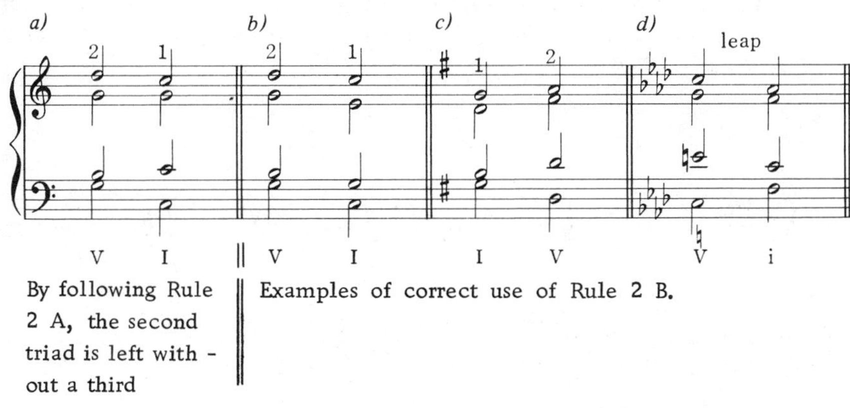

By following Rule 2 A, the second triad is left without a third

Examples of correct use of Rule 2 B.

"Similar motion" means in the same direction, as when all three voices move up, or all three voices move down. The bass may move in either direction in either circumstance. Rule 2B is valuable in the V–I or I–V progression when the soprano line is 2–1 or 1–2, or when there is a leap in the soprano line.

Note that in the V–I progression of Figure 4.40b, the leading tone does not ascend to the tonic, but skips down a third, contrary to its normal tendency. In this progression, the leading tone is found only in an inner voice (alto or tenor); the irregular resolution in the soprano is too prominent to be useful.

Fig. 4.41

Martin Luther, *Ein' feste Burg*

Assignment 4.11. Write authentic cadences using Rule 2B.

Rules 2C and 2D present alternate ways of part-writing the authentic cadence.

Part-Writing Rule 2C. In a progression of two triads whose roots in the bass are a fifth apart, move the third of the first triad up or down the interval of a fourth to the third of the second triad, hold the common tone, and move the other voice by step.

The effect of this procedure is a change of position, open to close or close to open, from one triad to the next. This procedure is found as a final cadence in many Bach chorales.

Fig. 4.42a

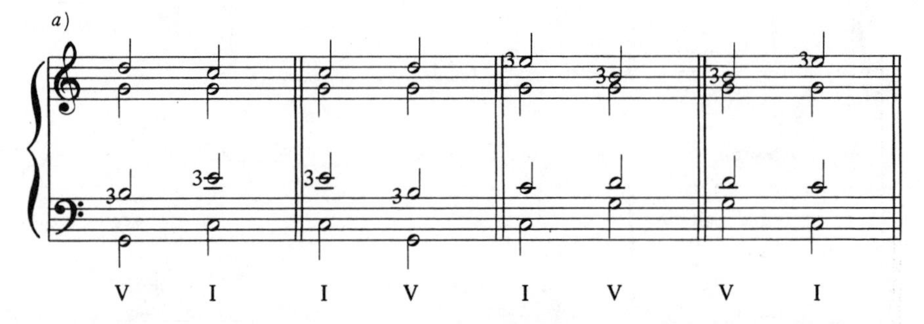

Fig. 4.42b

Bach, *Ermuntre dich, mein schwacher Geist* (#91)

Part-Writing Rule 2D. In an authentic cadence, the root of the tonic triad may be tripled, omitting the fifth of the triad.

Although this procedure is useful in any authentic cadence, it is often used to replace Rule 2B at the final cadence, allowing the leading tone to ascend to the tonic.

Fig. 4.43

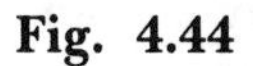

Fig. 4.44

Hymn: Toulon

Assignment 4.12. Write authentic cadences, using the part-writing procedures indicated.

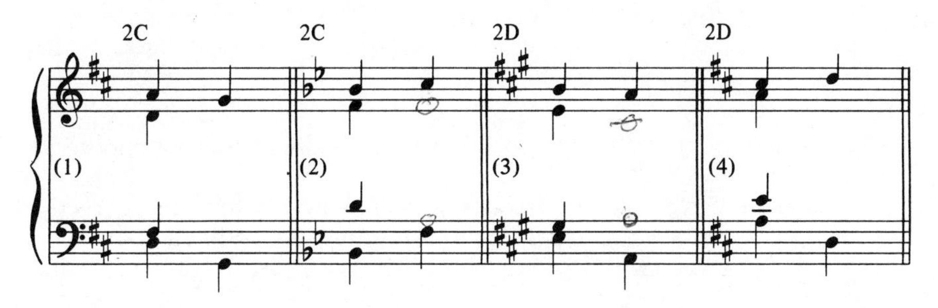

Writing Extended Exercises

In a series of I and V triads leading to a cadence, as in Assignment 4.13, one must analyze each pair of triads for its root movement and choose a suitable part-writing procedure. Figure 4.45 is a sample exercise; the steps for its solution follow, and Figure 4.46 is the completed exercise.

Fig. 4.45

Triads 1 to 2 Roots are a fifth apart. In soprano, the third of the first triad moves to the third of the second triad. Use Rule 2C.

Triads 2 to 3 Roots are a fifth apart. Common tone can be held. Use Rule 2A.

Triads 3 to 4 Roots are repeated. Use Rule 1. (There are two choices here: triad 4 in open position keeps voices in better range.)

Triads 4 to 5 Roots are a fifth apart. Common tone can be held. Use Rule 2A.

Triads 5 to 6 Roots are a fifth apart. Common tone cannot be held. Use Rule 2B. Alternate solutions: 1) the third of triad 5 can leap a fourth to the third of triad 6; use Rule 2C, and 2) since this is a final cadence, Rule 2D can be used.

Fig. 4.46

Which cadence should you choose? Since all are correct, choose the sound you prefer.

Sufficient practice in part-writing will allow you to write correctly without having to consider each progression as minutely as outlined above.

Assignment 4.13. Writing extended exercises.

Ear Training

The Dominant Triad

Exercise 4.1. Singing the I and V triads in a major key.

a) You will hear a single note played at the piano; this will be the tonic note of a major key. From this note, sing the tonic triad, using letter names. The fifth of the tonic triad is the same pitch as the root of the dominant triad. From this note sing the dominant triad using letter names.

Fig. 4.47

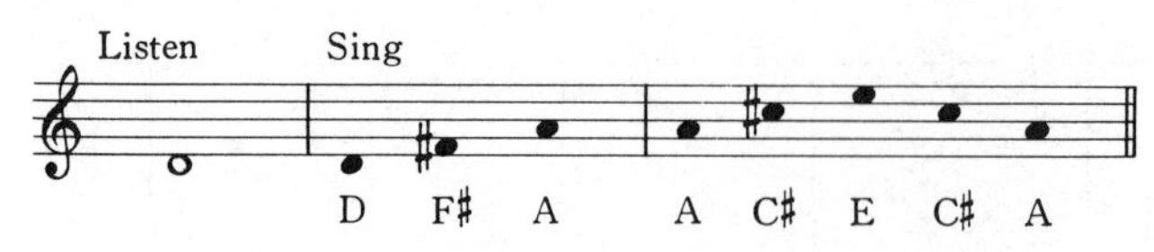

b) Sing the dominant triad immediately after hearing the tonic note.

Fig. 4.48

The Authentic Cadence

Exercise 4.2. Identifying the authentic cadence. You will hear a phrase of music at the piano. The last two triads will comprise an authentic cadence.

a) At the conclusion of the first playing, sing the tonic of the key.

b) During the second playing, sing the roots of the cadence chords.

c) During the third playing, sing the soprano line. Identify the cadence as perfect, imperfect, or half.

Fig. 4.49

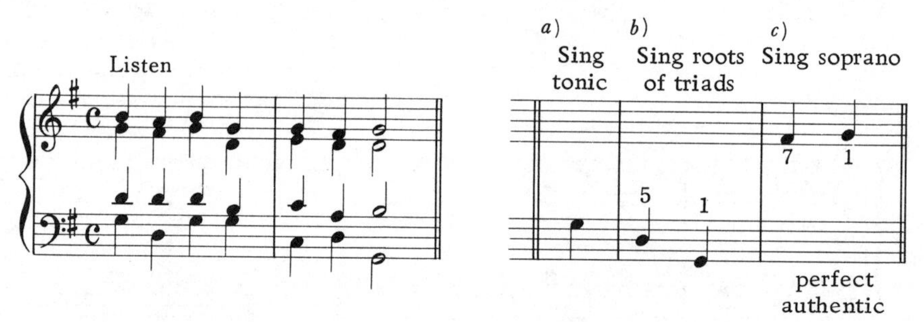

With continued practice, identify cadence completely in two hearings, then in one hearing.

Exercise 4.3. Writing the cadence from dictation. On staff paper, prepare a grand staff with treble and bass clefs, and with the key signature assigned.

a) Listen to a phrase of music, similar to Figure 4.49. Identify the cadence by name.

b) Below the staff, write V I if the cadence is perfect or imperfect; write I V if it is a half cadence.

c) Listen again and determine the direction of the movement of the two roots in the bass. Write the bass notes on the staff.

d) Listen for the soprano; write soprano notes on the staff, based on their scale step numbers.

e) Fill in the inner voices, using part-writing procedures from this chapter.

If Figure 4.49 had been the dictation exercise, the steps would appear as in Figure 4.50.

Fig. 4.50

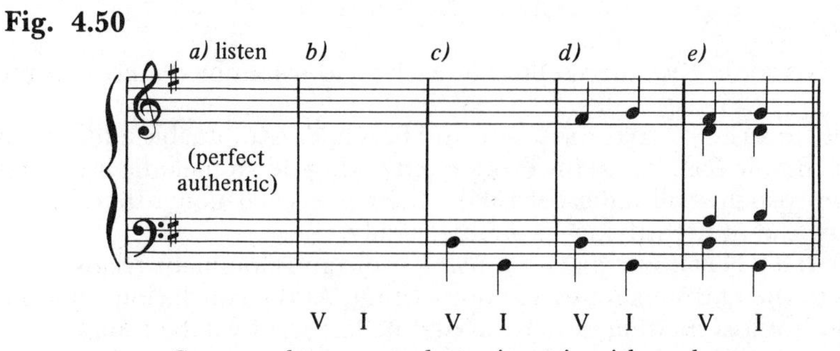

Some cadences can be written in either close or open position. Listen carefully for voice distribution before writing alto and tenor lines.

With practice, you should be able to complete all steps with no more than two hearings.

Harmonic Dictation

In harmonic dictation, the student listens to a series of chords in a musical phrase and identifies each according to the location of its root in the key, a process we have already begun in Exercise 4.3. A roman numeral (V and I at this point in our study) will indicate the root heard, and, as other types of triads are introduced, the type of roman numeral will indicate the quality of the sound (for example, I = major tonic triad, i = minor tonic triad, vii° = diminished triad on the seventh scale step, and so on.)

A successfully completed harmonic dictation exercise will indicate that the student knows on which scale step the harmony is built and the quality of the particular chord. This can be done without knowledge of the particular key in which the exercise is heard. What we are listening for is the harmonic relationship of each chord to the key center and the relationships of the chords to each other. Should this example be played as in Figure 4.51,

Fig. 4.51

the following answer would suffice to indicate the harmonic aspect of the music is understood:

V|I I|V I|V V|I ||

When the key is announced, the spelling of each triad will immediately become apparent.

The ability to write down the soprano and bass lines is a valuable addition to exercises in harmonic dictation. However, avoid taking down melodic lines first since these lines usually will indicate visually the correct harmony, thereby defeating the purpose of identifying harmony aurally.

Exercise 4.4. Harmonic dictation using tonic and dominant triads.

a) Listen to the entire exercise without writing. At the conclusion, sing the tonic note. (Do not assume that either the first or last triad will be tonic!)

b) On the second hearing, sing the root of each triad as the triad is played.

c) On the third hearing, sing the triad roots using the scale step number for each. This number will be the same as the roman numeral for the triad.

d) Write the chord numbers as the exercise is played.

As progress is made, eliminate steps *b* and *c*.

Keyboard Harmony

Authentic Cadences

You have already played single triads at the keyboard. To play a cadence, simply play two triads in succession, the choice of triads and position determined by the type of cadence and soprano line. For example, play a perfect authentic cadence in G major, soprano line 2–1.

Fig. 4.52

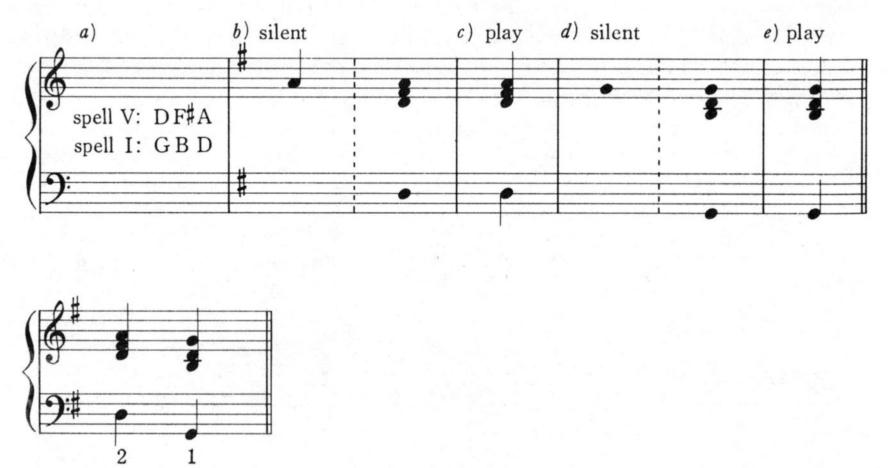

a. Spell the dominant and tonic triads
b. Locate the second scale step of G major on the piano; locate lower notes of the dominant triad, as in Exercise 2.18.
c. Play dominant triad.
d. Locate tonic note on the piano; locate other notes of the tonic triad.
e. Play tonic triad.

When using close position in the right hand, part-writing procedures will always be correct, and at the same time the cadence can easily be played. Open position (two notes in each hand) may be used, but this is slightly more difficult. Students should never resort to playing three notes in the left hand; although this may seem easier, the musical result is inferior. Musical voice leading procedures are impossible, and the sound of a cluster of notes in a low register is often harsh and unpleasant.

Exercise 4.5. Playing authentic cadences. In practicing each cadence below, use the circle of fifths (review Chapter 1, section 19). Start at any key and play the cadence in that key. Go to the next key of the circle, and continue around the circle until you arrive at the key from which you started.

a) Play the perfect authentic cadences:

Major:	2	1	7	1
	V	— I	V	— I

b) Play the imperfect authentic cadences:

Major:	2	3	5	5	5	3
	V	— I	V	— I	V	— I

c) Play the half cadences:

Major:	1	7	1	2	3	2	5	5
	1	— V	I	— V	I	— V	I	— V

Harmonizing Melodic Cadences

Many melodic phrases end with cadences consisting of two scale steps as practiced in Exercise 4.5. As a first step in learning to harmonize an entire melody, we will learn to harmonize these melodic cadences with harmonic authentic cadences. In Figure 4.53, we see two motives from a folk song with melodic cadences using scale steps 2–3 and 2–1, which can be harmonized with an imperfect authentic cadence and a perfect authentic cadence, respectively.

Fig. 4.53

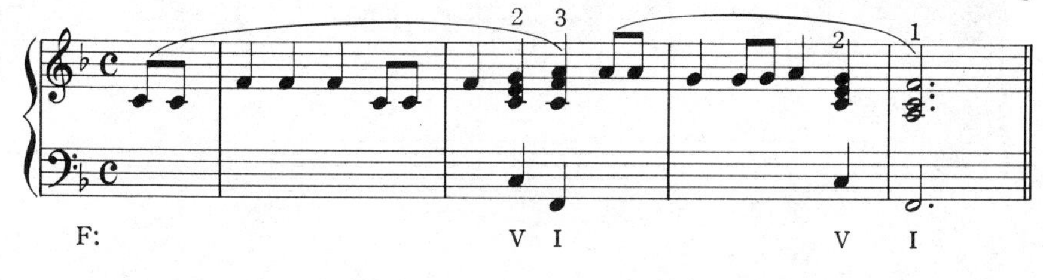

Exercise 4.6. Play these tunes (phrases from chorales and from well-known melodies), and supply a harmonic cadence at the point of the melodic cadence, as in Figure 4.53.

For additional practice, use the following melodies from sight singing books. Harmonize the cadence at the end of each phrase mark. When the given melody is in the bass clef, play it one or two octaves higher.

From *Music for Sight Singing,* melodies 10, 11, 16, 26, 29, 30, 33, 42, 58, 59, 63, 135. For the following, play only those phrases indicated in parentheses (e.g., "3, 4" means third and fourth phrase marks): melodies 6 (3, 4), 15 (2, 4), 20 (1, 2, 4), 25 (1, 2), 34 (1, 2), 38 (1, 2), 66 (2, 4), 94 (1, 2), 125 (1, 3, 4), and 127 (1, 2, 4);

From *More Music for Sight Singing:* melodies 266 (2, 4), 268 (2), 269 (2, 4), 271 (2, 4, 6), 272, 275 (1, 3, 4), 278 (1, 2, 6), 285, 286 (2, 3), 287 (1, 3), 296, 308 (1, 3), and 319.

In many melodic cadences the melodic clues, such as 7–1 or 2–3, are not quite as obvious, for the following three reasons.

1. The melodic cadence may contain one or more nonharmonic tones.

Fig. 4.54

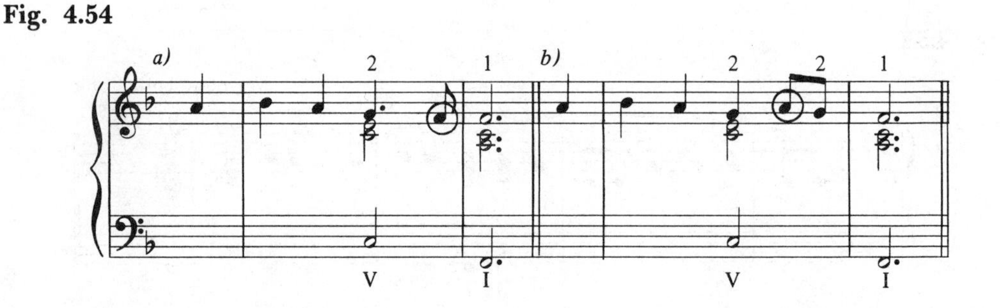

2. Several tones, harmonic or nonharmonic, may be found in either triad.

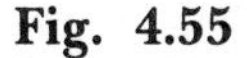
Fig. 4.55

3. The final melodic cadence may be 5–1, using the same notes as the roots of the triads. This parallel motion is generally considered poor, except in a strong final cadence.

Fig. 4.56

Exercise 4.7. Play these seven tunes, following directions from Exercise 4.6. For additional practice consult *Music for Sight Singing,* melodies 72 (2, 4) 81, 92, 93, 96, 109, 113, 127, 134, 175, 183; and *More Music for Sight Singing,* melodies 268, 274, 277, 279, 282, 298, 320, 322, 345, and 347.

Melody Harmonization Using Lead Sheet Symbols

An important objective in keyboard harmony is the development of the ability to harmonize a melody at sight, or at least after a short consideration. To do this you must not only understand what harmony is implied in the melodic line and the function of the nonharmonic tones included in the line, but also have sufficient keyboard facility to transform these theoretical ideas into a musical performance.

The preceding exercises are preliminary steps in achieving this goal. You have practiced V–I and I–V progressions so that they are easy to play in any key, and have combined this skill with a knowledge of the harmonic implications of the melodic cadence.

A technique of melody harmonization designed particularly for amateur musicians will also be helpful in our situation. For persons unable to evaluate the implications of a melodic line, a score consisting of a melodic line plus letter name symbols is often provided. The simple folk tune below uses only I and V chords, but instead of chord numbers the root of the necessary chord is given. By quickly spelling the chord, a simple but adequate accompaniment can be played without reference to harmonic or melodic implications.

Fig. 4.57

Such a score, of the kind shown in Figure 4.57, is often known as a *lead sheet* or *fake sheet.* This type of melodic presentation is found in most of the current series of public school music textbooks, primarily as an aid to the teacher with limited musical training. *Fake books* are well known in the popular music field; in these, the performer improvises upon the given tune and its accompanying letter-name symbols.

Of the many possible modes of performing a lead sheet, the following two are the simplest and at the same time yield a musically effective result.

1. Playing an Accompaniment Only. When someone else performs the tune, or when you sing or whistle the tune yourself, use a simple "oom-pah" style: Play the root in the left hand on the strong beat, and play the triad in the right hand on the weak beat (on 2 and 3 in triple meter).

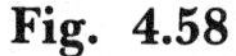
Fig. 4.58

Any soprano position may be selected for the first triad, but triads that follow should be connected by using the part-writing procedures already learned. Note that in going from measure 2 to measure 3 (I to V), Rule 2A was used.

2. Playing Melody and Accompaniment Together.

Fig. 4.59

Play the given chord on the down beat, three notes in the right hand and one in the left hand, with the melody note being the highest note in the chord. Play a chord again *a*) after a bar line (measures 1–2 above), or *b*) at the point a new chord is required (measure 3).

Practicing from lead sheets such as this will improve your keyboard facility, while careful observation of what you are doing will bring you insights as to the reasons for harmonic choices and nonharmonic usages.

Exercise 4.8. Playing a harmonization from a lead sheet.

*omit accompaniment on upbeats.

When the melody note (see asterisk above) is not part of the chord, substitute it for the note that follows:

Recommended highly for further practice is the text *Melodies to Harmonize With* by Frank D. Mainous (Prentice-Hall, Inc., 1978), in which the study of the harmonic aspect of melody correlates closely with the present text. For this assignment, use all the melodies, 1–58, in Chapter A, except for numbers 25, 31, 48, 50 and 53, which are in minor keys.

In the Mainous text, most dominant chords are marked with a 7 (C7, G♭7, and so on). For our present purposes the 7 can be omitted, though you may wish to experiment by including it. When the seventh of a V^7 chord appears as a melody tone, merely play a complete V triad with it.

Rules? Why Rules?

A composer writes in any way which best expresses his (her) ideas, and best pleases himself. While a competent composer will never be tied down to a set of given procedures, it is also true that he will usually be strongly influenced by his musical heritage and environment. This usually results in some degree of similarity in the works of composers of a specific chronological era and a specific geographical area. The compositions of Beethoven (19th century) and Schubert (19th century) are more alike than, say, those of Beethoven and Palestrina (16th century), or Beethoven and Schoenberg (20th century).

In looking back over a period of music composition, the music theoretician attempts to discover, clarify, and codify the procedures of composers of that period. For purposes of part-writing pedagogy, we have observed those part-writing procedures frequently and successfully used by composers in the period c. 1650–1900, and codified them into a set of "rules."

Our use of the term "rule" does *not* imply strict adherence. It is used in the same sense as when one says, "As a rule, the bus is late." This does not mean that the bus must always be late! Our rules simply show a few basic and certain ways of producing effective part-writing easily and quickly. As your skill in part-writing increases, you will often find that in certain situations, other procedures will produce even better musical results. These will be discussed throughout the text when applicable to the material under study.

Appendix 1, page 438, lists eleven basic procedures (rules) covering most part-writing situations, numbered, in this text, for ease of reference. It is *not* necessary to memorize rules by number; rather, use the appendix freely to find the procedure you need for a particular problem. With continuing practice in part-writing, you will find less and less dependence on recalling specific rules.

For some students with a strong musical background and/or a natural instinct or intuition for part-writing skills, Rule 11 (General Rule) may suffice. Most students, however, will benefit by studying Rules 1–10 individually, and carefully, applying each as it is presented in the text.

CHAPTER 5

The Minor Triad
Cadences in a Minor Key

Theory and Analysis

Upon examining the minor scale and the triads that are built on each of its scale steps (review Chapter 1, section 23), we find that the triad built upon the first scale step, the tonic, is a minor triad. This minor tonic triad (i) serves the same functions in a minor key as were ascribed previously to the major tonic triad in a major key. One of the most important of these is its function as the final goal of the harmonic progression in a minor key.

Fig. 5.1

The Minor Triad

The minor triad (Figure 5.2a) displays both similarities and differences when compared with the major triad. In both, the perfect intervals are identical (Figure 5.2b), whereas the locations of the major and minor intervals are reversed (Figure 5.3).

Fig. 5.2

Fig. 5.3

Minor Triad Spelling

Spelling minor triads should be practiced until any minor triad can be spelled quickly and accurately. Spelling may be accomplished in either of two ways.

1. When the root or fifth is given, you may spell the major triad from that note, and then lower the third. Example:

B♭ = 1. Major triad is B♭ D F; minor triad is B♭ D♭ F.
C♯ = 5. Major triad is F♯ A♯ C♯; minor triad is F♯ A C♯.

When the third is given, you may raise that note one half step, spell a major triad, and then lower the third. Example:

G = 3. Raise to G♯. Major triad is E G♯ B; minor triad is E G B.

2. With a knowledge of interval names and spellings, the minor triad may be spelled by interval. These are the intervals in the minor triad:

1 up to 3	Minor Third (m3)	3 down to 1
3 up to 5	Major Third (M3)	5 down to 3
5 up to 1	Perfect Fourth (P4)	1 down to 5
1 up to 5	Perfect Fifth (P5)	5 down to 1
3 up to 1	Major Sixth (M6)	1 down to 3
5 up to 3	Minor Sixth (m6)	3 down to 5
1 up to 1	Perfect Octave (P8)	1 down to 1
3 up to 3		3 down to 3
5 up to 5		5 down to 5

Assignment 5.1. Minor triad spelling.

a) Spell with letter names the minor triad when each of the following is the root. D, A, C, F, E♭, A♭, G♯, B, G♭, B♭.

b) Spell the minor triad when each of the following is the third. F, C, B♭, E, E♭, D, F♯, G♯, A, B, D♭.

c) Spell the minor triad when each of the following is the fifth. A, B, D, G, F♯, B♭, C♯, A♭, F, D♯.

Assignment 5.2. Based on a given triad, spell each of the intervals in the table of intervals. Example: C♯ minor triad.

m3	C♯ up to E	m6	G♯ up to E
M3	E up to G♯	M6	E up to C♯
P4	G♯ up to C♯	P8	C♯ up to C♯
P5	C♯ up to G♯		E up to E
			G♯ up to G♯

Do the same with triads from Assignment 5.1*a*, or others as assigned.

Cadences in a Minor Key

Authentic cadences in a minor key are similar to those in a major key. The tonic triad is usually minor (i), whereas the dominant triad is invariably major (V); this situation requires an accidental to show that the seventh scale step has been raised to provide a leading tone for the key.

Fig. 5.4

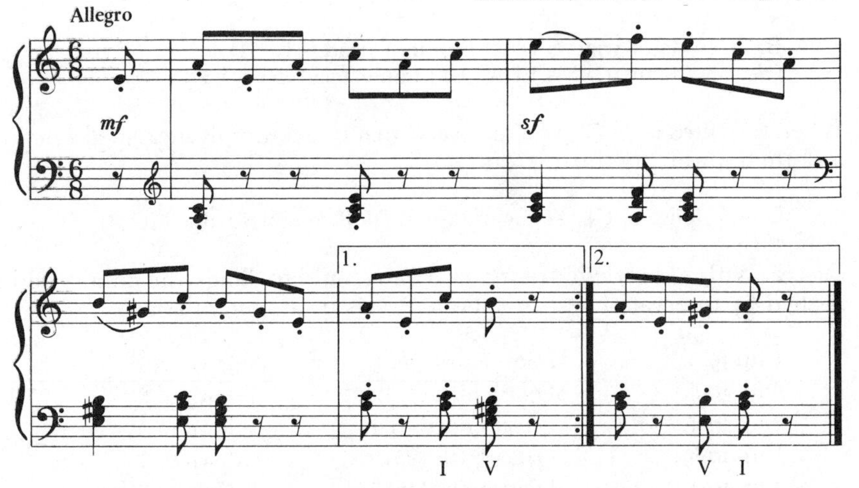

Unlike the almost inevitable final major triad in a major key, two alternate final triads can be found in minor keys, especially in music of the sixteenth, seventeenth, and early eighteenth centuries. During this time, the minor triad was often felt to be too dissonant for a concluding triad. In its place, composers used either a major triad, called a "picardy third" or "tierce de Picardie,[1] or a triad without a third (root and fifth only).

Fig. 5.5

Fig. 5.6

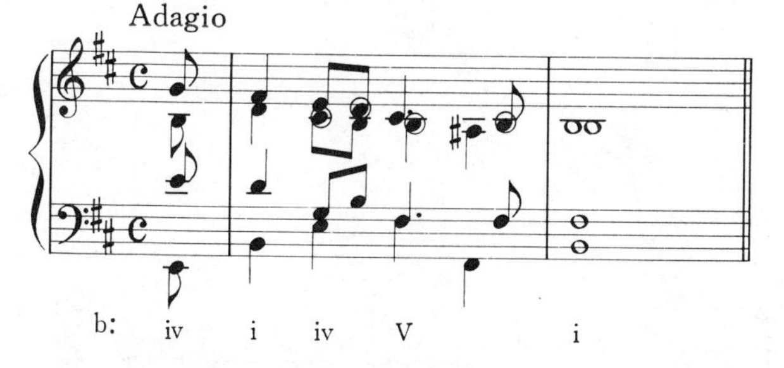

Assignment 5.3. Spell the tonic and dominant triads and the dominant seventh chord in each minor key. Start with A minor and continue around the circle of fifths (review Chapter 1, section 19).

	i	V	V^7
A minor	A C E	E G♯ B	E G♯ B D
E minor	E G B	B D♯ F♯	B D♯ F♯ A
etc.			

Assignment 5.4. Locate and identify by name and by chord numbers each cadence in these examples. Observe that not all cadences include only triads, as there may be any of these as well: nonharmonic tones, the V^7 chord, and chords in inversion. Indicate these as in previous assignments. Note that in the Bach chorales, the fermata (𝄐) indicates the end of a phrase, and therefore the location of a cadence.

[1]The origin and meaning of this term are unknown.

Bach, *Vater unser im Himmelreich* (#110)

(1)

Brahms, *Capriccio,* Op. 116, No. 1

(2)

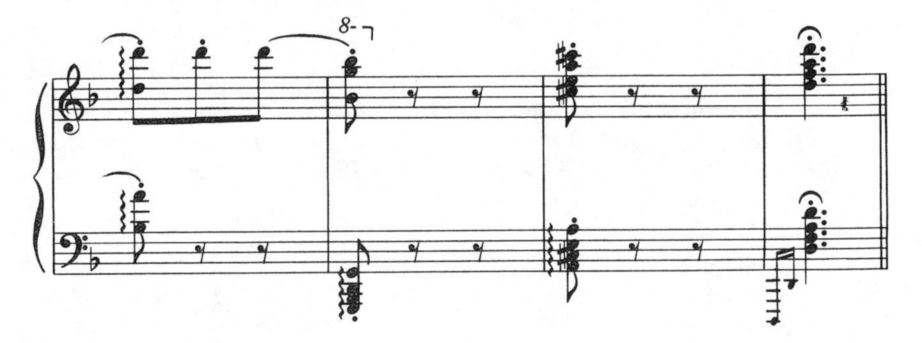

Bach, *Herzliebster Jesu, was hast du verbrochen* (#59)

(3)

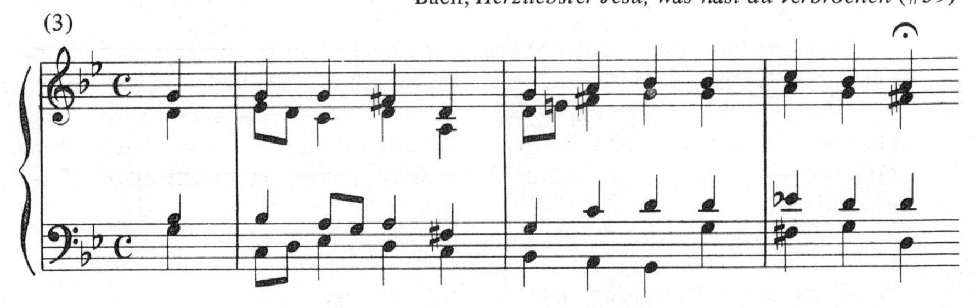

Bach, Cantata No. 78, *Jesu, der du meine Seele*
(4)

Torelli, Concerto for Violin, Op. 8, No. 8
(5)
Vln. I
Vln. II
Vla.
Bass

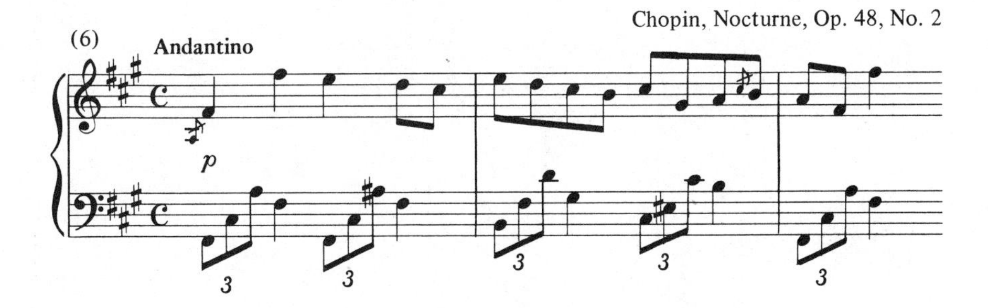
Chopin, Nocturne, Op. 48, No. 2
(6)
Andantino
p

Application

Written Materials

Part-Writing

Assignment 5.5. Write minor triads on the staff. Using each of the following letters as a root of a minor triad, write the complete triad in four voices, using the number after the letter name as the soprano note. Example: B♭ (3)

Fig. 5.7

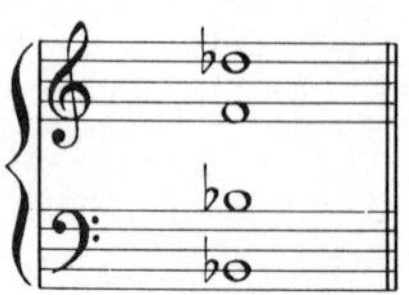

A (1), E (5), G (3), F♯ (5), C♯ (1), B (1), E♭ (5), G♯ (3), A♭ (1), D♯ (5).

Assignment 5.6. Write intervals from the minor triad on the staff. Using the table of intervals in Assignment 5.2, write all the intervals ascending and descending in each of the triads listed in Assignment 5.5 Example: B♭.

Fig. 5.8

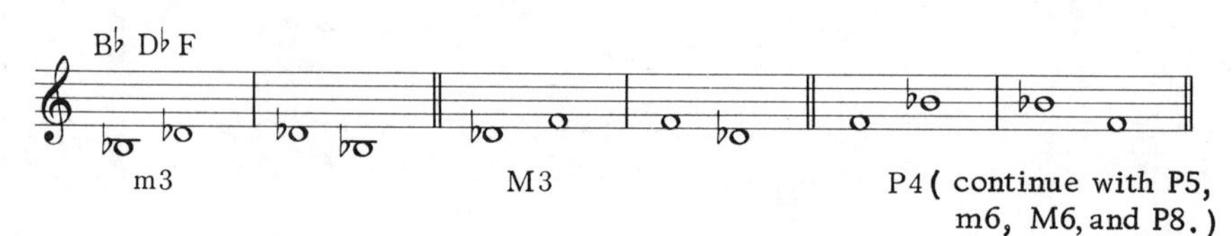

Assignment 5.7. Write each pair of repeated minor triads. Follow directions for part-writing given in Chapter 4. No new procedures are required.

Writing Authentic Cadences

The part-writing of authentic cadences in a minor key follows the same procedures as those described in Chapter 4. The only exception is the presence of an accidental appearing below some of the bass notes.

In a minor key, there are two possible dominant triads, depending on the form of the minor scale used.[2]

Fig. 5.9

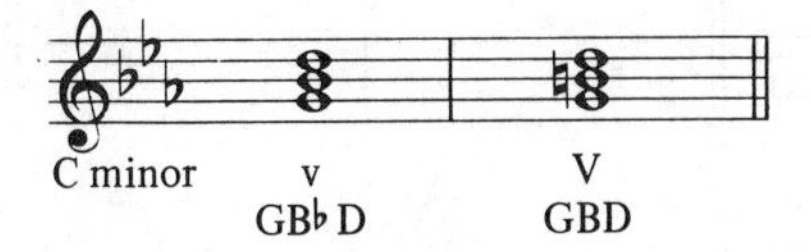

When the complete triad is not shown, there must be a way to indicate which of the two is meant. An accidental (♮, ♯, or ×) placed below the root in the bass voice will indicate that the third above the bass note is to be raised one half step, thereby creating a major triad.

Fig. 5.10

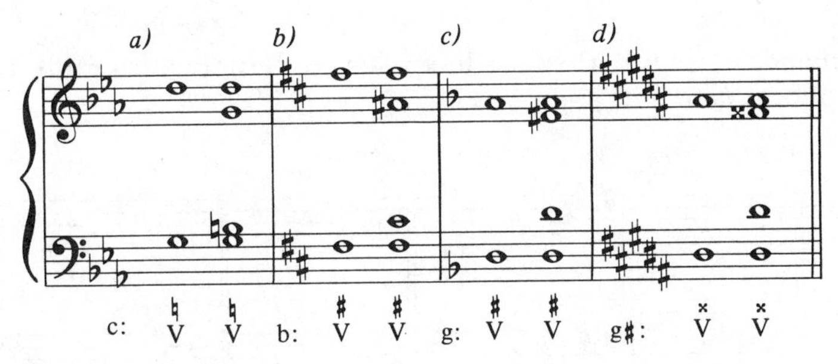

The Picardy third can be indicated in the same way.

Fig. 5.11

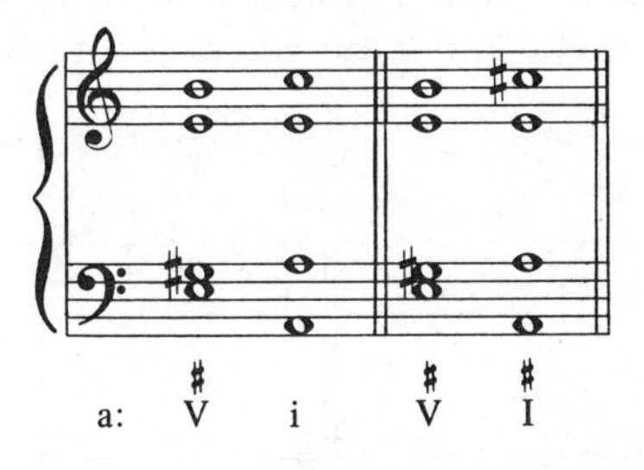

[2]The minor dominant triad (v) will be considered in Chapter 16.

These are the first of a group of symbols called *figured bass.* The system will be explained fully in Chapter 9.

Assignment 5.8. Writing authentic cadences. Fill in the missing notes and identify each cadence by its name and chord numbers.

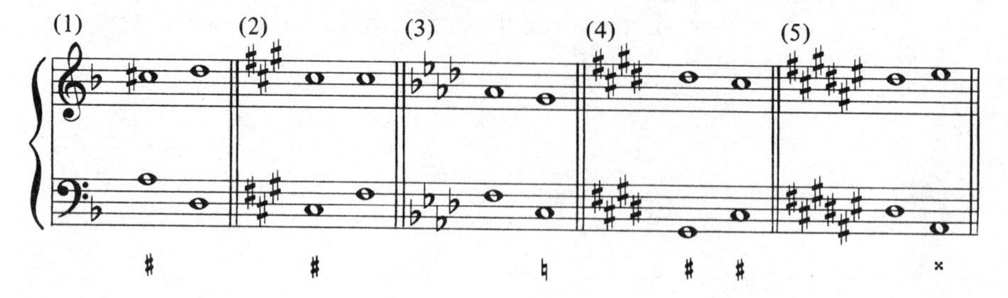

Assignment 5.9. Only the bass line is given. Supply a soprano line and complete by adding alto and tenor voices.

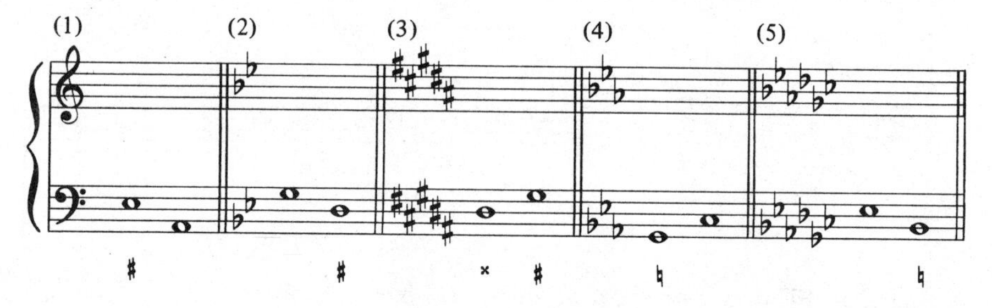

Assignment 5.10. Only the soprano is given. Supply a bass line (review directions in Assignment 4.11.) together with alto and tenor voices. Supply the necessary figured bass symbols.

Assignment 5.11. Writing extended exercises using tonic and dominant triads. Follow the procedure described in Assignment 4.13.

*Use Rule 2C.

*Use Rule 2C.

Ear Training

Hearing the Minor Triad

Ear-training drills for the minor triad listed below are similar in intent and procedure to the drills for the major triad found in Chapter 2. For more specific directions and illustrations, refer to like exercises in Chapter 2 as indicated. Exercises without such references are new to this chapter.

Exercise 5.1. (*cf.* Exercise 2.2.) Singing the minor triad

a) Listen to minor triads played at the piano. After each is sounded, sing the pattern 1–3–5–3–1.

b) Listen to the triad. Sing the root of the triad only.

Exercise 5.2. (*cf.* Exercises 2.3–2.5.) *a*) Play or listen to any given pitch. Call this pitch 1. Sing a minor triad from this pitch.

b) Call the given pitch 5. Sing the triad pattern.

c) Call the given pitch 3. Sing the triad pattern.

Exercise 5.3. (*cf.* Exercise 2.6.) Repeat Exercise 5.2, but instead of using numbers when you sing, sing with triad spellings.

Exercise 5.4. *a*) Repeat Exercise 5.2, but be prepared to sing either a major triad or a minor triad as directed by the instructor.

b) Repeat Exercise 5.3, but be prepared to sing either a major or minor triad with triad spellings.

Exercise 5.5. (*cf.* Exercise 2.9. Review Exercises 2.7 and 2.8 if necessary, using minor triads.) Identify the soprano note of a minor triad as 1, 3, or 5 of the triad when the triad is played at the piano.

Exercise 5.6. Listen to a series of major and minor triads, mixed. Identify the soprano note and indicate whether the triad is major or minor. For example, the answers to the examples below would be 5M, 3m, 1m, 3M (M = major, m = minor).

Fig. 5.12

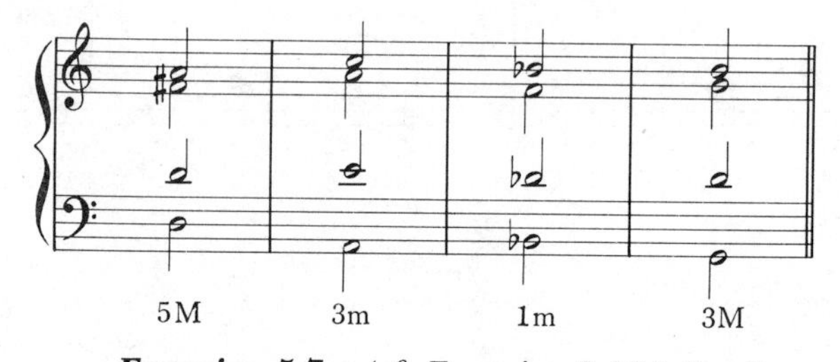

Exercise 5.7. (*cf.* Exercise 2.10.) Spell a minor triad when the triad is played at the piano and the name of the soprano note is given.

Exercise 5.8. Repeat Exercise 5.7, but expect to hear either a major triad or a minor triad. Spell the triad accordingly.

Intervals in the Minor Triad

Ear-training drills for intervals in the minor triad are similar to the drills for intervals in the major triad found in Chapter 2. The intervals studied here are the same as in the major triad, but in different contexts; for example, a major third is found as 3 up to 5 in a minor triad rather than as 1 up to 3 in a major triad.

Each exercise that follows is based on a similar exercise from Chapter 2 using the minor triad instead of the major triad as its basis.

Exercise 5.9. (*cf.* Exercise 2.11) Singing intervals from the minor triad by number. You will hear a minor triad played at the piano followed by a direction such as "Sing 1 up to 3."

Exercise 5.10. (*cf.* Exercise 2.12.) Singing minor triad intervals from a given pitch. You will hear one pitch played at the piano followed by a direction such as "Sing 5 down to 1."

Exercise 5.11. (*cf.* Exercise 2.14. Review Exercise 2.13 if necessary.) Identifying intervals from the minor triad aurally. You will hear an interval played at the piano. Identify the interval by its triad numbers, as found in the minor triad.

Exercise 5.12. (*cf.* Exercise 2.15.) Identify intervals aurally by naming the interval.

Exercise 5.13. (*cf.* Exercise 2.16.) Sing the interval when the name and direction of the interval is given and the first note of the interval is played at the piano.

Exercise 5.14. (*cf.* Exercise 2.17.) Writing intervals from the minor triad on the staff from dictation.

The Authentic Cadence

Exercise 5.15. (*cf.* Exercise 4.2.) Identify the authentic cadence in a minor key. If the cadence contains a Picardy third, indicate as much.

Exercise 5.16. (*cf.* Exercise 4.3.) Writing the authentic cadence from dictation in a minor key.

Exercise 5.17. (*cf.* Exercise 4.4.) Harmonic dictation in a minor key.

Keyboard Harmony

Playing Triads and Cadences in a Minor Key

Keyboard activity in minor keys will follow procedures already established for major keys in Chapters 2 and 4.

Exercise 5.18. (*cf.* Exercise 2.18.) Play a minor triad, using each pitch name in the circle of fifths. Play each with its root in the bass, and with the root, third, and fifth successively in the soprano.

Exercise 5.19. (*cf.* Exercise 4.5.) Play authentic cadences using the list found in Exercise 4.5, but substitute V–i for V–I, and i–V for I–V.

Exercise 5.20. (*cf.* Exercises 4.6 and 4.7, and the commentary preceding each.) Play these melodies, supplying a harmonic cadence at the point of the melodic cadence, as in Figure 4.53, page 91.

(1) Hymn: Windsor

Additional exercises include the following:
Music for Sight Singing, 45, 46 (1, 4), 47, 49, 51 (1, 2, 4), 52, 55, and 57; *More Music for Sight Singing,* 328 (2, 3), 330, 331, 338, 339, 341, 357, 358 (1, 2, 4), 360, 377 (1, 2, 8), and 384 (1–4).

Exercise 5.21. (*cf.* Exercise 4.8 and the discussion preceding it.) Play from the lead sheet in these five melodies. For a minor triad the symbol is the root name plus "m"; for example, Gm = G B♭ D.

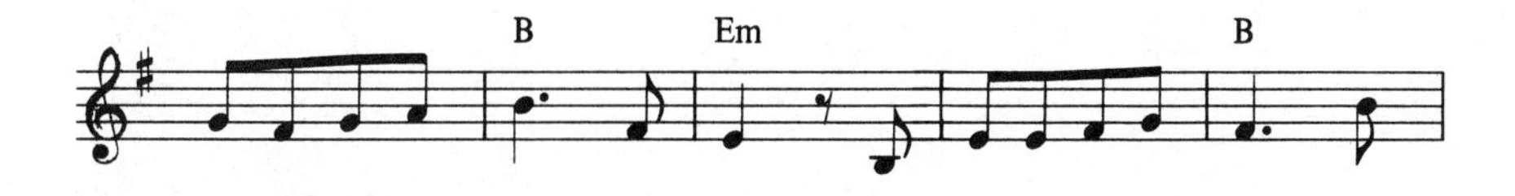

Additional melodies can be found in Mainous, *Melodies to Harmonize With*, numbers 25, 31, 48, 50, and 53.

CHAPTER 6

The Melodic Line

Study of this chapter may begin upon completion of the exercises in rhythmic reading and rhythmic dictation in simple time from Chapter 3. It is suggested that the study of sight singing and melodic dictation precede that of melodic composition.

Theory and Analysis

General Considerations

Most people, on hearing a piece of music, initially react to the melody. This is natural considering that, from a historical point of view, singing was probably the first musical act, and that, in the life of an individual, singing is often the first childhood experience of music. The earliest known music is melodic, and the importance of melody to our own time has not diminished, in spite of continual developments in the rhythmic and harmonic aspects of music composition.

The character of a given melody is a reflection of the historical era and geographical area from which it arose, either as a deliberate composition or as an extemporaneous expression, such as a folk song. The article "Some Varieties of Melodic Expression," included in this chapter, describes and illustrates several different types of melodies from various times and places.

Melodies of the common practice period as well as much twentieth century music influenced by the common practice period, such as popular music, church music, music for instructional purposes, television and radio commercials, and background music, all display similar characteristics of *pitch, harmony, meter/rhythm,* and *form.* These characteristics are given general definitions here as they relate to the whole body of melodic music of the common practice period. Each definition will be broadened by more detailed studies of both standard and exceptional melodic practices.

1. Pitch. Melodies are usually based on major and minor scales and the keys they represent.

Fig. 6.1

Beethoven, Sonata in C Minor for Piano, Op. 13
Allegro
phrase
Key: C minor
Meter: 1 2 1 2 1 2
Minimal Harmonization: i(CE♭G) V(GBD) i
phrase
1 2 1 2 1 2 1 2 1 2
V i V i

Fig. 6.2

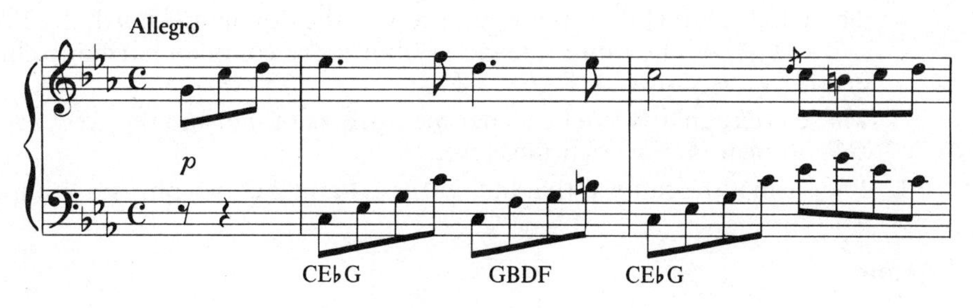
Allegro
p
CE♭G
GBDF
CE♭G

p
GBD
BDFA♭

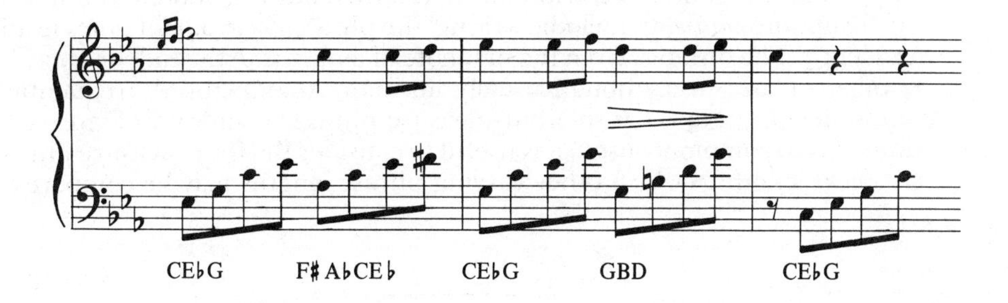
CE♭G
F♯A♭CE♭
CE♭G
GBD
CE♭G

2. Harmony. A melody will imply a certain chord progression (sometimes more than one). You have already experienced this in harmonizing lead sheet melodies in the preceding chapter.

3. Meter/rhythm. A melody will be found in a regularly recurring metric pattern, such as $\frac{4}{4}$ 1 2 3 4 | 1 2 3 4 ||. Successive measures will each contain the same number of beats, with a regularly recurring accent on the first beat of each measure. Rhythmic patterns within the measure will be so devised as to allow this regularity. (See the article "Another Metrical Concept" in this chapter.)

4. Form. A melody will conform to a formal structure, as discussed in Chapter 2 in relation to Figures 2.1 and 2.2.

To illustrate, here is a Beethoven melody (Fig. 6.1). Observe the following features:

a. It is based on the C minor scale.
b. Harmonically, it could simply imply i and V triads only, as shown in Figure 6.1. Try this melody at the keyboard like a lead sheet exercise. Play C E♭ G at the symbol i, and G B D at the symbol V. (In measure 5, combining the A♭ of the melody with G B D creates a variety of the dominant chord, the V^9 chord, G B D F A♭.) The more satisfactory but more complex harmony chosen by Beethoven is shown in Figure 6.2.
c. There are regularly two beats per measure (cut time) and the accent regularly falls on beat one of each measure.
d. The form is the same as that in Figures 2.1 and 2.2: two phrases, comprising a period.

Form

Most music is written in some orderly arrangement. In the music of the West, certain patterns of musical construction have come to be commonly (though not exclusively) used. These patterns are known as musical *forms.*

The term *form* refers to the shape or structure of the object or concept being described. In music, a form usually ends at a cadence point; a form begins either at the beginning of the piece or immediately after a cadence. Since a musical composition usually has more than one cadence, it usually contains a series of forms. These smaller forms, in turn, will often combine to make up a larger kind of form, the nature and description of which is determined by the number of cadences and nature of the material between cadences.

From this general description, we can turn our attention to the smallest of the forms, the *phrase.* In melodic writing, the phrase is a group of notes leading to a cadence. The distance from the first note of a phrase to the cadence may be any number of measures, though usually not more than eight. A frequently used phrase length in music is the four-measure phrase, as shown in Figure 6.3. Because it is so commonly used, it is useful to consider the four-measure phrase as a standard length to which other varying phrase lengths may be compared.

Fig. 6.3.

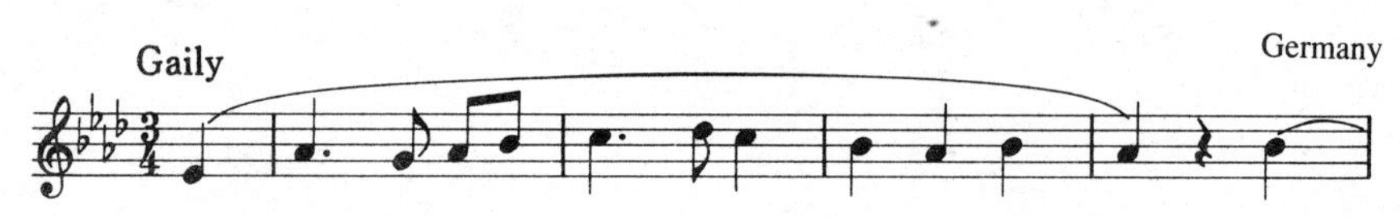

In this melody, the first phrase ends with a cadence on the tonic note, and the whole phrase is marked off with a phrase-mark extending from the first note to the last note of the phrase. A phrase may also consist of two or more distinct units, called *motives*. The phrase in Figure 6.4 is composed of two two-measure motives; the motives combine to make a phrase. The motive can be identified by the fact that it is a unit of melody smaller than a phrase, usually identifiable by a pause in the melodic line or in the rhythm. Note that the phrase-mark is used to indicate the length of the motive.

Fig. 6.4

Two phrases may combine to form a *period*. In the period the first phrase, called the *antecedent phrase*, usually ends with a half cadence, or occasionally with an imperfect cadence. The second phrase, called the *consequent phrase*, then ends usually with a perfect cadence, though again an imperfect cadence is possible.

Periods may be *parallel* or *contrasting*. A period is parallel when the two phrases are similar in some respect. Usually the beginning of each phrase is identical to the other, as in Figure 6.5, but any marked melodic similarity in the two phrases will justify the analysis of it as a parallel period. The similar melodic contour of each phrase in Figure 6.6 leads to its analysis as a parallel period. When the two phrases lack any specific or general melodic similarity, the period is contrasting, as in Figure 6.7.

Fig. 6.5 Parallel Period

Fig. 6.6 Parallel Period

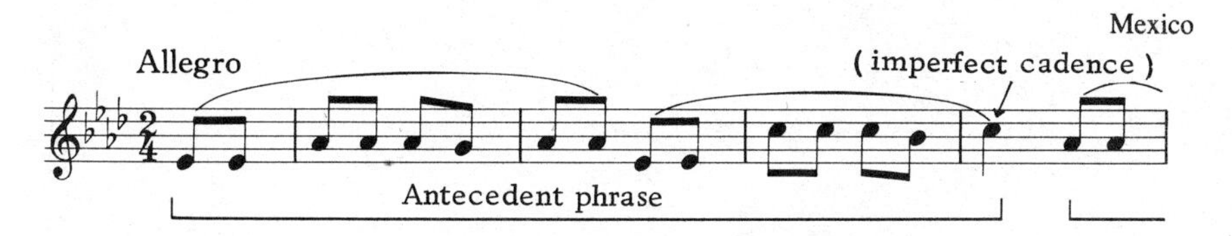

Fig. 6.7 Contrasting Period

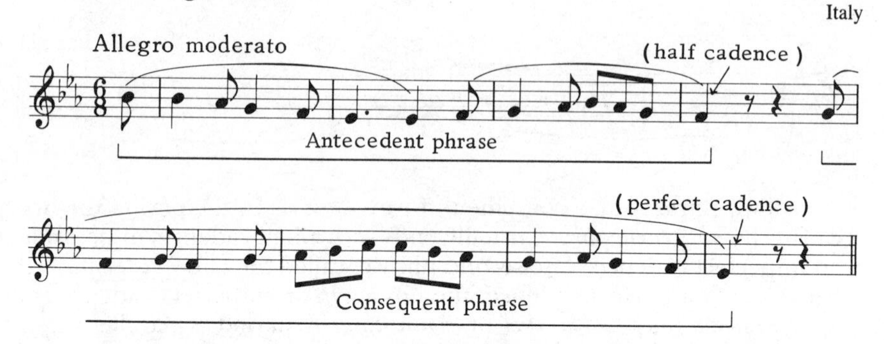

At times, successive phrases will each end with the tonic note. Since the perfect cadence marks the *end* of a formal pattern, these phrases cannot be combined into a larger form. The folksong in Figure 6.8 contains two four-measure phrases, each ending on the tonic note. Therefore, the song is not a period, but simply two phrases.

Fig. 6.8

Phrases are also classified according to the rhythmic placement of their first and last notes, that is, whether these notes occur on a strong beat or a weak beat of the measure. There are, of course, four such combinations, the most common of which are those with strong final tones.

First note	*Final note*
strong	strong
weak	strong
strong	weak
weak	weak

(The terms *masculine beginning* and *masculine ending* are sometimes used to refer to strong first and final notes, and the terms *feminine beginning* and *feminine ending* to weak first and final notes.)

Fig. 6.9 Strong first note; strong final note

Beethoven, Sonata in C Minor for Piano,
Op. 10, No. 1

Fig. 6.10 Weak first note; strong final note

Schubert, *Winterreise,* Op. 89,
"Der Lindenbaum"

Fig. 6.11 Strong first note; weak final note

Mozart, Sonata in A Minor for Piano, K.310

Fig. 6.12 Weak first note; weak final note

Mendelssohn, *Songs Without Words,*
Op. 19, No. 2

When two phrases combine to form a period, both phrases commonly display the same beginning and ending characteristics, as can be seen by reviewing Figures 6.5–6.7; however, other combinations are not infrequent, as in Figure 6.13.

Fig. 6.13

Often the close of the antecedent phrase of a period will be connected to the opening of the consequent phrase with one or more decorative pitches. Locating the cadence will help to identify the last note of the antecedent phrase; the notes between it and the beginning of the consequent phrase should not be considered to constitute a weak beginning of that phrase.

Fig. 6.14

Assignment 6.1. Analyzing form in melodies. Each of these melodies will be either a parallel period, a contrasting period, or two successive phrases. Copy out the melody and indicate *a)* the location and name of the cadence, using roman numerals V–I or I–V, *b)* the phrase lengths, by a bracket from the first to last note of the phrase, *c)* the nature (strong or weak) of the first and final notes of each phrase, and *d)* the name of the entire form. Use Figure 6.15 as a guide, and then continue with the melodies following it.

Fig. 6.15

Silcher, Alle Jahre wieder
strong
strong
I
V
antecedent phrase
half
cadence
strong
strong
V
I
consequent phrase
imperfect
authentic cadence
Form: Contrasting period.
(1)
Brahms, Symphony No. 1, Op. 68
(2)
France
(3)
Spain
(4)
Haydn, Sonata in C Major for Piano

For material similar to the preceding examples, see *Music for Sight Singing,* 1, 2, 6, 14, 20, 28, 35, 40, 42, 44, 45, 46, 48, 51, 55, 61, 66, 70, 72, 73, 74, 109, 111, 113, 127, and 132; and *More Music for Sight Singing,* 266, 268, 269, 272, 276, 279, 285, 294, 308, 311, 334, 339, and 360.

Pitch Considerations: Scale Steps and Larger Intervals

A melody in its simplest form may consist only of adjacent scale steps, as in Figure 6.16. Such melodies are relatively uncommon. See also the melody line of Figure 2.1, which contains only one interval larger than a second.

Fig. 6.16

At the other extreme, melodies made up exclusively of thirds or larger are also uncommon. In Figure 6.17, such intervals are used exclusively in measures 1–8.

Fig. 6.17

More usual is a melody incorporating both scale line passages and intervals larger than the scale step, as can be seen in most melodic lines, including those shown in Figures 2.2 and 6.1.

Scalar lines and intervallic leaps are not used indiscriminately, however. The following are some general considerations, pertaining particularly to the more simple type of melodic line. In more sophisticated styles, such as symphonies and concertos, melodies will often display considerably more freedom.

1. In a scalar line, four or five tones (and occasionally six) in the same direction is the usual limit (Figure 6.18a), although examples of a full octave (eight tones) are fairly common as in the first phrase of *Joy to the World* and in Figure 6.18b.

The longer the run in the same direction, the more likely it is that the first note of the run will be approached from the opposite direction and the last note left in the opposite direction (Figure 6.18a, measures 7–9 and 10–11).

Fig. 6.18

Haydn, Symphony No. 101

2. Skips (intervals of a third or larger) are usually limited to not more than two (but occasionally three) in the same direction, after which the melodic line progresses in the opposite direction. Such successive leaps are usually triadic, as in Figure 6.19, where the two leaps outline the G B D triad.

Fig. 6.19

England

When a seventh chord is outlined, three skips are possible.

Fig. 6.20

Germany

As an example of an exception to this rule Figure 6.21 shows three skips in the same direction; the third interval is not part of the G major triad. Note that the fourth note, E, seems merely to interrupt the normal arrival of the chord tone D.

Fig. 6.21

Mexico

A large leap (a fifth or larger) is usually approached from a direction opposite to the skip and left in a direction opposite to the skip, as in Figure 6.22. Also, observe this process with each large interval in Figures 6.18a and 6.18b.

Fig. 6.22

Bach, Minuet

3. The range of the melody (lowest note to highest note) must not exceed the range of the voice or instrument for which the melody is written. The ranges shown for part-writing voice lines on page 77 also apply here. Note the limited range of the folk songs included in this chapter. Instruments have a much wider range than the human voice. Their outer limits are included in Appendix 2, "Instrumentation."

In most melodies the highest tone, sometimes called the *climax note,* is not repeated within the phrase, and often not within the period. Its effectiveness is often lost upon repetition. The same is true of the lowest note *(anticlimax note)* though in its case the rule is not so strictly observed.

Assignment 6.2. Analyze these melodies, looking for these following features:

a) Scale lines. How many notes go in the same direction? How is the run in one direction approached and left?

b) Chord outline. What chords are outlined in a series of two or more skips.?

c) Large leaps. Is the leap 1) approached and left by similar or contrary motion, and 2) is it approached and left by scale step or by skip?

d) High and low notes. Check for the highest note and the lowest note in each phrase. Is either found twice or more?

e) Note any exceptional practices and try to determine why they were used.

Bracketed and circled notes in Figures 6.23 and 6.24 are explained after each figure.

Fig. 6.23

1. These skips outline the tonic triad. In measure 1, the last note is left in contrary motion. In measure 7, the first note is approached by contrary motion and left in the same manner.

2. The large skip is approached and left by contrary motion.

3. In the scale line of four or five notes, each is approached and left by contrary motion.

4. These skips outline the dominant seventh (V^7) chord, and each group is approached and left by contrary motion.

5. The low notes and high notes of each phrase are circled. Each phrase displays one of each.

Fig. 6.24

(consider repeated notes as a single note)

1. This scale line of 5 notes is approached from the same direction (the tonic-dominant leap is common) and left by contrary motion.
2. In this scale line of 6 notes, each group is approached and left by contrary motion (except the final note).

Analyze the following melodies, using the techniques just discussed.

Pitch Considerations: The Leading Tone

The leading tone (seventh scale step) must be treated with care. As its name implies, it *leads* to the tonic. When approached by step from below, the leading tone must progress to the tonic (Figure 6.25a). When preceded by the tonic note it may progress down by step, as in a scale (Figure 6.25b), or it may return to the tonic (Figure 6.25c). When it is part of an arpeggiated triad figure, its direction is determined by the direction of the arpeggio (except when it is found as the final note of the arpeggio, in which case it returns to tonic—Figure 6.25d).

Fig. 6.25

Minor Keys: The Sixth and Seventh Scale Steps

In a minor key, the sixth and seventh scale steps require particular attention. If the harmonic form of the scale is used, the interval of the augmented second results. Although this interval does have limited uses, it is generally avoided, especially in less sophisticated styles.

Fig. 6.26

As its name implies, the melodic form of the minor scale is generally used in melodic writing. When a melody ascends through a scale line from the dominant tone to the tonic tone, the sixth and seventh scale steps are usually raised.

Fig. 6.27

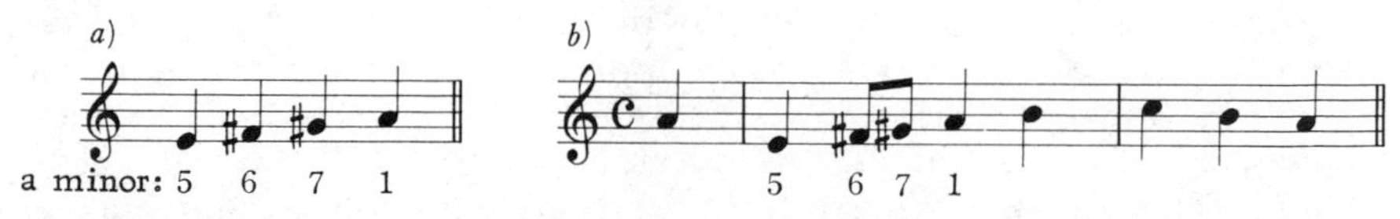

When the melody descends through a scale line from the tonic tone to the dominant tone, the seventh and sixth scale steps are usually lowered, as in the descending form of the melodic minor scale.

Fig. 6.28

When either the sixth or seventh scale step is used without the other in a step-wise passage, the seventh scale step is raised and proceeds up (Figure 6.29a), and the sixth scale step is lowered and proceeds down (Figure 6.29b).

Fig. 6.29

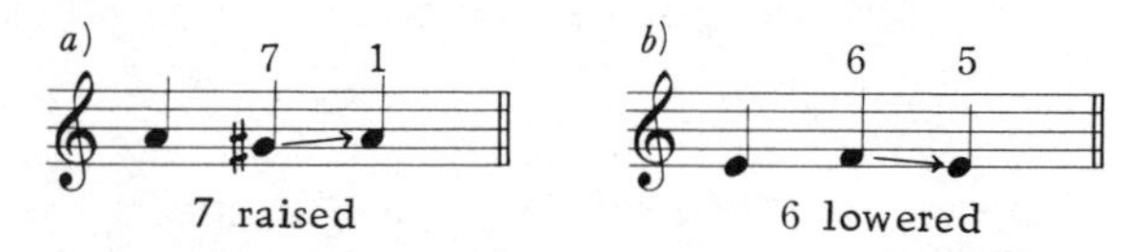

Occasionally, both the sixth and seventh scale steps are found in a step-wise passage but are not found between the tonic and dominant tones. In this case each note in the group of sixth and seventh scale steps is treated alike. If the last note of the group is the seventh scale step, all the notes of the group are raised (Figure 6.30a). If the last note of the group is the sixth scale step, all the notes of the group are lowered (Figure 6.30b).

Fig. 6.30

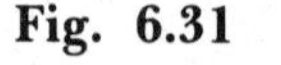
Fig. 6.31

When an arpeggiated form of all or part of the dominant (V) triad is used melodically, the raised seventh scale step may descend to the next chord tone.

Fig. 6.32

Often this V triad pattern is filled in with passing tones, with the result that it appears that the ascending form of the scale is used in a descending passage.

Fig. 6.33

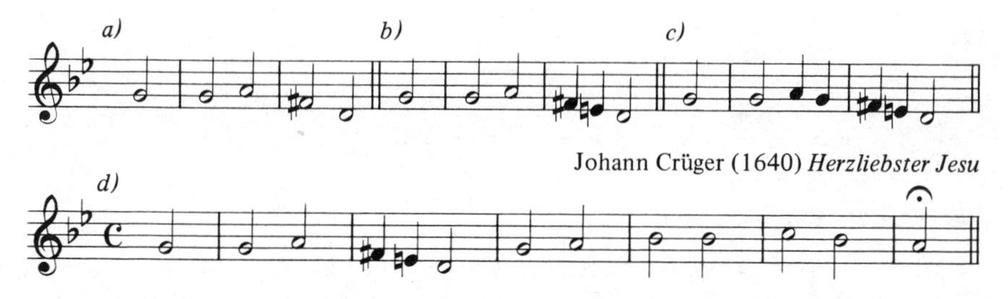

The dominant tone generally returns immediately to a note of the tonic triad, thus implying dominant-tonic harmony.

Assignment 6.3. Locate and explain the use of each sixth and seventh scale step in these melodies.

Repetition and Sequence

In the parallel period, we have seen the second phrase act in some ways as a repetition of the first. This repetition is sometimes exact, except for the last note or notes (as in Figure 6.5 and Assignment 6.1, parts 1 and 2) and sometimes the repetition is vague (as in Figure 6.6). Repetition within the phrase is just as valuable, both in preventing too many ideas from being included in the short space of four measures, and in emphasizing a good idea once it has been stated.

Exact repetition can be effective if it is not done to the point of monotony. In Figure 6.34a, the repeated figure alternates with contrasting material, whereas in Figure 6.34b the sense of repetition is not disturbed by the slight modification in measures 3–4.

Fig. 6.34

a) Spain

b) Spain

modified

Repetition may be modified by *inversion.* In this process, each note in the repetition of the given melodic figure progresses to the next note by the same interval, but in the opposite direction. Measures 5–6 of Figure 6.35 are the inversion of measures 3–4. (The quality of the interval, whether major or minor, is not considered, only the interval number. Measure 5 shows a major second down, answered in measure 7 by a minor second up).

Fig. 6.35

Sequence is similar to repetition, except that the repeated material appears at a new pitch level. This device thus allows similarity and variety simultaneously. Consequently, it is one of the most successful and widely used devices in music composition—not only in melody, but in rhythm and harmony as well. In Figure 6.36, the melodic and rhythmic element (the two usually go together) of measure 2 is repeated as a sequence in measures 3 and 4; it is designed in this way so that a perfect cadence will be reached at the end of the regular four-measure phrase.

Fig. 6.36

Figure 6.37 contains the following uses of sequence.

1. There is a sequence within measure 1–2.
2. Measures 3–4 are a sequence of measures 1–2.
3. There are three occurrences of the melodic figure, the last in inversion, in measures 5–6.
4. To conclude this very fine melody, measure 7 features, for contrast, the figure in reverse ( ) and measure 8 shows the inversion of the three-note figure located at the end of the antecedent phrase.

Fig. 6.37

Sequence need not be exact; it may be modified to some extent, as long as the aural impression of repetition is clear. The last two measures of Figure 6.38 are a sequence of the previous two measures, although they differ by one note.

Fig. 6.38

Assignment 6.4. Locate and describe examples of repetition and sequence in the following melodies.

a) In Assignment 6.1, (7) and (9); in assignment 6.2, (4) and (5); and Figures 6.1, 6.18b, 6.21, 6.22, and 6.31.

b) In *Music for Sight Singing,* melodies 5, 7, 15, 16, 18, 31, 33 48, 71, 72, 84, 88, 110, 114, 115, 118, 137, 139, and 144; and, in *More Music for Sight Singing,* melodies 273, 281, 282, 288, 289, 291, 298, 309, 346, 347, 348, 352, 355.

c) In the following melodies:

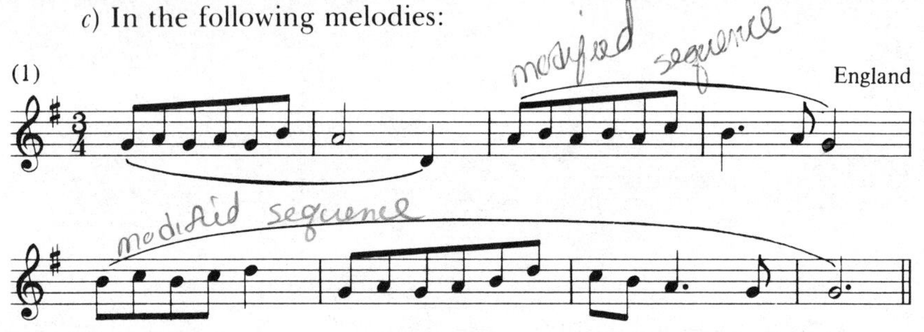

Implied Harmony

In all probability, melody from earliest times was performed by itself, without accompanying sounds or with only a rhythmic percussion accompaniment. Early in the history of Western music composition, however, accompanying pitch sounds were added, and, as time progressed, composers continually increased the complexity and sophistication of these additional sounds. We now take for granted that melody is virtually inseparable from accompanying sounds. In music of the common practice period, these sounds usually consist of chords and their progressions. It is often difficult, if not impossible, to determine whether the composer designed the melody to fit the chord progression or the chord progression to fit the melody. In most cases, it is probable that both were conceived simultaneously.

Some tunes, such as that in Figure 6.39, are so written that they immediately establish their own harmonic background.

Fig. 6.39

On the other hand, the melody of Figure 6.40 gives little clue to the harmony chosen to accompany it.

Even in contrapuntal music, where the most important aspect of the composition is the juxtaposition of two or more melodic lines, examples from the common practice period such as Figure 6.41 clearly show an implied harmonic background.

As a means of developing our ability to discover the harmonic implication of a melody, we will begin with easy folk songs, even though these were conceived and usually performed as single-line music. In the folk song repertoire of the Western World, most of these tunes based on major and minor scales (as opposed to modal scales) carry clear harmonic implications, as you have observed from playing melodies with lead sheet analyses in the previous chapter. Even though such tunes usually imply the simplest possible harmonizations, they can be harmonized differently using a wider range of harmonic material, as will be shown in later chapters. Figure 6.42a shows such a folk song, with lead sheet symbols for i and V only; Figure 6.42b shows the same tune with a more complex harmonization based on a wider variety of harmonic materials.

We will work at present only with tunes in which there is a clear harmonic implication of I (i) and V or V^7. The harmonic implication of such tunes can be discovered by observing one or both of the following two characteristics:

1. The chord is actually outlined in the melodic line. This chord outline can exist within an individual measure, as in the first two notes of the first full measure of Figure 6.42, or extend over several measures, as in Figure 6.39.

Fig. 6.40

Wolf, *Die ihr schwebt*

Fig. 6.41

Bach, Fugue in G Minor ("Little G Minor Fugue")

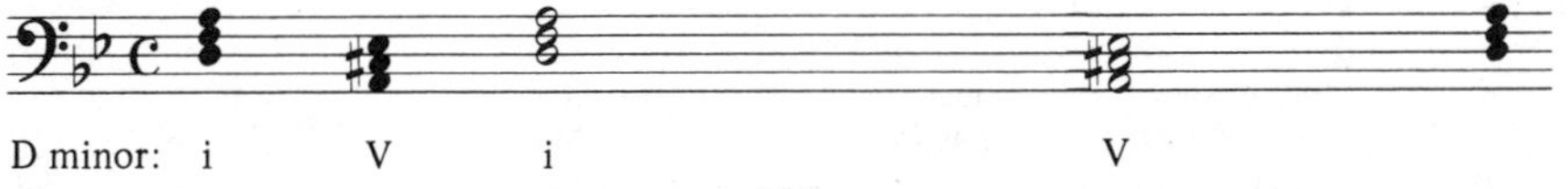

Fig. 6.42

Norway

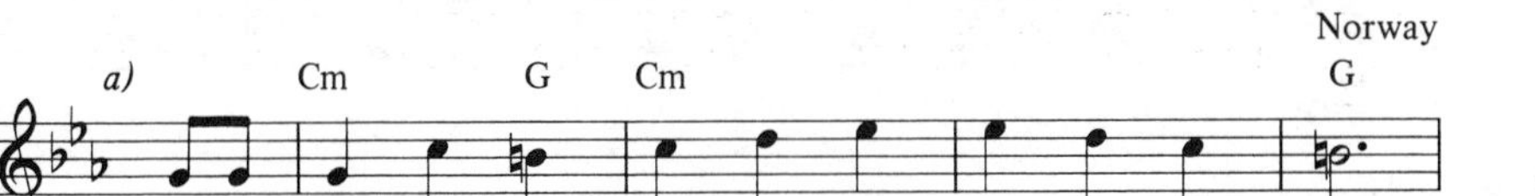

2. When there is no chord outline, the strong beat, or beats, of the measure may suggest the harmony. In Figure 6.43, measure one (the three repeated tonic notes—G—plus the final B) suggests a tonic triad (GBD), whereas in measure two, the A and F♯ on the principal beats suggest the dominant triad (D F♯ A).

Fig. 6.43

Chord changes may, of course, occur within the measure, as the melodic line dictates.

Fig. 6.44

Melody tones differing from the notes of the implied harmony are *nonharmonic tones.* (Used in this sense nonharmonic means that these tones are not part of the harmony sounding simultaneously with them. It is possible that a nonharmonic tone in one harmonization could be a harmonic tone in a different harmonization of the same melody).

The most common nonharmonic tone—the *passing tone*—is found stepwise between two different chord tones. When it occurs on a weak part of a beat it is an *unaccented passing tone* (UPT); when on an accented part of the beat it is an *accented passing tone* (APT). Also common is the *neighbor tone,* which is found stepwise between two notes of the same pitch; these are also unaccented (common) and accented (less common). They are also found as an upper neighbor (UN) and lower neighbor (LN). Several other varieties of nonharmonic tones will be considered in a later chapter.

Fig. 6.45

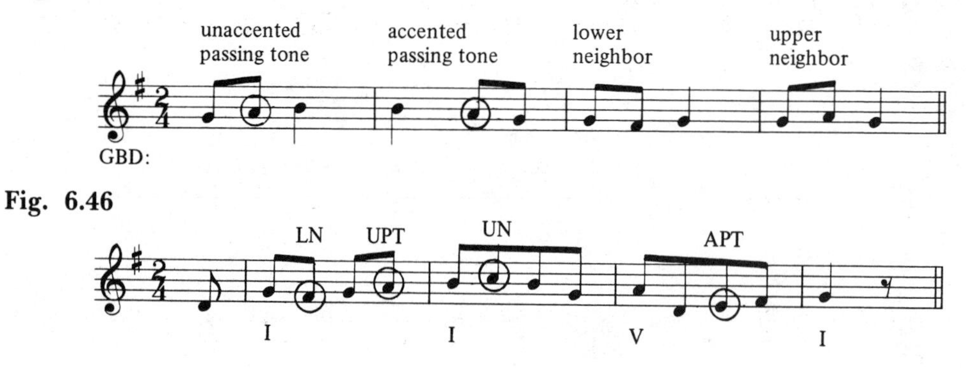

Fig. 6.46

One melody tone that is frequently encountered requires its own explanation. The fourth scale step of the key often implies the seventh of the V^7 chord. When used as a seventh, this fourth scale step almost always progresses downward, either by leap when part of an arpeggiated V^7 melodic line (Figure 6.47a), or by step in other instances (Figure 6.47b).

Fig. 6.47

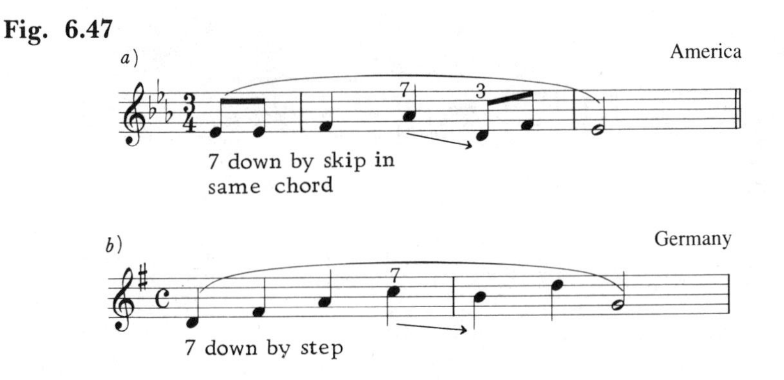

In rare cases where the seventh is allowed to ascend, the melodic line usually descends immediately after to effect a normal resolution of the seventh.

Fig. 6.48

Meter/Rhythm

The simplest kind of rhythmic pattern in a melody would be the use of single note value. Such melodies are uncommon. Melodic interest is heightened by contrast in the durations of pitches. This contrast can be very simple, as demonstrated by the melody of Figure 6.6, which consists of eighth notes only except for a single quarter note at the beginning of measures 4 and 8. The melody in Figure 6.8 is only slightly more complex. In rhythmic reading, observe how few rhythmic patterns are used in any one melody and how often rhythmic patterns are repeated, as in Figure 6.32.

A melodic sequence is, of course, almost invariably coupled with a rhythmic sequence, although rhythmic sequence can often be found without its melodic counterpart, as in Figure 6.35.

All of the melodic lines that we have studied thus far have been typical of music of the common practice period, in that they are found in recurring measures of equal length, with accents implied on the strong beat(s) of the measure. The differences between this practice and the concepts of an earlier period and of the twentieth century are described in the article in this chapter, "Another Metrical Concept."

Assignment 6.5. Analyze the implied harmony in each of these folk tunes. Place the chord numbers I, i, V or V^7 and the chord spelling below the staff, at the point where that chord replaces the previous chord. The only nonharmonic tones will be passing tones and neighbor tones. Circle each of them and identify them by the abbreviations UPT, APT, UN, or LN. The first tune has been analyzed for you.

Application

Written Materials

Melodic Composition

To the non-composer, the composition of a piece of music often appears to come about when a special musical gift is aided by an unexplainable source of inspiration. While the presence of both of these factors is certainly helpful, more important to a composer's accomplishments is a thorough knowledge of the materials with which he is working. Thus far in this chapter, we have investigated a number of simple melodies to discover their characteristics of pitch, rhythm, and form. By using this knowledge, it is entirely possible for anyone to produce at least an acceptable melodic line, and, more likely, one of considerable musical merit.

The well-known melody from Beethoven's ninth symphony (Figure 6.16) is a case in point, showing how a fine melody can be constructed from the simplest materials. In this melody

1. the scale line is used throughout and there are no intervals larger than a second;
2. the harmonic implications are of I and V only;
3. there is a rhythm pattern of repeated quarter notes, varied only at each cadence;
4. there is a simple eight-measure parallel period.

While the other melodies of this chapter display varying characteristics, all of them demonstrate that a good melody can be created with the simplest materials.

The following assignments will give you the opportunity to write original melodies. The test of a good melody is its "singability." Playing a melody on the piano will not necessarily reveal a defect, since almost any melody can easily be played. If, when you are singing, you find the melody contains an awkward interval or section, try to determine the cause of the defect. Then rewrite the melody as much as necessary until it is easily singable.

Assignment 6.6. Melody writing. Continue each of these melodic beginnings to form a four-measure phrase. Indicate the implied harmony by using the symbols I and V, or i and V, and circle any notes that are not part of these triads. Observe the specific directions given with each example.

(1) End with a perfect cadence.

(2) Use sequence and end with a perfect cadence.

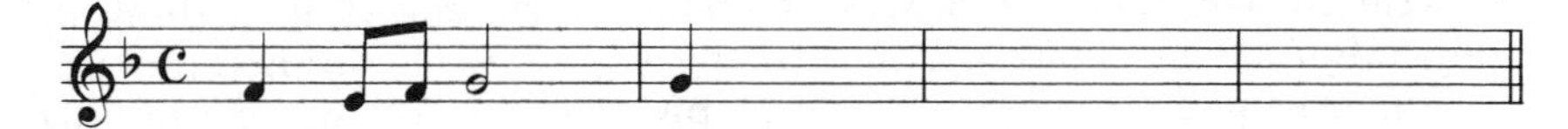

(3) Use sequence and end with a half cadence.

Assignment 6.7. Melody writing. Use any of the phrases from the examples in Assignment 6.6 as the first phrase of a period, and experiment with both parallel and contrasting periods. If your phrase from Assignment 6.6 ends with a perfect cadence, rewrite it so that it ends with a half or imperfect cadence and then continue with the consequent phrase.

Assignment 6.8. Melody writing. Write completely original periods, following your instructor's directions for such factors as clef, key, time signature, use of sequence, and so on. Edit each melody by indicating motives or phrases with phrase marks, and by including a tempo indication and dynamic markings.

Ear Training

Melodic Dictation

In melodic dictation, the student is asked to write on the staff a melody he hears performed. This skill improves on that of rhythmic dictation by adding the ability to write the correct pitch. Success in melodic dictation, as in rhythmic dictation, depends upon the ability to memorize the melody dictated. Therefore, review the comments and directions for the development of musical memory found on page 62.

Exercise 6.1. Melodic dictation, simple time, and major keys. Here is a suggested procedure:

a) The name of the key will be given by the instructor. Write the key signature on the staff, treble or bass as assigned.

b) The time signature will be given. Write it on the staff.

c) While making a conductor's beat and tapping the background beat, listen to the melody being played by the instructor.

d) On the second playing, sing the melody along with the piano. (You may delete this step once you have gained sufficient experience.)

e) Sing the melody without the piano, still conducting and tapping. (Delete this step with sufficient experience.)

f) Sing aloud or mentally, as directed, the tonic triad (1–3–5–3–1), and determine the letter name of the first note of the melody.

g) Write the melody on the staff. If it seems particularly difficult, first write the rhythm above the staff.

h) Listen to a final playing and check your work.

Here is an alternate procedure:

a) The name of the first note will be given by the instructor. Write this on the staff.

b) After hearing the melody, sing the tonic note of the key and then the first note of the melody. Determine the relationship of the first note to the tonic sound to discover the key of the melody. Write the key signature on the staff. Here is an example: G is given as the first note. You sing the melody, followed by its tonic note. If G is a major third above tonic, then you know that the key is E flat.

Exercise 6.2. Melodic dictation, simple time, and minor keys. Follow the same procedure as that in Exercise 6.1.

Exercise 6.3. Melodic dictation, compound time, and major keys. Follow the same procedure as that in Exercise 6.1.

Exercise 6.4. Melodic dictation, compound time, and minor keys. Follow the same procedure as that in Exercise 6.1.

Another Metrical Concept

If one were accustomed only to music in the style of the common practice period, and acquainted with meter and rhythm only as they are presented in Chapter 3 of this text, one might believe that all music is made up of regularly recurring measure lengths, each with regularly recurring strong and weak beats. Although metrical patterns of the latter kind have been used since early times in music meant for dancing or marching, music compositions of the greatest composers of the fifteenth and sixteenth centuries often display a metrical system markedly different from these.

These composers, who were to their period what Bach and Beethoven were to the Baroque and Classical periods, made their greatest accomplishments in vocal contrapuntal music. This style is based on the simultaneous sounding of two to eight, and sometimes more*, independent melodic lines. In pre-seventeenth century practice, each of these lines was written as a sep-

*For instance, the motet *Spem in alium*, by Thomas Tallis, c. 1550, is written for eight five-voice choirs, thus giving a total of 40 independent melodic lines.

arate score, as are band and orchestra parts today. Also, these voice lines were written without bar lines, as shown in this example of the beginning of the bass and tenor lines from a three-voice work by Palestrina.

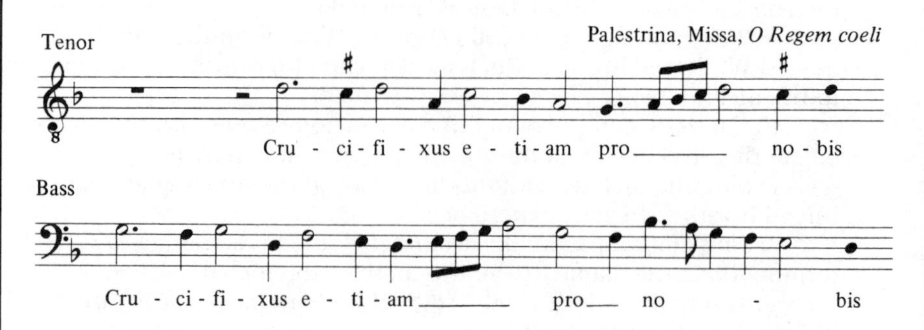

The vocal performer in the fifteenth and sixteenth centuries, like the instrumental musician today, read his part without visual reference to the parts for other voices; this is in contrast to today's full choral scores. And yet, without such reference and without bar lines, how was the meter determined by the performer? It was done by observing the natural accents of the text.

Cru- ci- fi- xus e- ti- am pro no- bis
(He was crucified for us)

In the music, each of these implied accents marks the beginning of a metrical group, and each group may be of like or different length from the previous or following group. If we place a bar line and an appropriate time signature before each accented note, each voice will consist of measures showing differing numbers of beat durations (and hence differing time signatures), and the resulting bar lines of the two voices will not always coincide.

Observe that the accented syllables usually appear on a longer note value, or at the beginning of a *melisma* (a group of notes on one syllable) longer than the previous note value. Accents such as these are caused by the relationship of long and short note values and are called *agogic* accents. In the preceding illustration, the only exception is the penultimate note in the tenor voice, a strong syllable on a metrically weak note to allow for a cadence on the next beat.

Modern editions of this early music are usually barred in the same way as today's music, that is, in measures of equal length. In the complete score for three voices shown below, one can see that the bar lines are at odds with the actual fluctuating meters, thus often giving the impression of syncopation (and unfortunately, often being performed as such). Look now at the

alto voice to determine the location of the accents and the duration of each metric group. Also, observe the rhythmic freedom of each individual voice line, and the nonconformity of the agogic accents in all the voices, which gives this music its particular charm in a performance, lending it an effect generally absent from most of the music of the common practice period.

The accidentals *above* certain notes in this example are indications of *musica ficta* (*false music*). Before the sixteenth century, many chromatic alterations were not written in the music on the assumption that the performer knew where they were needed. In modern editions of this early music, accidentals are placed above the notes to indicate the probable use of *musica ficta*.

Use of the regularly recurring bar line, so common in music of the seventeenth through nineteenth centuries, is often referred to as the "tyranny of the bar line." Harking back to sixteenth century rhythmic practice, twentieth century composers have broken this tyranny in many ways, one of them being the use of successions of measures in differing time signatures**. Another method, as shown in the example below, is the use of beaming and dynamic markings. Time signatures have been added in parentheses above the staff to show an interpretation of the actual meter changes.

Bartók, Quartet No. 4

**See examples in *Music for Sight Singing,* Chapter 19, and in *More Music for Sight Singing,* Part 2, melody 782 ff., and in Parts 5 and 6.

Some Varieties of Melodic Expression

Since melody exists in all parts of the world, and has existed presumably from prehistoric times up to the present, we can assume that it has displayed many forms and characteristics. A few examples will show the contrast between these other forms and the characteristic melodies of the period of Western music (c.1600 through c.1900) being discussed in this chapter.

The following chant-like aboriginal melody, which has been placed in notation by researchers, certainly shows no harmonic implication, no regular metric system, and too few notes to establish a feeling for scale or key. However, a rudimentary form is established when the passage of repeated D's followed by repeated B's is started over again in measure 5.

(Let us hurry, the wind is fierce and keen.)

The next example is taken from the earliest known body of Western music, the Gregorian chant of medieval times. (c.800 A.D.). It displays a scale pattern of E F G A B C D E, with tonic on E. This scale is known as the Phrygian mode, and is one of several scale systems, known as *modes*, that were in use before 1600. By the beginning of the common practice period, this system had been reduced to two scales, now called major and minor.

Both the medieval modes and the present major and minor modes are based on half steps and whole steps only. In Eastern Europe, the Near East, and in the Arab countries of Asia and Africa, scales containing one or two augmented seconds (three half steps, or a step and a half) are a major part of their harmonic resources. In the next examples, the augmented seconds are

E♭–F♯ and B♭–C♯, and the entire scale is D E♭ F♯ G A B♭ C♯ D. In Eastern Europe this scale is often known as the *Hungarian minor scale* or the *Gypsy minor scale.**

Folk music of Western European cultures has consistently made use of scale patterns that are the same as the medieval modes. This tune is based on the Mixolydian mode (G A B C D E F G).

(Further comment on modal writing in composed music is included in another article in this chapter, "Another Metrical Concept.")

Since the common practice period, melody has often abandoned the tonal concept and has proceeded in many directions. The most dramatic of these is called the twelve-tone system of music, in reference to the twelve tones of the chromatic scale. Its basic premises are that no note may be repeated until the other eleven have been sounded, and that the so-called *row* of twelve tones, which is established before the composition is begun, will be used consistently throughout (see the following Schönberg example).

*Further examples of medieval modes can be found in *Music for Sight Singing,* Chapter 17, and in *More Music for Sight Singing,* Part 4. Examples of melodies from other cultures can be found in *More Music for Sight Singing,* Part 6.

Characteristic of this melody is its angularity—the predominance of wide skips (also seen in the Brahms example, Figure 6.17)—and the inadmissibility of any harmonic implication (also seen to some extent in the Hugo Wolf example, Figure 6.40).

Although these few illustrations can only serve as small samples of the wide variety of melodic practices found in different regions and eras, they should serve to point out those characteristics that differentiate melodies of the common practice period from those of other cultures and other times.

CHAPTER 7

The Alto and Tenor Clefs

Theory and Analysis

The C clef is universally used in music, though not as commonly as the treble and bass clefs. The C clef sign or indicates the location of middle C on the staff.[1] It is particularly useful for those instruments whose range extends from the middle part of the bass clef to the middle of the treble clef. Using C clefs avoids excessive ledger lines.

Fig. 7.1

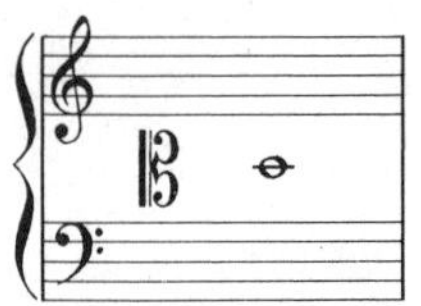

Fig. 7.2

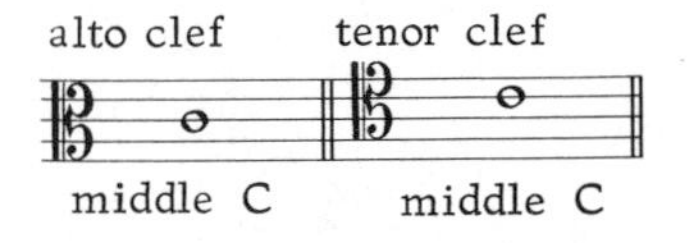

When the C clef is found on the third line of the staff, it is known as the *alto clef*, used by the viola and by the trombone. When the C clef is found on the fourth line of the staff, it is known as the *tenor clef*, and is often used by the violoncello, the bassoon, the trombone, and occasionally by the double bass. Illustrations of actual usages of these clefs follow.[2]

[1]Early versions of the C clef can be seen on pages 39–40.

[2]A score in which each part or voice line is on a separate staff, as in Figure 7.3, is known as an *open score*.

Fig. 7.3

Fig. 7.4

Fig. 7.5

These two clefs, together with the treble and bass clefs, are the only ones remaining in common use today from a system of ten different clef signs used in music before 1750. The other six clefs are seen in Figure 7.6.

Fig. 7.6

These clefs can be found in very old editions of music and in many modern publications of pre-nineteenth-century music.

Exercise 7.1. Learn the names of the lines and spaces of the alto clef. Check your ability in the following two ways:

a) Name the pitch when the line or space is given. Example: fourth line: answer, E.

b) Name the line or space when the pitch name is given. Example: F; answer, first line or fourth space.

Exercise 7.2. Learn the names of the lines and spaces of the tenor clef. Follow the procedures of the previous exercise.

Figure 7.7 shows how sharps and flats for the key signatures are placed on the alto and tenor clefs. Observe that the patterns are the same as for the treble and bass clefs, except for the sharp keys on the tenor clef. Starting with the first sharp on F (second line), succeeding sharps are in a pattern, up a fifth, down a fourth.

Fig. 7.7

Assignment 7.1. Write the signature for each major and minor key in both the alto and tenor clefs.

The Vocal Tenor Clef

In the term *vocal tenor clef*, the word *tenor* refers to the tenor voice rather than to the tenor C clef. Although, for the range of the tenor voice, the tenor C clef is ideal, the abandomnent of the C clefs for vocal purposes left no suitable clef available. The treble clef now commonly serves the tenor voice. Although music so written is an octave higher than actual pitch, this method does avoid excessive ledger lines.

In choral writing, the treble clef is also commonly used when the tenor part is on its own staff. However, increasing use is now made of the treble clef signs shown in Figure 7.9 to indicate transposition an octave lower. Also, the C clef on the third space shows actual pitch, but this clef is used infrequently.

Fig. 7.8

Fig. 7.9

Key Transposition Using Clefs

The various clefs are useful in transposing music from one key to another. Music in the treble clef, for example, can be read in a key a step (half or whole) higher by 1) substituting the alto clef, 2) substituting the appropriate key signature, and 3) "thinking" pitches in the new clef an octave higher.

Fig. 7.10

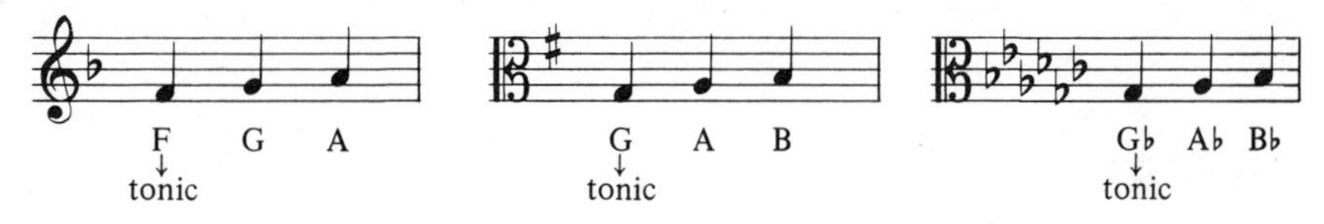

Again in the tenor clef, one can transpose down a step (half or whole) in the same way.

Fig. 7.11

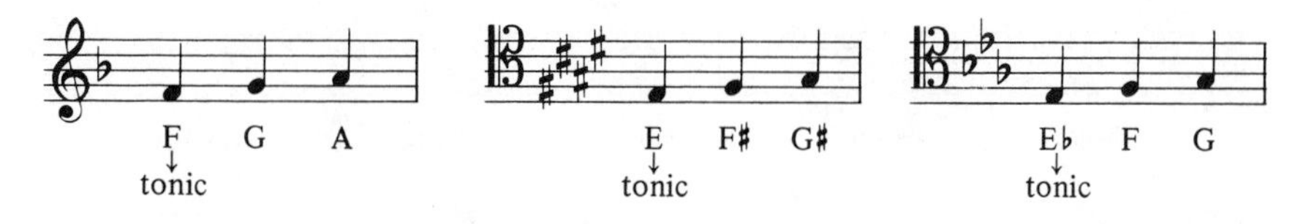

When accidentals appear in a melody, as is common in the minor scales, they may need to be changed to accommodate the new key.

Fig. 7.12

By making use of the various G and C clefs shown in Figure 7.6, you can transpose a given key to any other key—valuable practice for any performer needing skill in quick transposition.

Fig. 7.13

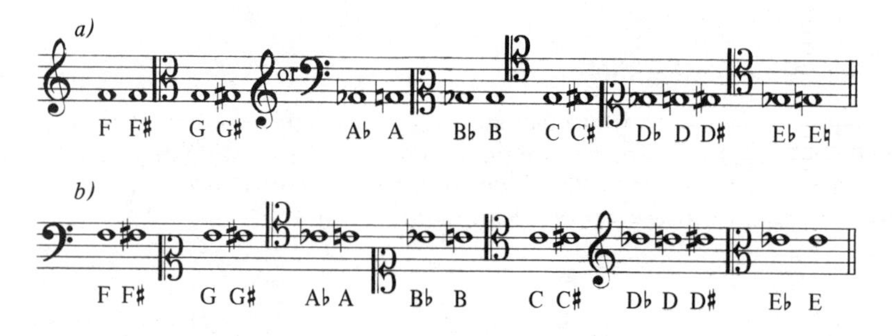

Written Materials

Assignment 7.2. Writing intervals in the C clefs. Write the second note of the given interval *a*) in the alto clef and *b*) in the tenor clef.

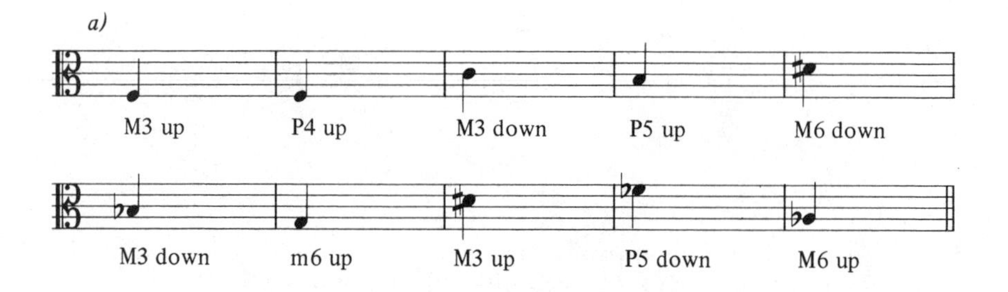

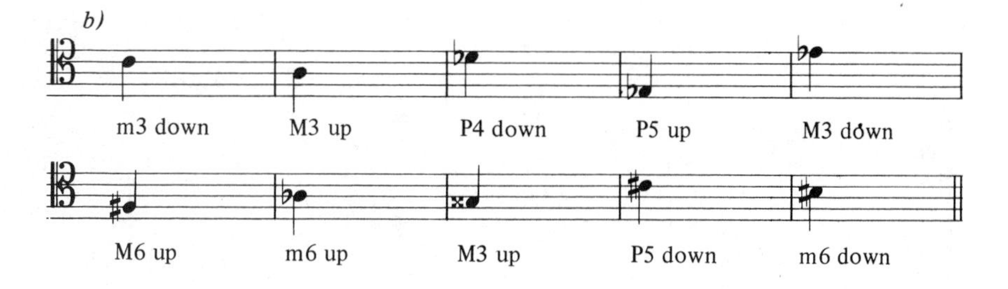

Assignment 7.3. Writing cadences in open score. Write each cadence in four parts, one part to a staff, using clefs as shown below. Example: F major, $\overset{2}{\text{V}}$–$\overset{1}{\text{I}}$ (2 1 indicates scale step progression; in F major, G–F).

Observe:

(1) Brace connecting the staves in open score.

(2) Use of stem direction for a single melodic line on a staff.

Write these cadences in the same manner.

	2	1		1	7
G major	V	I	D minor	i	V
	7	1		2	3
E major	V	I	F minor	V	I
	3	2		5	5
B♭ major	I	V	F♯ minor	V	i
	5	3		1	2
D♭ major	V	I	G♯ minor	i	V

Assignment 7.4. Writing cadences in open score. Rewrite several cadences from Assignment 7.3, using the treble clef for soprano and alto voices, and the

vocal tenor clef for the tenor voice. The following example uses the same progression as the example in Asignment 7.3.

Assignment 7.5. Part-writing in open score. Soprano and bass lines are given. Prepare an open score of four staves, either as in Assignment 7.3 or as in Assignment 7.4, as assigned. Copy in the soprano and bass lines shown below, and fill in the alto and tenor lines. For additional practice, use the soprano and bass lines from Assignment 5.11.

Assignment 7.6. Transposition. Place a clef before each of these notes so that the given note sounds the pitch A. Clefs to be used are those in Figure 7.6 as well as the treble, bass, alto, and tenor clefs.

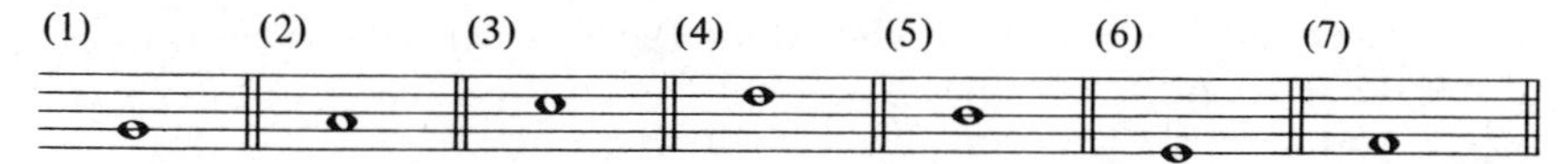

Assignment 7.7. Transposition. Use the melodies in Assignment 6.4. Name the possible key or keys when the alto or tenor clef is substituted for the given clef.

Example:

a) Note that the tonic is in the second line (key of G, treble clef).

b) Replace the treble clef with the alto clef. Remove the key signature.

c) Note that the second line (tonic) is now A or A♭. The signature for either key may be used.

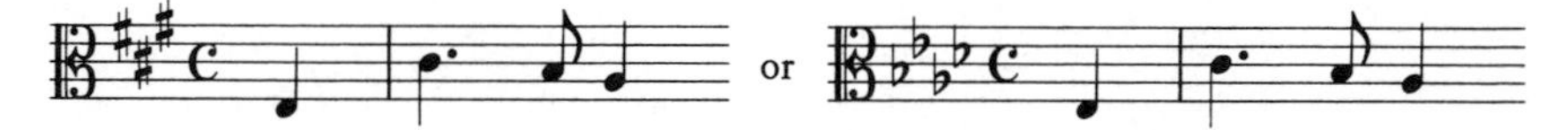

d) Follow this same procedure using the alto clef in melodies 1–8 of Assignment 6.4.

e) Follow this same procedure using the tenor clef in melodies 1–8 of Assignment 6.4.

Assigment 7.8. Transposition. Use the melodies in Assignment 6.5 listed below. Name the clef needed (clefs from Figure 7.6. included) to transpose the melody to the given key.

Example: Transpose melody 1 to the key of F major. Tonic is on the second line. If second line is F, the tenor clef is required.

Continue with these following melodies from Assignment 6.5:

Melody 1 to A major
Melody 2 to A♭ major; to F major
Melody 3 to G♭ major; to D major
Melody 5 to C minor; to G♯ minor
Melody 7 to A minor; to E minor

Ear Training

Exercise 7.3. Write intervals from dictation in the C clefs. The name of the clef, alto or tenor, and the name of the first note will be given. Listen to the interval and write the second note on the staff.

Exercise 7.4. Melodic dictation. Dictation exercises will now be given in both the alto and tenor clefs. Remember that the C clef indicates *middle C,* and place your melody on the staff accordingly.

CHAPTER 8

The Subdominant Triad

Theory and Analysis

Spelling the Subdominant Triad

The subdominant triad has its root on the fourth (subdominant) scale step of the key. In a major key, the triad is a major triad. In a minor key, the subdominant triad is usually minor, but when melodic considerations require the use of the raised sixth scale step, it is major.

Fig. 8.1

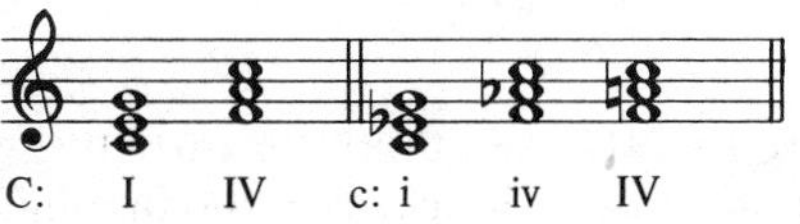

Assignment 8.1. Spell the subdominant triad in each major key.

Assignment 8.2. *a*) Spell the minor subdominant triad in each minor key. *b*) Spell the major subdominant triad in each minor key.

Plagal Cadences

Like the dominant triad, the subdominant triad can occur during the course of the phrase and also as part of a cadential progression. Cadences using the subdominant and the tonic triads are known as *plagal cadences,* and may be found in the same forms as authentic cadences. Figure 8.2 shows these as they occur in major keys. If we place four flats in the key signature of these examples, this same figure will illustrate these cadences in F minor (iv = B♭ D♭ F, i = F A♭ C). Use of the major subdominant triad in a minor key will be explained in Chapter 9.

The plagal cadences are:

1. Perfect plagal The progression IV–I or iv–i, in which the subdominant triad has its root in the bass and the final tonic triad has its root in both bass and soprano. See also Figure 8.3.

2. *Imperfect plagal* The progression IV–I or iv–i, in which the final tonic triad is found with its third or fifth in the soprano and/or the bass, or in which the bass note of the subdominant triad is the third or fifth. The commonly used soprano lines are 6–5, 4–3, and 1 up to 3. See also Figure 8.5, soprano line 6–5.

3. *Half* A little-used cadence, the progression I–IV or i–iv. See also Figure 8.6.

Fig. 8.2

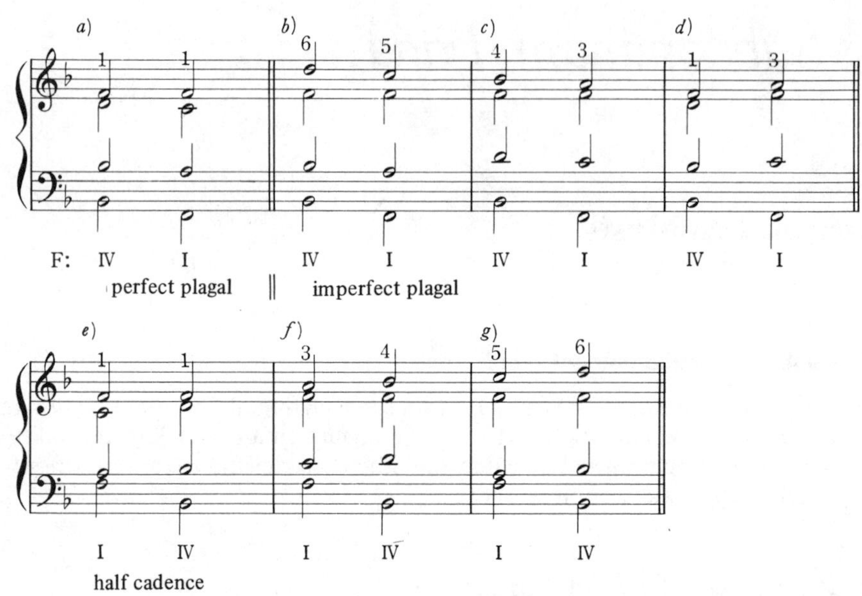

These cadences are much less frequently used than the authentic cadences. Their appearance usually follows an authentic cadence, as in the familiar "Amen" at the close of a hymn tune.

Fig. 8.3

In this piano postlude to a Brahms *lied,* an extended plagal cadence follows the authentic cadence of measures 9–10.

Fig. 8.4

In this excerpt from the *Messiah,* the phrase preceding the final plagal cadence is itself an extended plagal cadence.

Fig. 8.5

The infrequent plagal half cadence is shown in this Bach chorale phrase. You may recall a similar cadence from the first phrase of *Auld Lang Syne.*

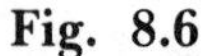

Fig. 8.6

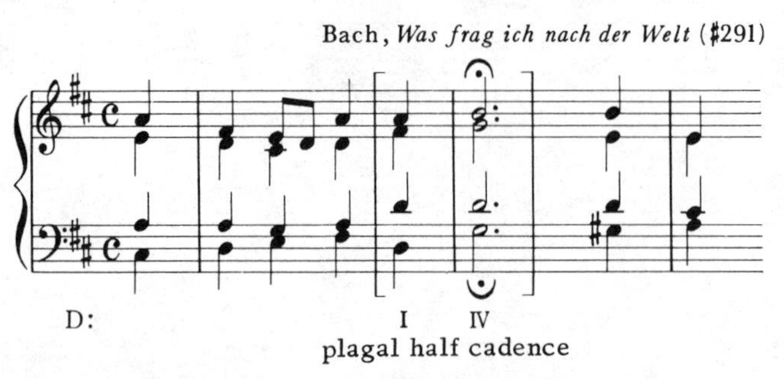

Assignment 8.3. Identify each of these cadences by name (e.g., imperfect plagal). A few authentic cadences are included.

The Progression IV–V, iv–V

The most frequent use of the subdominant triad is its progression to the dominant; the reverse (V–IV, V–iv), on the other hand, is little used. When IV precedes V at the cadence, the progression IV–V–I or iv–V–i is often known as a "full cadence."

Examples from literature using only I, IV, and V, all as triads and all in root position, are uncommon. An example can be seen in measures 1-3 of Figure 8.11. The examples from Assignment 8.4 show that usually one or more of these triads is in inversion and that the dominant triad is often found as a V^7 chord.

Fig. 8.7

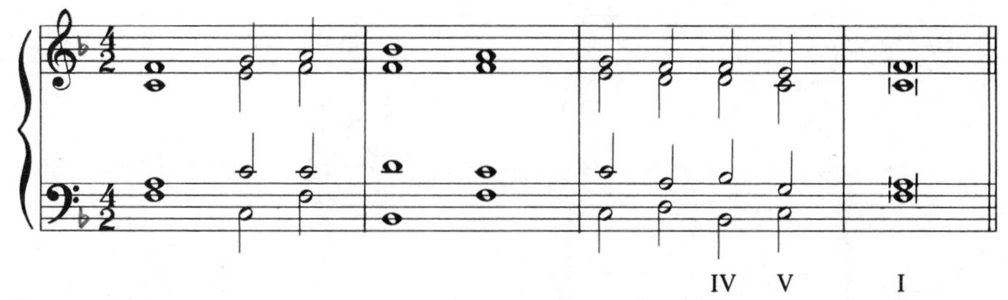

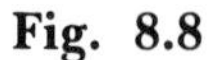
Fig. 8.8

These three chords, (I, IV, V, or I, IV, V^7) are widely used as the principal "guitar chords," especially for strumming along with a simple folk tune or with many of the "country and western" tunes of popular music culture.

Fig. 8.9

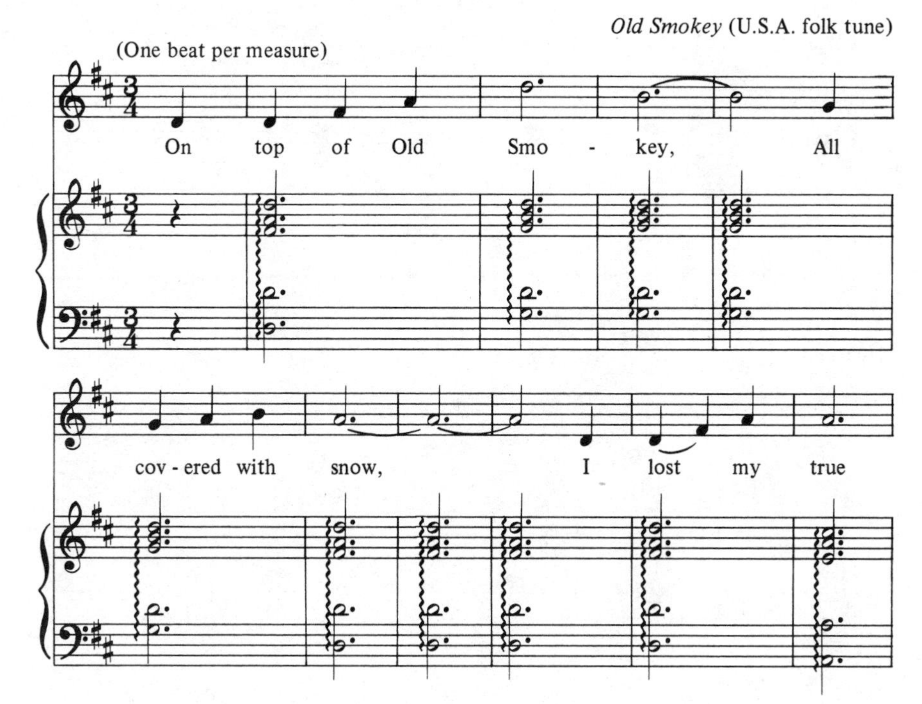

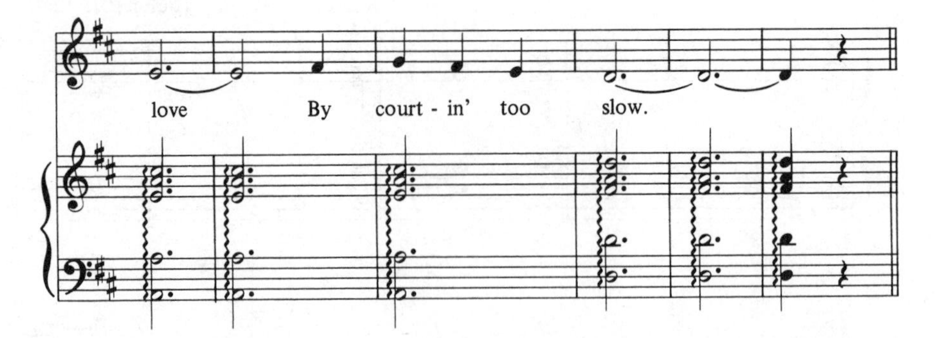

Assignment 8.4. Harmonic analysis. Analyze these excerpts using the symbols I, IV, V, or V^7. Circle all nonharmonic tones.

(1) Schubert, *Ländler*

(2) Schubert, *Impromptu*. Op. 90 No 4

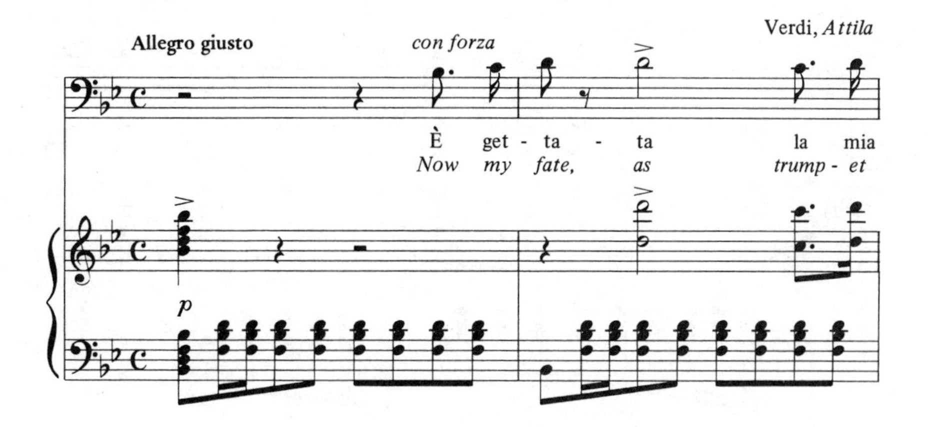
Verdi, *Attila*
Allegro giusto
con forza
p
È get - ta - ta la mia
Now my fate, as trump - et

sor - te; Pron - to so - no a - d'o - gni
call - ing, Leads me where mar - tial hon - or

guer - ra; S'io ca - drò, ca - drò da
wait - eth: If I fall, then no - bly

The Subdominant Triad in Melodic Writing

Intervals from the subdominant triad can be used effectively in melodic writing, although they are used less frequently than intervals from tonic and dominant triads.

Fig. 8.10

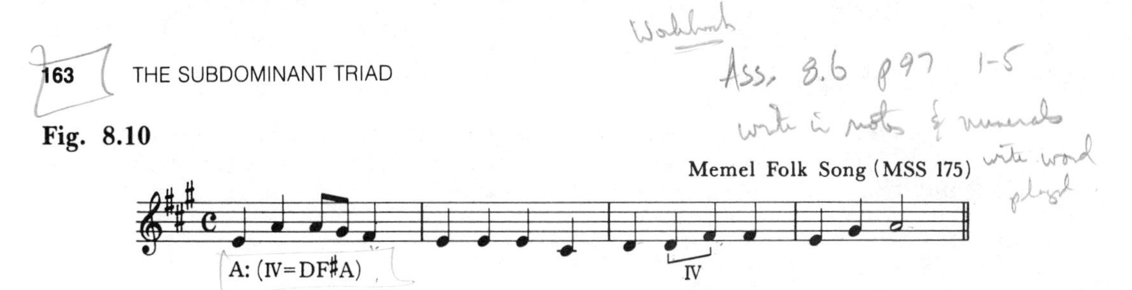

Assignment 8.5. Locate intervals from the subdominant triad in these melodies.

For additional melodies, see *Music for Sight Singing,* Chapters 6 and 7; and *More Music for Sight Singing,* numbers 276, 279, 281, 290, 291, 292, 301, 306, 324, and 325.

Application

Written Materials

Writing the Progression IV–I

In the progression IV–I or I–IV (iv–i or i–iv), the triad roots are a fifth (fourth) apart. Use of Rule 2, Triads with Roots in the Bass a Fifth Apart, will successfully connect these triads.

Fig. 8.11 Use of Rule 2A.

See also Figures 8.2 (except *d*), 8.3, 8.5, 8.6.

Fig. 8.12 Use of Rule 2B.

See also Figure 8.2d, and Figure 8.11, measure 2.

Fig. 8.13 Use of Rule 2C.

Assignment 8.6. Writing plagal cadences. Fill in the alto and tenor voices. Identify each cadence as perfect, imperfect, or half. All require use of Rule 2A only. Write in open score as directed.

Assignment 8.7. Writing progressions using Rules 2B and 2C. Fill in the alto and tenor voices. Include a roman numeral analysis.

Assignment 8.8. *a*) Part-write cadences when the bass line only is given. Supply any correct soprano lines. Both authentic and plagal cadences are included.

b) Part-write cadences when the soprano line only is given. Be sure the bass note is always the root of the triad. Both authentic and plagal cadences are included.

Assignment 8.9. Write the following cadences in major or minor keys, as assigned.

a) The perfect plagal cadence (1–1).
b) The imperfect plagal cadence in two positions (6–5, 4–3).
c) The half cadence in three positions (1–1, 3–4, 5–6).

Writing the Progression IV–V

Writing the progression IV–V or iv–V, with the roots in the bass a second apart, requires a new procedure.

Part-Writing Rule 3. In a progression of two triads whose roots in the bass line are a second apart, move the three upper voices to the nearest triad tones in contrary motion to the bass.

Fig. 8.14

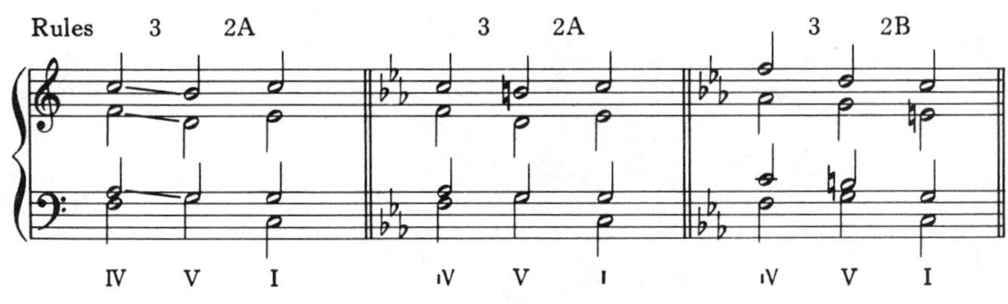

Fig. 8.15

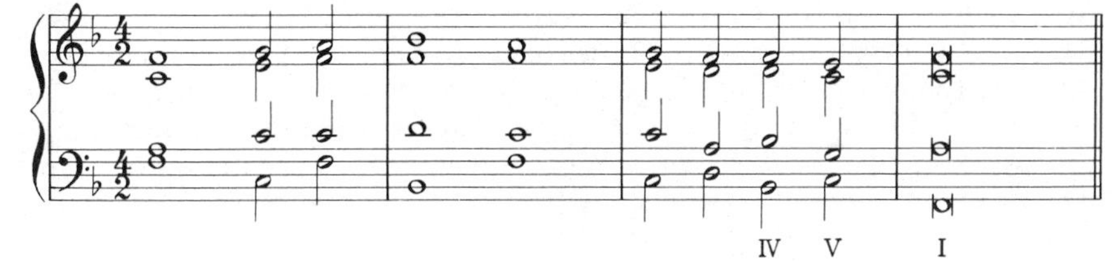

Fig. 8.16

Violation of this rule is one of the most frequent causes of the appearance of three weaknesses in part-writing most likely to plague the beginning student.

They are, as shown in Figure 8.17a:

1. parallel perfect fifths.
2. parallel octaves.
3. the melodic augmented second.

Figure 8.17b shows how these weaknesses appear in part-writing when Rule 3 is not observed.

Fig. 8.17a

Fig. 8.17b

Attempts to avoid parallel octaves by changing the direction of one of the two notes involved do not produce successful results. Figure 8.18a shows a parallel octave between the alto and bass voices. In Figure 8.18b, an attempt was made to avoid the octave by moving the bass down a minor seventh instead of up a major second. These are still parallel octaves but they are called, in seemingly contradictory language, *parallel octaves by contrary motion.* There are, in our illustration, two *f*'s going to two *g*'s in the same pair of voices. Use of Rule 3 in Figure 8.18c eliminates the offending octaves.

Fig. 8.18

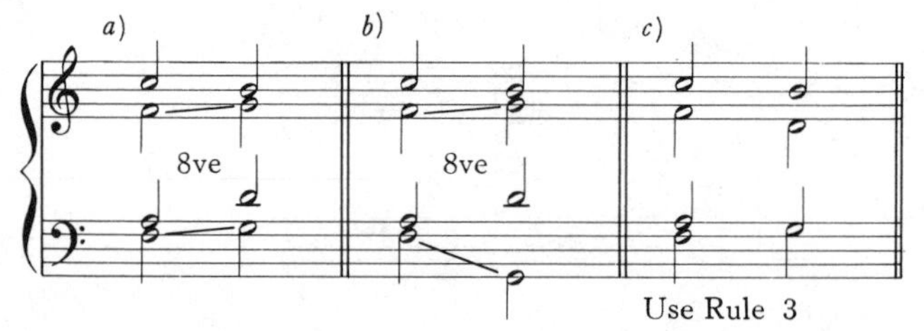

These octaves, which are usually contrary, can be used, however, at final cadences.

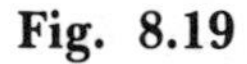

Fig. 8.19

Fig. 8.20

Parallel fifths by contrary motion are likewise to be avoided. Those in Figure 8.21 have been caused by violation of Rule 2B.

Fig. 8.21

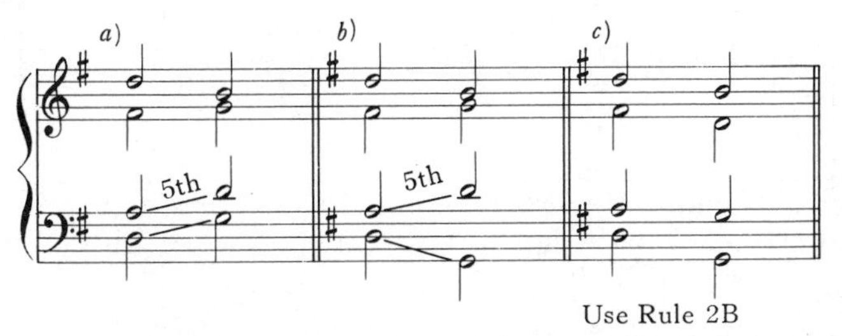

Note, however, that octaves or fifths repeated on the same pitches are *not* considered parallel; the use of these *stationary* octaves or fifths is acceptable.

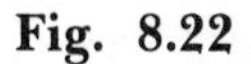

Fig. 8.22

Also to be avoided is the melodic augmented second (an interval one half step larger than a major second). It appears in the tenor line of Figure 8.23, and is caused by not following Rule 3. Note also the resulting unwanted doubled leading tone. For further discussion of these particular problems, see the article, "The Three Demons of Part-Writing" in this chapter.

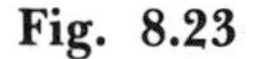

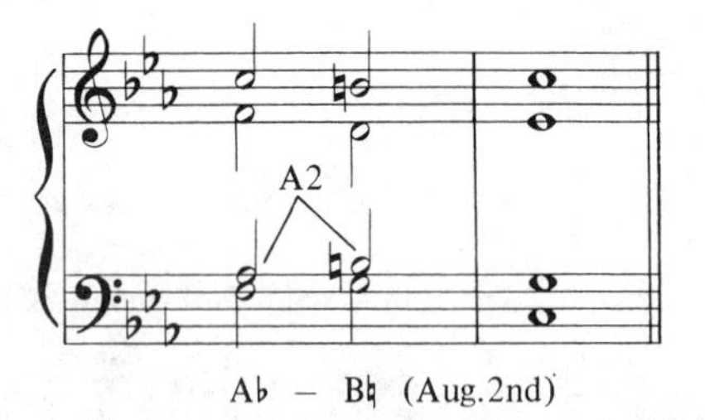

Assignment 8.10 *a*) Write cadences as found below. Write chord numbers below the staff.

b) Write, on staff paper, the progression I–IV–V–I or i–iv–V–i, in the following keys or in other keys as assigned. Write in open score, with C clefs if so assigned.

E♭ major	A♭ minor
B major	C♯ minor
F♯ major	F minor
D♭ major	D♯ minor

Assignment 8.11. *a*) Fill in alto and tenor voices using part-writing procedures studied thus far. Make harmonic analysis by placing correct roman numeral below each bass note.

b) Solve exercises in open score, as assigned.

(1)

(2)

(3)

(4)

(5)

Assignment 8.12. Supply soprano, alto, and tenor lines above a given bass line. In writing a soprano line, observe the rules for melody-writing previously studied, particularly the treatment of the leading tone. The soprano note should be changed when the bass note is repeated. Make an harmonic analysis.

Assignment 8.13. Harmonize melodies, supplying the alto, tenor, and bass parts. Follow this procedure.

a) Determine the key. Check not only the key signature, but sing the melody through, observing the nature of the cadence to determine whether the melody is major or minor.

b) Write in the chord numbers for the cadence below the bass staff.

c) Write in chord numbers leading up to the cadence.

d) Write the bass line, each note being the root of the chosen chord.

e) Fill in the inner parts.

Ear Training

Learning to hear the subdominant triad can be accomplished by using the procedures for hearing the dominant triad presented in Exercises 4.1–4.4. Refer to these for full directions.

Exercise 8.1. (*c.f.* Exercise 4.1, page 87) Singing the subdominant triad from any given note.

a) Listen to given tonic pitch.
b) Sing up a perfect fourth to the subdominant tone.
c) Sing the subdominant triad with letter names.

Fig. 8.24

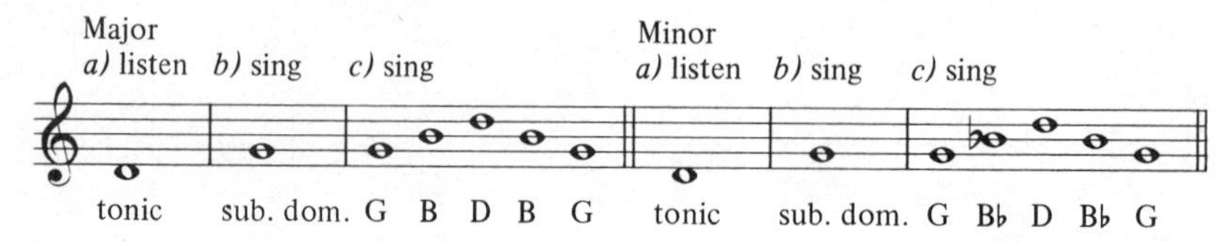

Exercise 8.2. Singing the progression I–IV–V–I or i–iv–V–i in any key. Sing each triad from its root, using letter names.

Fig. 8.25

Exercise 8.3. (*c.f.* Exercise 4.2.) Identifying the plagal cadence. Here is a sample exercise.

Fig. 8.26

Exercise 8.4. (*c.f.* Exercise 4.3.) Writing the plagal cadence from dictation.

Exercise 8.5. (*c.f.* Exercise 4.4 and the preceding material headed "Harmonic Dictation.") Harmonic dictation using I, IV, V and i, iv, V triads. Here is a sample exercise.

Fig. 8.27

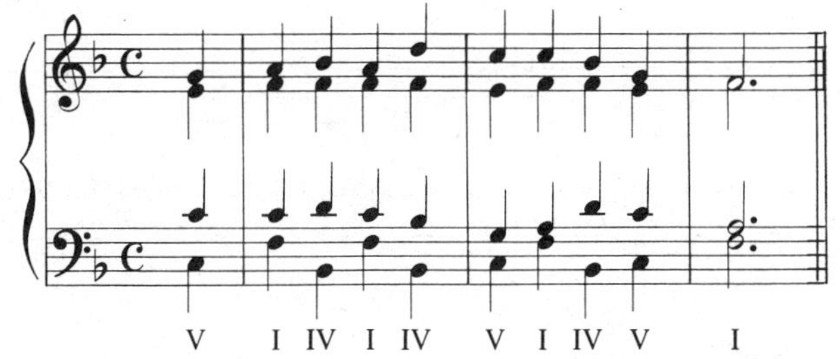

Keyboard Harmony

Plagal Cadences

Exercise 8.6. Playing plagal cadences at the keyboard. Follow the directions given in Exercise 4.5 and the preceding discussion, substituting the IV or iv triad for the V triad.

a) Play the perfect plagal cadence.

Major	1	1	Minor	1	1
	IV	— I		iv	— i

b) Play the imperfect plagal cadences.

Major	6	5	4	3
	IV	— I	IV—	I
Minor	6	5	4	3
	iv	— i	iv —	i

c)Half cadences are not common; they are shown in Figure 8.2e if practice is desired.

Exercise 8.7. Harmonizing melodic plagal cadences at the keyboard. Following directions given in Exercise 4.6 and the preceding discussion, harmonize all cadences, authentic and plagal, in the following melodies.

The Progression I–IV–V–I

Exercise 8.8. Playing the progression I–IV–V–I and i–iv–V–i at the keyboard. Play the progression with the tonic triad in each of its three soprano positions. Play it in all major and minor keys, and following all part-writing rules. In Figures 8.29b and 8.30b the melody may end on the tonic note if we use Rule 2B in the V–I cadence.

Fig. 8.28 Major Key:

Fig. 8.29 Minor Key:

Melody Harmonization

Exercise 8.9. Harmonizing a melody with lead sheet symbols. The procedure is the same as that for I and V triads (review "Melody Harmonization" in Chapter 4, page 94).

Additional melodies may be found in Mainous, *Melodies to Harmonize with,* Chapter 8, melodies 59–104.

Exercise 8.10. Melody harmonization at the keyboard. The melodies of Assignment 8.13 may be used at the keyboard. Play the appropriate chord for each soprano note. For further practice, copy out each melody in various keys. Using melody 1 from Assignment 8.13 as an example, this can be done as follows:

a) Note the key; in this case, B♭ major.

b) Identify each soprano note by its scale number.

Fig. 8.30

c) Choose a new key, F for example. Write the melody in the new key by using the same scale numbers.

Fig. 8.31

d) Harmonize the melody in the key of F major at the piano.

The Three Demons of Part-Writing

Well, not really demons. But many students, exasperated by their frequent and unwanted appearances, are ready to believe in some evil force at work!

There is nothing inherently wrong with parallel fifths, parallel octaves, and melodic augmented seconds. Any sound one can conceive is right for a person if it pleases him. In the same way any sound is right for a particular era, or in a geographical area, if it pleases the listeners of that time or place. However, during the period in Western music from about 1000 to 1900 A.D., these three sounds have generally *not* pleased composers or listeners, and consequently have not been characteristic elements in the music of the West.

Ironically, the earliest known music for more than one voice line—the simultaneous sounding of a chant melody and the same melody a perfect fifth lower—produced, of course, a series of perfect parallel fifths.

However, the monotony of this harmonic sound was replaced by the more interesting sounds of contrary motion at around 1000 A.D., and from that time right up to our own parallel fifths have been almost nonexistent in Western musical culture. They can be found occasionally, however, as in this excerpt from a Mozart sonata.

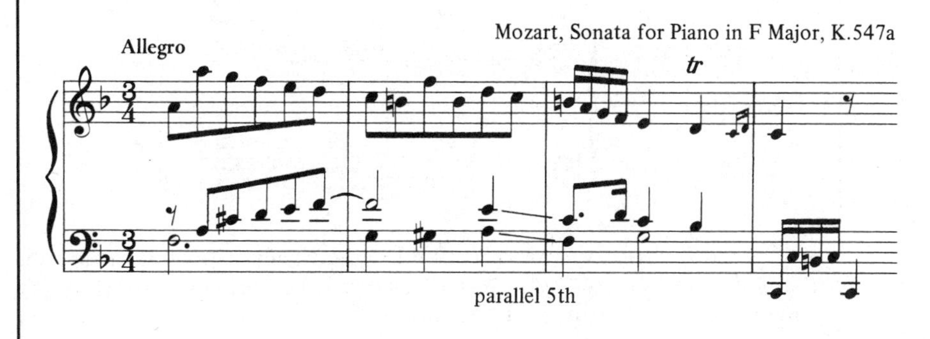

They have also been used to achieve special effects, as in the opening of the second act of *La Bohème,* where they accompany a scene of general confusion.

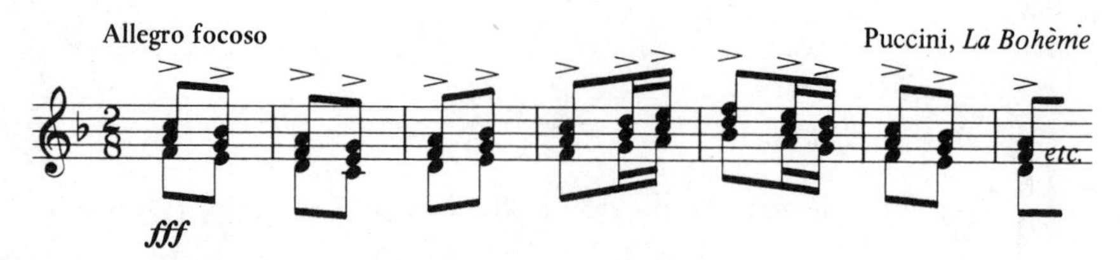

And yet in the twentieth century, and probably beginning with the music of Debussy (1862–1918), parallel fifths have regained their respectability after nearly a thousand years of neglect, and are universally acceptable in contemporary music practice (see the Ravel excerpt below).

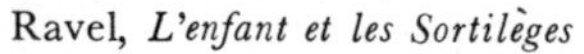

Parallel octaves are of two varieties, one acceptable, the other not. An octave is merely the repetition of a given pitch at another level, higher or lower. When the two notes sound simultaneously, both sounds represent the same note. When two *different* voice lines move in octaves, then these octaves represent only one moving sound, and the effect is the loss of one voice line. In the example below the four-voice structure is reduced to three by this parallelism.

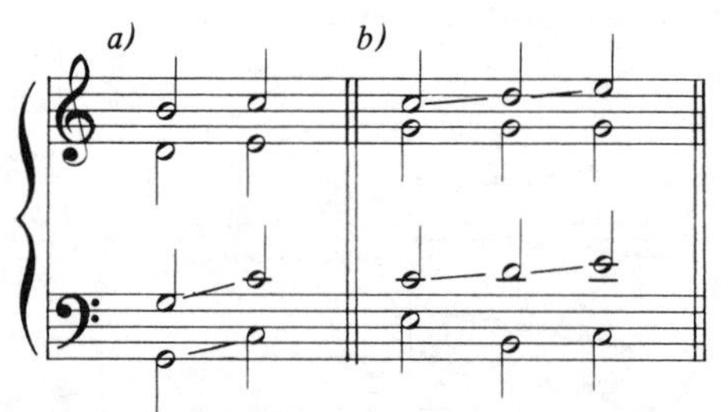

Parallel octaves are acceptable when they represent a doubling of a single voice line, as is common in instrumental and keyboard music. The following example appears to include five voice lines, but actually the melody in the treble clef has simply been doubled in the bass clef, and both represent the same voice line.

Beethoven, Sonata in E Major for Piano, Op. 14, No. 1

The melodic augmented second is a characteristic element in many Near Eastern and oriental scales (review the article "Some Varieties of Melodic Expression" in Chapter 6). The interval is sometimes used in Western music to give a flavor of Orientalism.

Saint-Saëns, *Samson and Delilah*

This interval also has its place in certain limited passages in Western music. These will be discussed later, as they have little relation to the elementary concepts now under discussion.

CHAPTER 9

The Triad in Inversion

Theory and Analysis

A triad (or any chord) is said to be in *inversion* when some note other than the root is in the bass. When the third is in the bass the triad is in *first inversion;* when the fifth is in the bass, the triad is in *second inversion.* Since there are three possible soprano positions and three possible bass positions in a triad, a total of nine combinations of soprano and bass tones exists.

Fig. 9.1

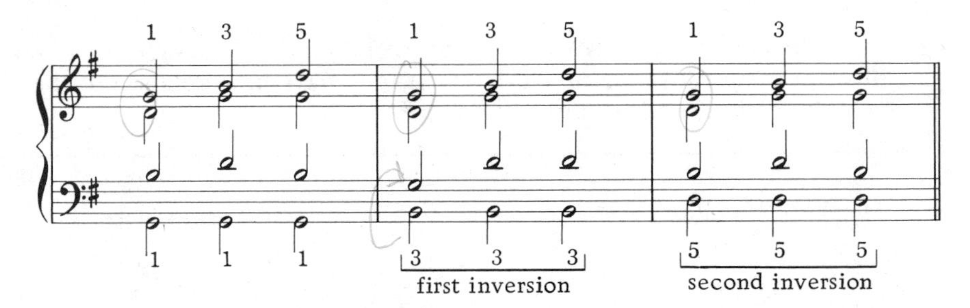

Chords in inversion are found in musical compositions for two reasons.

1. To give variety to the vertical sound. A composition consisting of chords with root in bass only is less interesting musically than alternation of chords with root in bass and chords in inversion.

2. To allow the bass line to be more melodic. When roots in the bass only are used, the bass line will consist mostly of large intervals. Use of inversions allows more step-wise movement and smaller skips in the bass line.

Figures 9.2 (chorale) and 9.3 (instrumental) each display a bass line in which more than half of the chords are in inversion. The improvement of the bass as a melodic line can easily be heard by comparing the actual bass line with a line consisting only of chord roots, especially when each of these is heard against the principal melodic line of the music, as shown in part *b* of each example. In Figure 9.2b, the "alto" becomes the melody in measure three when the soprano voice becomes static on the pitch D.

Fig. 9.2

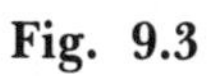
Fig. 9.3

Beethoven, Sonata for Piano, Op. 28

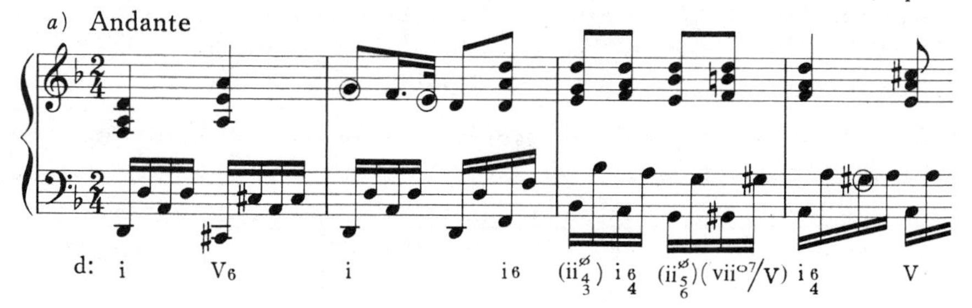

These excerpts demonstrate one of the most important concepts in the composition of music, the two-part structure existing between the bass line and the melodic line. These two voices, played by themselves, will sound like a good two-voice composition; the judicious use of inversions is the major contributing factor in this effect.

Figured Bass Symbols

The use of the symbols ♯, ×, or ♮ below a bass note was included in the discusion of part-writing in Chapter 5. These symbols are a part of a larger system known as *figured bass* or *thorough bass.* Dating from the seventeenth and eighteenth centuries, figured bass was used by composers in writing music and by performers in playing their compositions (see the article "Figured Bass" in this chapter). Although no longer used for these purposes, figured bass still has a real pedagogical value, in that it helps students to learn part-writing techniques.

Two important aims in the study of harmony are 1) the ability to choose effective chord progressions and 2) the ability to connect a series of chords in such a way that the horizontal melodic lines produced are musical and performable. Both of these skills are required simultaneously when writing original music or setting harmonizations to existing melodies. But first it is desirable to learn each skill separately, putting them together when each technique is satisfactorily established. Figured bass is a compact, shorthand device that can be used to describe the harmonic structure above a bass note. When the student knows that a series of bass notes with figured bass will describe a harmonic progression, he is left free to concentrate on part-writing techniques (until it is time to combine part-writing with harmonic choice).

An arabic numeral, or figure, under a bass note *always* indicates the size of an interval *above the bass note.* Two or more numbers, together with the given bass note, will spell the entire chord. Certain combinations of numbers will quickly indicate whether the bass note is the root, third, or fifth of the triad. The figuration $^5_3$ indicates that the bass note is the root of a triad.

In Figure 9.4, $^5_3$ indicates that the interval of a third and the interval of a fifth should be placed above the bass note G (the G in the soprano results from normal doubling and is usually not noted in the figuration). Thus, $^5_3$ usually indicates that the bass note is the root of a triad.

Fig. 9.4

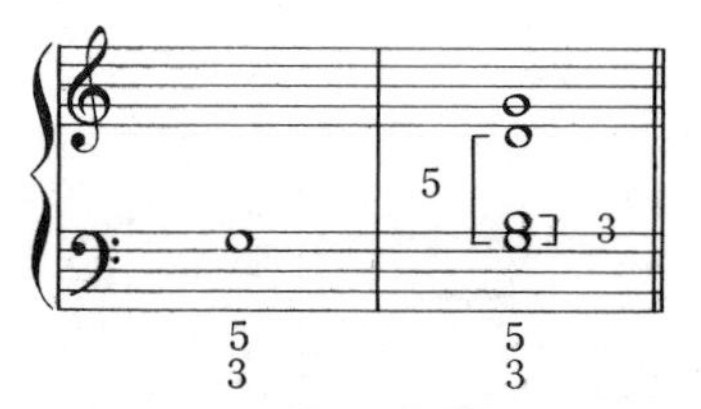

In actual practice, when the bass note is the root of a triad, the $^5_3$ is usually not written, but is understood to be below the bass note. If one or more of the notes above the bass require an accidental, then those numbers only, with accidentals, appear. An accidental used without a number always refers to the third above the bass note. A slash through a number means the same as a sharp before a number.

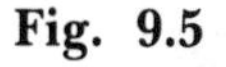

Fig. 9.5

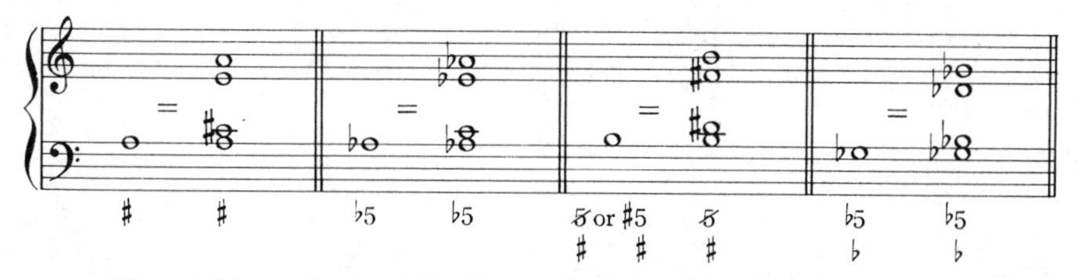

Figured bass does not indicate open or close structure, nor does it indicate soprano position. All possible arrangements of a triad with the root in the bass will be served by the same figured bass symbol.

Fig. 9.6

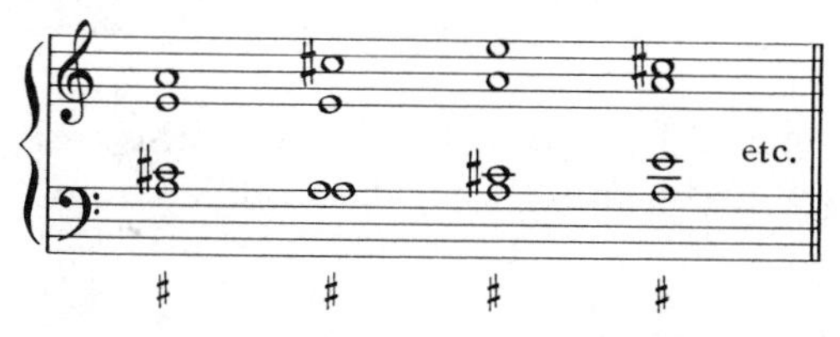

With a key signature, the figured bass calls for that letter name above the bass indicated by the signature. A ♮ (natural sign) is used to cancel out an unwanted accidental in the key signature.

Fig. 9.7

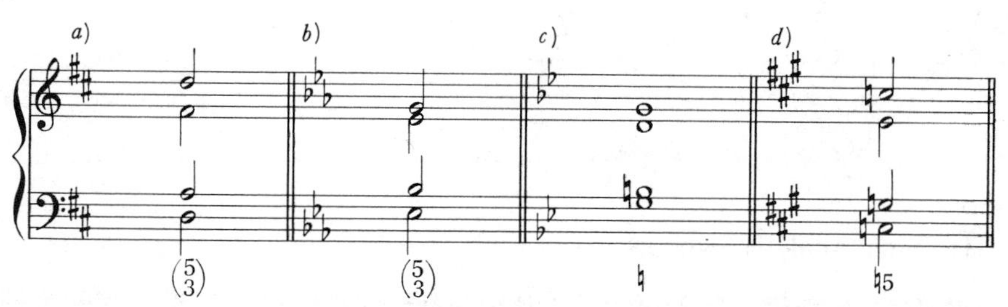

Minor triads (or any other type of chord) can be indicated by figured bass.

Fig. 9.8

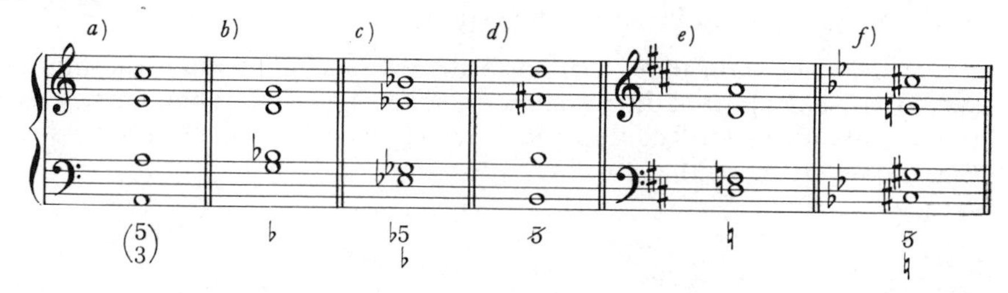

For *first inversion,* the symbol 6 is ordinarily used. The complete symbol is $^{6}_{3}$, meaning that there can be found above the bass note an interval of a third and an interval of a sixth (Figure 9.9a). Generally, the 3 is omitted but understood to be present (Figure 9.3b). When it is necessary to raise or lower the third above the bass, the symbols $^{6}_{\sharp}$ or $^{6}_{\flat}$ are used (Figure 9.9c, d). The symbol 6̸ in Figure 9.9d is commonly used to indicate that the sixth above the bass is raised. ♯6 serves the same purpose, and ♭6 indicates that the sixth above the bass is lowered (Figure 9.9e).

Fig. 9.9

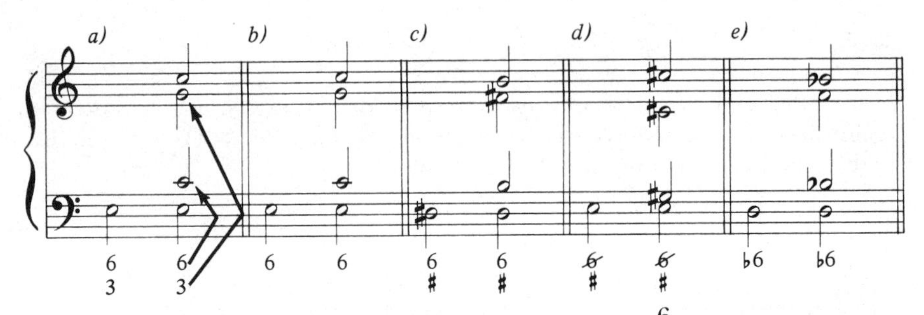

For *second inversion,* the figured bass symbol is $^{6}_{4}$, and in this case neither number is ever omitted although either number may be modified by an accidental.

Fig. 9.10

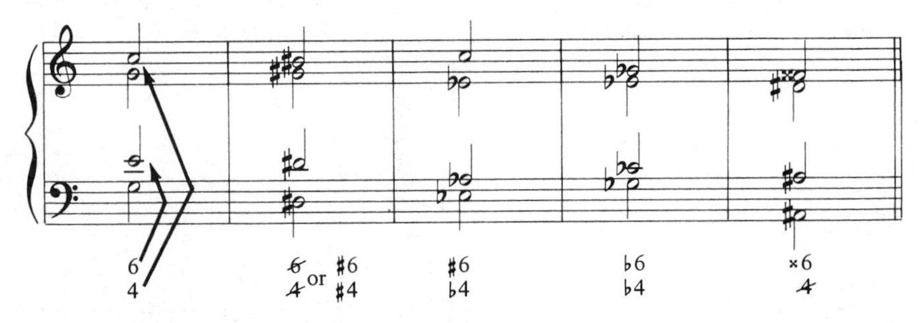

Harmonic Analysis Symbols

Inversion may be indicated in the roman numeral chord designation by placing a figured bass symbol to the right and a little below the roman numeral, 6 for first inversion and $^{6}_{4}$ for second inversion. Examples: IV_6 = IV triad in first inversion; $i_{\substack{6\\4}}$ = i triad in second inversion.

Chromatic indications are not ordinarily included when the figured bass symbol is used as part of the roman numeral designation. When the key is known, the roman numeral will correctly spell the chord, while the figured bass will indicate the inversion of that spelling.

Figure 9.11 shows an excerpt in the key of F minor, although the signature is that for F major. For the chord in second inversion, measure 3, we find $\flat{}^{6}_{4}$ in the figured bass, but i^{6}_{4} (no flat) in the harmonic analysis symbol. Because we know that the music is in F minor, we also know that i^{6}_{4} spells F A♭ C in that key, and therefore a flat in this symbol would be redundant.

Fig. 9.11

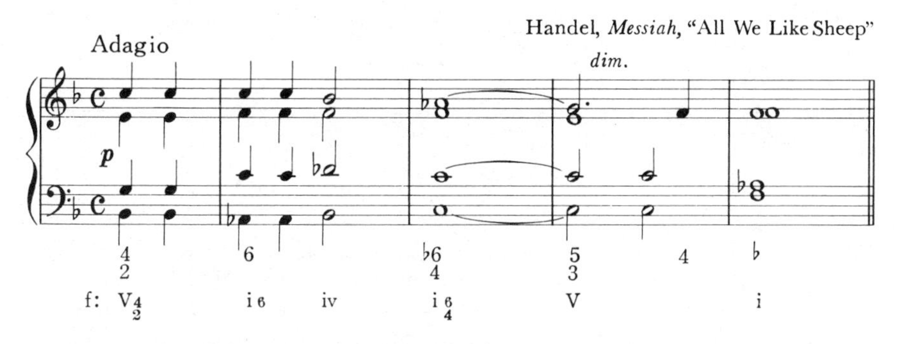

Use of the First Inversion

The first inversions of the tonic, dominant and subdominant triads can be used freely to create a bass line having maximum melodic interest. Note, in Figure 9.2, how a series of four first inversions (three triads and one seventh chord plus a judicious use of a passing tone) creates a scalar line in the bass voice. In measures 1–2 of Figure 9.3, a first inversion alternates with a root position triad to avoid the monotony of constantly sounding roots in the bass.

Use of a first inversion makes possible two new uses of triads previously studied.

1. V_6–IV_6 (major only[1]). The use of first inversions in succession is common, as demonstrated in Figure 9.2. In this situation, chord progressions that might otherwise be ineffective become quite useful, including the progression V_6–IV_6.

Fig. 9.12

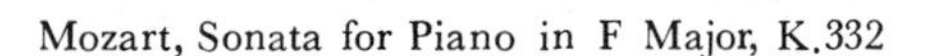

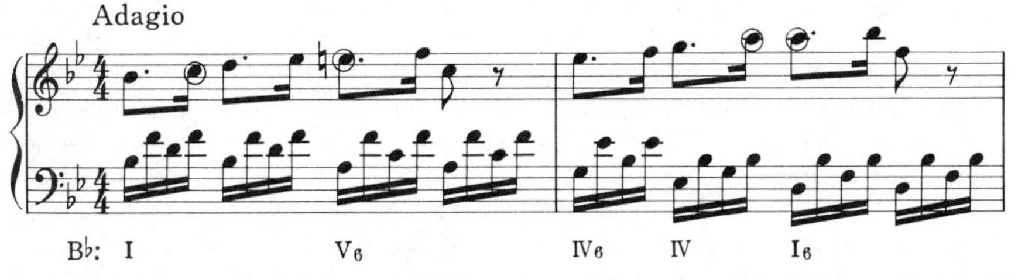

[1]v_6–iv_6 can be used in a minor key. The minor dominant triad will be studied in Chapter 16.

2. *The IV triad in a minor key.* Ordinarily, the subdominant triad in a minor key is a minor triad (iv). The third of this triad is the sixth scale step; when it is found in an ascending melodic line, it is raised one half step, as in the melodic minor scale, causing the triad to become major (IV).

Fig. 9.13

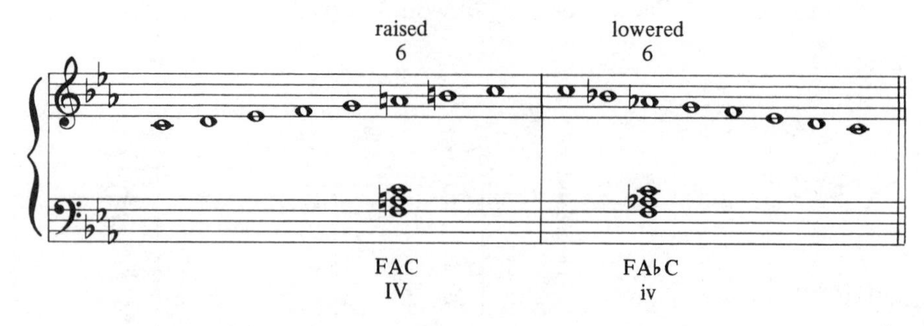

The ascending scale line from dominant to tonic (in C minor: G A♮ B♮ C) can be found in any voice line, but we must limit our study of it at present to its use as a bass line.[2] Figure 9.14 shows this ascending scale line, in G minor, with the raised sixth (E) producing the IV_6 triad followed by the raised seventh (F♯) in the V_6 triad. Note that the iv_6 (C E♭ G) would produce a melodic augmented second (E♭–F♯). See Bach chorale 185 for another example.

Fig. 9.14

Anon. (c. 1670) *Nun sich der Tag geendet hat*

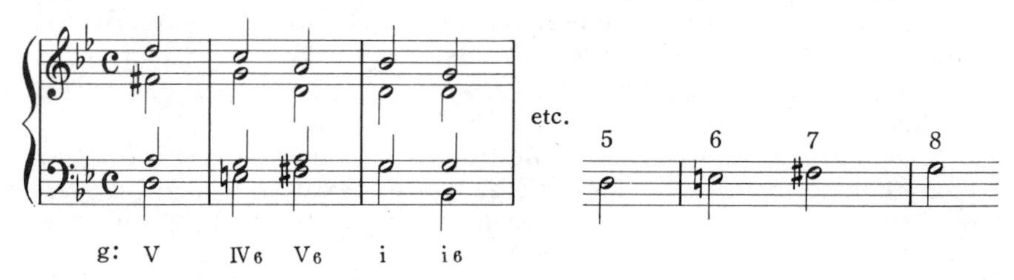

Use of the Second Inversion

In contrast to the liberal use of triads in first inversion in the eighteenth and nineteenth centuries, the second inversion is restricted to a limited number of specific musical situations. This is because of the dual nature of the six-four sonority. Upon observing the penultimate chord of Figure 9.3, one clearly sees the triad spelling D F A, i in D minor. Yet, if asked to sing the root of this chord upon hearing it, most persons will respond by singing the bass note A, the root of the V triad in D minor. This contradictory interpretation of the lowest note of the six-four chord is caused by the presence of a perfect fourth above the bass note. From earliest times in the history of Western music, the perfect fourth above the lowest sounding note has been considered a dissonance, requiring a downward resolu-

[2]In other voices, the chord following IV is rarely V, but often vii°_6, as studied in Chapter 12.

tion to the nearest consonance, a third (major or minor) above this same lowest sounding note (figured bass: 4 3). Therefore, in the penultimate chord of Figure 9.3, if the fourth above the bass is considered a dissonance resolving to a third above the bass (D—C♯), then the A in the bass is considered the root of a V triad, lasting two beats, as in Figure 9.15c.

Fig. 9.15

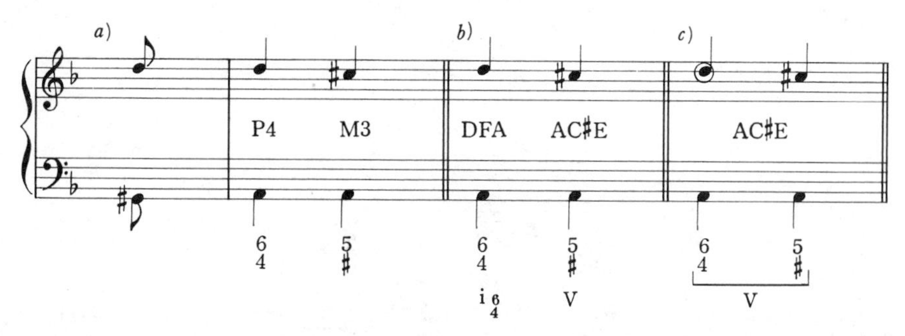

For purposes of instruction, we will consider the six-four sonority as a triad built above its fifth, as in Figure 9.15b, but in writing and listening, the dissonant function of the perfect fourth above the bass should always be kept in mind.

Of the few specific uses of triads in second inversion, only one, the *cadential six-four,* will be considered in this chapter.[3] As its name implies, this six-four appears at the cadence in the progression $\mathrm{I}_{\substack{6\\4}}$–V–I. Since $\mathrm{I}_{\substack{6\\4}}$–V is actually the V triad with added dissonance, as shown in Figure 9.15, the complete cadence is really just an elongated V–I cadence, but as such, it is one of the most frequently used cadences in music of common practice period styles.

The cadential six-four normally appears on the strong beat of the measure (Figures 9.11 and 9.16), although in triple meter it often appears on the second beat of the measure (Figure 9.17), thus allowing the final tonic triad to appear on the strong beat.

Fig. 9.16

[3]See Chapter 16 for other uses. The tonic six-four chord in measure 3 of Figure 9.3 shows one of these other uses, a *passing six-four* chord.

Fig. 9.17

Hymn: St. Martin's

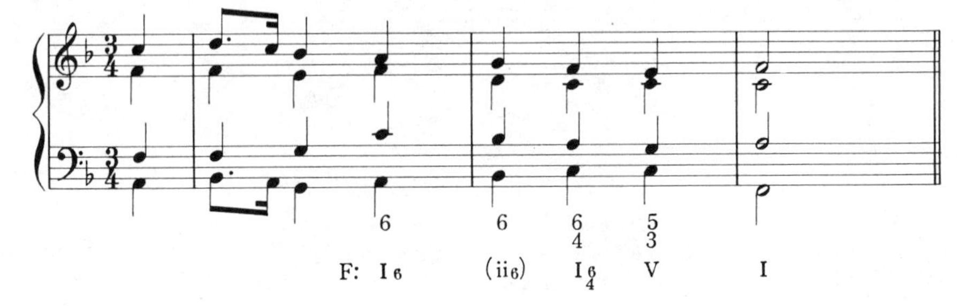

Although a "full" cadence can be created with this progression, such as IV–$\text{I}_{\substack{6\\4}}$–V–I in Figures 9.11 and 9.16, far more frequently found is the cadence ii_6–$\text{I}_{\substack{6\\4}}$–V–I, seen in Figure 9.17 and discussed more fully in Chapter 13.

Assignment 9.1. Analysis. These excerpts are from early German chorales. Place an appropriate figured bass symbol below each triad in inversion (symbols not yet studied have already been placed for you). On the third staff and using chord roots only, write the bass line, and compare the two bass lines for musical effectiveness. In excerpt 1, the first four beats have been completed for you.

(Bach, #'s 47, 110, 267, 292)

(1) **Vater unser im Himmelrich* (1531)

*The cadence in measure 4, iv_6–V, is known as a *Phrygian cadence.* See Chapter 16.

These chorale tunes have been reharmonized by Bach. The Bach chorale numbers are given to allow you to make an interesting comparison of harmonization techniques. Excerpts 2 and 3 are the final measures of their respective chorales.

Application

Written Materials

Writing the Triad in First Inversion

New doubling procedures apply when the triad is found in inversion. In first inversion, a common procedure is to double the soprano note and to retain one each of the remaining triad members.

Fig. 9.18

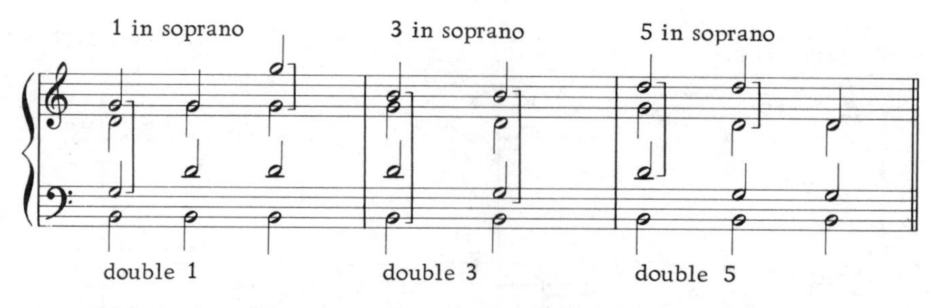

Assignment 9.2. *a)* Write single triads in first inversion when soprano and bass note are given.

b) Write single triads when bass note only is given. Write each example in each of the three possible soprano positions.

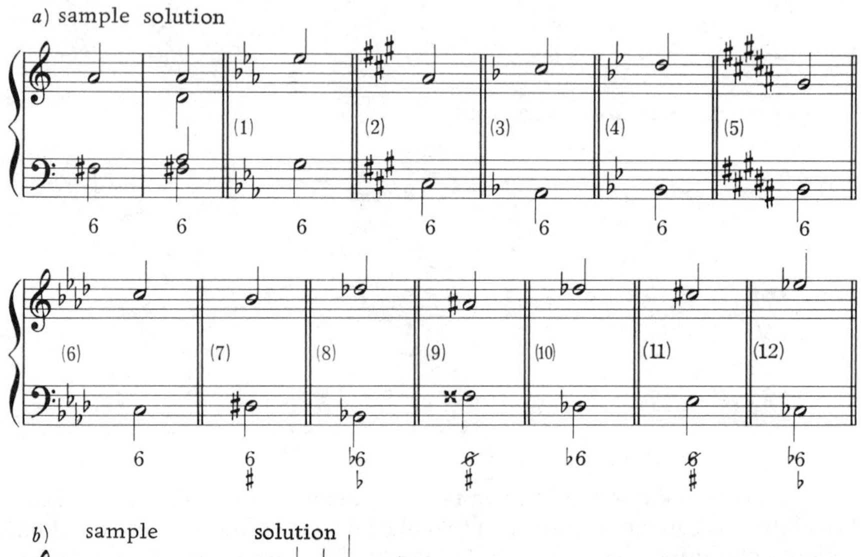

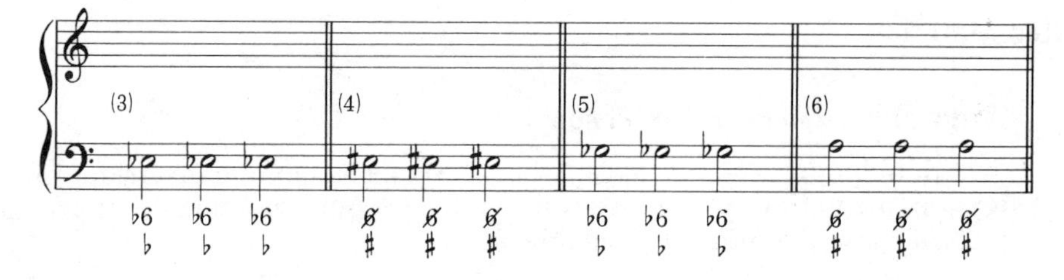

Writing to or from a Triad in Inversion[4]

When writing a triad in first inversion and connecting it with any triad with its root in the bass, the primary part-writing consideration is the correct approach to the doubled note and the correct resolution of the doubled note. It is possible for each of the two doubled notes to move in three different ways in relation to each other: by contrary motion, by oblique motion, and by similar motion. Figure 9.19 shows these movements in the resolution of the doubled note, while Figure 9.20 shows these movements towards the doubled note of the triad in first inversion.

Fig. 9.19

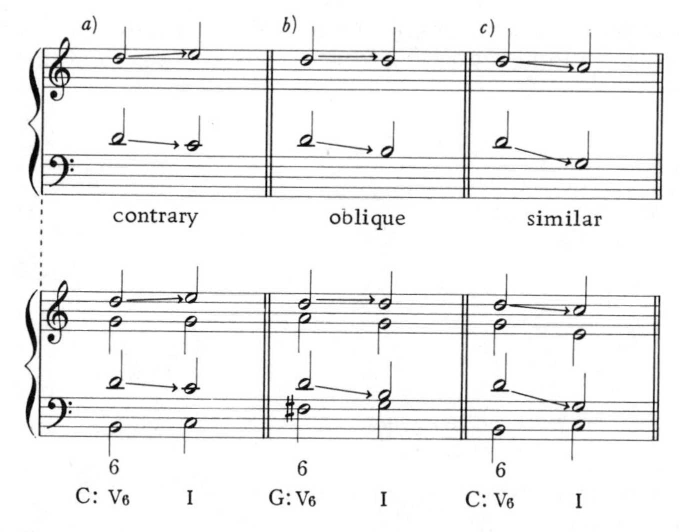

Fig. 9.20

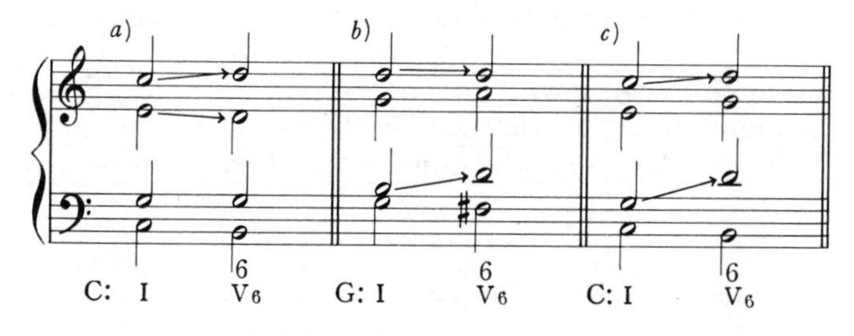

It is always best to use contrary or oblique motion in approaching and leaving the doubled note. In Figure 9.21, contrary motion is used exclusively at every occurrence of a triad in first inversion.

[4]The procedures described here and expressed as Rules 6A and 6B (on page 440) refer to *all* triads in *any* inversion and to any triad containing an unusual doubling, as will be presented later.

Fig. 9.21

Similar motion is ordinarily necessary only in unusual cases where one voice must be brought into a better range (Figure 9.22) or to effect a change of position (Figures 9.19c, 9.20c).

Fig. 9.22

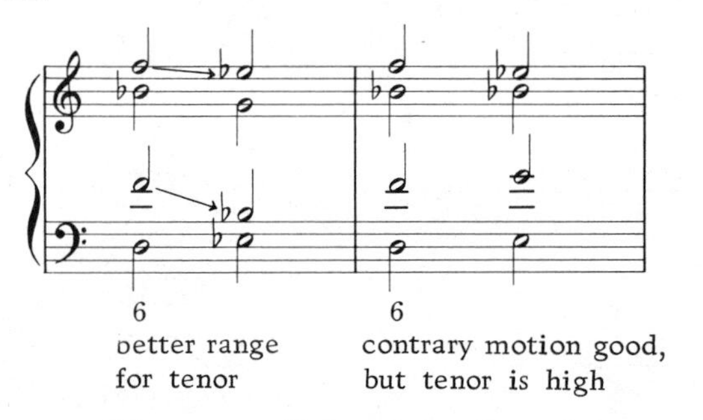

The most efficient procedure for part-writing to or from a triad in first inversion is as follows (Figure 9.23):

Step 1. Complete the first of the two triads.

Step 2. Approach or resolve doubled note by contrary or oblique motion if possible.

Step 3. Fill in remaining voice with note necessary to produce normal doubling. When doubled note moves by contrary or oblique motion, the remaining voice usually moves by step or remains stationary, rarely moving by leap.

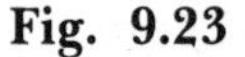
Fig. 9.23

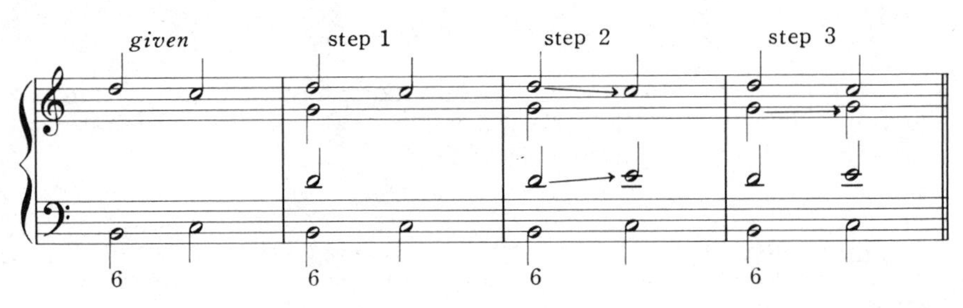

Part-Writing Rule 6A.[5] When writing to or from a triad in any inversion, write the two voices moving to or from the doubled note *first,* using contrary or oblique motion between the two voices, if possible. When using similar motion, care should be taken to avoid parallel fifths and octaves.

Assignment 9.3. Write pairs of triads, following Rule 6A. As usual, place chord numbers below each bass tone.

Writing Successive Triads in First Inversion

When triads in first inversion are used in succession it is impossible for each of these triads to be found with the usual doubling in the same pair of voices, since parallel octaves and fifths will result.

Fig. 9.24

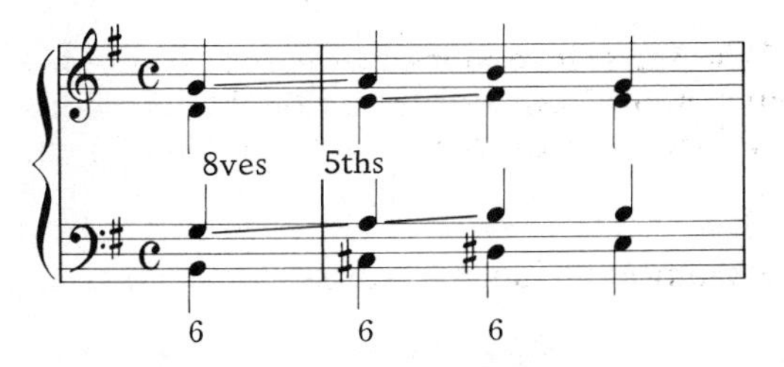

There are two ways to remedy this situation. First, each triad in inversion may have a different doubling, if necessary.

[5]Part-writing rules are not numbered consecutively in the text, but are numbered for ease of reference in Appendix 1, "The Essentials of Part-Writing."

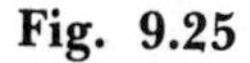
Fig. 9.25

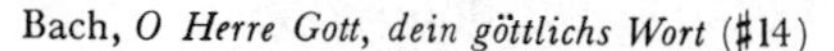
Bach, *O Herre Gott, dein göttlichs Wort* (♯14)

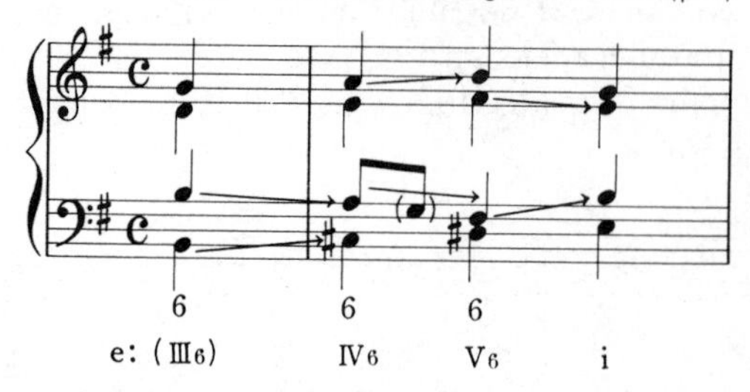

When using unusual doublings such as these, *avoid doubling the leading tone of the key, or any altered note* (such as the raised sixth scale step in minor). In the example above, Bach has succeeded in resolving each doubled note by contrary motion, has avoided doubling the raised sixth and seventh scale steps, and has moved from triad to triad with a minimum of motion. This example deserves careful study.

Second, it is often possible, especially when there are only two first inversions in succession, to double the soprano note in each triad, but in different pairs of voices (Figure 9.26). Writing IV_6—V_6 or V_6—IV_6 can usually be accomplished by this method.

Fig. 9.26

Part-Writing Rule 6B. When first inversions of triads are found in *succession,* each succeeding triad must either have a different doubling, or normal soprano doubling may appear in different pairs of voices. Avoid doubling the leading tone or any altered tone.

Assignment 9.4. Write examples of successive first inversions using Rule 6B.

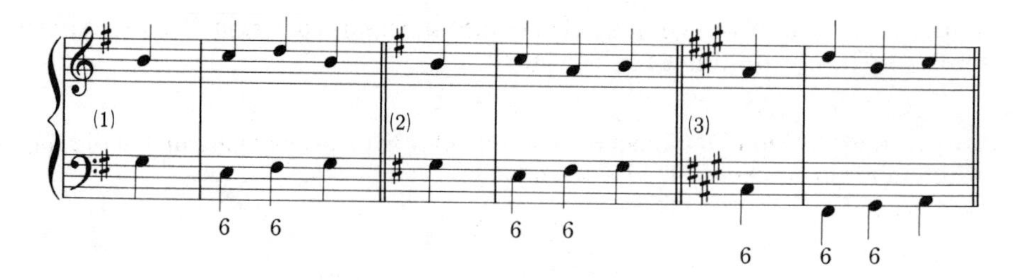

Writing the Triad in Second Inversion

Doubling. When a triad is found in second inversion, the fifth of the triad (the bass note) is usually doubled. Approach the doubled note using Rule 6A. See Figures 9.11, 9.17, and 9.27.

Approach to the bass note. 1. The bass note can be approached by step. Using the triads studied thus far, IV and IV_6 will precede $I_{\substack{6\\4}}$ in this manner.

2. The bass note can be approached by leap from another position of the tonic triad, I–$I_{\substack{6\\4}}$ or I_6–$I_{\substack{6\\4}}$. Given that the tonic six-four is actually a dominant harmony, spelled temporarily like tonic (review Figure 9.15 and the discussion of it), the progression is really I–V.

Fig. 9.27

Resolution of the Six-Four. Following the $I_{\substack{6\\4}}$, the intervals of the sixth and of the fourth above the bass each move down stepwise to members of the V triad. (Exceptions will be noted in Chapter 16.)

Fig. 9.28

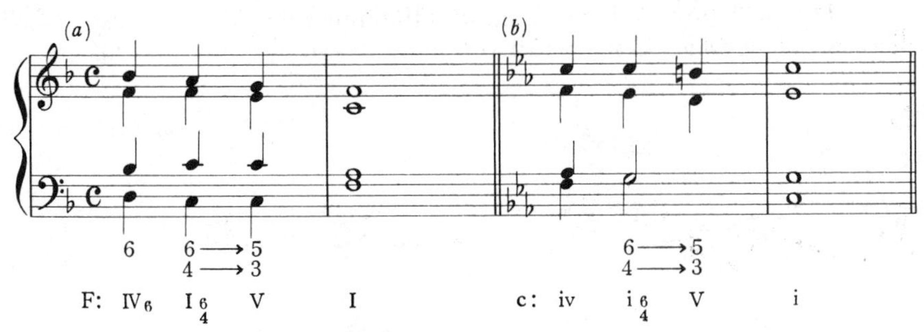

Assignment 9.5. Fill in inner voices. Make an harmonic analysis.

Other Part-Writing Considerations

1. The Melodic Augmented Fourth. This interval is usually avoided in melodic writing, and therefore should not appear in any voice line in four-part writing. Both tones of the interval have strong resolution tendencies, the upper tone resolving up and the lower tone resolving down. Therefore, changing direction after the large leap is not satisfactory, as seen in Figure 9.29a.

The problem is solved by leaping the interval of the diminished fifth, thus allowing a melodic change of direction as shown in Figure 9.29b.

Fig. 9.29

This interval is necessary in the progression IV–V_6, among others, as shown in Figure 9.30a.

2. *Overlapping voices.* When two adjacent voices (tenor and bass for example) ascend simultaneously, the lower voice should not ascend to a pitch above the higher of the two original tones. This also applies to the upper voice when two tones are descending. See Figure 9.30b-e. Although examples may occasionally be found in music (e.g., the last phrases each of Bach chorales 46, 48, and 107), this procedure is comparatively infrequent and should be avoided by the student at this time, unless no other part-writing procedure is effective.

These overlapping voices may often be eliminated simply by changing the direction of one part, as in Figure 9.30c. In other cases, it will usually be necessary to change the position of the first of the two triads, or, if this is impossible, to change the position of a triad appearing before the pair in question.

Part-Writing Rule 7. Triad position may be changed 1) at a repeated triad; 2) using Rule 2C; 3) at a triad in inversion or a triad with unusual doubling.

In Figure 9.30d, changing the position of the second of the two V triads prevents the overlapping parts. In Figure 9.30e, it is necessary that the IV triad be in close position. This is possible only if the inner voices of the previous I_6 triad are changed.

Many part-writing difficulties other than the above can be solved by going back to a point where Rule 7 may be applied and rewriting the subsequent material.

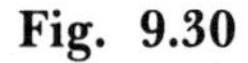
Fig. 9.30

Assignment 9.6. *a)* Write extended exercises (the soprano and bass lines are given). Make an harmonic analysis.

b) The bass only is given. Write the soprano line and fill in alto and tenor voices. Make an harmonic analysis.

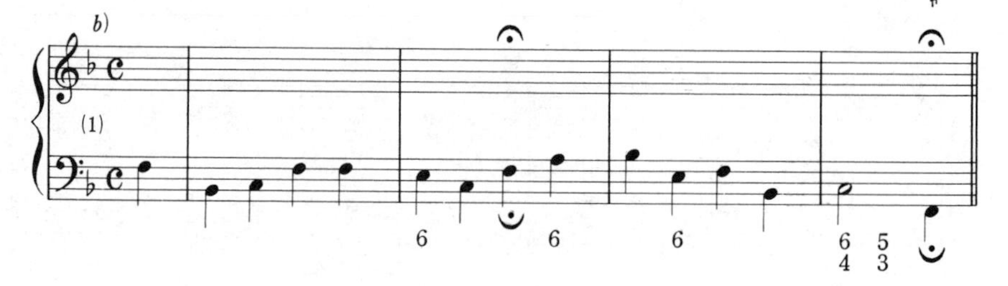

Assignment 9.7. Write on the staff the following progressions based on the given chord symbols. Other keys may be used.

a) G Major — I V_6 I
b) D♭ Major — I V_6 I
c) E Major — I IV_6 V I
d) G Minor — i V_6 i
e) B Minor — i iv_6 V i
f) F Minor — i IV_6 V_6 i
g) A Major — I IV $I_{\substack{6\\4}}$ V I

h) D♭ Major — $\frac{3}{4}$ I I_6 I | V V_6 V | I IV V | I ||

i) B Major — $\frac{4}{4}$ I | IV_6 V_6 I I | IV V I ||

j) F♯ Minor — $\frac{2}{4}$ i V_6 | i i_6 | iv V | i||

k) D Minor — $\frac{4}{4}$ V_6 | i i iv V_6 | i iv $i_{\substack{6\\4}}$ V | I ||

l) A♭ Major — $\frac{3}{4}$ V | I IV V_6 | I I_6 I | IV_6 $I_{\substack{6\\4}}$ V | I ||

Performance of Part-Writing Exercises

Actual performance of part-writing exercises will allow the student to hear the musical effect of his efforts, particularly the effectiveness of the individual parts. Such performance may be accomplished in one of two ways.

As a Choral Performance. Copy out each of the four parts on separate pieces of paper for distribution to members of the class.

As an Instrumental Performance. Each of the four parts may be played on such orchestral or band instruments as are available in the theory class. Each of the four parts must be written separately for the use of individual players. Writing for instruments involves technical considerations ordinarily studied as instrumentation. An understanding of the following elementary principles of instrumentation will suffice in writing exercises for performance.

1. Range. Each instrument has one low note below which it cannot play, and an upper range above which its tones are unsatisfactory or difficult. Music written for an instrument must conform to this limitation.

2. Transposition. For some instruments, music is written with pitches differing from the actual sound. A clarinet in B♭, for example, sounds B♭ when the written pitch is C.

3. Clefs. Some instruments use clefs other than the treble and bass clef. The viola uses the alto clef almost exclusively, while other instruments use C clefs as needed.

Details concerning these three principles will be found as Appendix 2. Study these carefully before writing, and consult the player about the problems in playing his particular instrument.

Figure 9.31 illustrates the first few measures of the second exercise in Assignment 9.6 as written for clarinet in B♭, viola, horn in F, and 'cello. Such a combination is not usual, but could occur in a classroom situation, and illustrates use of clefs and transposition.

Fig. 9.31

Assignment 9.8 Rewrite exercises from Assignments 9.6 and 9.7. Using an open score, write for instruments as assigned.

Ear Training and Music Reading

Exercise 9.1. Listening to triads in inversion. *a*) Identify the bass note of a major triad as 1, 3, or 5 when the triad is played at the piano. Follow the same procedure used when identifying the soprano note—sing the triad from the root, sing the bass note, and identify the bass note by number.

b) Identify the bass note of a minor triad as 1, 3, or 5. Follow directions outlined in *a* above.

c) Identify the bass note when major and minor triads are played, as 1M, 5m, 5M, 3m, and so on.

d) Identify both soprano and bass note when major and/or minor triads are played.

e) Spell the triad and the soprano note when the spelling of the bass note is given, or spell the triad and the bass note when the soprano note is given.

Exercise 9.2. Write the triad in inversion from dictation when the bass note is given. Procedure:

a) Place the given bass note on staff.
b) Spell the triad after hearing it played.
c) Write the soprano note on the staff.

Exercise 9.3. Harmonic dictation, first and second inversion of triads. Taking harmonic dictation with inversions follows the basic procedure outlined in Exercise 4.4 with additional steps listed below. This procedure will remain valid for the remaining harmonic dictation exercises in this course of study.

Step 1. Prepare a great staff with treble and bass clefs. Leave space for key signature. Write in time signature as announced.

Step 2. Listen to dictation exercise all the way through without writing. Then sing the tonic key aloud or silently, as instructed. Here is a sample exercise.

Fig. 9.32

Step 3. Upon the second hearing, sing aloud or silently the root of each triad as it is played, and write its number below the bass staff:

V | i i IV V | i iv i V | i ||

Step 4. As the exercise is replayed, listen for the bass note of each triad. If the third is in the bass, add subscript "6" to chord number. If the fifth is in the bass, add "$^6_4$".

V | i_6 i IV_6 V_6 | i iv i^6_4 V | i ||

Step 5. The key signature will be given (in our example, two sharps). Write in the bass line. If the chord numbers and inversion symbols are correct, the pitch name of each bass note can be ascertained. Rehearing the exercise at the piano will indicate the direction of intervals, up or down. Listening to the bass line as a melodic line will confirm the accuracy of the series of chord numbers or reveal points of error.

Fig. 9.33

Step 6. Listen to the exercise again, this time taking down the soprano line. Optionally, the inner voices may be filled in, either by listening or by following part-writing rules.

As an alternate procedure, the key signature may be given in Step 4. Write the bass line, then indicate the inversion in the chord symbols.

Keyboard Harmony

Exercise 9.4. Play any major or minor triad in first or second inversion, with any member of the triad in the soprano. As in previous keyboard performances of single triads, play each triad in inversion with three notes in the right hand and one in the left, using correct doubling. Example: Play the first inversion of the D major triad, with its fifth in the soprano.

Fig. 9.34

Play these triads, or others as assigned. Soprano note is indicated in parentheses.

First Inversion:	Major—C(1), E♭(5), A(3), B(1), D♭(5)
	Minor—D(1), G(5), F♯(3), B♭(1), D♯(5)
Second Inversion:	Major—A(3), F(1), G♭(5), E(1), C♯(3)
	Minor—A(1), F♯(5), B(3), G♯(1), E♭(1)

Exercise 9.5. Play these progressions in each major and minor key. The first three are written out. Also, try each exercise beginning with one of the two other soprano positions of the opening tonic triad.

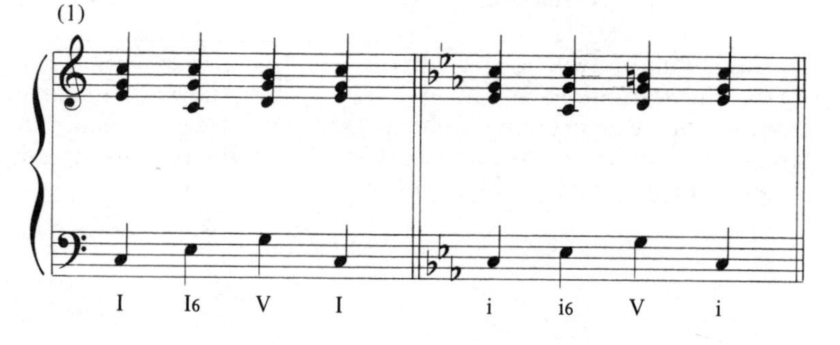

(4) I I_6 IV V I; i i_6 iv V i
(5) I IV_6 V_6 I; i IV_6 V_6 i
(6) I IV $I_{\substack{6\\4}}$ V I; i iv $i_{\substack{6\\4}}$ V i
(7) I IV_6 $I_{\substack{6\\4}}$ V I; i iv_6 $i_{\substack{6\\4}}$ V I

Exercise 9.6. Play part-writing exercises from Assignments 9.3–9.6. Transpose to other keys.

The Theory of Inversion

The fact that a chord can be inverted—that, for example, E–G–C is the same chord as C–E–G, only inverted—appears so plain to us now that we assume the concept must have been known to the very earliest composers. In reality, however, the seemingly "simple" fact of harmonic invertibility only became formally established in the year 1722 by Jean Phillipe Rameau (1683–1764) in his *Traité de l'harmonie reduite à ses principes naturels* (*Treatise on Harmony Reduced to its Natural Principles*).

To understand why the concept of the chord and its inversion came so late, we must once again look back to the beginnings of composition in Western music. The earliest known music is melodic, that of the chants of the medieval church.

Music in two voices, two melodic lines together, appeared in the ninth century, with the chant also stated a perfect fifth higher than the original melody and with both lines sung simultaneously.

This simple device of sounding two melodies simultaneously, known as *counterpoint,* evolved first through independence of direction in the two lines,

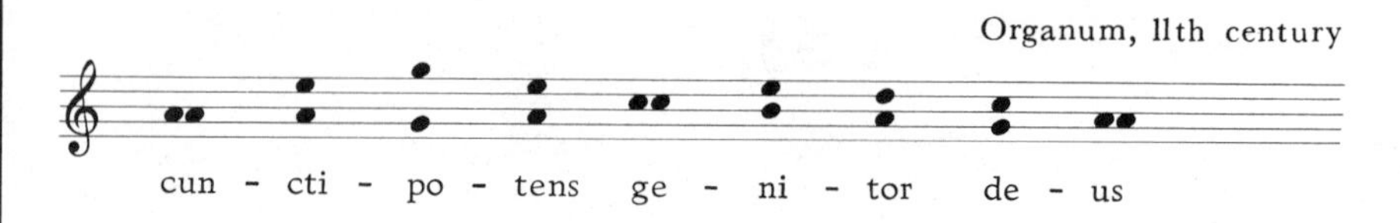

then with independence of rhythm,

followed by the addition of more and more melodic lines,

and reaching its culmination in the *polyphonic* (many-voiced) contrapuntal writing found in the masterworks of the late sixteenth century.

These first five excerpts are reprinted by permission of Harvard University Press, Cambridge, Mass., from Davison and Apel, *Historical Anthology of Music,* Vol. I (1949).

Palestrina (1525-1594), *In Dominicus Quadragesima*

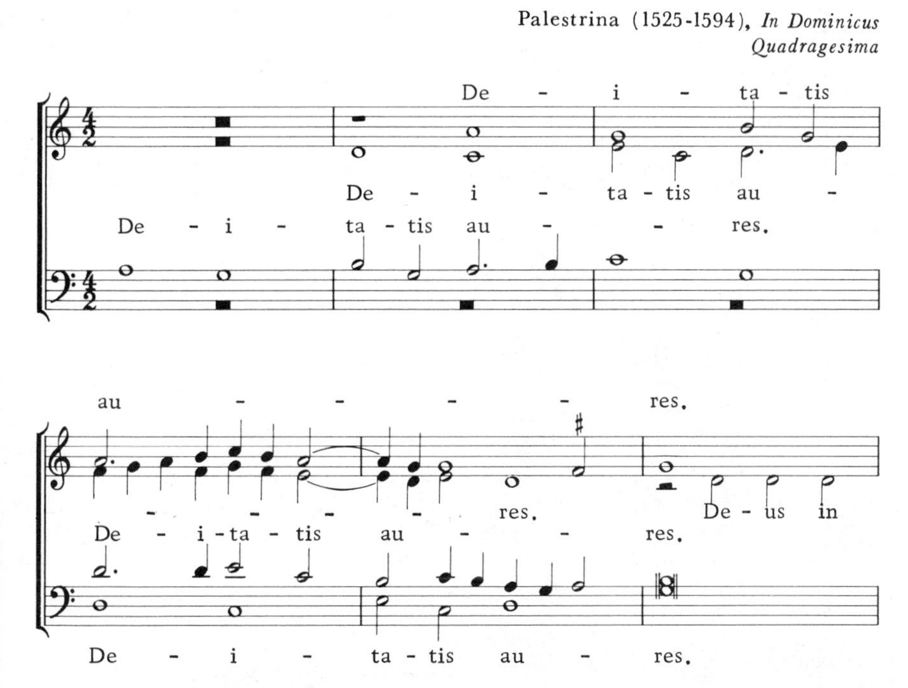

In all of these developments, the primary compositional concern was the setting of voice lines against each other. The harmonic aspect was controlled exclusively by making sure that intervals above the lowest sounding notes were consonant with these notes (though specific dissonances in well-defined situations were allowed). Hence, the first vertical sonority in measure 4 of the Palestrina example we would call a D minor triad, but in the sixteenth century it would have been described simply as a minor third and a perfect fifth above the D in the bass. On the fourth beat of the measure, we see from the bass up the notes C–E–A, to us the first inversion of an A minor triad, but at that time a major third and a major sixth above the C in the bass. Only the major triad occurring at the end of a composition was given an identity, and called the *trias harmonica* (harmonic triad).

The impetus of performance and composition through the use of figured bass (see the article, "Figured Bass," in this chapter) heightened awareness of the harmonic aspect of music. Many theoreticians during this time attempted a rational explanation of this new concept, but none was successful until the theories of Rameau appeared, approximately one hundred and twenty-five years after the introduction of figured bass. Rameau's proof of the invertibility of a chord or of an interval was arrived at through the principle of the "identity of the octave." In the interval of the octave both notes sound identically; therefore, the octave actually represents a single pitch of the same name. It should follow that any interval of a chord that is changed only by an octave transposition of one or more of its notes has not really been changed at all.

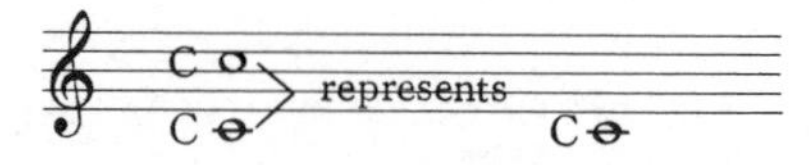

Thus E G C is C E G, the same triad but in a different form, the first inversion, and G C E is C E G, but in second inversion.

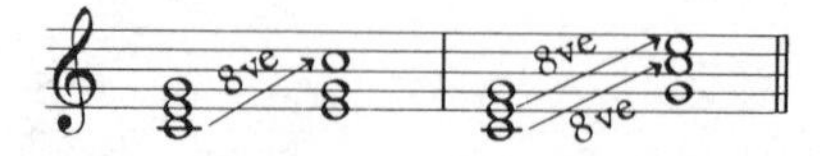

But why is C the fundamental note of this triad rather than E or G? The answer to Rameau was based on an acoustical phenomenon well known as far back as early Greek times, and said to have been discovered by Pythagoras (sixth century B.C.). We take a string that when played sounds C. If we press a finger at the half-way point on the string and play on one half of the string, the note produced is another C an octave higher. If we place the finger to divide the string in thirds, and play on one third of the string, we get a pitch G an octave and a fifth above the original note. Here are the pitches derived from the first six divisions of a string sounding C.

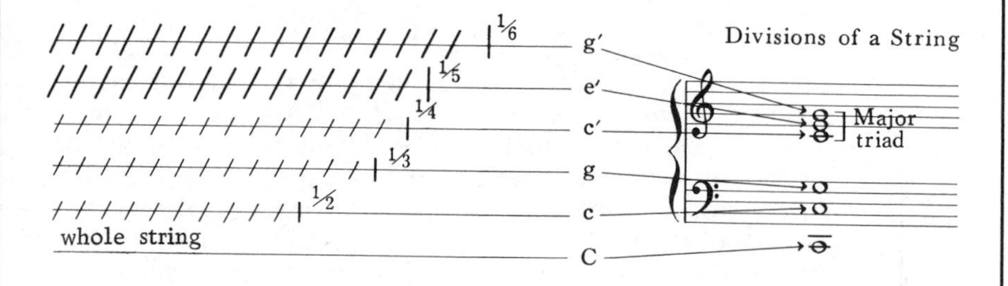

Rameau observed that each note created by dividing the string was directly related thereby to the entire string, the source from which the upper tones are derived. In our illustration, the triad c^1 e^1 g^1 is derived from the division of an original string sounding C. c^1 is in an octave relationship to the original C; it therefore represents the fundamental or generating tone and becomes the root or fundamental of the triad, no matter in what order the triad notes are arranged.

Another acoustical phenomenon, the *overtone series* (described in Appendix 3, "Elementary Acoustics"), displays the same relationship of intervals as that found in the division of a string. Although discovered by Joseph Sauver, a blind and deaf music theoretician, twenty years before his own theories, Rameau pointed to the overtone series as further confirmation of his work once he had become acquainted with it. In the following overtone series on C, the C E G triad appears as partials numbered 4, 5, and 6, comparable to the fourth, fifth, and sixth divisions of the string.

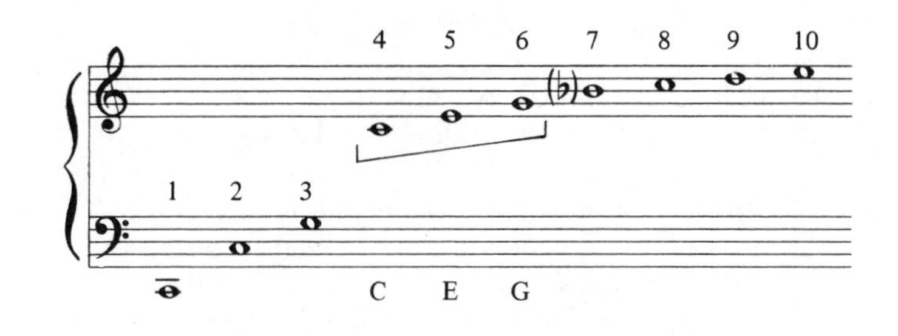

Intervals are invertible in the same manner. Moving the lower note up an octave or the upper note down an octave changes the interval only by the ratio of 1 : 2. Since this ratio indicates the octave, which in turn represents the fundamental, the two intervals are inverisons of each other. P5 and P4 are inversions of each other; m3 and M6 are inversions of each other.

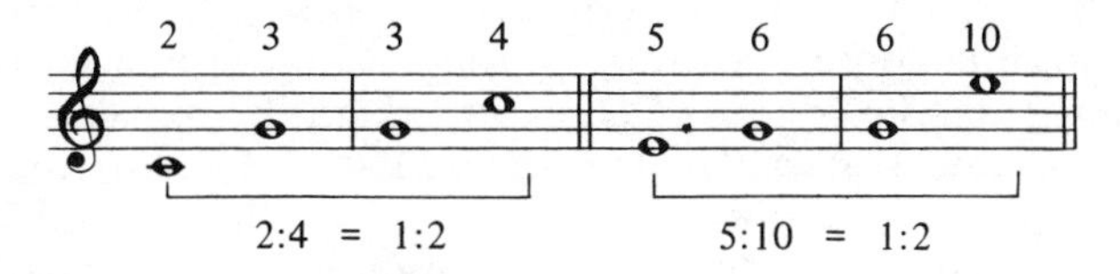

Having found that all chords have roots and that the root remains constant when the notes are rearranged, Rameau next sought to discover the underlying principle governing the progression of one chord to another. Rameau said that these progressions are based upon movement of the roots of chords, whether or not these roots are in the bass. In looking at the intervals from the division of the string and from the overtone series, he noted that the first interval to appear above the fundamental and its repetition, the octave, is the fifth. Therefore, root movement should be best when the roots are a fifth apart. This can be shown by taking a piece of music and extracting the roots, placing these on a third staff, as in the following example. It should be kept in mind that there are three possible root movements, by

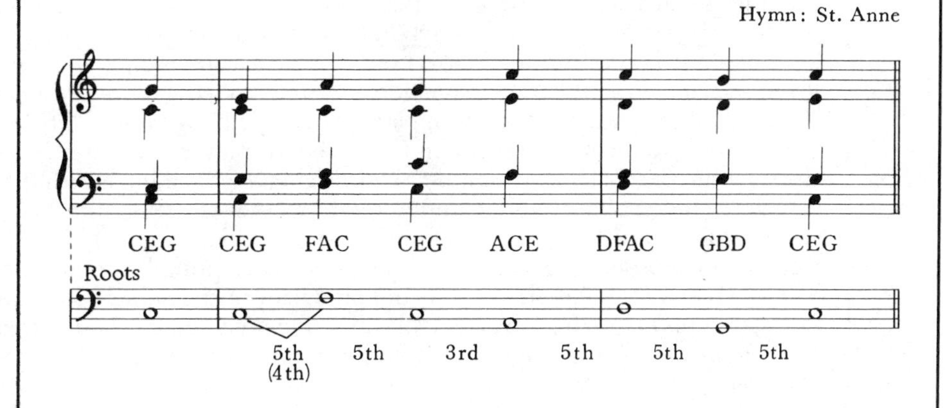

fifth, by third, and by second. According to the theory of inversion, the effect of the fourth is the same as the fifth (C up to F is the same as C down to F), the sixth is the same as the third (C up to A is the same as C down to A), and the seventh is the same as the second (C up to B is the same as C down to B).

In this part of his theory, Rameau was correct; subsequent analysis has shown that in the music of almost every composer during the years 1600–1900, the majority of root movements were by the interval of the fifth. Rameau's reasoning that root movement by thirds should be next best and root movement by seconds least best has been reversed by the practice of composers.

But on the whole, Rameau was eminently successful in discovering satisfactory principles of chord construction and chord progression. Chords have roots that may or may not be in the lowest sounding voice, and chord succession is a function of the movement of these roots, movement by the fifth being the best. These principles allow us to identify a chord by numbering the chord according to the location of its root in the scale, and to study the relationship of chords through the movements of their roots.

Music written after the time of Rameau and up to c. 1900 can, for the most part, be studied and analyzed by the principles first outlined by Rameau. It is because of this fact, and in spite of the large number of composers and diverse styles in this three-century span, that we can study the music of this period under the single subject heading of harmony.

Figured Bass

In its four-hundred-year history, figured bass has functioned in three distinct areas of musical endeavor. It began as a solution to a performance problem, then, during the Baroque era, became an important compositional device, and finally, today, serves as a widely used aid in the learning of harmony and part-writing.

Its history dates from the late sixteenth century. You may recall from reading the article, "Another Metrical Concept," in Chapter 8, that vocal music of the time was written on separate pages for each of the voices. And although much of this music was written without accompaniment (*a capella*), it was the custom of the time to include instrumentalists informally, playing any or all of the vocal parts or even playing them without singers. The problem we have spoken of arose when the keyboard player tried to read all of the separate parts of a work simultaneously when performing it with the ensemble. The problem was compounded by the fact that in this pre-seventeenth century music, each line was a melodic line, and all of the lines were superimposed on each other to create a contrapuntal composition (as we have seen in the Palestrina excerpt in the previously mentioned article).

A solution to the keyboard player's dilemma came when someone thought of using the bass part only and of writing nubmers under or over certain bass notes to indicate the intervals above those notes. The performer quickly calculated the intervals above the bass and played these notes as a group—as a *chord.* As the music evolved, the succession of chords harmonized with the contrapuntal composition, even though it was in direct contrast to the melodic intent of the composition.

Although a concept of harmony, as opposed to one of counterpoint, was stirring in the sixteenth century, this practice of playing from a figured bass—of preparing a solo line and a figured bass line—actually provided composers with the impetus to write chordally. The first such music in this style was written by Lodovico Viadanna, in or about the year 1596. The style was eagerly accepted and practiced by most compsers, and thus harmony soon replaced counterpoint as the predominant characteristic of music.

The following example is taken from Caccini's *Le Nuove Musiche ("The New Music")*, published in 1601. Only the vocal solo line and the bass line with figuration were written by the composer. The rest of the notes represent one possible interpretation, called a "realization," of the figured bass.

Giulio Caccini (1550?-1618), *Sfogava con le stelle*

Early figured bass examples, such as that of Caccini, often used numbers higher than eight to indicate compound intervals (10 = 8ve + 3rd). Except for nine in certain circumstances, these large numbers were soon discarded. The player seeing 6 for example, could play the sixth above the bass in any convenient octave.

Composition using figured bass continued throughout the mid-eighteenth century, and included many of the great vocal and instrumental works of Bach, Handel, and their contemporaries.

Whereas keyboard performers of this period improvised freely over the given figured bass lines, today's performers prefer to purchase a copy of the score with the keyboard part already written out. Thus, if one purchases the Handel violin sonatas in two different editions, one gets two different keyboard realizations. There is no reason, however, why any player cannot improvise or write out his own keyboard parts to these compositions.

When looking at original figured bass lines, one notices that the method of writing for figured bass varied from composer to composer. For example, the markings #6, 6#, 6+ and 6̸ all mean the same thing. Symbols are often missing when the composer thinks the harmony is obvious, but at times they are present when they seem unnecessary. The figured bass symbols shown in examples in this book are authentic to their historical period, but of necessity their style cannot be attributed to any one composer.

With the end of the eighteenth century, figured bass, together with improvisation and casual interpretation of the music score, became a thing of the past. Composers now wrote exactly what they wanted played, and since that time it has been considered an artistic necessity for the performer to reproduce as exactly as possible the composer's intentions. But the twentieth century has seen a revival of the improvisatory and casual aspects of music, particularly in jazz groups and in scores for aleatoric music, which give both performers and conductors choices of what to play and how to play it.

CHAPTER 10

Rhythm: Subdivision of the Beat

Theory and Analysis

The Subdivided Beat

Musical examples studied thus far in rhythmic reading, rhythmic dictation, and sight singing have utilized the divided beat only. By dividing equally each of the divided beats, subdivision of the beat results.

Fig. 10.1

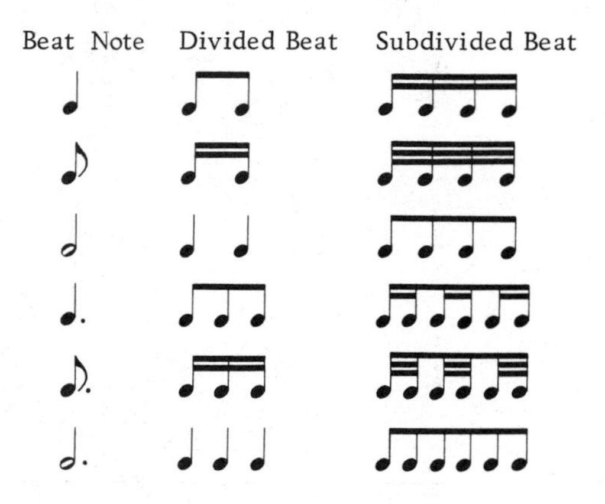

Application

Ear Training and Music Reading

Exercise 10.1. Reading rhythmic patterns . While making a conductor's beat and tapping the divided beat, read the following examples of subdivided beat. Read each line as many times as necessary before proceeding to the next line. Using the guide numbers at the left in Figures 10.2–10.6, read lines in random order as designated by instructor.

a) Simple time

Fig. 10.2

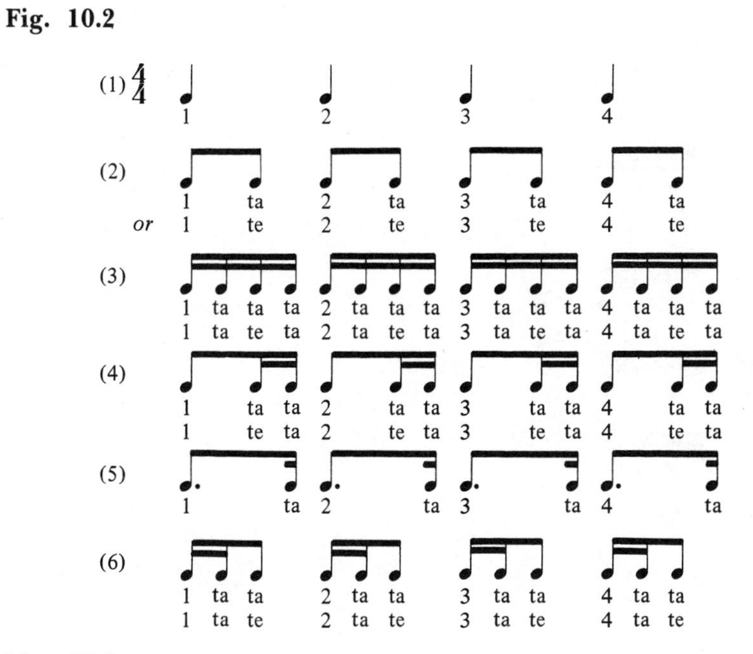

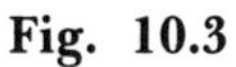

Fig. 10.3

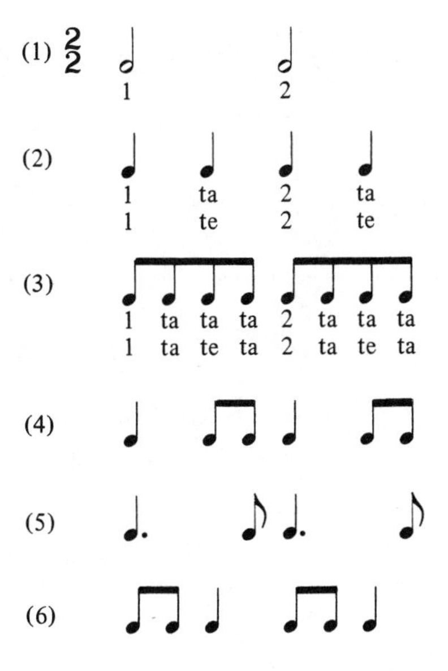

Fig. 10.4

b) Compound time

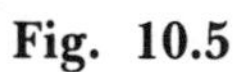

Fig. 10.5

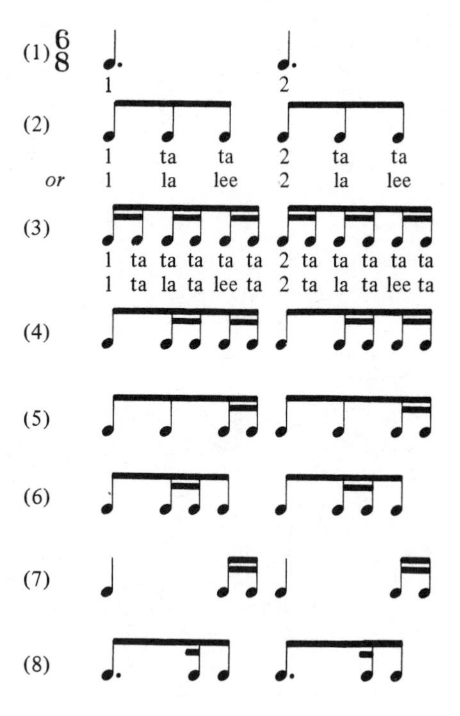

Fig. 10.6

c) Triple meter in fast tempo. When music in triple meter ($\frac{3}{4}$, $\frac{3}{8}$, etc.) is performed at a very fast tempo, it is usually counted one beat per measure, with each beat divided into three parts. Therefore, the effect is that of compound time, one beat per measure.

Fig. 10.7

(1)  $\frac{3}{4}$ ♩ ♩ ♩ | ♩ ♩ ♩ $\frac{3}{8}$ ♪ ♪ ♪ | ♪ ♪ ♪

1	ta	ta	1	ta	ta
1	la	lee	1	la	lee

Note that each group of two measures of $\frac{3}{4}$ in Figure 10.7 looks like one measure of $\frac{6}{4}$ in Figure 10.6 with a bar line added after the equivalent of three quarter notes. Continue reading from Figure 10.6 as though the time signature were $\frac{3}{4}$ and the extra bar line placed accordingly.

In the same way, each group of two measures of $\frac{3}{8}$ in Figure 10.7 looks like one measure of $\frac{6}{8}$ in Figure 10.5. Continue reading in Figure 10.5 as though the time signature were $\frac{3}{8}$ and the extra bar line placed accordingly.

Review "The Conductor's Beat" in Chapter 3, page 57.

Exercise 10.2. Rhythmic reading.

a) In *Music for Sight Singing*, read the rhythm of melodies 142–145 and 221, and of all melodies in Chapters 11–13.

b) In *More Music for Sight Singing*, read the rhythm drills in Part I, Sections H–K, pages 17–26. Also, read the rhythm from melodies containing these problems, beginning at melody number 385 (triple time, one in a measure), number 395 (simple time, four divisions to the beat), and number 413 (compound time, six divisions to the beat).

Exercise 10.3. Rhythmic dictation. Rhythmic dictation utilizing the subdivided beat will be given at this time by your instructor. Follow the directions for rhythmic dictation on page 61.

Exercise 10.4. Melodic dictation. After you have begun sight singing study of materials in Exercise 10.2, you will be given comparable problems in melodic dictation.

CHAPTER 11

Nonharmonic Tones; Harmonizing Melodies at the Keyboard

Theory and Analysis

In previous studies of cadences (page 70) and of harmonic implications in melodic lines (page 131) you have been introduced to the concept of nonharmonic tones, specifically the passing tone and the neighbor tone. These, together with several other varieties of nonharmonic tones, fulfill two important functions in music composition:

1. The addition of the dissonant effect of these notes furnishes the necessary contrast to the purity of repeated and unrelieved consonance.
2. When using triads only, voice lines are often melodically dull and rhythmically static. The addition of nonharmonic tones can improve both the melodic flow and the rhythmic interest in each of the melodic lines, as can be seen by comparing the following phrase from a Bach chorale with the same phrase with its nonharmonic tones deleted.

Fig. 11.1

Bach, *Herr Jesu Christ, du höchstes Gut* (#294)

The several classifications into which nonharmonic tones may be placed are described in the following paragraphs. Table 11.1, which follows this discussion, and is found on page 228, lists these classifications and their basic characteristics. The complete Bach chorale seen in Figure 11.24, page 228, includes most of these types of nonharmonic tones, except the upper neighbor and pedal. Each type is identified by its abbreviation (e.g., UPT) as stated in the definitions below.

Definitions of Nonharmonic Tones[1]

Nonharmonic tones may be identified and classified by the relationship of the dissonance (the nonharmonic tone) to the harmonic tones that precede and follow it. To identify most nonharmonic tones, it is necessary to analyze the *three* notes involved: 1) the harmonic tone preceding the dissonance, called the note of approach, 2) the dissonance itself, and 3) the harmonic tone following the dissonance, called the note of resolution.

1. Passing Tone. A passing tone is a nonharmonic tone that is found stepwise between harmonic tones of a different pitch. These may be either unaccented (UPT) or accented (APT).

Fig. 11.2

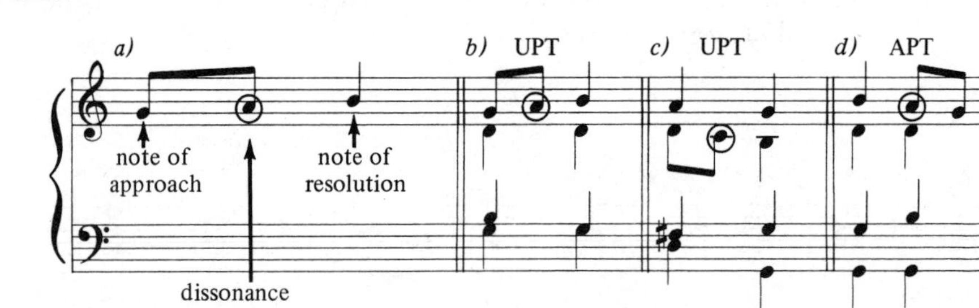

[1]There are in current use many names and conflicting definitions for the various nonharmonic tones. For comment on this problem, see "Terminology Variants" on page 233.

Fig. 11.3 Unaccented passing tones.

Fig. 11.4 Accented passing tones.

Passing tones are sometimes found in succession when they are necessary to fill in the interval between two harmonic tones.

Fig. 11.5

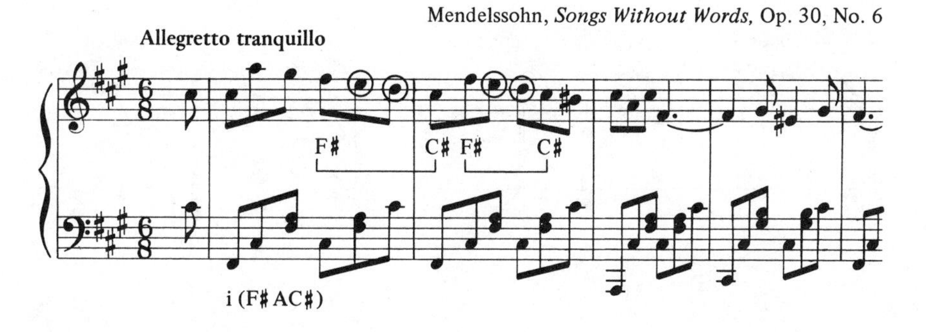

Most nonharmonic tones can be found with chromatic alterations, as in Figure 11.6, which shows successive passing tones between members of the A C E triad in measure one, and the E G♯ B D chord in measure two.

Fig. 11.6

Nonharmonic tones in general are frequently found in pairs, and occasionally in groups of three. The first and last phrases of this Bach chorale show passing tones in pairs, both in similar and contrary motion.

Fig. 11.7

2. *Neighbor Tone.* A neighbor tone is a nonharmonic tone found stepwise between two harmonic tones of the same pitch. The two varieties are upper neighbor (UN) and lower neighbor (LN), both of which may be found unaccented or accented.

Fig. 11.8

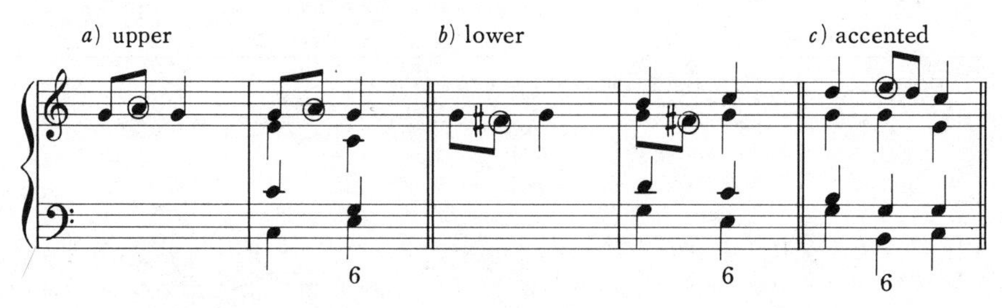

Figure 11.9 shows both the lower neighbor and the upper neighbor in pairs, and in measure 3, a chromatic lower neighbor and a single upper neighbor. Single neighbor tones can also be found in Figures 11.3, 11.5, and 11.6.

Fig. 11.9

3. Suspension. Suspension (S) occurs when a nonharmonic tone is approached by a note of the same pitch and resolved down by stepwise motion. The note of approach is often tied into the dissonance.

Fig. 11.10

The dissonance sounds here even though the note is not actually written at the point of dissonance.

Fig. 11.11

Bach, *Schaut, ihr Sünder* (#171)

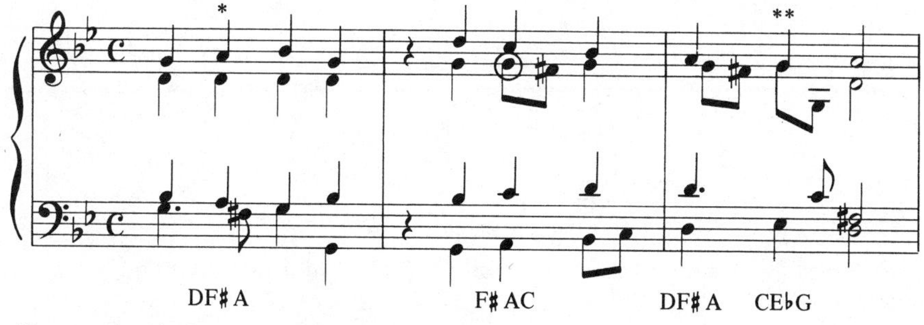

*Suspension in bass voice on beat 2.
**Suspension in tenor voice on beat 2.

A suspension in which the dissonance resolves *upwards* is known as a *retardation* (R). These are not common, and in many of these the real downward resolution is only slightly delayed by the upward movement.

Fig. 11.12

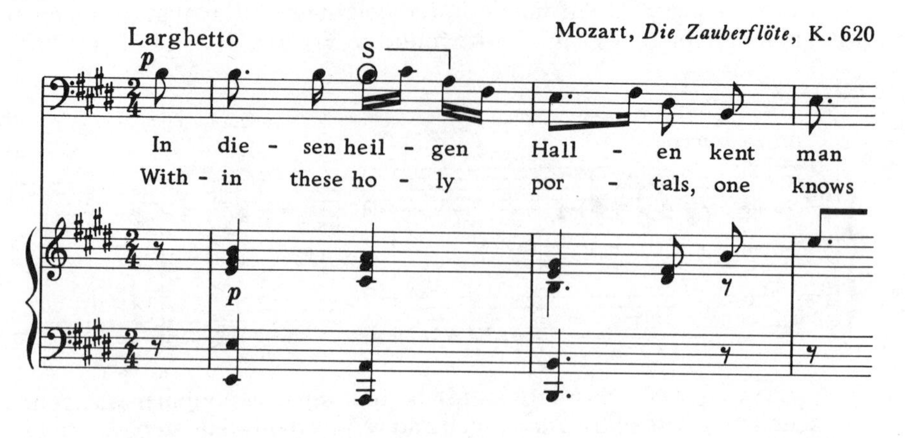

Further discussion of suspensions (in Chapter 15) will include figured bass types, chain suspensions, multiple suspensions, and varieties of resolution.

4. *Anticipation.* An anticipation (A) is a nonharmonic tone that sounds the same pitch as the harmonic tone following it. It anticipates a tone of the following chord. The anticipation is usually approached by step. Anticipations are most commonly used at cadences. There is a single anticipation in Figure 11.13a, and a double anticipation in b.

Fig. 11.13

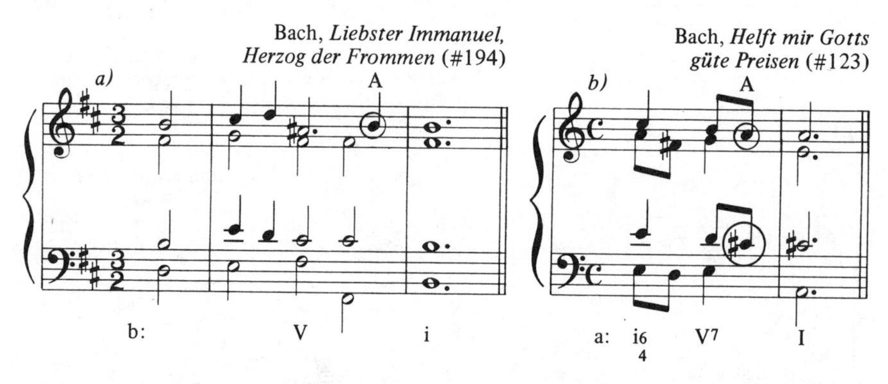

5. *Appoggiatura.* An *appoggiatura* (App) is a nonharmonic tone approached by leap and resolved by step. The resolution is usually in the direction opposite to the leap. See Figure 11.14–11.16.

One sometimes encounters resolution in the direction of the leap. In Figure 11.17, measure one, the leap up to the leading tone is continued upwards. In measure two, both C♮ and E♭ appear to be appoggiaturas to D♭, but it is more likely that there is a changing tone figure (see 7, following) D♭ C♮ E♭ D♭, interrupted by the tonic note G♭.

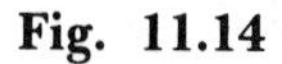

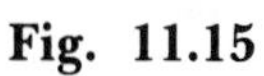

Fig. 11.16

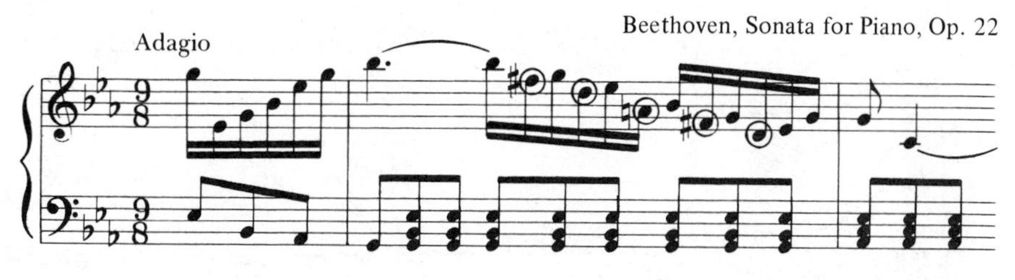

Fig. 11.17

In Figure 11.18, measures 1–2, the four-note (32nd note) figure on beat three opens with a chromatic lower neighbor tone. Each repetition of the same figure in measure three lacks its previous preparation, so that the first note of the figure now sounds as an appoggiatura.

Fig. 11.18

6. *Escaped Tone* (*Escape tone; Échappée*). An escaped tone is a non-harmonic tone approached by step and left by leap (ET). The resolution is usually in a direction opposite to that of the approach.

Fig. 11.19

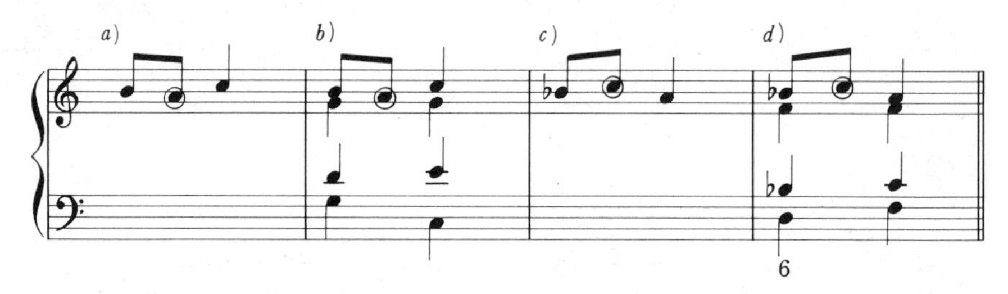

Fig. 11.20

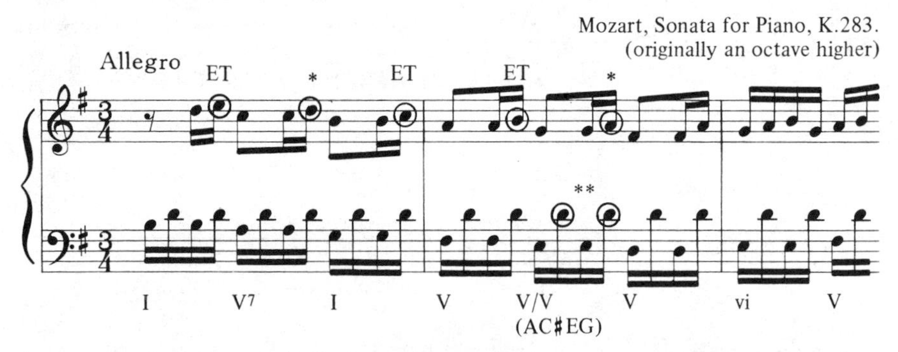

*When the three-note melodic figure is repeated in sequence, the third note is sometimes dissonant, sometimes consonant, yet functions melodically the same each time. Some musicians would prefer to identify each occurrence of this third note as a decorative pitch without particular name, or to call each an escaped tone, thereby assigning equal importance to each occurrence.

**The pitch d^1 that occurs throughout the bass clef of this excerpt is a *pedal tone* (see number 8, *Pedal point*). At this point it is dissonant, replacing C♯, of A C♯ E G. V/V means a chord in dominant relation to the V chord: A C♯ E G is dominant of D F♯ A (see Chapter 18).

7. *Changing Tones.* This figure involves four notes, the middle two of which act as successive upper and lower neighbors or vice versa. The fourth note is usually the same as the first, although sometimes it is another chord tone (CT).

Fig. 11.21

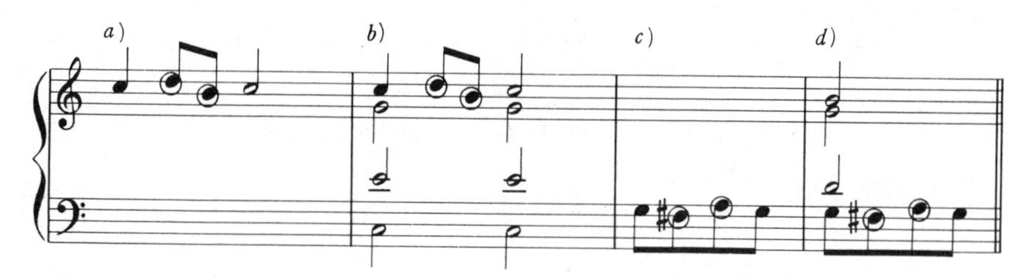

Fig. 11.22

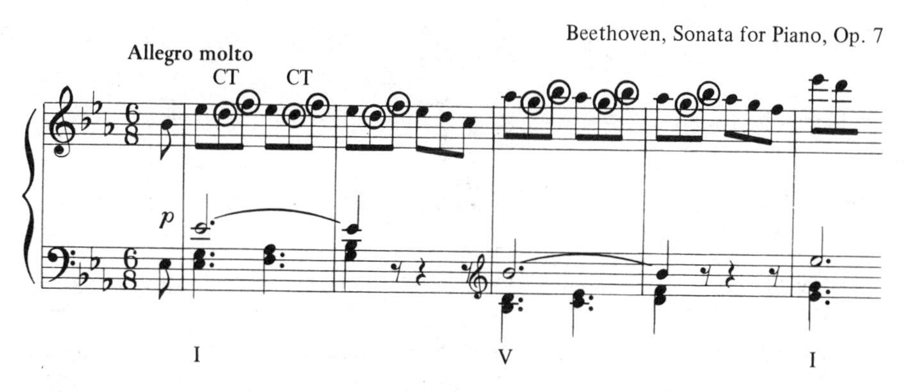

8. *Pedal Point (or Pedal; Organ Point).* The pedal point is a note sustained in one voice while in the other voices the harmonies are changing. It often occurs in the bass voice, whence the name pedal, referring to the practice of holding down one note with the foot on the pedal of the organ. When the sustained tone is found as the highest voice, it is known as an *inverted pedal;* when the sustained tone is found in an inner voice, it is known as an *inner pedal* or *internal pedal.* (P). While being sustained, the pedal pitch may sometimes be consonant and sometimes dissonant. Figure 11.23 is an example of a common use of the pedal in the bass. The pedal of Figure 11.20 is in an inner voice, hence it is an inner pedal. The keyboard figuration allows the pedal pitch to be sounded only on every other note, but the aural effect is that of a sustained note.

Fig. 11.23

TABLE 11.1 NONHARMONIC TONES

Name of non-harmonic tone	*Abbreviation*	*Example*	*Note of approach*	*Note of resolution*	*Direction of resolution*
Passing tone, unaccented	UPT		Step-wise	Step-wise	Same direction as approach
Passing tone, accented	APT		Step-wise	Step-wise	Same direction as approach
Neighboring tone, upper	UN		Step-wise	Step-wise	Opposite to approach
Neighboring tone, lower	LN		Step-wise	Step-wise	Opposite to approach
Suspension	S		Same note	Step-wise	Down
Retardation	R		Same note	Step-wise	Up
Anticipation	A		Step-wise	Same note	Same note
Appoggiatura	App		By leap	Step-wise	Opposite to leap
Escaped tone	ET		Step-wise	By leap	Opposite to approach
Changing tones	CT		Step-wise	Step-wise	Same note as note of approach
Pedal Point	P	Held note --			

Fig. 11.24

Bach, *Jesu, Jesu, du bist mein* (♯244)

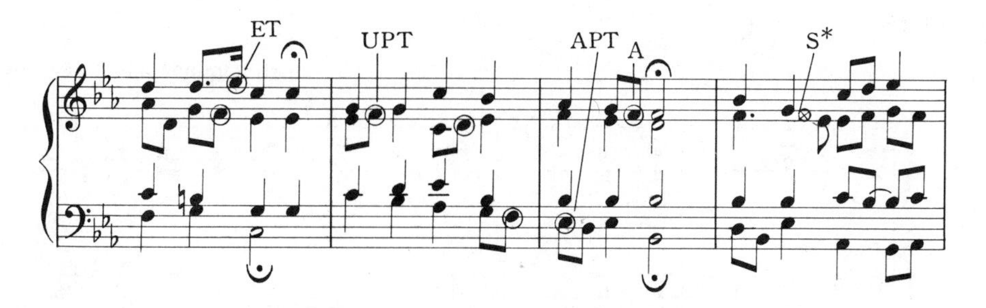

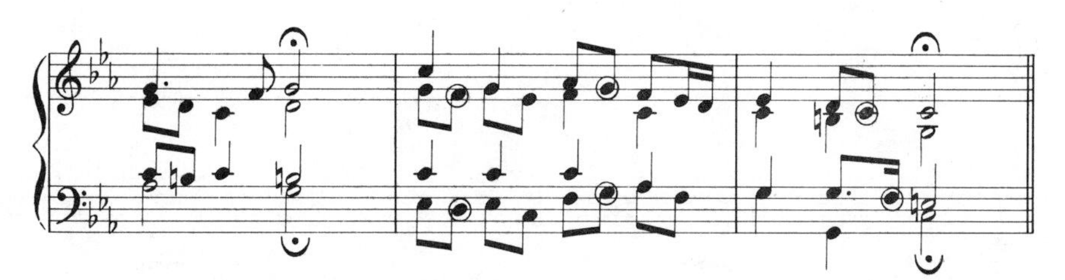

*⊗ = note held over sounds non - harmonic at this point

Less Common Uses of Nonharmonic Tones

In examining music scores, you will occasionally find nonharmonic tones used in ways that vary slightly from the preceding definitions or in more complex situations.

1. Successive Different Nonharmonic Tones. We have already discussed the use of successive passing tones (see Figures 11.5 and 11.6). Successions of two different nonharmonic tones are also possible.

Fig. 11.25

As an alternate analysis to the preceding one, the A♭ may be considered as a suspension, and the preparation as being decorated with an upper neighbor, B♭.

Fig. 11.26.

2. *Simultaneous Different Non-Harmonic Tones.* Combinations of any two, and sometimes three, different nonharmonic tones are possible. The only limitation (also true of simultaneous similar nonharmonic tones) is that each nonharmonic tone must in itself be used correctly, and that each must be consonant with any other nonharmonic tone. In Figure 11.27, a lower neighbor and an escaped tone sound together, the two being found at the interval of a major sixth. (This melody is the same as that in Figure 11.1. Compare the two harmonizations.)

Fig. 11.27

A more striking example shows an anticipation and a passing tone together, each moving correctly but the pair resulting in parallel fifths.

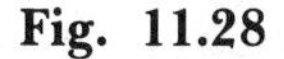
Fig. 11.28

The term *appoggiatura chord* is often applied to a group of nonharmonic tones, regardless of type, that sounds over a bass note from a different chord. It is often found as V or V^7 over the tonic note in the bass at the cadence.

Fig. 11.29

3. Unprepared Nonharmonic Tone. This tone occurs when the first note of a melodic line begins with a dissonance. It is usually termed an appoggiatura.

Fig. 11.30

4. "Harmonic" Nonharmonic Tone. This contradictory designation refers to a tone that is nonharmonic to the written or implied harmony, but that has no dissonant interval between it and any other voice at the moment it sounds. This happens frequently in music for less than four voices. In measure two below, for instance, the D♯'s obviously do not create a G♯ B D♯ harmony; rather, the D♯'s are dissonant against the E G♯ B stated at the beginning of the beat.

Fig. 11.31

At the asterisk in the next figure, the chord appears to be A C E, but sounds like V (C E G) of the authentic cadence. The note G is not found in any of the lower voices, which means that when the upper neighbor note A resolves, the C major triad is found with its usual doubling.

Fig. 11.32

5. *Nonconforming Nonharmonic Tones.* The nonharmonic tones we have examined thus far have been easily definable. Frequently, however, one will find examples, either singly or in combination, of other nonharmonic tones that conform to the spirit of our definitions in general, but that cannot be fully explained by any single definition. The wide variety of uses to which such tones can be put is limited only by the imagination and ingenuity of the composer. Most examples are unique; each can be explained only through its context and through any perceived similarity it may have to conventional nonharmonic tones.

The observable note of approach to the retardation (R) in Figure 11.33 is the note D in measure two, with the implication that it is repeated on the next beat. But at this point it is the other two notes of the V triad that are heard, as they skip from one side to the other of the implied note. These three notes, B♭ D F plus the A♭ in the soprano, also form a V^7, thus giving the effect of an appoggiatura chord against the tonic triad in the bass clef. If you review the discussion of Figure 11.17, you will find that the nonharmonic tones of measure two belong in this nonconforming category.

Fig. 11.33

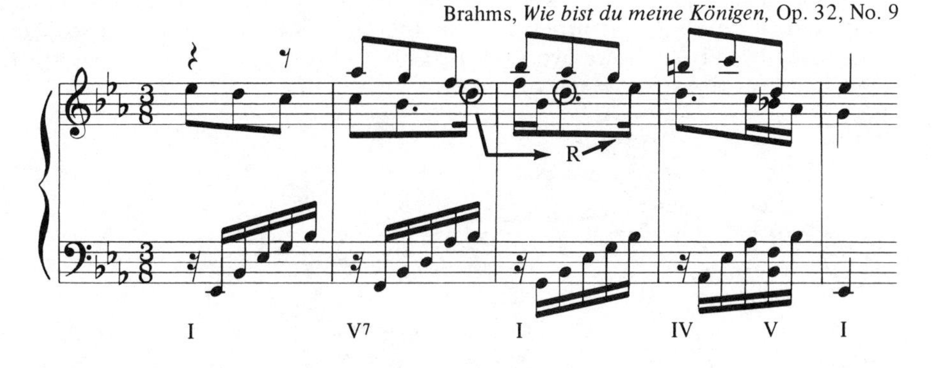

Terminology Variants

Terminologies for the various nonharmonic tones and the definitions of these terminologies very widely and have never been standardized. Nonharmonic tones in general are often known as *non-chord tones, foreign tones, accessory tones,* and *bytones.*

Nonharmonic tones are usually classified in one of two ways. In the first system, each nonharmonic tone is named and defined according to the relationship of the dissonance to the harmonic tones that precede and follow it. Nonharmonic tones listed in the previous pages of this chapter have been named and defined according to this principle. Even within this system, other names are often used for terms described earlier in this chapter and as shown in the list of alternate names at the end of this section.

In the second system, nonharmonic tones are defined according to rhythmic placement. Any nonharmonic tone that is sounded on an accented beat or part of a beat is known as an *appoggiatura,* this term including the suspension figure (as defined on page 223) when there is no tie into the dissonance. When the tie is present, then the dissonant tone is known as a *suspension.* Unaccented nonharmonic tones carry names similar to those already present or in the list of alternate names below.

Of all the nonharmonic tone designations, only the terms unaccented passing tone, anticipation, and pedal point appear to mean the same thing in all systems of nonharmonic tone terminology. The following list presents some of the more frequently used alternate names for terms listed in Table 13.1.

Neighboring Tone: (1) changing tone (when occurring on a weak beat), (2) auxiliary, (3) returning note, (4) turning tone, (5) appoggiatura (when appearing on a strong beat).

Appoggiatura: (1) neighboring tone (when occurring on a strong beat), (2) unprepared neighbor, (3) cambiata, (4) incomplete neighbor, (5) passing tone or turning tone reached by leap.

Escaped Tone: (1) neighboring tone (when occurring on a weak beat), (2) incomplete neighbor, (3) passing tone or turning tone left by leap.

Changing Tone: (1) double neighbor, (2) cambiata.

Suspension: appoggiatura (when not tied to note of approach).

Accented Passing Tone or *Accented Neighboring Tone:* appoggiatura.

Finally, some systems consider harmonic structures on weak beats, or on strong beats that are weaker than surrounding strong beats, to be multiple nonharmonic tones, grouped as "passing chords," "neighbor chords," and the like. Figure 11.34 shows two such neighbor chords, at *a* on the weak third beat and at *b* on the strong beat of measure two.

Fig. 11.34

The name *appoggiatura* is also given to a small note appearing before a principal note in a melody. This appoggiatura receives half of the value of the note following, unless the note following is a dotted note, in which case the appoggiatura receives two thirds of the value of the following note.

Fig. 11.35

This appoggiatura is not to be confused with the *grace note,* a note which looks like an appoggiatura but with a slash across the stem (𝅘𝅥𝅮). The grace note is performed without specific time value and as quickly as possible.

Fig. 11.36 Haydn, *The Creation*

The above is not a complete survey of the appoggiatura. The notation and the use of the appoggiatura, as well as the other nonharmonic tones, is often directly related to the historical period in which the device is used. For complete information, the student is referred to articles on nonharmonic tones in standard musical reference works, such as *Grove's Dictionary of Music and Musicians* and the *Harvard Dictionary of Music.*

Analysis of Nonharmonic Tones

1. Nonharmonic Tones in Chorales. The chorales of Johann Sebastian Bach offer unlimited opportunity for study of nonharmonic tones. Each of the four melodic lines in any chorale displays many of them. To identify these nonharmonic tones, it is necessary first to spell the chord; those notes not belonging to the chord will be nonharmonic tones that can be positively identified by relating the dissonant note to its preceding and following notes.

The examples for analysis may contain chords not yet studied. In such cases, merely arrange the notes in a series of thirds to spell the triad or chord; any remaining notes will be nonharmonic.

Fig. 11.37

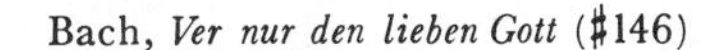
Bach, *Ver nur den lieben Gott* (♯146)

Note that when an accented nonharmonic tone is used, the chord tone is the note following the accented nonharmonic tone, as in the third chord (E G♯ B) above.

The identification of the note located at the interval of a seventh above the root is sometimes difficult because it often seems to be a chord tone (seventh of a chord) and a nonharmonic tone at the same time. For the present, consider such tones as chord tones when they are accented, and as nonharmonic when they are unaccented.

Fig. 11.38

Assignment 11.1. Identify the nonharmonic tones that are circled but not already labeled, in Fig. 11.24. Use abbreviations as given in Table 11.1.

Assignment 11.2. *a*) In the following phrases from Bach chorales, circle and identify each nonharmonic tone. Be sure to spell each harmonic sonority before detemining which notes are nonharmonic.

Bach, *Schmücke dich, O liebe Seele* (#22)

(2)

b) Copy out phrases from the Bach chorales listed below. Circle all nonharmonic tones and identify each.

Chorale No. *2, first phrase*
5, last phrase
49, first phrase
111, first phrase
120, first phrase
167, first, second, and third phrases
201, first phrase
219, first phrase
256, first and second phrases
260, entire chorale
280, first and second phrases

2. *Nonharmonic Tones in Instrumental Music.* Music for instruments, including the keyboard, is generally not written in block chords. Proper analysis depends upon locating the beginning and ending of an harmonic structure and combining the pitches within this duration. The analysis of the "broken chords" of Figure 11.39 should be obvious, and in Figure 11.40 the aural impression of tonic and dominant is clear, even though the four voices function as contrapuntally independent lines. Once the harmonic structure has been established, the remaining tones can be analyzed by using the appropriate nonharmonic tone terminology.

Fig. 11.39

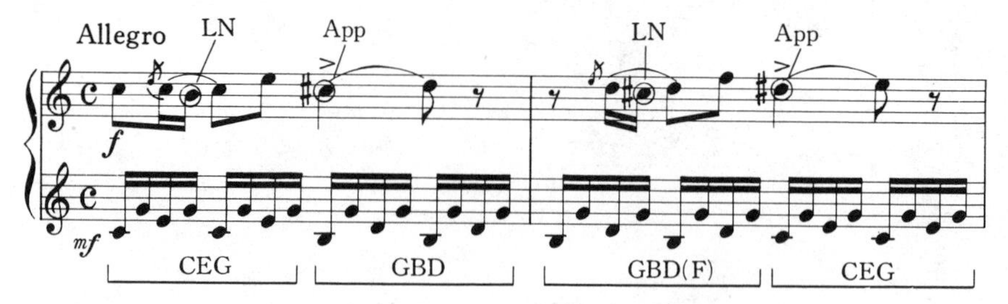

Fig. 11.40

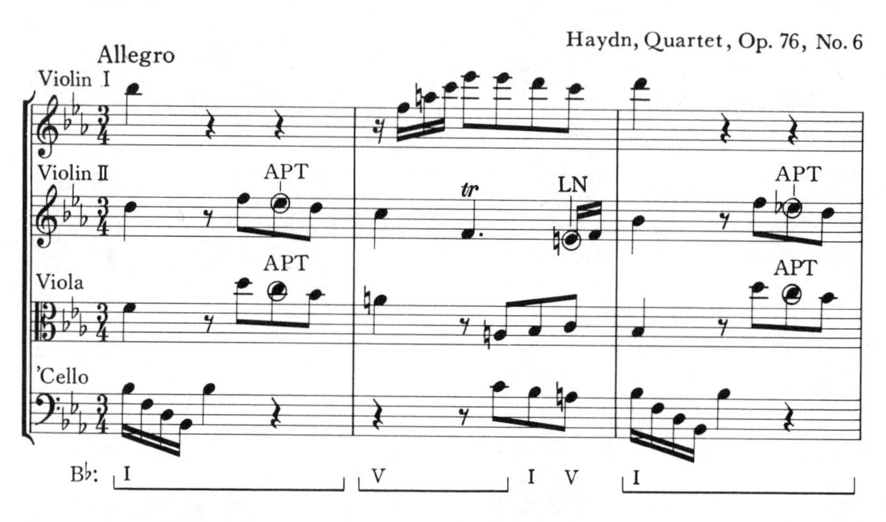

Assignment 11.3. Analysis of nonharmonic tones in instrumental music. Indicate a harmony by chord spelling or by roman numeral (spellings of a few chords other than I, IV, and V are given). Circle each nonharmonic tone and identify it by its abbreviation .

(2) Beethoven, Sonata for Piano, Op. 22

(3) Chopin, Mazurka, Op. 59, No. 2

Assignment 11.4.[2] From the music scores listed below, copy out the measures indicated. Below the bass line write in chord spellings and the chord numbers (only I, IV, V, and V^7 chords will be found). Circle all nonharmonic tones and identify each with proper abbreviation.

Measure 1 in any composition is the *first complete* measure. Repeats indicated by repeat signs are not numbered. First endings are not numbered. Grace notes need not be analyzed.

Beethoven, Sonata for Piano No. 5 (Op. 10, No. 1), second movement, measures 1–9.

Chopin, Mazurka No. 16 (Op. 24, No. 3), measures 1–12.

Mendelssohn, *Songs Without Words*
No. 12 (Op. 30, No. 6), measures 15–21
No. 37 (Op. 85, No. 1), measures 1–5

Mozart, Sonatas for Piano
G Major, K. 283, first movement, measures 1–10
A Major, K. 331, third movement, last 31 measures

Schumann, *Album for the Young,* Op. 68
No. 8, measures 1–8, 9–16
No. 11, measures 25–28
No. 19, measures 1–4

Additional examples will be found in the *Workbook* accompanying this text. Similar examples will be found in Arlin *et al, Music Sources* (Prentice-Hall, Inc., 1979), and in Murphy and Melcher, *Music for Study* (Prentice-Hall, Inc., 1960).

Melody Harmonization: Determinants of the Harmonic Background of a Melodic Line

Up to this point you have studied the harmonization of a melody in two ways.

1. At the keyboard, you have harmonized melodies from lead sheet symbols. Since the harmony was given, little or no attention to the function of the nonharmonic tones was necessary.

2. You have written harmonizations of melodies, below each note of which you supplied a chord, either I, IV, or V (i, iv, or V).

[2]Assignments in harmonic analysis in this text will be found in one or or more of these sources: Bach, *371 Chorales,* Beethoven, Sonatas for Piano (numbers 1–12 only), Chopin, Mazurkas, Mendelssohn, *Songs Without Words,* Mozart, Sonatas for Piano, and Schumann, *Album for the Young,* Op. 68.

The latter type of melody is actually not common in music literature, being limited almost solely to a portion of the church hymn repertoire. Most music, whether a melodic line or a full orchestral score, is a judicious combination of chord tones and nonharmonic tones. If one gives careful consideration to the following four factors, one can learn to recognize chord tones and non-chord tones in a melodic line, and to choose a chord progression that correlates satisfactorily with these melodic implications.

1. Chord Succession. Although any chord can precede or follow any other chord, investigation of music in the common practice style reveals that composers generally favor some progressions and shun others. Of the three chords studied thus far, only one of the possible combinations, V–IV, is used infrequently.

Common		*Less Common*
I–V	IV–I V–I	V–IV
I–IV	IV–V	

A review of melodies having lead sheet symbols in previous chapters will demonstrate the extensive use of all possibilities except V–IV. Therefore, in choosing chord progressions at this time, care should be taken to use V–IV only when no other possibility exists.

Fig. 11.41

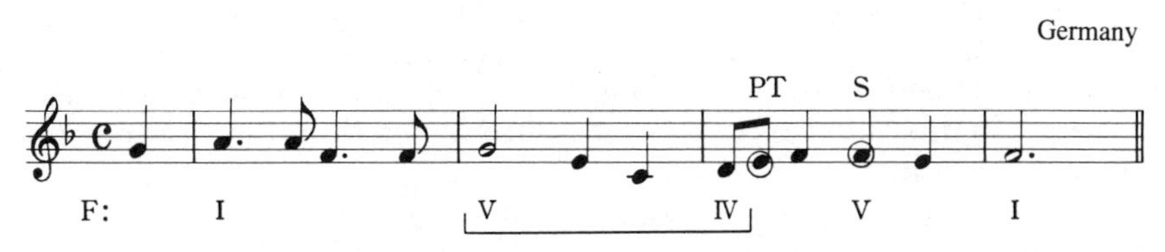

Occasionally, the fourth scale step in the melodic line will imply the seventh of a V^7 chord. In this case, it is only necessary to add a V triad to make a complete V^7 chord.

Fig. 11.42

A IV triad harmonization would be possible in the third full measure of the example above. Since both IV and V^7 are technically correct, the choice will be dictated by the individual student's musical taste.

Care should be taken that each phrase end with some form of cadence, authentic or plagal. In the following example, the end of the phrase could be harmonized with successive I triads, but this is unmusical because of the lack of a cadence.

Fig. 11.43

2. *Tempo.* As a rule of thumb, it can be said that ordinarily a new chord or a repetition of a previous chord will be placed at each principal beat in the measure, for example, two chords per measure in $\frac{2}{4}$ time, three chords per measure in $\frac{3}{4}$ time, two chords per measure in $\frac{6}{8}$ time, and so on. In a very slow tempo, more chords per measure may be needed, while in a very fast tempo, the call is for fewer chords per measure. In Figure 11.44 the melody to be harmonized has been given three different tempi markings to illustrate the effect on chord selection. If this melody is marked *very slow,* as in *a,* then the tempo is felt as six beats per measure, indicating the desirability of changing the chord on each of those beats where a change of melody note occurs. In the more common moderate tempo *b,* the chord changes are more likely to occur on the strong beats of the measure, in this case two beats per measure. When the tempo is rapid, one chord per measure often suffices, as in *c.*

Fig. 11.44

It cannot be specifically stated how slow or fast the tempo must be before determining how often a chord change is desirable. This can be determined only by careful study of the melody and applying one's own aesthetic judgment.

3. Use of Nonharmonic Tones. After determining the frequency of harmonic change, based on the chosen tempo, one factor determining chord choice will be the location of nonharmonic tones in the melody. More often than not, the strong beats in a melody will be part of a harmonic structure, whereas intervening notes will be other chord tones (including the seventh of V^7) or nonharmonic tones, as shown in Figures 11.42 and 11.44.

At times, however, a melody note on the beat will imply a nonharmonic tone, as in measures 6 and 7 of Figure 11.45.

Fig. 11.45

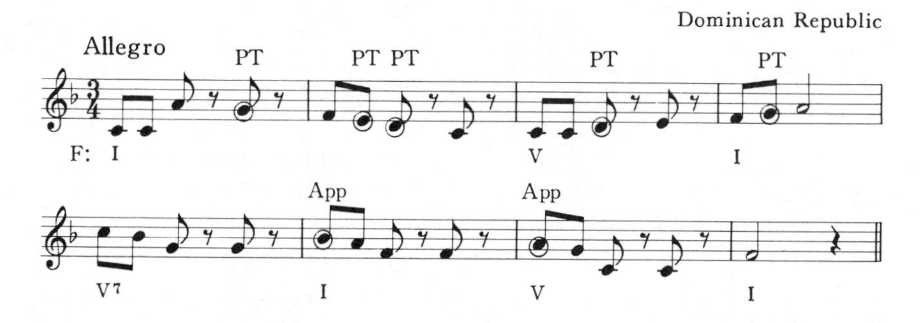

Should you attempt, in measures 5–8, to make the first beat of each measure a chord tone, the resulting progression would be V^7–IV–I–I, which includes the poor harmonic movement V–IV, and the progression I–I, which is where the V–I cadence should be (unless V were placed on the last C, which would be questionable at the tempo indicated).

Lastly, in some instances, a note on the beat may imply *either* an harmonic tone or a nonharmonic tone.

Fig. 11.46

4. *Harmonic Rhythm.* The rhythmic pattern established by the frequency of chord change is known as *harmonic rhythm.* In an example such as that in Figure 11.47, in which the harmony changes on each beat, its harmonic rhythm can be expressed by a series of like note values.

Fig. 11.47

It is also possible for music to cover several measures with no change of harmony at all, resting in an harmonic rhythm pattern of a single long-held note.

Fig. 11.48

These are extremes in the application of harmonic rhythm. More common are patterns in which the harmonic rhythm changes on successive measures or on successive strong beats,

Fig. 11.49

or in which the harmonic rhythm pattern is more irregular.

Fig. 11.50

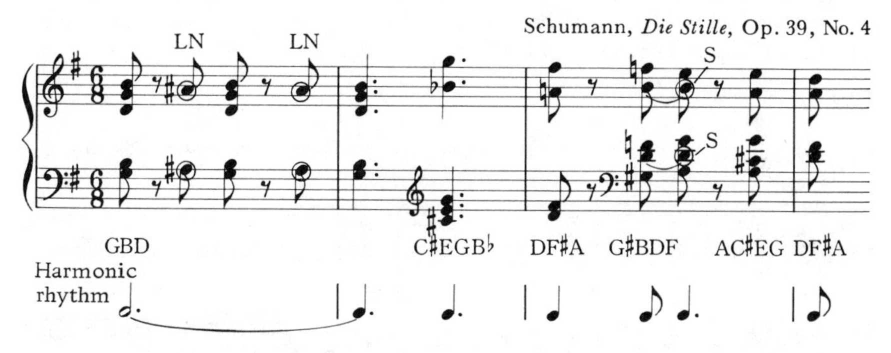

Typical harmonic rhythm patterns of the period show these characteristics:

1. Chords may be changed on any beat of the measure.
2. When a change of chord appears on a strong beat of the measure, it may extend into following beats.

3. When a change of chord appears on a weak beat of the measure, it should not be repeated on a following stronger beat. A new chord should appear on the following stronger beat.
4. When a change of bass note appears on the weak beat of a measure, this note is not repeated on the following strong beat.

Fig. 11.51

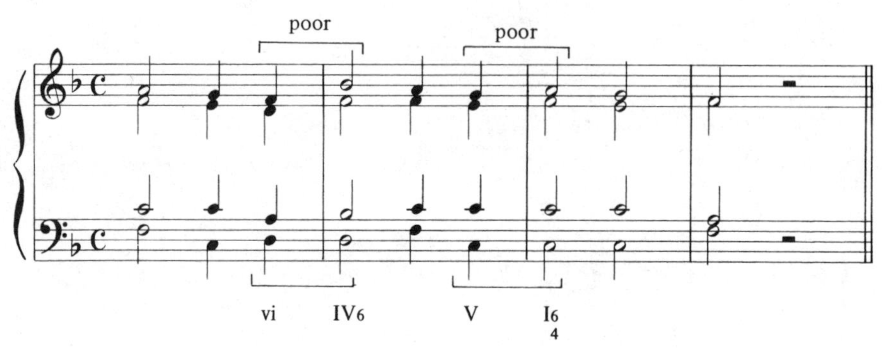

With the chords studied thus far, this situation can only occur in the progression V–I^6_4. Since the I^6_4 in Figure 11.51 functions as V with nonharmonic tones, there is actually no harmonic movement between these two chords, and therefore its rhythmic placement is ill chosen. The progression vi–IV_6 shows one of the many situations that can arise even when a greater variety of chord choice is available. Even though there is a change of harmony here, the harmonic rhythm is poor.

5. Exceptions to general principles of harmonic rhythm: *a*) The chord appearing on the opening weak beat of the piece or of a phrase may be repeated on the following strong beat (Figure 11.52a), or, no harmony at all may appear at these points (Figure 11.52b).

Fig. 11.52

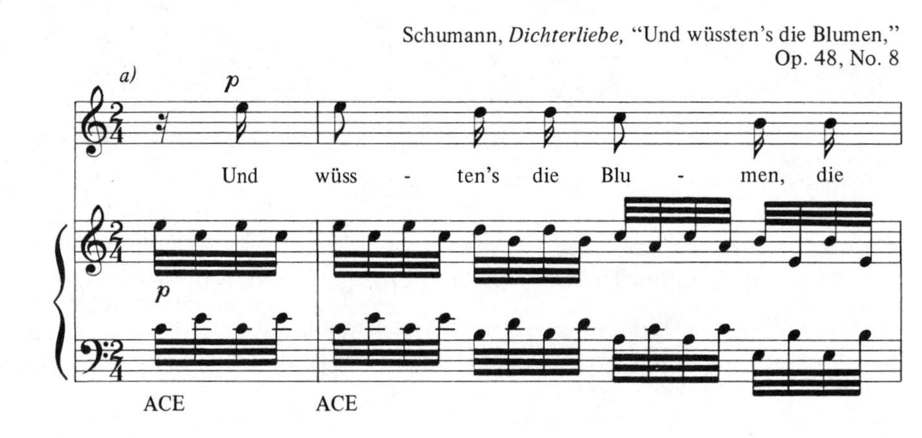

Schumann, *Dichterliebe,* "Und wüssten's die Blumen," Op. 48, No. 8

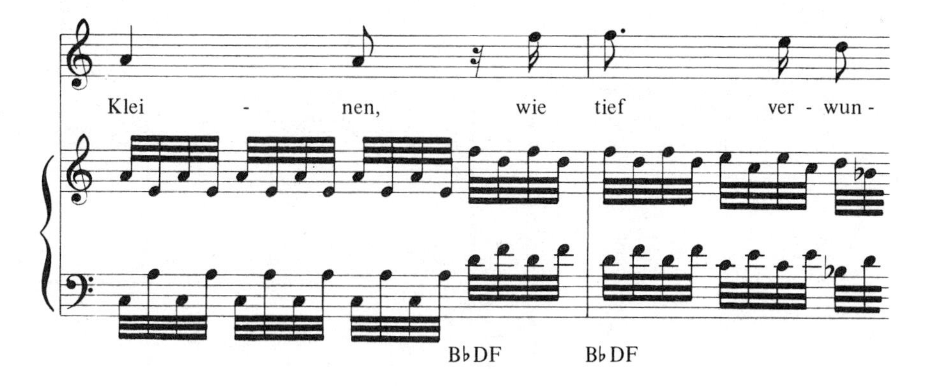

b) A new phrase or motive beginning on a strong beat may repeat the harmony of the previous weak beat.

Fig. 11.53

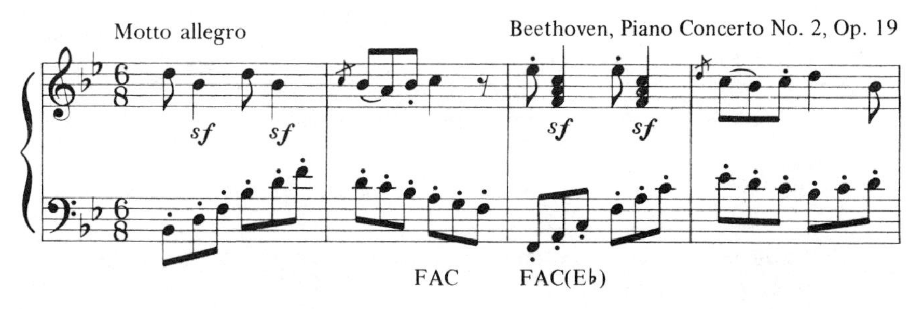

The following melody has been harmonized in two different ways to show the effect of both incorrect and correct applications of the principles of harmonic rhythm. Although the chord succession in both is satisfactory, observe how in harmonization *a* several chords appearing for the first time on weak beats are held over into strong beats, thus achieving an harmonic rhythm pattern that includes rhythm values tied over from weak to strong beats. This rhythmic effect, called *syncopation,*[3] is generally avoided in harmonic rhythm of the common practice style.

[3]Syncopation results when stress is placed on weak beats rather than on strong beats. This is often accomplished by accenting the weak beat or tying a weak beat into a strong beat.

Fig. 11.54

On rare occasions you may encounter a melody so constructed that an irregular harmonic rhythm pattern will offer the most acceptable harmonization.

Fig. 11.55

Assignment 11.5. Harmonic analysis of a melodic line. Follow these steps:
a) Copy out the melody.
b) Play or sing the melody and choose an appropriate tempo.
c) Locate each melodic cadence and supply it with a harmonic cadence.

d) Based on your choice of tempo, choose an harmonic progression that leads up to the cadence. Indicate the nonharmonic tones. Consider different possibilities when they're available. Here are four possible solutions for a single tune.

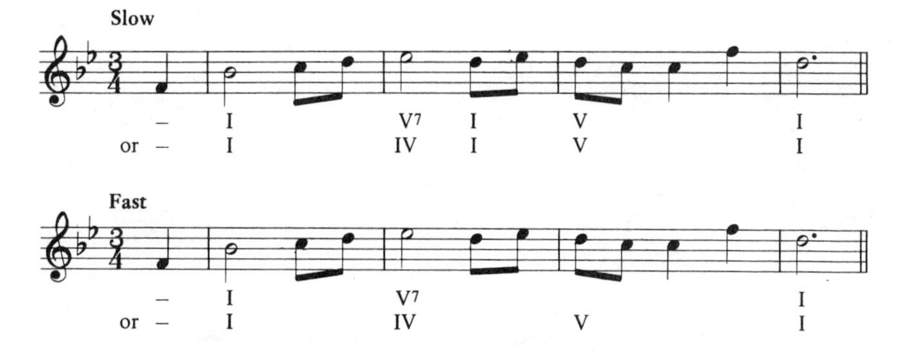

e) Correlate this assignment with Exercise 11.1 (page 255), playing the melodies at the keyboard. When alternate harmonizations are available, choose the one that you feel is the most effective musically.

Melodies are grouped in four categories.

Group I: Easy; tonic and dominant triads only.

In these additional melodies from sight singing texts, if the melody is in the bass clef or a C clef, copy it out in the treble clef.

Music for Sight Singing: melodies 15, 30, 32, 33, 55, 72, 93, 101, and 107.

More Music for Sight Singing: melodies 272, 274, 279, 303, 311, 320, 332, 335, and 339.

Group II: Easy; tonic, dominant, and subdominant triads.

Music for Sight Singing: melodies 126, 174, 193, 195, and 313.

More Music for Sight Singing: melodies 290, 313, 321, 330, 341, and 345.

Group III: Melodies slightly more difficult, using any or all of the tonic, dominant, and subdominant triads.

*The fourth scale step here can also be harmonized with V^7 (Group IV). Watch for this possibility in other melodies from groups II and III.

Music for Sight Singing: melodies 52, 57, 66, 70, 78, 90, 111, 147, 160, 165, 193, 195, 203, 327, and 330.

More Music for Sight Singing: melodies 278, 291, 294, 295, 299, 308, 314, 318, 322, 326, 336, and 365.

Group IV: Melodies in which a fourth scale step requires a V^7 chord, or is a choice equal to or better than IV.

Music for Sight Singing: melodies 2, 4, 5, 6, 17, 18, 31, 44, 56, 60, 90, 113, 115, 117, 118, 159, 167, 175, 198, 303, and 308.

More Music for Sight Singing: melodies 267, 269, 275, 284, 285, 287, 288, 292, 298, 316, 319, 324, 331, 340, 349, and 369.

Application

Written Materials

The principles and technqiues of writing nonharmonic tones will be found in later chapters: passing tones and neighboring tones, Chapter 13; suspensions, Chapter 15; and appoggiaturas and escaped tones, Chapter 16.

KEYBOARD HARMONY

Combining Analytical and Accompaniment Skills

The ability to analyze a melodic line as developed in this chapter and the skill in playing an accompaniment as developed in earlier chapters can now be combined so that a melody can be harmonized at the keyboard without using lead sheet symbols. The simultaneous application of these skills requires, of course, that you as performer be adequately prepared in the keyboard skills that have been previously presented. Particularly important is the ability to play the chord progression exercises accurately and without hesitation in all major and minor keys:

To review these exercises, see Exercise 4.5, page 91, playing authentic cadences; Exercise 8.6, page 175, playing plagal cadences; and Exercise 8.8, page 176, playing the progression I–IV–V–I or i–iv–V–i.

In all previous keyboard exercises involving single triads and triads in succession, you have been directed to play with three notes in the right and one in the left.[4] In so doing, you have been playing in close position, giving you maximum assurance that part-writing procedures will be correct, particularly since in keyboard playing, vocal range is not a consideration. Keyboard harmonization, then, simply amounts to playing chord progressions already known, but with a melody superimposed, as shown in Figure 11.56. Note that it is not necessary to repeat the

Fig. 11.56

[4]The use of two other methods of keyboard accompaniment is discouraged. In the first, block chords in root position are played in the left hand. Obviously, parallel fifths always result, and the concentration of pitches in a low register usually produces thick, muddy sounds.

In another common practice, the left hand plays a chord selected from the progression I–IV$^{6}_{4}$–V$^{6}_{5}$–I, producing the aural effect of the desired chord progression with a minimum of finger movement. This also produces all the undesirable musical effects described above, plus frequent doubled leading tones that usually resolve to tonic by parallel octaves, as well as frequent occurrences of other parallel octaves and fifths. While this procedure may suffice for amateurs or for avocational interest, professional musicians should be satisfied only with a performance that is technically correct and aesthetically pleasing, especially when this skill is to be used in the teaching of other persons. The methods of keyboard harmonization described in this chapter are admittedly a little more difficult than the two "short cut" methods described. But students who have practiced keyboard exercises in previous chapters to the point of playing with ease and accuracy should experience little difficulty in learning to harmonize a melody so that it sounds professionally competent and pleasing to the ear.

triad on every beat. The triad once played need not be repeated until a change of triad, though often, as in our figure, if a single triad lasts more than one measure, it may be repeated on the next downbeat. Use the sustaining pedal on the piano to keep the harmonic sound alive between actual playing of the triads.

Other styles of playing as shown in Figure 11.57 (*a* and *b*) may be attempted by those with more keyboard proficiency. The left hand accompaniment figure of *b* can be adapted to any meter scheme, as shown in *c*.

Fig. 11.57

It will often be found useful to harmonize a cadence with the tonic six-four chord, especially with a soprano line 3–2–1 or 1–7–1. The tonic six-four can be preceded by the tonic or subdominant triad, but should not be preceded by the dominant triad. It must appear on a strong beat of the measure, or may appear on the second beat in triple time, and is followed by the dominant triad. See Figure 11.58.

When playing a triad with an accented nonharmonic tone (review page 232), remember that the nonharmonic tone is temporarily replacing a harmonic tone, with the complete triadic harmony appearing on the following weak beat. In Figure 11.59 at the asterisk, the suspension G temporarily replaces the triad tone F♯. Therefore, play the triad tones D and A with the suspension G; when the G resolves to F♯ on the next beat, the complete D F♯ A triad appears. Measures two and three of this figure include similar examples.

Fig. 11.58

Fig. 11.59

Students working in pairs can practice keyboard harmonization and sight singing simultaneously. While one student sings the melody (or plays it on an instrument), the other will accompany him. In this procedure, the melody need not be played by the keyboard player; instead, he may divide the accompaniment figure between the two hands. A few such methods of accompaniment are shown in Figure 11.60.

Fig. 11.60

Exercise 11.1. Play melodies with accompaniments of tonic, dominant, and subdominant triads at the keyboard, using piano accompaniment styles as shown in Figures 11.56–60.

a) Practice melodies from Assignment 11.5 for which you have already provided an analysis, beginning with the easy melodies of Group I, page 249, and continuing with Group II, page 249, Group III, page 250, and Group IV, page 251.

b) Play melodies from Exercise 4.7, page 93, and Exercise 8.7, page 175, in which you have already harmonized the cadences.

c) Play melodies from *Music for Sight Singing* and/or *More Music for Sight Singing*, as listed in Groups I, II, III, and IV for Assignment 11.5, pages 249–51. When any of these melodies appears in the bass clef or one of the C clefs, transpose it one octave higher and play it as though it were in the treble clef.

CHAPTER 12

Secondary Triads
Principles of Chord Progression
The Diminished Triad
The Leading Tone Triad

Theory and Analysis

The Secondary Triads

The secondary triads in a key are those built on scale steps other than I, IV, and V. In a major key, these triads are:

Fig. 12.1

In a minor key, alternate forms of the triads appear because of the use of different forms of the minor scale.

Fig. 12.2

Note that in minor the roots of the two submediant triads (VI and vi°) are on different scale steps (lowered sixth and raised sixth). The same is true of VII and vii° (lowered seventh and raised seventh scale steps). In each of these cases, the triad number indicates the scale step on which the triad is built.

VI always refers to a triad built on the lowered sixth scale step.
vi° always refers to a triad built on the raised sixth scale step.
VII always refers to a triad built on the lowered seventh scale step.
vii° always refers to a triad built on the raised seventh scale step.

Other chord spellings are infrequently found on these scale steps (for example, A C♯ E or B♭ D♭ F in C minor), and any exceptions will be noted as encountered.

Principles of Harmonic Progression[1]

In studying the three principal triads (I, IV, V), there has been little difficulty in determining the progression of one triad to the next. We found that both the dominant and subdominant triads can progress directly to the tonic of the key, the goal of the harmonic progression, and the tonic, in turn, may progress to either. The subdominant also progresses easily to the dominant; only the reverse of this progression was found to be infrequently used.

With the addition of the secondary triads, making a total of seven diatonic triads, we find it theoretically possible for any one triad to progress to any one of six other triads. It might seem that we should be at liberty to follow any triad by any other triad. But before making such an assumption, we should ask, "Are there any restrictions governing the choice of chord succession?" If we should attempt to answer this question by looking in composed music for an example of each possible chord progression, the answer would be "No," since diligent search would certainly and eventually reveal an example of any possible succession of two chords. But by the time we had located every possible chord progression, we would have noted that certain chord progressions appear over and over again, while others appear infrequently or rarely. Composers have not chosen to utilize all possible chord progressions equally; an understanding of the style of the commom practice period is dependent in part on knowledge of the relative frequency of use of the various and numerous chord progressions available, and the reasons for variance in frequency.

Progression of chords, one to another, is always described in terms of root movements, that is, the intervallic distance between the roots of the two successive chords in question, regardless of the actual bass notes (inversions) used.[2] These intervallic distances can only be three: the fifth, the third, and the second. The fourth, the sixth, and the seventh are merely the inversions of these (a root movement *C* up to *G*, a fifth, is the same as a root movement *C* down to *G*, a fourth), while progression by the same root note or its octave is static.

Root movement *down by fifth* accounts for a large percentage and often a majority of the chord progressions in the music of most composers. This is the movement of the authentic cadence (V–I), which is so effective in establishing a sense of key. It has been surmised by many theoreticians that the basic quality of the downward fifth lies in its relationship to the first interval (other than the octave) in the overtone series:[3] a fifth, 3 down to 2.

[1]This survey treats the subject of triads to be studied in this and following chapters. It should be reviewed periodically during the remainder of the course.

[2]Review the article "The Theory of Inversion" in Chapter 9.

[3]Review Appendix 3, "Elementary Acoustics."

Starting with this root movement (downward fifth), we will list all possible root movements to discover what chord progressions occur in each type of movement. In each series, a bracket indicates those progressions most commonly found in music literature. (Chord numbers for major keys are used in this discussion and in Table 12.1, but refer equally to minor keys unless otherwise noted. Diminished triads are usually found in first inversion: vii°_{6} and ii°_{6}.)

Progressing *down by fifth* (up by fourth) produces the series:

I—IV—vii°—iii—vi—ii V—I (in minor VII–III)

Progressing *up by fifth* (down by fourth) produces another series:

I—V—ii—vi—iii—vii°—IV—I

Progressing *down by second* produces the series:

I—vii°—vi—V—IV—iii—ii—I (iii–ii_6 only)

while progressing *up by seconds* produces:

I—ii—iii—IV—V—vi—vii°—I

The series produced in progressing *down by thirds* is

I—vi—IV—ii—vii°—V—iii—I

and *up by thirds* is

I—iii—V—vii°—ii—IV—vi—I

Codifying the above information, we find that

1. I (tonic) can progress to any other triad. It may also interrupt any common progression, e.g., vi–I–IV.
2. Any triad, except vii°, may progress to V.
3. Placing the remaining progressions in the following diagram shows that, once sounded, a chord usually gravitates towards tonic, from left to right in the diagram. The four exceptions to this movement are shown beneath the diagram.

Major:		iii →	vi →	ii or IV →	V or vii° →	I
Minor:	VII →	III →	VI →	ii° or iv →	V or vii° →	i

Others (major and minor): V–vi, iii–ii_6, iii–IV, vi–iii–IV

For your reference, Table 12.1 lists the common progressions from any given chord. With few exceptions it is valid for seventh chords and altered chords, as well as triads.

TABLE 12.1 THE COMMONLY USED CHORD PROGRESSIONS

	Chord Progression
I	I may progress to any other chord. Any chord may progress to I when I interrupts a progression listed in this table (e.g., ii—I—V).
ii	May progress to V or vii°
iii	May progress to ii6, IV, V, or vi.
IV	May progress to I, ii, V, or vii°
V	May progress to I or vi.
vi	May progress to ii, IV, or V; also, vi—iii—IV.
vii°	May progress to I; in minor, VII—III.

Other Common Progressions

There are three additional cateogries of harmonic progression. In these, the progression standing alone is infrequently used, but in special situations it can be considered equally deserving of use as any common progression.

1. First Inversions in Succession When a bass line moves by step and each note is the third of a chord, any resulting succession of chords is acceptable.

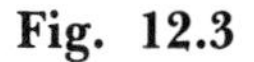

2. *Harmonic Sequence.* A harmonic sequence is a series of chords with a regularly recurring pattern of root movements, a series in which any resulting pair of triads or chords is acceptable. The pattern is usually described by the intervals of the root movement, for example, down a fifth, up a fourth, down a fifth, and so on, as shown in the root pattern of Fig. 12.4:

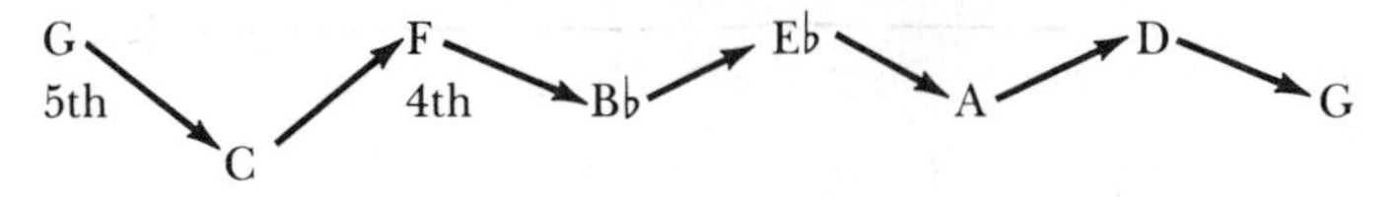

Fig. 12.4

Any other regular pattern of root movements can be used, such as third down, second up, third down, etc. or, as in Figure 12.5, the pattern fourth down and fifth up, I–V–ii–VI, the latter chord being altered.

3. *Chromatic Bass Line.* When the bass line ascends or descends by a series of half steps, any chord succession resulting is usually satisfactory. Further discussion and illustration of this type of chord movement will be presented during the study of altered chords in *Advanced Harmony.*

A survey such as this serves merely to show all the possibilities from which a composer may choose and to provide a source for a list of those progressions that composers from the seventeenth through the nineteenth centuries used with any degree of frequency. At the present time, our study of harmony will concern itself principally with those progressions indicated in Table 12.1 as commonly used progressions, while study of the remainder will be considered in later chapters and in *Advanced Harmony.*

By restricting yourself at present to these progressions, you will be able to make immediate and effective use of harmonic materials with a minimum chance of error in chord choice, whether it be in melody harmonization at the keyboard or on paper or in original composition. Knowledge of the commonly used progressions will be found valuable in taking harmonic dictation; knowing what to

Fig. 12.5

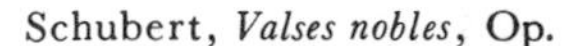

Schubert, *Valses nobles*, Op.

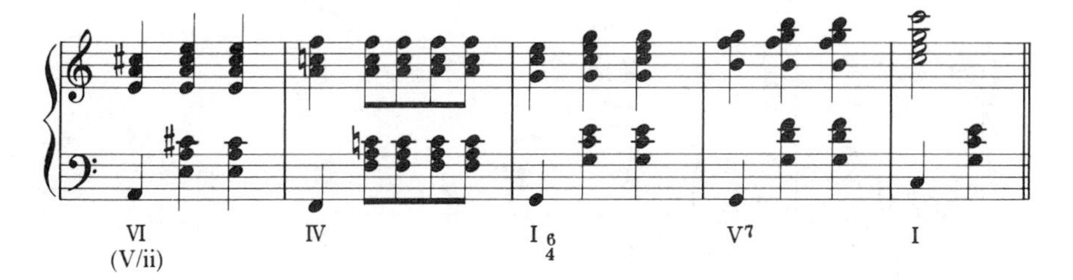

listen for and what to expect next after a given chord will be found most helpful in developing your harmonic listening ability. A complete understanding of this and following chapters will be made easier and clearer if Table 12.1 is memorized now.

The Diminished Triad

The diminished triad is composed of two minor thirds. The resulting distance between the root and the fifth of the diminished triad is the interval of a diminished fifth (one half step smaller than a perfect fifth); the interval of the diminished fifth, when inverted, becomes an augmented fourth.

Fig. 12.6

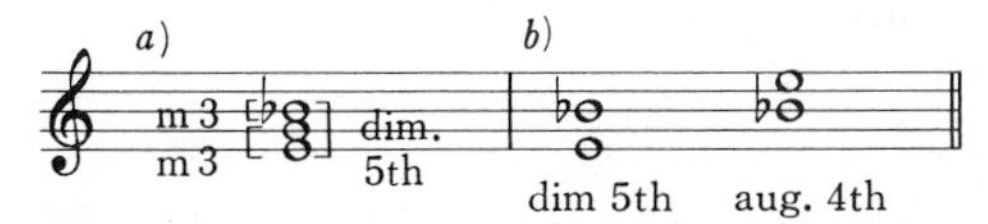

Because of the interval of the diminished fifth, the diminished triad is classified as one of the dissonant triads.[4] Both the interval of the diminished fifth and its inversion, the augmented fourth, are known commonly as a tritone, referring to the fact that the interval is composed of three whole steps (six half steps). The interval equally divides the octave.

[4]Consonant triads are defined (in the historical period under study) as those containing consonant intervals: the octave, perfect fifth, perfect fourth, major and minor thirds, major and minor sixths. Triads or chords containing other intervals are dissonant.

Fig. 12.7

The diminished triad is most frequently used in first inversion. Typical examples of its use are seen in Figures 12.8 and 12.9.

Fig. 12.8

Bach, *O Welt, sieh hier dein Leben* (#117)

Fig. 12.9

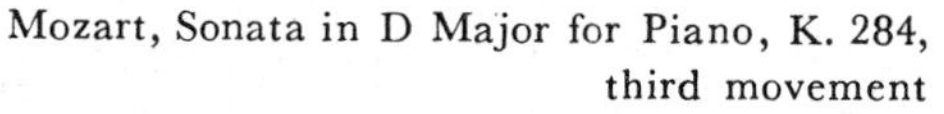

Mozart, Sonata in D Major for Piano, K. 284, third movement

The diminished triad, either vii° or ii°, may appear with its root in the bass when it occurs during the course of a harmonic sequence, as shown in Figure 12.4, where the ii° triad is seen with its root in the bass.

The Leading Tone Triad

The triad on the leading tone is a diminished triad in both major and minor keys. Its symbol is vii°, and it is ordinarily found in first inversion, vii°_{6}, as in Figure 12.8.

Assignment 12.1. Spell the vii° triad in each major and minor key.

The vii° triad bears a striking resemblance, both in sight and sound, to the V^7 chord. The vii° triad looks like the upper three notes of the V^7 chord and is often symbolized as $V^7_{\circ}$, meaning a V^7 with its root missing (in C: $V^7_{\circ}$ = B D F; V^7 = G B D F). There is, however, a major difference between these two chords. In

Fig. 12.10

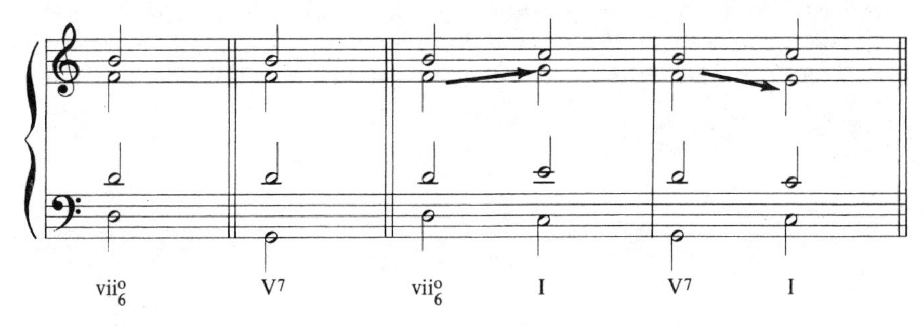

progressing to the tonic, the seventh of V^7 always resolves down. In the vii° triad, the fifth (which would be the seventh of the V^7 or $V^7_{\circ}$) always resolves up.

In progressing to the tonic, the vii° triad has the aural effect of a dominant chord, and for this reason can be freely used in place of V in this situation. Two specific placements of vii° far outnumber the other remaining possibilities:

1. Between the tonic triad and its first inversion (Figure 12.11) or reverse (Figure 12.14).

Fig. 12.11

2. In the progression IV–vii°6.

Fig. 12.12

Examples *a* and *b* in Figure 12.12 and Figure 12.8 show the vii$^{\circ}_{6}$ used after IV when the melody ascends stepwise. This is a very common harmonization of the ascending sixth and seventh scale steps. Were the progression IV–V used, parallels could easily result. In the same progression in a minor key, the raised sixth scale step requires a major subdominant triad (IV, instead of iv).

Fig. 12.13

Assignment 12.2. Harmonic analysis. Make an harmonic analysis of these excerpts from pre-Bach chorales. Describe the use of each leading tone triad. Also, see examples in the workbook.

Johann Crüger, *Herr, ich habe misgehandelt* (1649)

Assignment 12.3. Harmonic analysis. In each of the first phrases from the following Bach chorales, locate the vii°6 triad and describe its use: 3, 26, 42, 103, 111, 145, 167, 171, and 183.

Application

Written Materials

Writing the Diminished Triad

Only the use of the first inversion of the diminished triad will be considered at this time. Root position is used in harmonic sequence (see the ii° in Figure 12.4). Use of second inversion is very rare.

The common voice distribution for any diminished triad in first inversion is two thirds, one root and one fifth (bass note doubled), except that when the triad is found with the fifth in the soprano, the fifth is usually doubled (two fifths, one root, one third).

Fig. 12.14

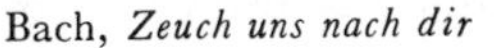

Bach, *Zeuch uns nach dir*

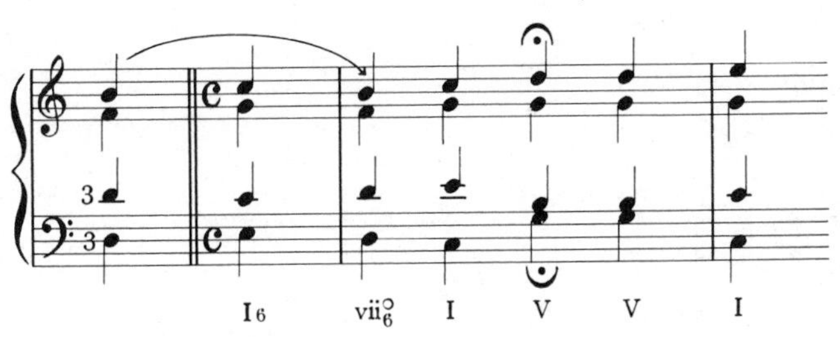

Fig. 12.15

Assignment 12.4. Writing diminished triads. Double the third when the root or third is in the soprano; double the fifth an octave lower when the fifth is in the soprano.

Writing the Leading Tone Triad

1. Use of Rule 6A. Since the leading tone triad is usually found in first inversion, use Part-Writing Rule 6A: *Approach and resolve each doubled tone by contrary or oblique motion.* Each example of the vii°6 in this chapter shows application of this procedure.

Fig. 12.16 (See next page)

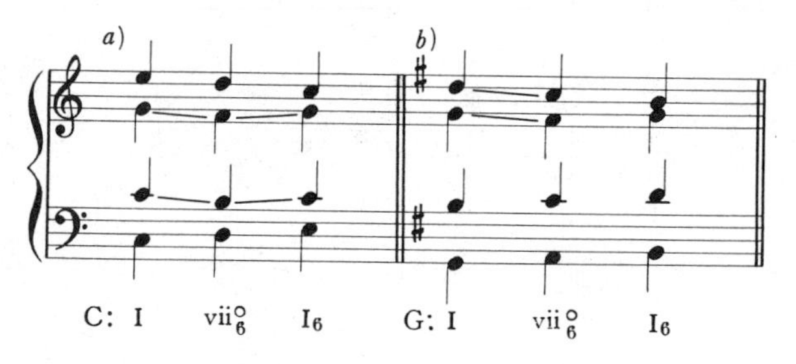

2. *Unequal Fifths.* This term describes a diminished fifth preceded or followed by a perfect fifth in the same pair of voices. The visual effect is that of parallel fifths, but as these are unequal in size they are perfectly acceptable. (See Figure 12.16)

3. *vii°₆ with the fifth in the soprano.* As a soprano tone, the fifth of the vii°₆ triad (or any diminished triad) normally descends, as in Figure 12.15. It may progress upwards when found in a melody line moving in similar motion with the bass at the interval of a tenth (an octave plus a third).

Fig. 12.17

Bach, *Vater unser im Himmelreich* (#47)

Assignment 12.5. Part-writing. Fill in alto and tenor voices. Be particularly careful of the approach and resolution of all doubled notes in triads in first inversion. As usual, write in triad numbers below the bass part.

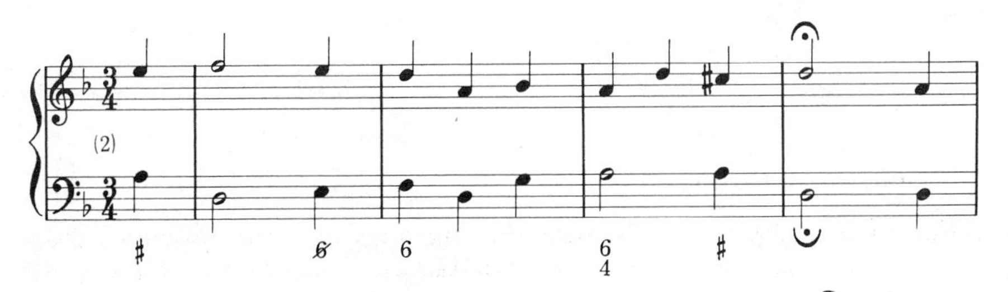

Assignment 12.6. Part-writing, bass line only given. Supply the melody line and fill in alto and tenor parts.

Assignment 12.7. Write in four voices the following progressions.

a) D Major	$\frac{3}{4}$V | I_6 vii^{o}_{6} I | IV_6 I^{6}_{4} V | I ||
b) G♭ Major	$\frac{4}{4}$I | IV vii^{o}_{6} I I_6 | IV V I |
c) G minor	$\frac{2}{4}$V | i i_6 | vii^{o}_{6} i | iv V | i ||
d) B♭ minor	$\frac{4}{4}$V | i i IV* vii^{o}_{6} | i iv i^{6}_{4}V | i ||

Melody Harmonization

The Triad in Inversion. In harmonizing melodies from previous chapters, we have always placed the root of the triad in the bass. The result has usually been a series of large skips in the bass voice. Though it is more acceptable to have such skips in the bass than in the other voices, it is preferable that the bass line be made more melodic, either by reducing the number of large leaps or the size of these leaps. This can be accomplished by the use of triads in inversion. Compare the bass lines of the two examples below, the first of which is a Bach chorale and the second the same harmonization with the root of each chord in the bass part.

*Third or fifth of triad in soprano.

Fig. 12.18

When harmonizing a melody, the triad to be used for each melody note should be chosen first. With the use of inversions, it now becomes necessary to decide which triads will be in inversion and which will have the root in the bass, and therefore the complete bass line should be written *before* the alto and tenor lines. The soprano and bass together should make a good two-part composition.

When the bass line moves with the soprano, their related movements can be in any one of four directions:

1.) *contrary motion* to each other

2.) *oblique motion*—soprano stays on same tone while bass moves, or soprano moves while bass maintains the same tone

3.) *similar motion* to each other

4.) *stationary motion*—both soprano and bass repeat their tones.

Fig. 12.19

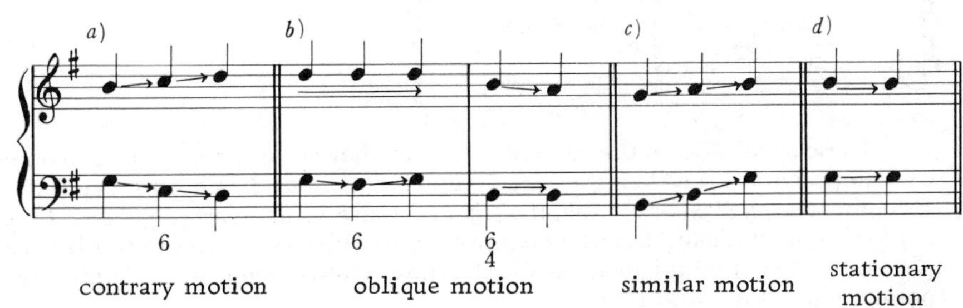

By extracting the soprano and bass only from Figure 12.18 we can find the following types of motion.

Fig. 12.20

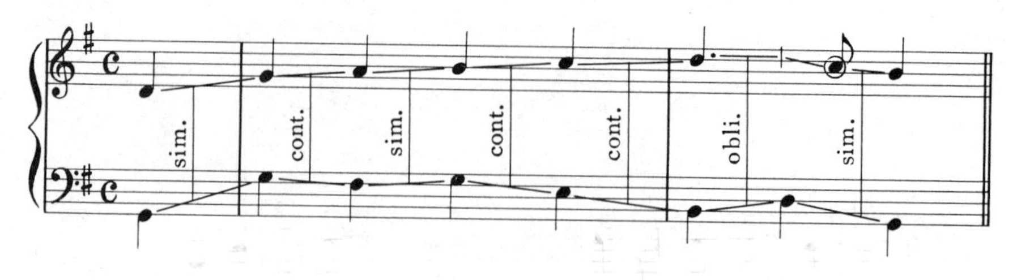

Of the four types of motion, contrary and oblique are the most frequently used, although similar motion is good when found as intervals of thirds or sixths between soprano and bass[5] (See Figures 12.18 and 12.20, the progression from the third to fourth chord.) Inversions should be chosen to make the bass line progress more by intervals of seconds and thirds than by larger leaps. Note, however, that cadences are usually more effective when their triads have roots in the bass. For the present, the first inversion only will be used, except that the I^6_4 may be used at a cadence.

By following the preceding directions, several possible bass lines can be found to fit a given melody, final choice to be dictated by musical taste. The following examples show how each of two melodies could be harmonized in a number of different ways.

[5]At this point, consideration should be given to the "hidden octave" and the "hidden fifth" (sometimes called "direct octave" and "direct fifth"). A hidden octave occurs when two voices progress in similar motion to a perfect octave; a hidden fifth occurs when two voices progress in similar motion to a perfect fifth.

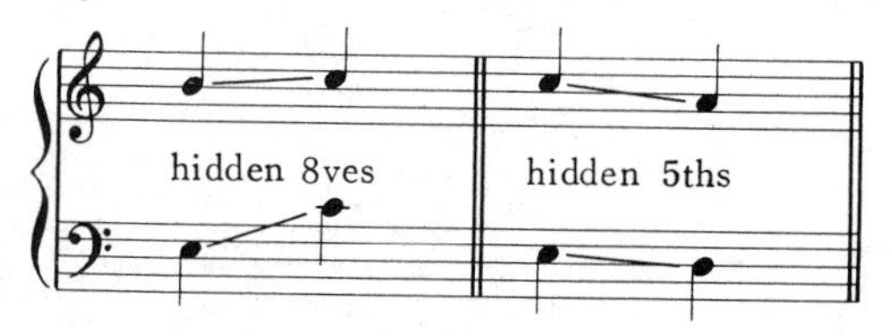

These need concern the student *only* when they occur between the two outer voices of a composition. Even then they are acceptable when *a*) the chord is repeated (Figure 12.20, first two chords) or *b*) when the triad roots are a fifth apart (Figure 12.14, progression I–V at the fermata). In other circumstances hidden octaves and fifths between outer voices often do not sound good. Any such octave or fifth should be used only after careful consideration of its aural effect.

Fig. 12.21

a) all roots

b)

c)

d)

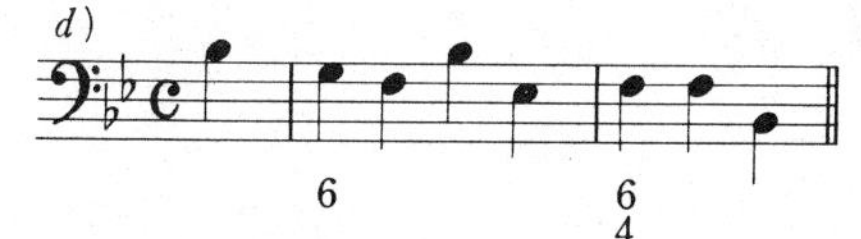

e)

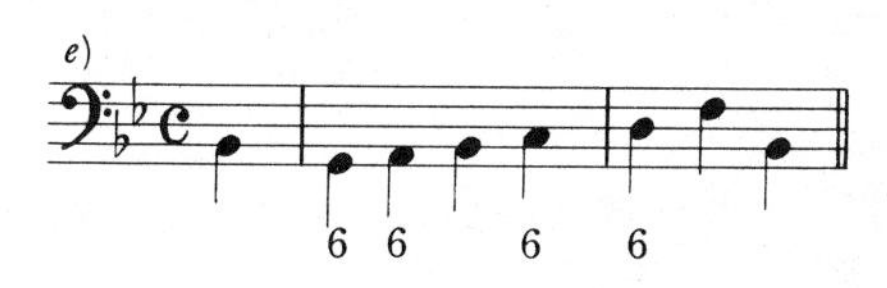

Fig. 12.22

a) all roots

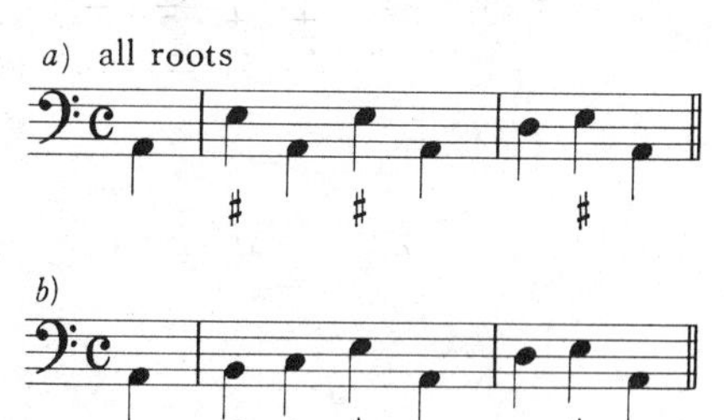

b)

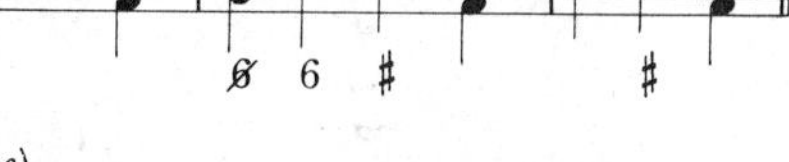

c)

d)

e)

Assignment 12.8. Melody harmonization. Supply harmony and three lower voice parts when melody only is given. As this is a problem in diminished triads, use the vii°_{6} triad wherever practicable.

Assignment 12.9. Write original exercises using the four triads studied to date. Write four-measure phrases or periods, as assigned. Write for voices or instruments, as assigned. Pay particular attention to *a*) chord choice, *b*) harmonic rhythm, *c*) melodic writing, and *d*) the bass line. In addition, indicate the tempo of your composition and include dynamic markings.

Ear Training and Music Reading

The Diminished Triad

Exercise 12.1. Singing diminished triads. From a given pitch, sing a diminished triad, calling the given pitch 1, 3, or 5, as directed, or sing with pitch names when the name of the given pitch is supplied.

Fig. 12.23

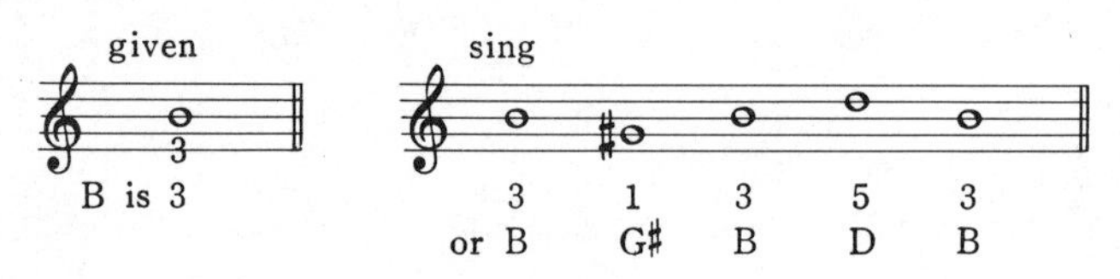

Exercise 12.2. Identifying the soprano when the diminished triad is played. For this ear training exercise, the diminished triad will be played in first inversion only. Follow this procedure:

a) Listen to the triad.

b) Sing the triad from root, bearing in mind that the bass tone heard is always "3."

c) Sing the soprano note.

d) Identify the soprano note as 1, 3, or 5.

e) Spell the triad when the name of the soprano note is given.

Exercise 12.3. Identifying the tritone by ear. Since the diminished fifth and the augmented fourth are exactly the same size, it is impossible to differentiate between them unless a chord is sounded at the same time.

Fig. 12.24

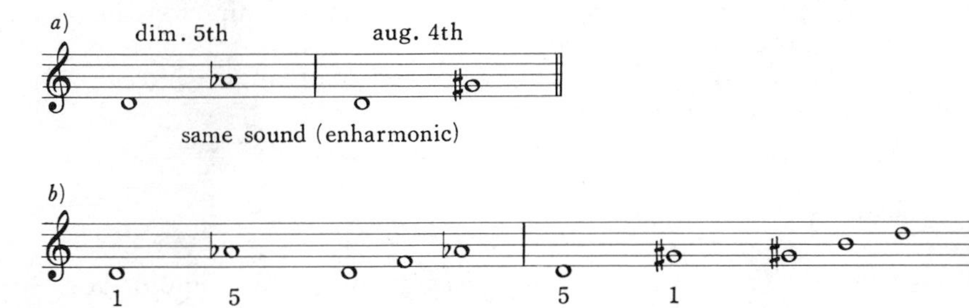

Procedure:

a) Listen to the interval; listen to the triad played in first inversion, from which the interval is taken.

b) Sing the triad from the root, singing 1–3–5–3–1.

c) Sing the interval using correct numbers.

d) Identify the interval by name; if the numbers are 1 up to 5 or 5 down to 1, it is a diminished fifth; if the numbers are 5 up to 1 or 1 down to 5, it is an augmented fourth.

Fig. 12.25.

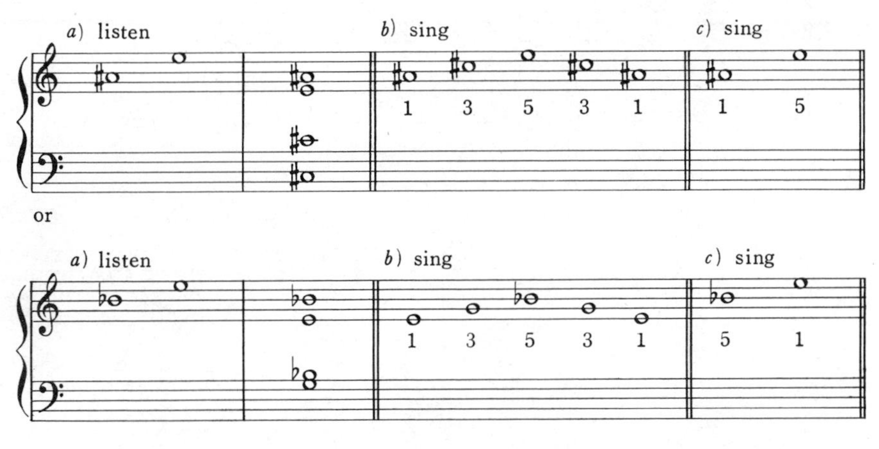

Spell the interval or write it on the staff when the name of the first note is given.

The Leading Tone Triad

Exercise 12.4. *a*) Singing the leading tone triad. In the given key (major or minor) sing the progression I–vii°–I or i–vii°–i. Sing each triad from its root with the letter names.

b) Sing the progression I–IV–vii°–I or i–IV–vii°–i in the given key.

Exercise 12.5. Harmonic dictation. The vii° can easily be identified, because it is a diminished triad and generally progresses directly to the tonic triad. Any or all of the following steps will be helpful in distinguishing the various triads studied thus far.

a) After listening to dictation exercise, write down the *type* of each triad, using the symbol *M* for major, *m* for minor, and *d* for diminished.

b) Sing with scale numbers or with letter names as directed, the root of each triad as the progression is played.

c) Sing each triad with the numbers 1–3–5, or sing each triad with correct spelling in the given key, as directed.

Keyboard Harmony

Exercise 12.6. Play these cadences in any major or minor key.

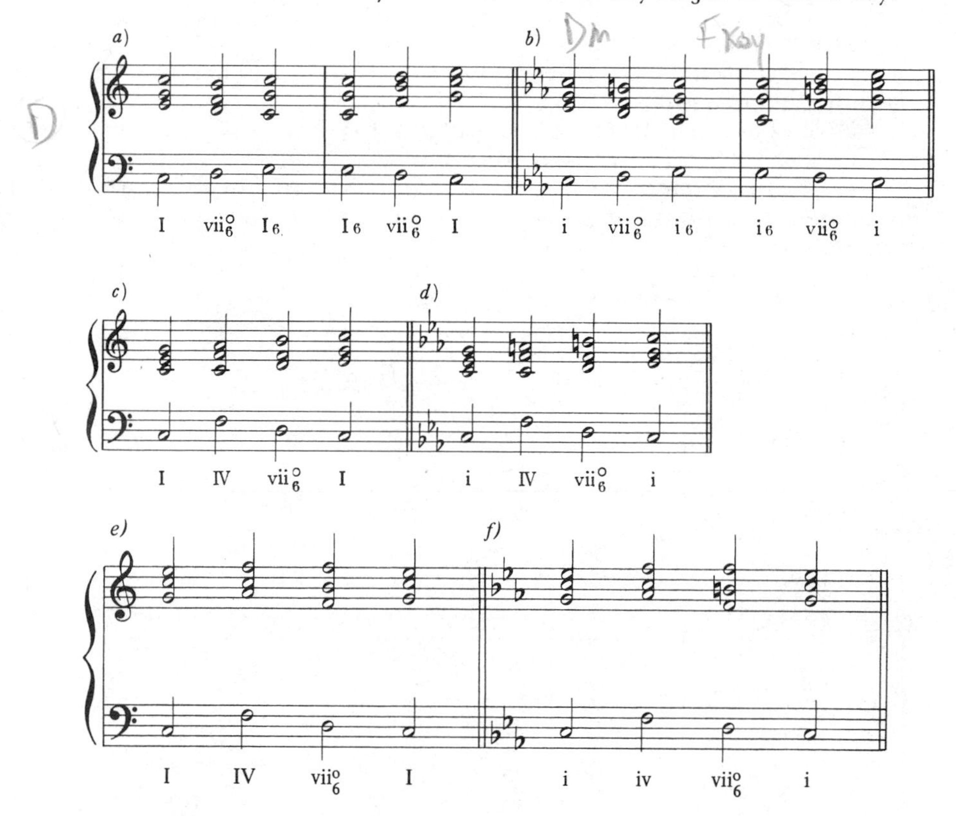

Exercise 12.7. Play the examples from Assignments 12.5 and 12.8 at the keyboard.

The Devil in Music

This uncomplimentary term (from the Latin *Diabolus in musica*) was applied in Medieval times (*c.* 1200) to the interval of the tritone. Composers and writers in music theory found it a difficult interval to understand or to use. Although it equally divides the octave (see Figures 12.6 and 12.24) in doing so it causes two different intervals to appear, each made up of the same number of scale steps (three whole steps). These intervals, the diminished fifth and the augmented fourth, lack the stability of the commonly used consonances: the octave, fifth, and the thirds and sixths. As a consequence, their use in music was severely limited until the seventeenth century. Any melodic use was forbidden, either as a direct skip (*a*) or as the outward limit of a series of notes in one direction (*b*).

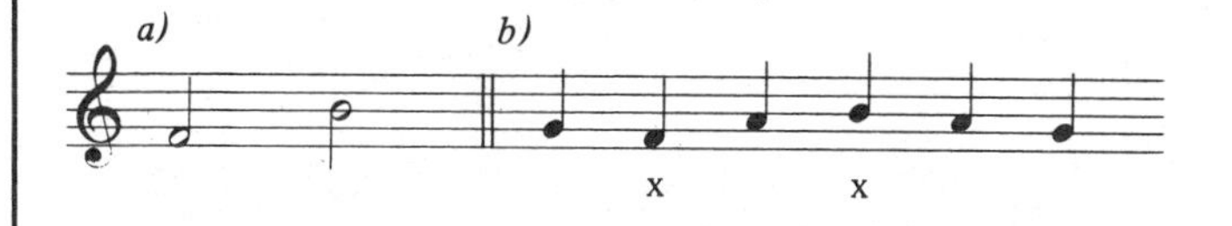

Harmonically, a tritone could appear between any two upper voices in music written for three or more voices. At that time, the consonance or dissonance of a vertical structure was determined by the consonance or dissonance of each upper note in relation to the lowest sounding note. At the asterisk in the following example, we find what looks like the first inversion of the G♯ B D (diminished) triad. In pre-seventeenth century terms, this sonority consists of a sixth above the bass (B up to G♯) and a third above the bass (B up to D). Both intervals are consonant, and therefore the vertical sonority is consonant. The resulting augmented fourth (D up to G♯) was not considered in this process.

Palestrina, *Missa, Spem in alium*

Restrictions against the tritone began to disappear in the seventeenth century, when the tritone emerged as a harmonic interval in its own right, even when found above the lowest sounding note.

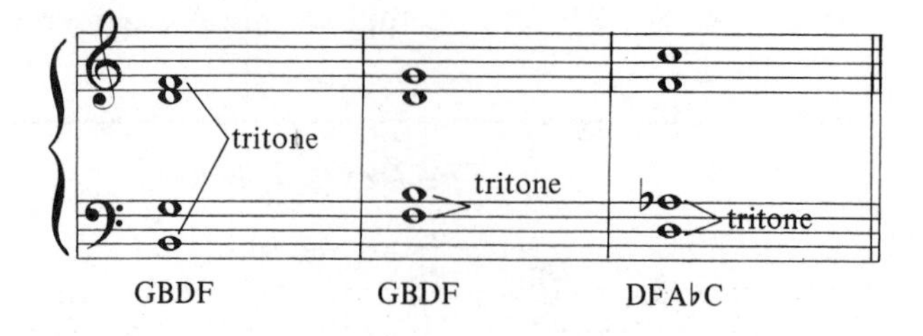

The tritone is particularly important in the dominant seventh chord, where the resolution of the tritone positively establishes a feeling of key.

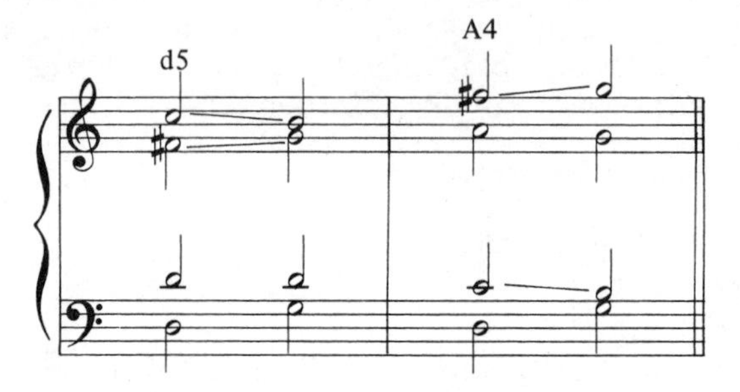

Made up of tritones, the diminished seventh chord became one of the most characteristic sounds of nineteenth century music. When inverted, the chord continues to produce tritones, a property not exhibited by any other chord. The sound of these simultaneous tritones tends to destroy the feeling of tonality, especially when they are sounded at length or follow each other in succession.

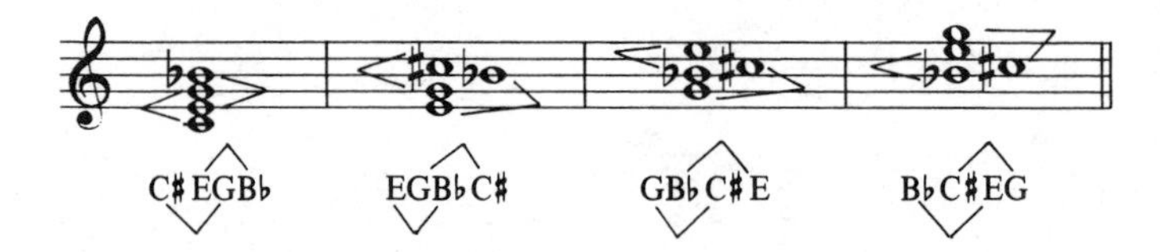

The ambiguity of the tritone in its diminished fifth–augmented fourth relationship (same sound, different spelling) was often capitalized upon by nineteenth century composers. In the following example, the sustained tritone C–F♯, is first part of a D F♯ A C chord, then as an implied C–G♭, part of the A♭ C E♭ G♭ chord. (Since the tritone is tied throughout the passage, it is obvious that the composer, for performance reasons, has not changed the F♯ to G♭. The interval in parentheses shows the actual harmonic spelling.)

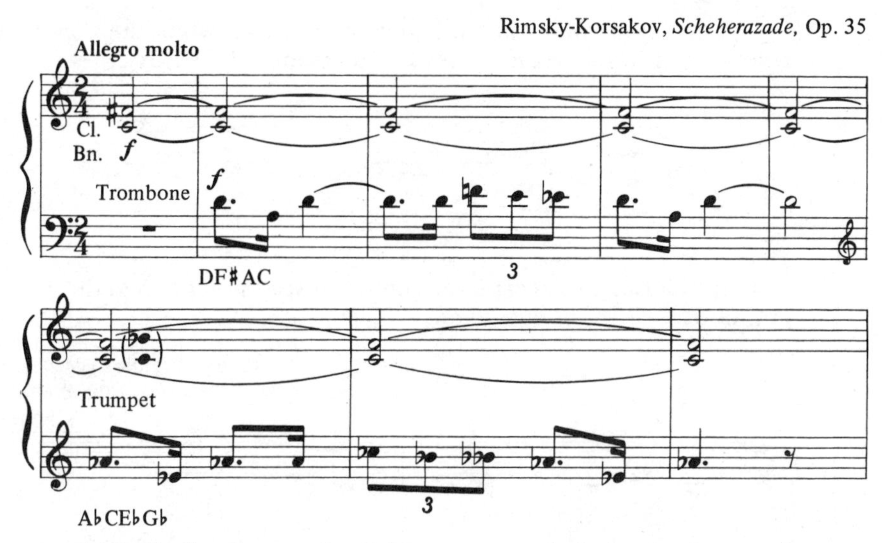

Melodically, the music of the seventeenth through nineteenth centuries shows no restriction in the use of the diminished fifth, since after the leap it is possible to change direction in accordance with the strong tendency of each tone.

On the other hand, the melodic augmented fourth was infrequently used. After making the leap, the second note of the interval wants to continue in the same direction.

Twentieth century music, in its quest for means to avoid the strong sense of tonic pervading music of previous eras, makes frequent use of the tritone. The opening of the following example shows the augmented fourth as the outer limtis of the melody (C♯–G).

The whole tone scale, which contains seven whole steps and has four tritones within its octave, is new to the twentieth century.

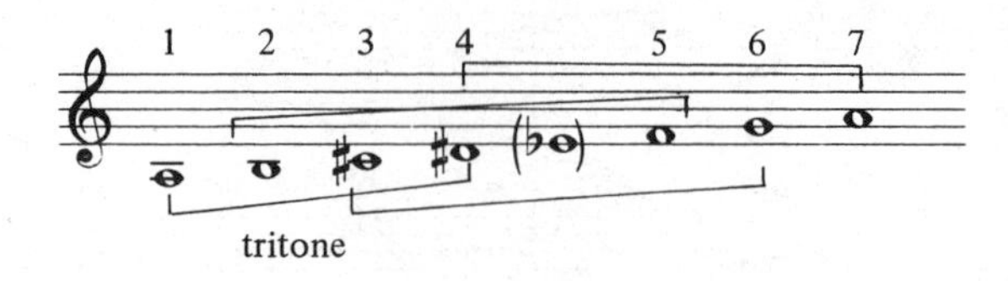

In the Bartók excerpt, the composer uses notes 1–5 in the right hand, and notes 3–7 in the left hand.

Bartók, *Hagsorok egeszhangokbol (Whole-tone Scale),* from *Mikrokosmos*

We will conclude with an example of an extended use of the augmented fourth, one of the many current uses of this interval.

Britten, *War Requiem,* Op. 66

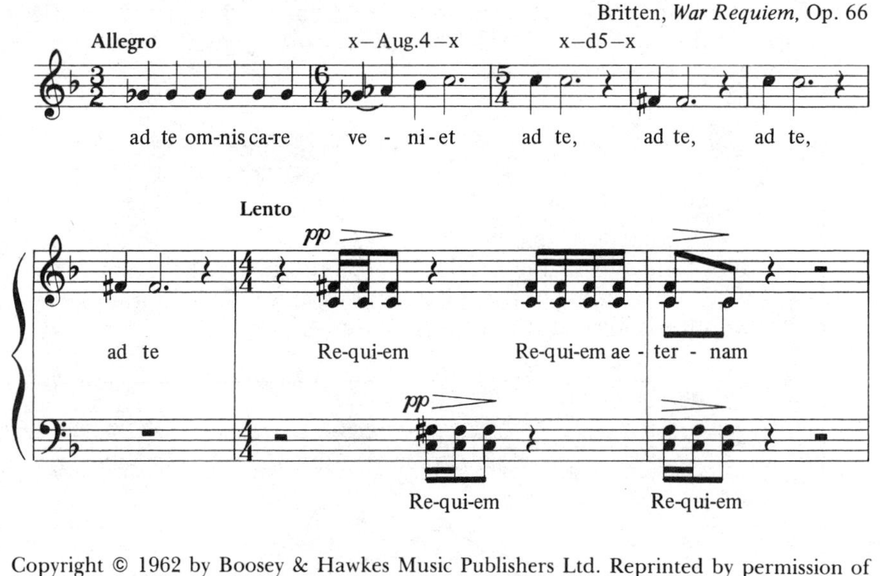

CHAPTER 13

The Supertonic Triad

Theory and Analysis

The supertonic triad has much in common with the subdominant triad: IV and ii have two tones in common (C: IV = FAC; ii = DFA), and both commonly progress to one of the dominant chords, V, $I_{6 \atop 4}$ or vii°. For this reason, the supertonic chords are said to be chords of subdominant function. As the chord leading to the V–I cadence, the supertonic actually shows a greater frequency of usage than the subdominant.

In a major key, the supertonic triad is a minor triad (ii). In a minor key it is a diminished triad (ii°) or a minor triad (ii) when used in conjunction with the melodic minor scale.

Fig. 13.1

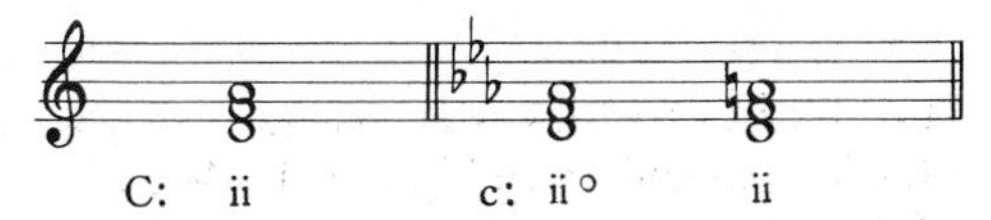

Assignment 13.1. Spelling the supertonic triad.

a) Spell the ii triad in each major key.
b) Spell the ii° triad in each minor key.
c) Spell the ii triad in each minor key.

Use of the Supertonic Triad

Unlike each of the three principal triads, the supertonic triad is most frequently found in first inversion. The progressions ii_6–V–I or ii_6–$I_{6 \atop 4}$–V–I, or in minor with ii°_{6}, are among the most commonly used progressions in all music.

Fig. 13.2

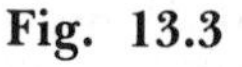
Fig. 13.3

The supertonic triad with its root in the bass is much less common than in first inversion. It is useful in a major key, as shown in Figures 13.4–13.5, but is not ordinarily found in a minor key (except in a harmonic sequence) since it is a diminished triad, ii°.

Fig. 13.4 ii-I$_{6 \atop 4}$

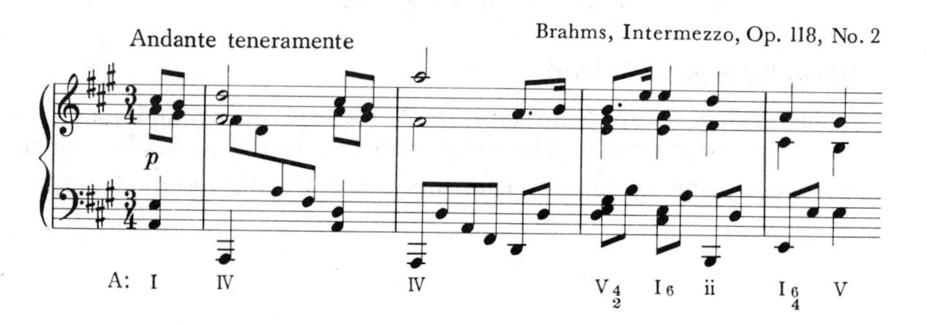

Fig. 13.5 I-ii-V

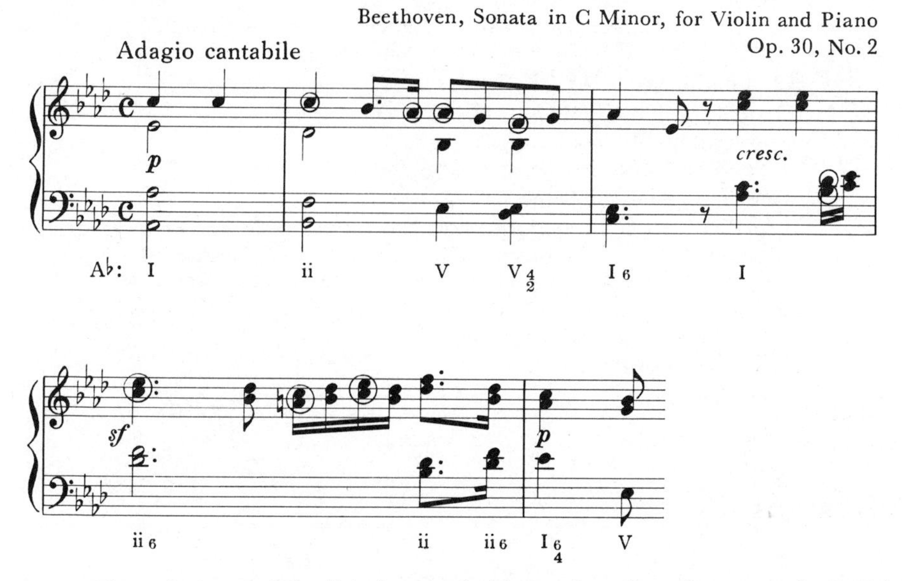

The existence of the ii (minor) triad in a minor key, for example, D F A in C minor, is in most cases questionable. Its fifth, the sixth scale step, generally ascends to the leading tone, with the result that the sonority is better analyzed as a vii$^{\circ}_{6}$ triad with an accented passing tone (review "harmonic" nonharmonic tones, page 231).

Fig. 13.6

Bach, *Wo soll ich fliehen hin* (#25)

The lower analysis in Figure 13.6 is possible, of course. When one encounters these ambiguous nonharmonic tones, the choice of analysis is often perplexing as it depends upon the tempo of the composition and the aural impression of the passage upon the listener.

Assignment 13.2. Harmonic analysis. The following excerpts contain examples of the supertonic triad and triads previously studied. Spell each chord, identify it by number and inversion, and identify nonharmonic tones.

Workbook for Elementary Harmony, Chapter 13
Beethoven: Sonatas for Piano
No. 1 (Op. 2, No. 1), fourth movement, measures 59–68
No. 15, (Op. 28), third movement, measures 1–8
Chopin: Mazurka No. 23 (Op. 33, No. 2), measures 1–8.
Mendelssohn: *Songs Without Words*
No. 8 (Op. 30, No. 2), measures 5–8
No. 39 (Op. 85, No. 3), measures 1–3
Mozart: Sonatas for Piano
G Major, K. 283, first movement, measures 36–38 (in D major)
C Major, K. 279, first movement, measures 1–4, 31–33 (in G major)
D Major, K. 284, third movement, variation 7, measures 1–3
Schumann: *Album for the Young,* Op. 68
No. 20, last 8 measures
No. 22, measures 1–4

Application

Written Materials

Alternate Doubling in Minor Triads

In the I, IV, and V triads previously studied, the preferred doubling common to all was the doubling of the root. In so doing, the tonic, subdominant, or dominant tones of the scale were doubled. This same scale-step doubling is satisfactory for the secondary triads as well, and in the case of ii_6 and ii°_6 it is actually preferred. Since the third of the supertonic triad is the subdominant tone, it is commonly doubled.

Fig. 13.7

Writing the Supertonic Triad

Most progressions in which the supertonic triad is found can be written with part-writing procedures already presented.

Rule 2A or 2B:	ii–V. See figure 13.8a and b. See also Figure 13.5.
Rule 3:	I–ii. See Figure 13.8a and b. See also Figure 13.5.

Rule 6A, 6B: Any progression to or from ii_6 or ii°_6. See Figure 13.8c. See also Figures 13.2 and 13.3. When used in first inversion, the supertonic triad is only rarely found with its fifth as a soprano note.

Procedures for connecting triads whose roots in the bass are a third apart, as in the progression IV–ii, will be considered in Chapter 15.

Fig. 13.8

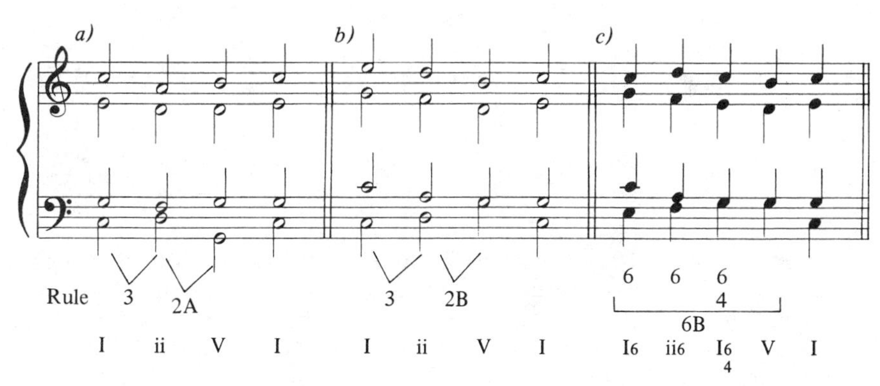

Writing Passing Tones and Neighboring Tones

The writing of any type of nonharmonic tone can be accomplished by the observance of one general procedure:

Part-Writing Rule No. 8 When a nonharmonic tone is used, it temporarily replaces a harmonic tone. Write the triad with normal doubling if possible and substitute the nonharmonic tone for one of the triad tones. Introduce and leave the nonharmonic tone according to the definition of the particular nonharmonic tone being used.

Application of this procedure to the unaccented passing tone and unaccented neighboring tones is very simple. A triad tone progresses by step to the dissonance and continues by step to the next harmonic tone. The dissonance is a substitute for the harmonic tone just left.

Fig. 13.9

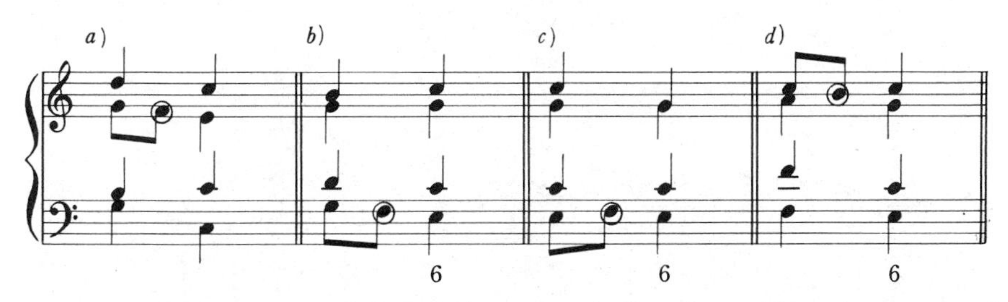

The importance of Rule 8 is more obvious in writing the accented nonharmonic tones. The dissonance and the accompanying chord are sounded simultaneously, with the dissonance then resolving to a chord tone. In establishing the doubling at the point of dissonance, the dissonant note should be considered a temporary substitute for the note that follows. In Figure 13.10a, the triad containing the dissonance would ordinarily include only one third. Since the resolution of the dissonance *is* the third, the dissonance represents the third temporarily; sounding the third with the dissonance produces incorrect doubling, as Figure 13.10b shows.

Fig. 13.10

In Figure 13.11 at the asterisk, the A in the tenor temporarily replaces the following G♯ so that there is conventional doubling at the resolution of the passing tone. In Figure 13.12 at each asterisk, the accented passing tone resolves to the root of a triad, so that the simultaneous sounding of the dissonance and its resolution is satisfactory.

Fig. 13.11

Fig. 13.12

Care must be exercised when writing a nonharmonic tone at the interval of a seventh above the *root* of a chord, even if the root is not in the bass. This dissonance creates the aural effect of a seventh chord; therefore, this dissonance must resolve downwards.

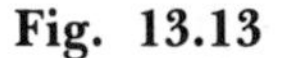

Fig. 13.13

Passing tones and neighboring tones, as well as other nonharmonic tones, are commonly found as double or triple dissonances (two or three dissonances sounding simultaneously) or in combination with each other. Figure 13.14 shows at (1) and (2) double passing tones, at (3) a lower neighbor sounding together with two passing tones in contrary motion and at (4) an upper neighbor and a passing tone sounding together. Simultaneous nonharmonic tones are ordinarily harmonic with each other; for example, at (1) in the next figure, the double passing tones are a third apart. Review "Simultaneous nonharmonic tones," page 230.

Fig. 13.14

Bach, *Ver Gott vertraut, hat wohl gebaut* (♯137)

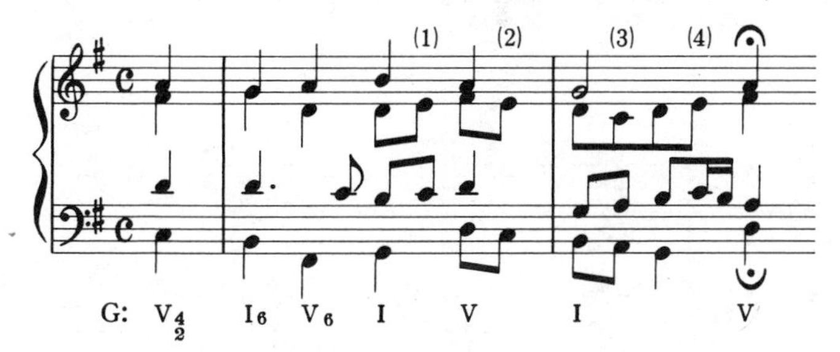

Figured Bass Symbols for Nonharmonic Tones

There are no standard figured bass symbols for nonharmonic tones; symbols are used that will best express the particular musical situation at the time. Very often, two or more figures will be found under a single bass note, the larger number usually on top.

Fig. 13.15

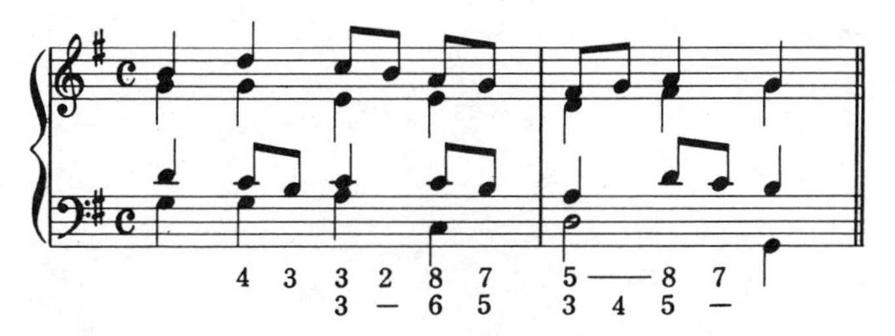

These will be read in the same manner as the figuration for second inversion, $^{65}_{43}$. Each horizontal line of figuration is read from left to right, indicating a melodic progression at the given interval above the bass. When the bass note changes, the number or numbers under the new bass note have no connection with the numbers under the previous bass note. The figured bass of Figure 13.15 is read as follows:

87 — octave above bass (in tenor) moves to seventh above bass;
65 — at same time, sixth above bass (in soprano) moves to fifth above bass.

5–87
345– — third above bass (in soprano) moves to fourth, then to fifth above bass; dash(–) indicates previous number is held; at the same time, fifth above bass (in tenor) is held, then leaps to the octave and proceeds to seventh above bass.

Assignment 13.3. Writing the supertonic triad. Fill in alto and tenor voices. Supply harmonic analysis below the staff. Continue to write some exercises as assigned, in open score, as described in Assignment 7.4.

(6)

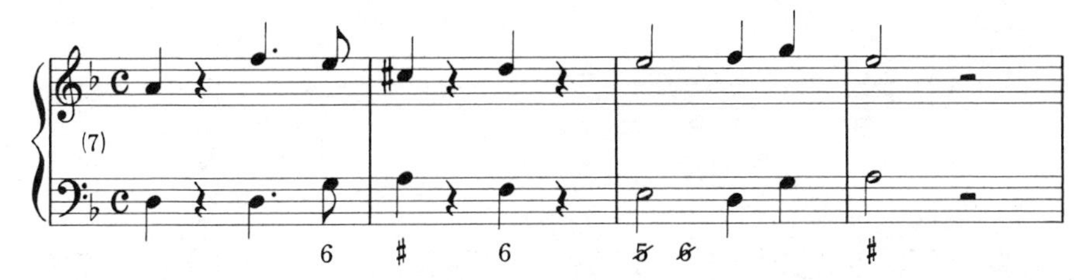
(7)

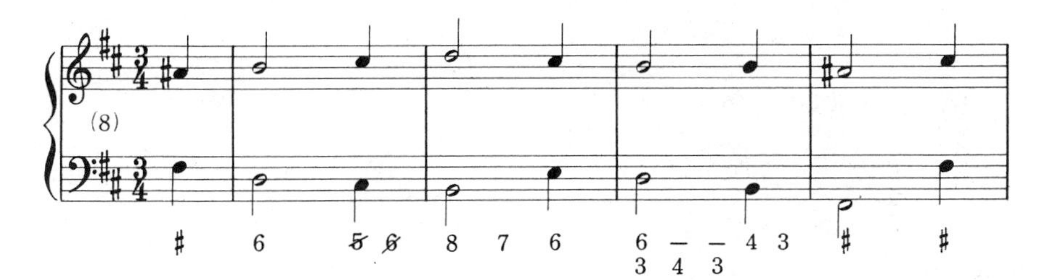
(8)

Assignment 13.4. Add soprano, alto, and tenor voices when bass line only is given. Do not add nonharmonic tones at this time (see Chapter 16). Make an harmonic analysis.

Assignment 13.5. Write the following harmonic progressions in four parts. Choose a time signature, and write a progression that is rhythmically interesting and displays acceptable harmonic rhythm.

a) E♭ Major	I ii_6 I_6 vii°_{6} I IV V I
b) F minor	V i i_6 vii°_{6} i ii°_{6} V i
c) B Major	V I_6 V_6 I I ii_6 V I I IV vii°_{6} I ii_6 $\text{I}_{\substack{6\\4}}$ V I

In the following progressions, no inversions are indicated. Choose inversions that will make a good bass line.

d) A Major	I I IV vii° I vii° I ii I V I
e) B minor	i iv V i vii° i i V V i ii° i V I
f) D♭ Major	V V I IV vii° I ii vii° I ii I V I

Melody Harmonization Using the Supertonic Triad

The supertonic triad is useful in harmonizing the second and fourth scale steps of the key. The sixth scale step harmonized with the supertonic triad (fifth of the triad as soprano note) is uncommon in major. In minor it is rare: Doubling the fifth of a diminished triad means that the lowered sixth scale step is doubled, making resolution awkward at best, and any other doubling emphasizes the tritone too strongly.

Assignment 13.6 Harmonize these melodies, using the supertonic and leading tone triads where appropriate. Use either two staves, two voices on each staff, or open score with C clefs, as assigned.

Ear Training

Exercise 13.1. Singing the supertonic triad.

a) In a major key: Sing the tonic triad of the given key; sing the supertonic note and sing the ii triad with letter names.

b) In a minor key: Sing the tonic triad of the given key; sing the supertonic note and the ii° with letter names.

c) Same as *b* but sing the ii triad.

Exercise 13.2. Sing with letter names each of the following chord progressions in the given key.

Major key: I ii V I; I ii vii° I
Minor key: i ii° V i; i ii vii° i

Example: i–ii°–V–i in F minor

Fig. 13.16

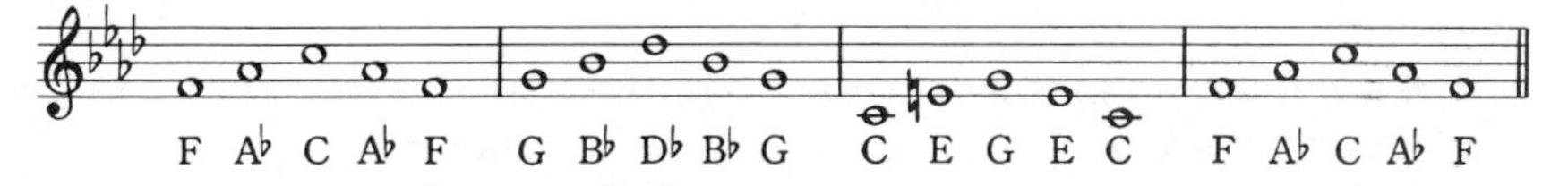

Exercise 13.3. Harmonic dictation exercises will now include the supertonic triads studied in this chapter. Listen with extra care to the two triads of sub-

dominant function (ii and IV). Since the supertonic triad is commonly found in first inversion, its bass note is the *same* as the root of the subdominant triad, and the two are easily confused. When you recognize subdominant function and the fourth scale step in the bass, listen to the chord quality before making your decision.

Fig. 13.17

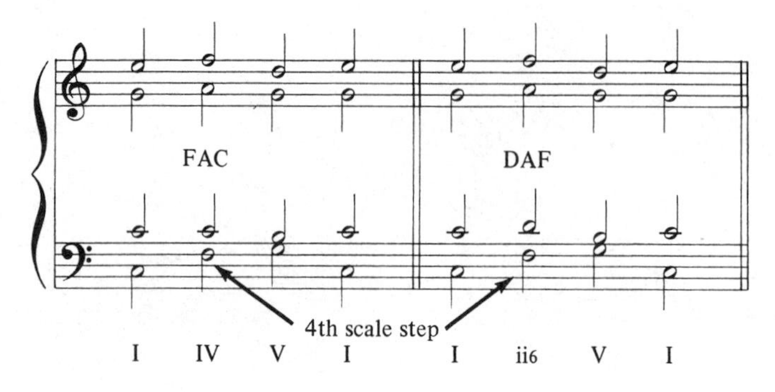

Keyboard Harmony

Exercise 13.4. Playing the supertonic triad at the keyboard.
a) Play the progression I–ii$_6$–V–I in all major keys.
b) Play the progression i–ii$^{\circ}_6$–V–i in all minor keys.
c) Play the progression I–ii$_6$–I$_6$—V–I in all major keys.
d) Play the progression i–ii$^{\circ}_6$–i$^{6}_{4}$–V–i in all minor keys.

Fig. 13.18

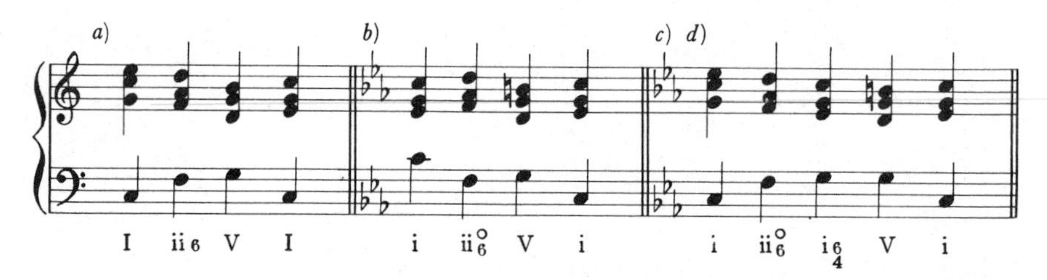

Harmonizing a melody at the keyboard. The vii° triad and the ii or ii° triad can be found useful in harmonizing a melody at the keyboard in two different ways.

1. Although most melodies can be harmonized with I, IV, and V, portions of some melodies are better harmonized with other triads.

a) When the melody ascends by step after a IV triad, the vii$^{\circ}_6$ is ordinarily used.

Fig. 13.19

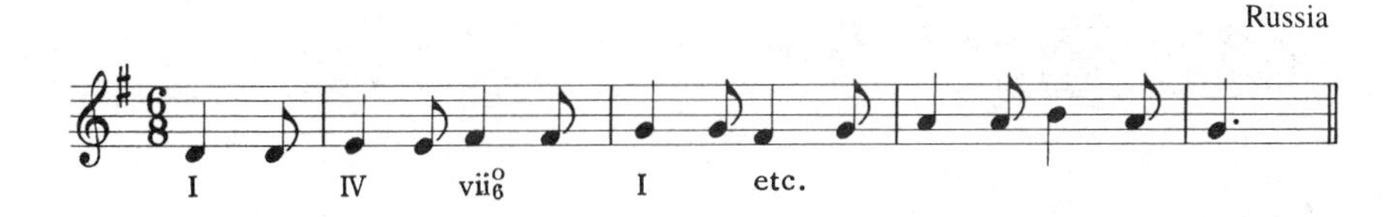

b) When the melody outlines a supertonic triad, the same triad is ordinarily found in the harmonization.

Fig. 13.20

In the above example, the melody at "ii" outlines a ii triad and therefore cannot be harmonized by I, IV, or V.

2. The vii° and ii (or ii°) triads can often be used to give variety to a harmonization, instead of using only I, IV, and V.

Fig. 13.21

Harmonizations can also be made more interesting through use of inversions—the first inversion during the course of the phrase and the I^6_4 at the cadence.

Exercise 13.5. Harmonizing a lead sheet melody. Triads marked "dim." (vii° and ii°) are diminished and should be played in first inversion. Any triad analyzed as supertonic will be more effective in first inversion. Recommended places for chords in second inversion are marked ($^6_4$). Continue your practice in Mainous, *Melodies to Harmonize With,* Chapter C, "Supertonic Triads."

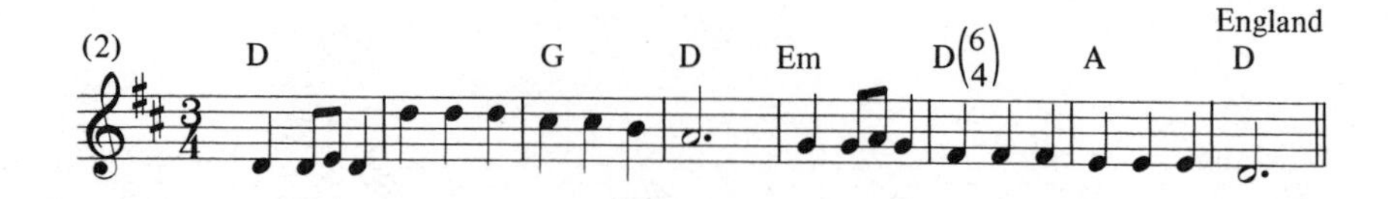

Exercise 13.6. Harmonizing melodies at the keyboard.

a) Harmonize these melodies, using leading tone and supertonic triads where appropriate.

*use appoggiatura chord (see page 231)

b) Continue your practice in the following sources. Melodies marked with an asterisk include an appropriate place for a leading tone triad.

Music for Sight Singing: melodies 2, 5, 7*, 58*, 65, 71*, 87, 107*, 124, 173, 204, 205, 206, 208, 313, 317, 320*, 353*, 368, and 373.

More Music for Sight Singing: melodies 266, 268, 282, 287, 288, 291, 293, 302*, 308, 315*, 337*, 348, 349, 358*, 395*, 406, 434, and 477.

CHAPTER 14

The Melodic Line (II): Melodic Extension; The Medieval Modes

Theory and Analysis

Form: Melodic Extension

Although the regular four-measure phrase and the eight-measure period appear frequently in music, phrases and periods of shorter and greater length are also of common occurrence. These often will be found to be extensions or contractions of the four-measure and eight-measure groupings studied in Chapter 6. Use of extended or contracted phrases, along with regular phrase lengths, helps to avoid the monotony of a constant succession of regular phrase lengths. There are many ways of modifying the regular phrase length; some of the more important ways are shown below.

1. Repeating a part of a phrase.

Fig. 14.1

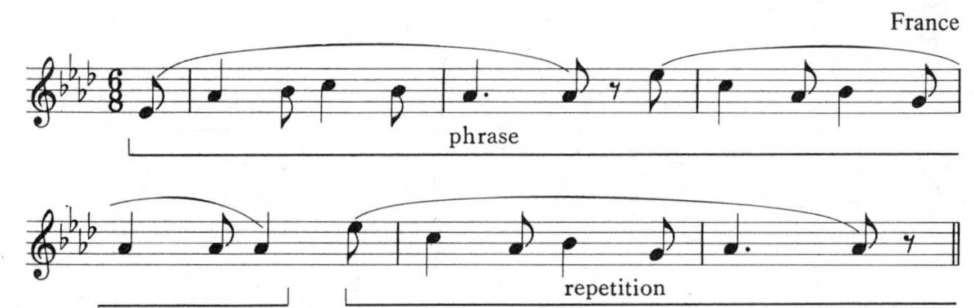

Exact repetition of an *entire* phrase is not extension. Since a phrase and its repetition are considered a single phrase, they cannot be considered as a period.

2. Evading the cadence at the end of the phrase, allowing the melody to continue further to the ultimate cadence.

Fig. 14.2

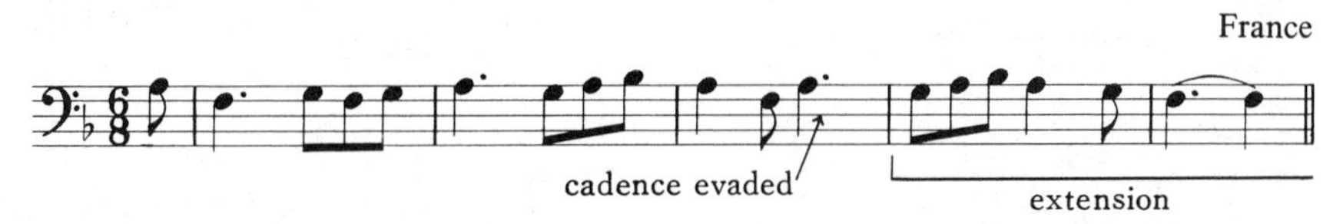

Without the evasion and extension, the phrase might have appeared as a normal four-measure phrase.

Fig. 14.3

3. Using a sequential pattern during the course of the phrase.

Fig. 14.4

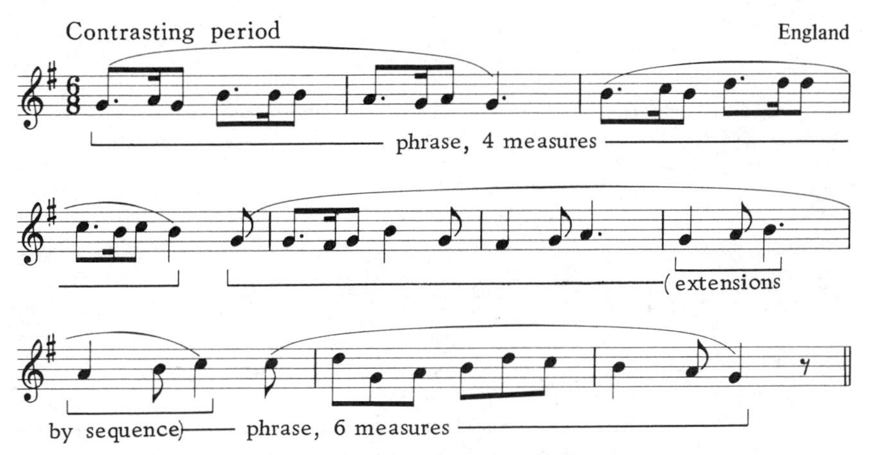

Without the two measures of sequence, the consequent phrase would be a normal four-measure phrase.

Fig. 14.5

Observe, however, that a sequence in itself does not necessarily indicate the presence of an extension. A normal four-measure phrase may contain a sequence, as shown in Figure 6.36.

4. Lengthening by additional measure.

Fig. 14.6

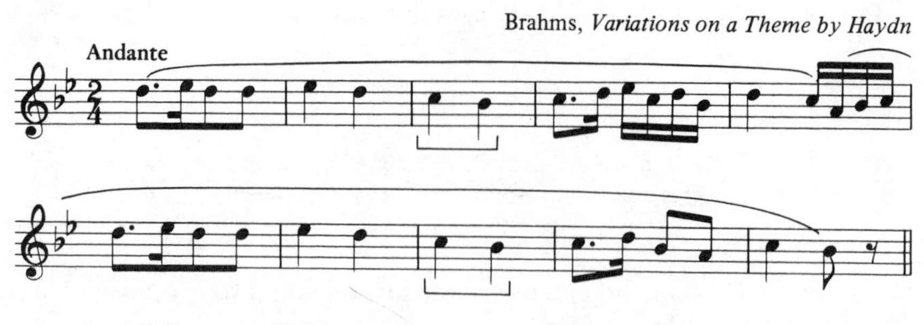

5. Adding an additional motive to the phrase.

Fig. 14.7

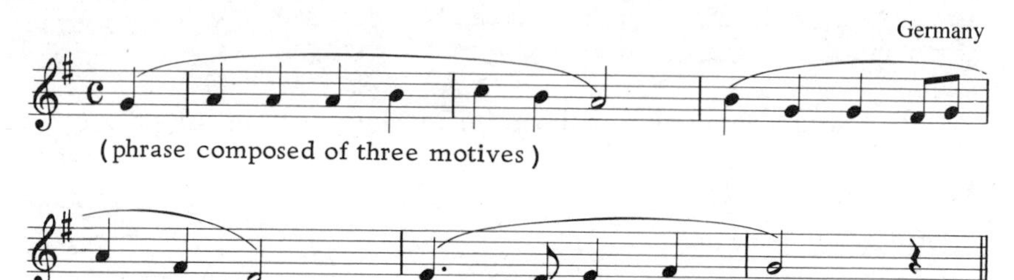

6. Occasionally phrases may be more or less than four measures in length. The following is a six-measure phrase, made up of two three-measure motives.

Fig. 14.8

In some instances, a two-measure phrase or an eight-measure phrase may be considered a regular phrase length.

a) When the tempo is very fast or when each measure contains only a few notes, an eight-measure phrase may be considered regular. The extremely rapid tempo of Figure 14.9 (one beat to the measure) produces a phrase of only eight beats in eight measures, comparable in sound to four measures of two beats each.

Fig. 14.9

b) When the tempo is very slow or when each measure contains many notes, a two-measure phrase may be considered regular. In Figure 14.10, the extremely slow tempo allows the completion of a phrase in a two-measure span.

Fig. 14.10

The Phrase Group and the Double Period

Two additional forms, each larger than the period, can be constructed by the addition of phrase lengths.

1. The *phrase group* consists of three or more phrases (very often three) each of which differs melodically from the others. Usually, each of the first two phrases

ends with a half cadence or an imperfect cadence and the last phrase ends with a perfect cadence.

Fig. 14.11

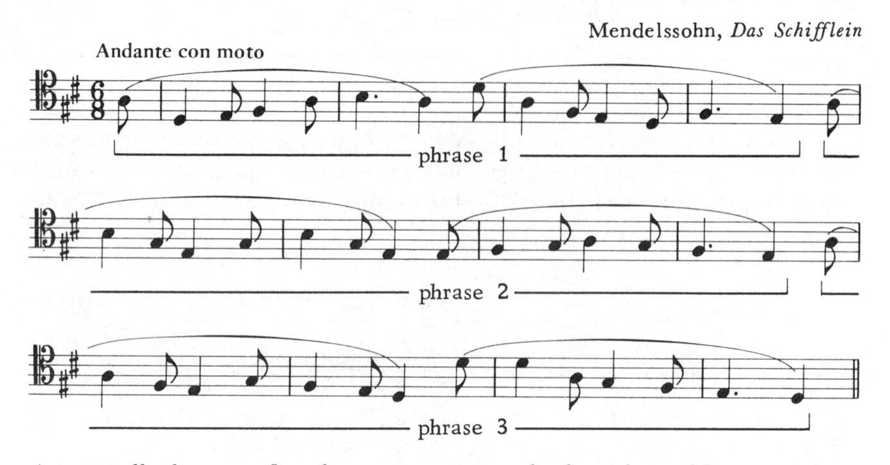

Any or all phrases of a phrase group may be lengthened by extension.

2. The *double period* consists of four phrases. Each of the first three phrases ends with a half cadence or an imperfect cadence, the last with a perfect cadence. Phrases one and three are usually similar to each other and very often identical, or nearly so, as in Figure 14.12. A form consisting of four different phrases (quite common in folk music) is usually considered a phrase group but could be identified as a double period.

Fig. 14.12

This example can be analyzed conveniently by assigning alphabet letters to each of the four phrases, the same letter for identical or nearly identical phrases and different letters for differing phrases. Thus the melody can be anlayzed as *a b a c* since the first and third phrases are identical, and the second and fourth phrases differ from *a* and from each other. In cases where phrases show some degree of similarity, the prime symbol (′) is used with the repeated letter, as in the next example, where the form is described as *a b a b′*

Fig. 14.13

No two successive phrases are identical in the double period, since simple phrase repetition would result. A melody analyzed as *a a b c* would be a phrase group, since *a* is simply a repeated phrase and not a period.

Any or all phrases of the double period may be found with extensions or in irregular lengths, as described previously.

Extension in Motivic Development

Extensions are often used as a location for the development of a melodic idea from the principal part of the phrase. In the next example, from Haydn's "Quinten" ("Fifths") Quartet, the consequent phrase of the period shows a rather long extension, used to develop a motivic idea from measure 3. First this three-note idea is repeated in sequence, either exact or modified. The climax note, d^3, then turns down stepwise, as a two-note figure. This figure, in turn, is repeated four times, leading to the final two measures of the basic four-measure phrase.

Fig. 14.14

Assignment 14.1. Analysis of form. Analyze the form of each of the following examples. Supply the following information:

a) the beginning and ending of each phrase;
b) the form of the entire melody;
c) the location and descriptions of extensions;
d) the location of any phrases other than those of four-measure length;
e) the location of any idea later developed, and a description of the process of development.

(4) J. Steffan

(5) **Presto** Haydn, Sonata in E♭ Major for Piano (1776)

Andante Borodin, Quartet

(6) Cello

Assignment 14.2. Analysis of form. Copy out these melodies and excerpts as assigned. Follow the directions for Assignment 14.1.

Music for Sight Singing: melodies 5, 22, 25, 51, 56, 71, 79, 80, 85, 91, 101, 103, 134, 149, 161, 164, 171, 180, 200, 231, 244, 249, 314, 354, 384, 385, 387, and 393.

More Music for Sight Singing: melodies 267, 270, 271, 274, 275, 281, 282, 283, 284, 292, 293, 295, 299, 304, 309, 312, 314, 336, 356, 358, and 367.

Beethoven, Sonatas for piano
- No. 12 (Op. 26), first movement, measures 1–16
- No. 17 (Op. 31, No. 2), measures 1–31
- No. 19 (Op. 49, No. 1), measures 33–49

Mozart, Sonatas for piano,
- C Major, K. 330, third movement, measures 1–10

F Major, K. 332, first movement, measures 1–12 and 94–111
F Major, K. 533, third movement, measures 1–12
Fantasia and Sonata, K. 475, third movement of sonata (Allegro assai), measures 1–16
Mendelssohn, *Songs Without Words*
No. 12, measures 7–21
No. 21, measures 9–32
No. 29, measures 1–21
No. 30, measures 1–15
No. 37, measures 1–17

The Medieval Modes

Music from Medieval times to the seventeenth century was characterized by the use of six scale patterns, rather than the two, major and minor, in use in the common practice period. These are like the major and minor scales in that each of these modes consists of seven scale steps, but they differ in that the location of the whole steps and half steps varies in each. Tonics of these modes are known as *finals*. When the range of the melody is generally between the lower and upper final, the mode is said to be *authentic*, and when it is roughly between the dominants of the mode, it is said to be *plagal*. For the latter, the prefix hypo- becomes part of the name of the mode (e.g., Hypodorian).

Authentic Mode Number	*Mode*	*Spelling/Half Steps*	*Plagal Mode Number*
I	Dorian	D E F G A B C D 2 3 6 7	II
III	Phrygian	E F G A B C D E 1 2 5 6	IV
V	Lydian	F G A B C D E F 3 4 7 8	VI
VII	Mixolydian	G A B C D E F G 3 4 6 7	VIII
IX	Aeolian	A B C D E F G A 2 3 5 6	X
XI	Ionian	C D E F G A B C 3 4 7 8	XII

A mode on B, called Locrian, is theoretical. Because it had a tritone from its tonic to dominant, it was not considered practical or useful.

These modes can easily be related to the present major and minor modes for easy identification.

Dorian:	Like natural minor with a raised sixth scale step.
Phrygian:	Like natural minor with a lowered second scale step.

Lydian:	Like major with a raised fourth scale step.
Mixolydian:	Like major with a lowered seventh scale step.
Aeolian:	Like natural minor.
Ionian:	Like major.

The Kyrie below is an example of the Mixolydian mode. Note the use of a scale on G, but with F natural used throughout except for an F♯ at the cadence.

Fig. 14.15

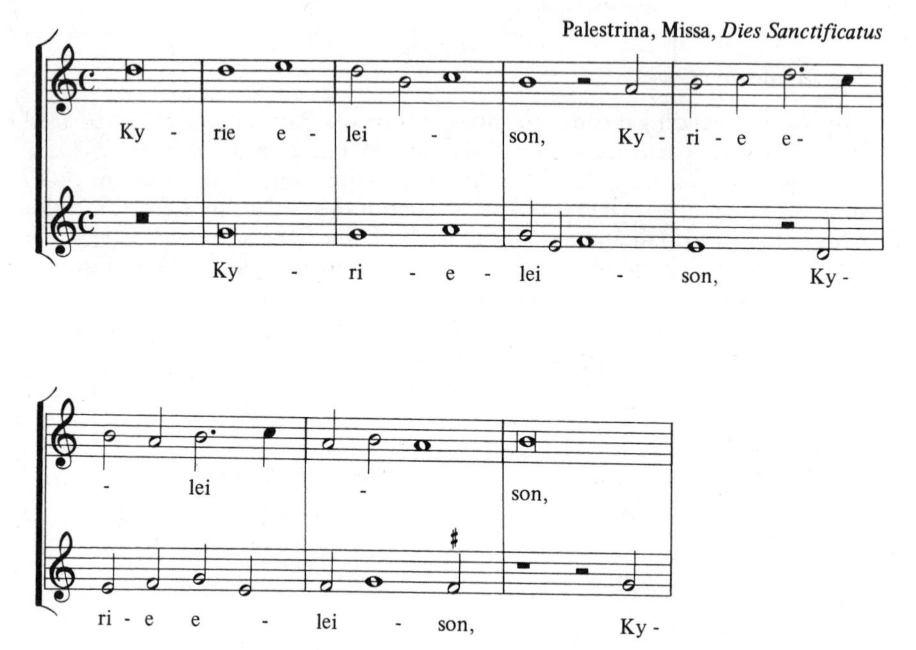

The F♯ at the cadence is one example of a system known as *musica ficta,* or *false music.* The accidental, though not written in the music, was assumed to be present by both the composer and the performer (it is now placed above the note in modern scores). The cumulative effect of the various rules of *musica ficta* was to eventually reduce the modes, except for the Phrygian, to major and minor. For example, changing the F in Mixolydian to F♯ creates a major scale.

Many of the Bach chorales are based on hymn tunes written in the modes that were common a century or more before Bach's time. One of the best known, *O Haupt voll Blut und Wunden* (*O Sacred Head Now Wounded*), a tune in the Phrygian mode, was originally a secular love song ("My heart is perplexed by a maiden.")

Fig. 14.16

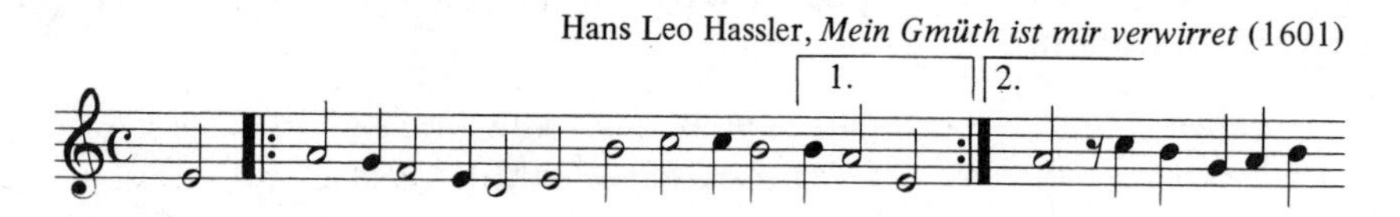

Bach harmonized this tune both in Phrygian and in major, as shown by these two versions of the final phrase.

Fig. 14.17

Transposition of Modes

Before the seventeenth century, modes had been written only on the scale steps listed, or transposed a fifth higher (fourth lower), adding one flat to the signature.

Fig. 14.18

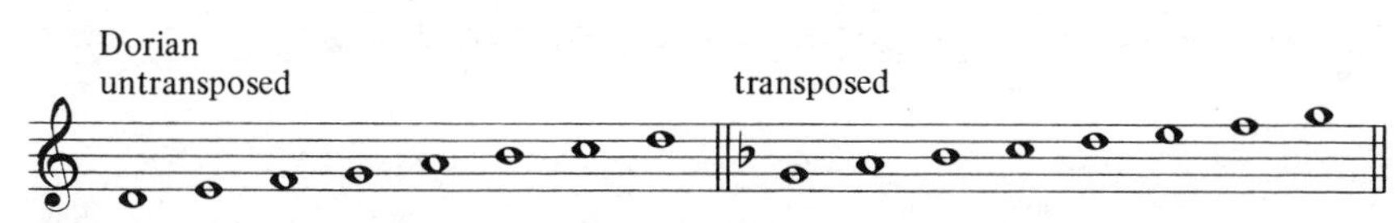

Other transpositions are useful for at least two reasons. First, much of the world's folk music is modal. Collectors and transcribers do not always place these tunes in untransposed modes. Second, these modes, though virtually absent from composed music during the common practice period, are again being used in our own time in both serious music and in music of popular culture.

Transposition to any beginning pitch is possible, and can be done easily by recalling the relationship of each mode to either the major or minor mode. In Example 14.18, Dorian is similar to natural minor but with a raised sixth scale step.

To transpose to G, spell a G natural minor scale and raise the sixth scale step, E♭ to E. To transpose to E, do the same, and the scale E F♯ G A B C♯ D E is the result.

Assignment 14.3. Spell each of these modes, Dorian, Phrygian, Lydian, and Mixolydian, on each pitch of the circle of fifths. For example:

Mixolydian: G A B C D E F G
D E F♯ G A B C D
A B C♯ D E F♯ G A etc.

Assignment 14.4. The following folk songs are notated in transposed modes. Identify the mode of each. Procedure: Ask yourself 1) Is the scale more like major or minor? (check the third scale step); and 2) what scale step differs from the major or minor scale determined in step 1? Example:

1. The scale is more like major.
2. The seventh scale step is lowered. The mode is Mixolydian.

Note: The key signature used for modal writing may be the same as the closest major or minor key, as above, or may include just the accidentals for the particular mode—in the example above, five flats.

Studies in the medieval modes may be continued by consulting Chapter 17 of *Music for Sight Singing* and Part 4 of *More Music for Sight Singing.*

Application

Written Materials

Melody Writing

In previous study and practice in melody writing (Chapter 6), you were limited to the simple phrase and period, and to the use of tonic and dominant implied harmony. The larger forms in this chapter, the addition of the subdominant and supertonic triads, and your more complete knowledge of nonharmonic tones make possible the composition of melodies of considerably more musical interest.

Use of intervallic leaps, which are larger than scale steps, can now have several analytical implications.

1. The interval(s) may outline a chord. In most melodies, scale steps and small intervals predominate, as in Figure 14.19, which includes intervals implying the ii triad and the V^7 chord.

Fig. 14.19

2. Melodies consisting predominantly of intervallic leaps can also be musically satisfactory. Note the use of sequence in this fugue subject.

Fig. 14.20

3. Each note of the interval can represent a different chord (a chord change occurs as the interval is sounded).

Fig. 14.21

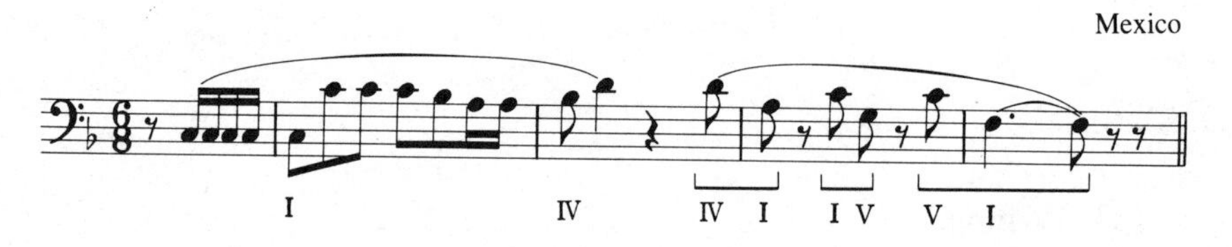

Two such leaps in the same direction are not common, but can occur.

Fig. 14.22

4. The interval may be a leap from a chord tone to a nonharmonic tone,

Fig. 14.23

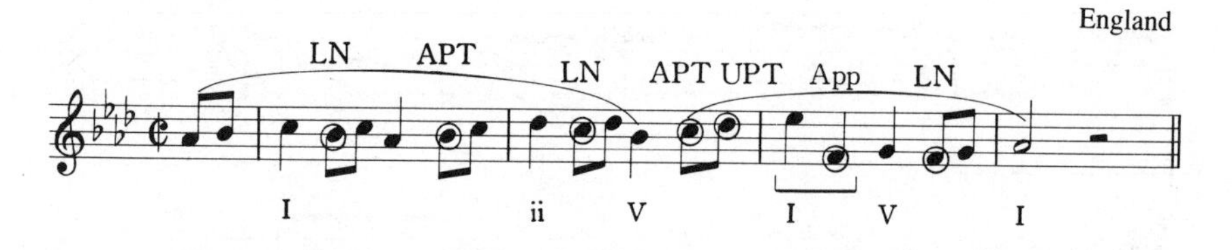

or, in the case of an escaped tone, from a nonharmonic tone to a harmonic tone.

Fig. 14.24

5. In the melodic sequence, the same leap in successive figures may hold differing implications.

Fig. 14.25

Extension in melodic writing is particularly important, in that it helps to avoid the monotony of a constant four-measure metric repetition. Extension is most useful in the development of ideas already inherent in the phrase. At its simplest, the one-measure addition in Figure 14.6 is a sequential repetition of the descending scale step of the previous measure. At the other extreme is the well-known opening of Beethoven's Fifth Symphony, where the first five measures act as an introductory extension, with the following phrase built on its idea.

Fig. 14.26

More common are the developmental processes shown in Figure 14.14 and in the excerpts from Mozart and Borodin in Assignment 14.1.

Assignment 14.5. Melody writing. Write original melodies in various forms, as assigned. Use extensions and/or development of motive as studied in this chapter. Make a *complete analysis,* including *a*) an analysis of the form, as shown in Figure 14.4, *b*) an analysis of the implied harmony as shown in Figure 14.23, *c*) identification of nonharmonic tones, and *d*) a description of any developmental procedures used. Refer to the workbook for preliminary exercises to aid you in this experience in original composition.

Assignment 14.6. Modal melody writing. Choose one of the medieval modes and write phrases or periods as assigned. This work will be done best if you become better acquainted with the style through singing and studying modal melodies in your sight singing books.

Ear Training

Exercise 14.1. Listening for formal structures. Listen to a phrase with extensions. How many measures are there? Where is the extension, and how was it accomplished? On successive hearings, write the melody.

Exercise 14.2. Listening for larger structures. Listen to a melody, a period or longer. How many phrases are there? Describe the cadence of each phrase. What is the complete form? Locate and describe any extensions you hear.

Exercise 14.3. Singing modal scales. From a given pitch, sing each of the modal scales on "la" as directed.

Exercise 14.4. Singing modal scales. From a given pitch name, sing with letter names the scale of the given mode.

Exercise 14.5. Melodic dictation. Listen to a modal melody. Decide if the third of the scale is major or minor. Then listen for the characteristic note of the mode and identify the mode by name.

Exercise 14.6. Melodic dictation. Given the first note of the melody, write the melody from dictation. Use either of the types of key signatures described in Assignment 14.4.

Keyboard Harmony

Exercise 14.7. Playing modal scales. Play any modal scale from any given note. Be sure to spell the scale first, either aloud or mentally.

CHAPTER 15

The Submediant and Mediant Triads

Theory and Analysis

The two remaining secondary triads are built on the submediant and mediant tones of the scale; both are minor triads (vi and iii) when found in a major key (Figure 15.1a) and both are major triads (VI and III) when found in a minor key (Figure 15.1b). Because of the altered sixth and seventh degrees in the minor scale, two additional triads are possible in a minor key. These are the vi° and the III+, diminished and augmented triads (Figure 15.1c). Because of the infrequent use of the two latter triads, they will not be considered in this chapter.

The submediant and mediant triads are used almost exclusively with their roots in the bass. In the following discussion of these triads, root position only is meant unless otherwise indicated.

Fig. 15.1.

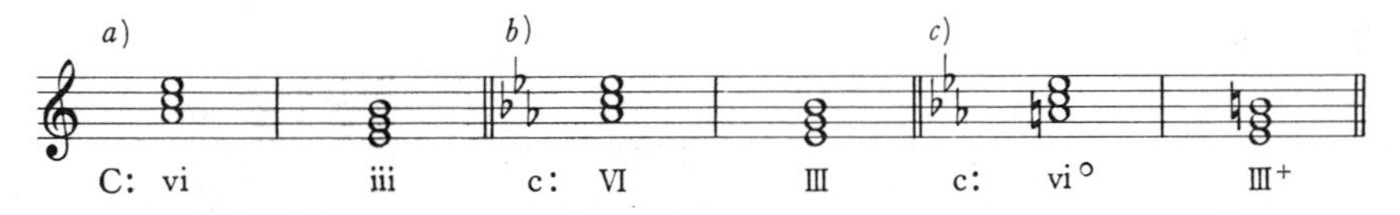

Assignment 15.1. Spelling the submediant and mediant triads.

a) Spell the submediant triad in each major and minor key.

b) Spell the mediant triad in each major and minor key.

In terms of resolution, the submediant triad is one of the most versatile of triads (as shown in Table 12.1, Table of Commonly Used Chord Progressions), resolving regularly to the supertonic, subdominant, and dominant triads, as well as to the mediant when the mediant is followed by the subdominant. Only the progression to the leading tone triad is little used. The submediant triad is usually preceded by the tonic or dominant triad or, less often, by the mediant triad.

The mediant triad has less opportunity for display, its resolution being limited usually to the submediant and subdominant triads, and preceded only by the tonic except in the special progression vi–iii–IV (VI–III–iv).

Root Movement by Downward Thirds

With the inclusion of the submediant triad, it is possible to construct a harmonic pattern based on root movement by thirds. Of all the possible root movements by thirds, the progression I–vi–IV–ii (in whole or in part) is of most common occurrence.

Fig. 15.2 I–vi–IV–ii

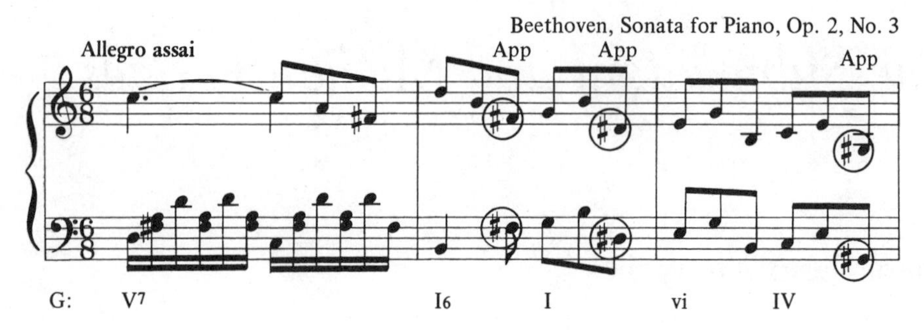

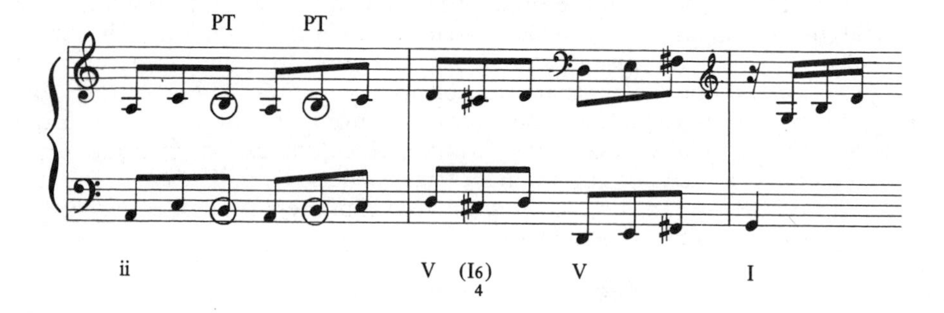

Fig. 15.3 i–VI–iv

C. H. Graun (1701-1759) *Der Tod Jesu*

Because of the similarity in the sounds of IV and ii_6, the progression vi–ii_6 gives the impression of descending root movement by thirds.

Fig. 15.4 I–vi–ii$_6$

Root Movement by Downward Fifths

The most useful progression from the submediant is to the supertonic, either with the root in bass or in first inversion. Figure 15.4 shows the progression vi–ii$_6$, whereas Figure 15.5 shows resolutions of vi to both ii and ii$_6$.

Fig. 15.5 vi–ii; vi–ii$_6$

Progression from the mediant by downward fifth, which might seem to be an excellent progression since this type of root movement is so common, is actually uncommon when compared with other approaches to vi and other progressions from iii.

Fig. 15.6 iii–vi

Root Movement by Seconds; The Deceptive Cadence

Both the submediant and mediant triads are commonly found in an upward progression by second: V–vi and iii–IV and the comparable progressions in minor. The only progressions by downward second used with any degree of frequency are vi–V and VI–V, and occasionally iii–ii$_6$.

When the progression V–vi or V–VI occurs at a cadence point, it is known as a *deceptive cadence*. The reason for the name becomes obvious from study of Figure 15.7. In each cadence, the V triad seems to demand resolution to the tonic triad, but instead the submediant triad is found as the resolution. (Note carefully that the first phrase of Figure 15.7 is in the key of F, while the second phrase is in the key of C.)

Fig. 15.7 V–vi

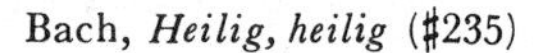

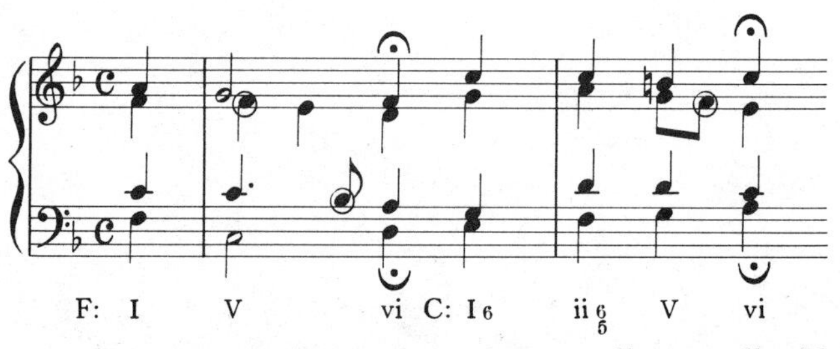

This progression may appear equally as well within the phrase.

Fig. 15.8 V–VI

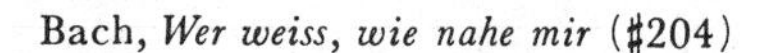

The deceptive effect of this progression combined with nonharmonic tones can be particularly effective. In Figure 15.9 a double suspension occurs simultaneously with the VI triad.

Fig. 15.9 V–VI

The deceptive progression is effectively used at the climactic moment in operatic arias or duets, as in the following duet for tenor and bass from the pen of Verdi. Note, beginning in measure three, the root movement III–VI–II–V, a series of downward fifths (but all major triads). These are secondary dominant chords, in this case in a series. This subject will be introduced in later chapters.

Fig. 15.10

By resolving down by step, the submediant triad immediately reaches the dominant, thereby bypassing the intermediate resolution of IV and/or ii.

Fig. 15.11 VI–V

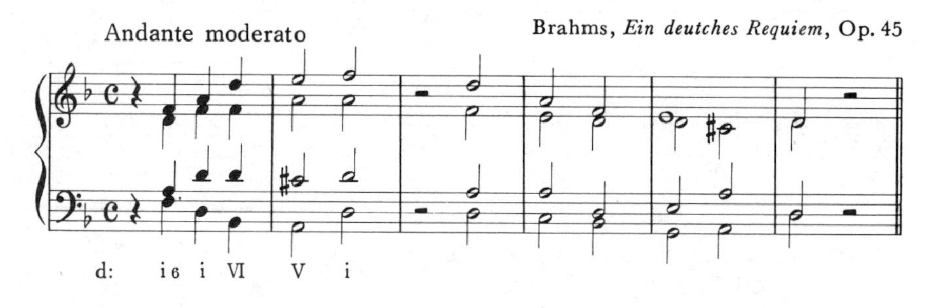

The resolution of the mediant to the subdominant is much more widely used than the resolution by downward fifth to the submediant. This progression is widely used to harmonize a descending scale pattern, 1–7–6–5.

Fig. 15.12 iii–IV

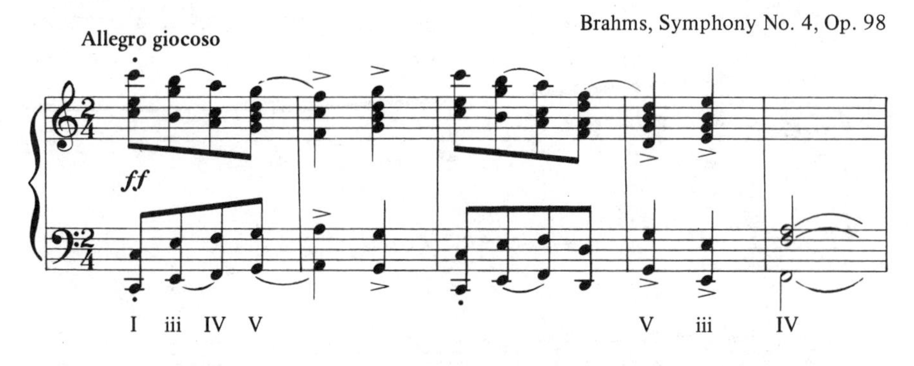

Note also, in Figure 15.12, the less commonly used V–iii progression.

The vi–iii–IV Progression

A common progression is the vi–iii–IV (VI–III–iv). Having vi precede iii is uncommon unless IV follows; this progression, vi–iii–iv, is the only one in the Table of Commonly Used Progressions consisting of three items. Figure 15.13 shows the entire descending E♭ major scale harmonized, beginning with the vi–iii–IV. The scale could have been harmonized starting with I–iii–IV, as at *b*.

Fig. 15.13 Vi–iii–IV

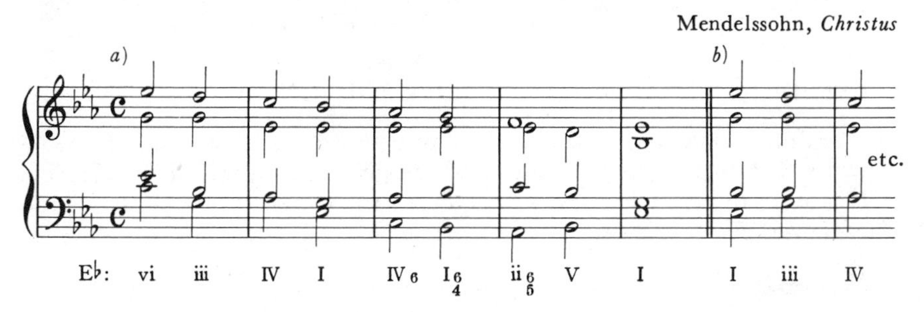

In Figure 15.14a, the melody of measures 1–2 of the first phrase is repeated in measures 5–6 of the second phrase. Both phrases include the progression vi–iii–IV, but the progression is located differently in each phrase. In the first phrase, the progression falls on the second, third, and fourth melody tones, and in the second phrase it falls on the first, second, and third melody tones (Fig. 15.14b).

Fig. 15.14

Substitution of ii or ii° for IV or iv after the mediant triad is possible because of the striking similarity of the subdominant and supertonic triads (review page 290). This example in a minor key shows the progression VI–III–ii°6 rather than the common VI–III–iv.

Fig. 15.15 VI–III–ii°6

Ambiguous Spellings

Vertical sonorities that look like submediant and mediant triads but are actually other triads with a nonharmonic tone included are rather common. Since they can easily be confusing, two examples are given here.

The following excerpt from Chopin contains two such examples. At measure 2, the triad is *not* F A C, but A C E with a suspension Figure F. What appears to be a iv–VI–i progression in measures 1 and 2 is in reality simply iv–i, as hearing the passage will confirm. (It is important to remember that in analysis you are analyzing *sound,* not merely the way notes look on paper!)

Fig. 15.16

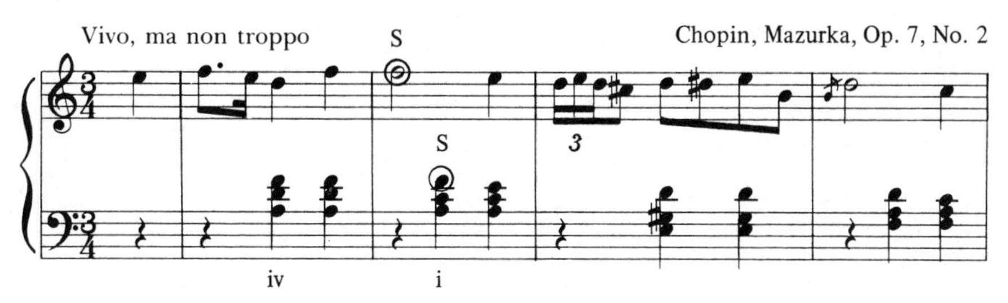

Now apply a similar analysis to measures three and four.

In a similar situation in a minor key (Figure 15.17), the sonority at the asterisk is spelled A♭ C E, an augmented triad, III+ in the key of F minor. Again the aural effect of the authentic cadence indicates that the A♭ in the soprano is a nonharmonic tone, this time an appoggiatura.

Fig. 15.17

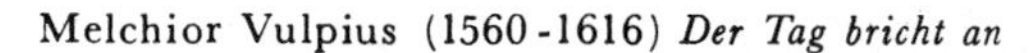

Special Use of the Tonic Triad in a Chord Progression

The tonic triad is often found between the two triads of a commonly used progression. In Figure 15.18, placing the tonic triad between vi and IV only temporarily interrupts a common chord progression. Such placement of a tonic chord can be made between the two triads of any progression studied thus far, for example, ii–I–V, iii–I–IV, and so on.

Fig. 15.18

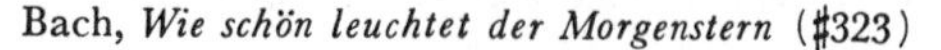

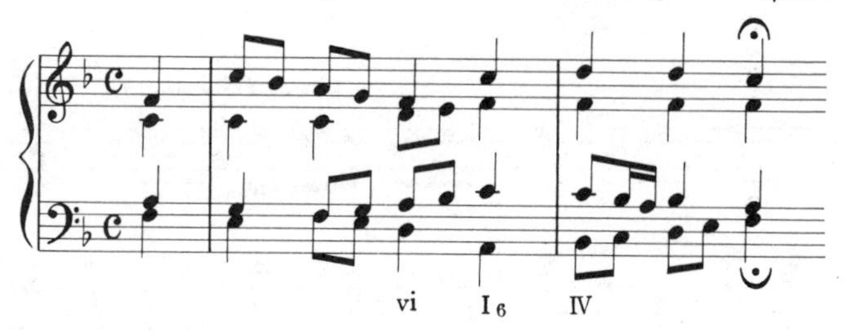

The Submediant and Mediant Triads in Inversion

The submediant and mediant triads may commonly be found in first inversion when they are part of a harmonic sequence or a series of chords in first inversion (these will be discussed in the next chapter). Otherwise, these triads in first inversion usually appear *only* when the bass note of the previous triad is held over to become the third of the submediant or mediant triad: I–vi_6 and V–iii_6. Any other uses are quite rare, and their appearance in second inversion is almost nonexistent.

Fig. 15.19

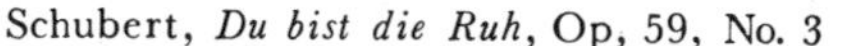

Assignment 15.2. Harmonic analysis. Analyze the harmony and identify the nonharmonic tones of these excerpts.

(1) Andante con moto
Schubert, Symphony No. 5
*

*V/ii = CEG

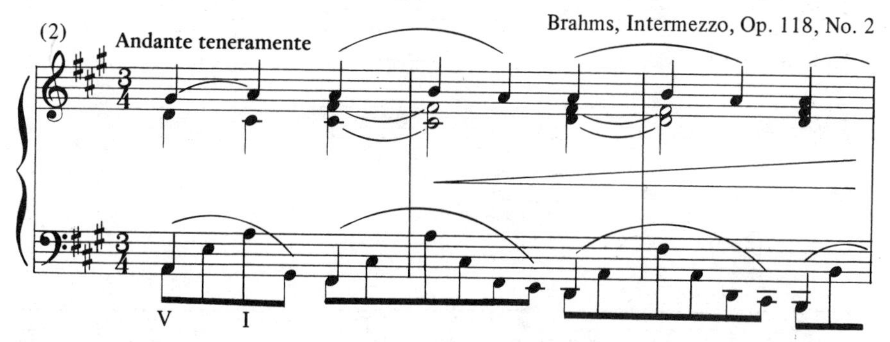
(2) Andante teneramente
Brahms, Intermezzo, Op. 118, No. 2
V
I

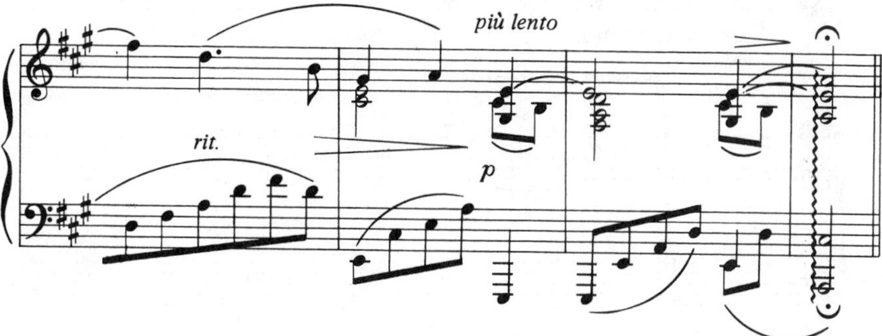
più lento
rit.
p

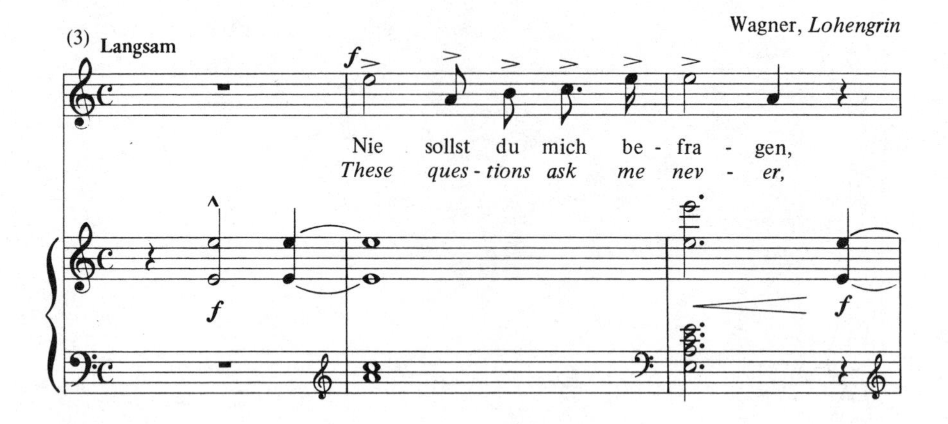
Wagner, Lohengrin
(3) Langsam
f
Nie sollst du mich be - fra - gen,
These ques - tions ask me nev - er,
f
f

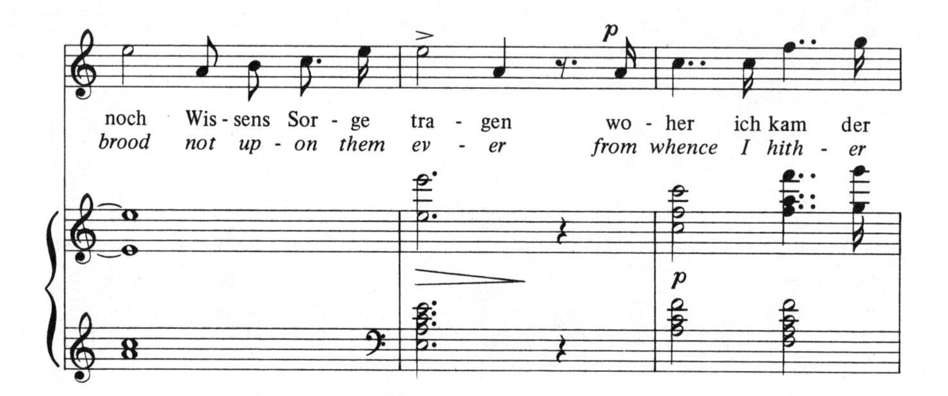
p
noch Wis - sens Sor - ge tra - gen wo - her ich kam der
brood not up - on them ev - er from whence I hith - er
p

Fahrt, noch wie mein Nam' und Art!
came, nor what my race and name!

Haydn, Quartet, Op. 76, No. 2

(4)

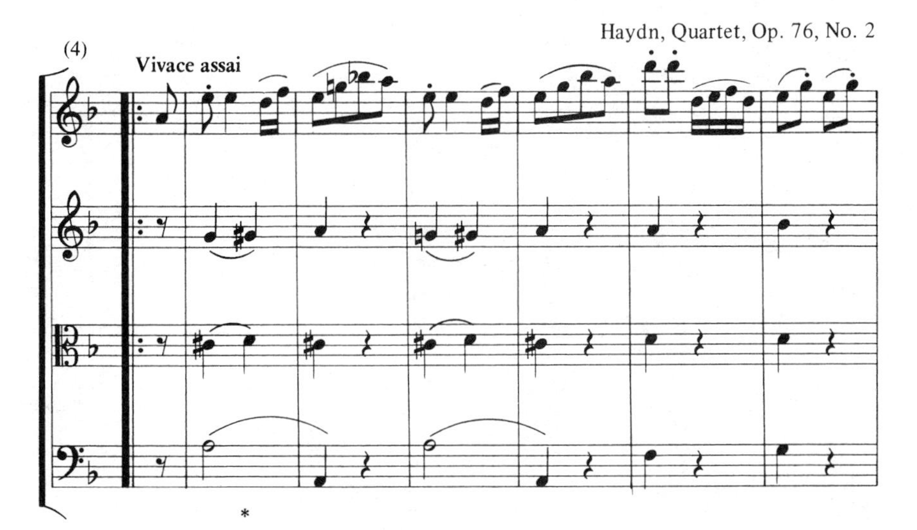

*EG♯BD = V^7/V, though at this tempo (vivace), you may wish to consider the notes in the second violin and viola parts as nonharmonic tones.

(5)

Schubert, Sonata for Piano, Op. 120

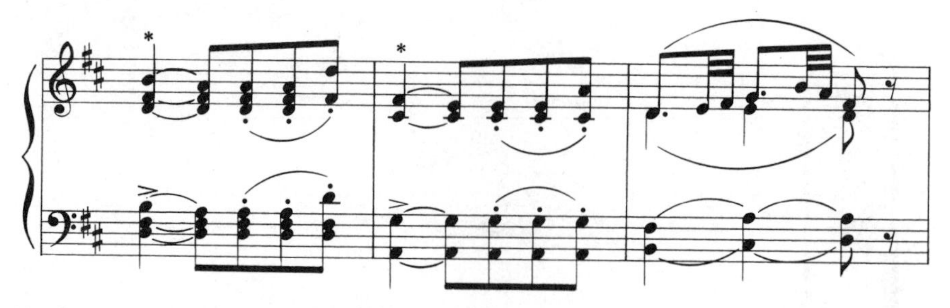

*Is the soprano note at each of these points a chord tone or a nonharmonic tone?

Assignment 15.3. Analyze the harmony and the nonharmonic tones of the following excerpts (Workbook, Chapter 15, Assignment 15.2).

Mozart, Sonatas for Piano
  C Major, K. 545, second movement, measures 12–16
  B♭ Major, K. 333, third movement, measures 13–16
  D Major, K. 284, third movement, variation 11, measures 1–3
  D Major, K. 311, second movement, last 8 measures
Schumann, *Album for the Young,* Op. 68
  No. 9, measures 1–4; No. 37, measures 9–16
Mendelssohn, *Songs Without Words,* No. 7 (Op. 30, No. 1), measures 1–6

Application

Written Materials

The Submediant Triad

Part-writing procedures previously presented can be of use in many of the progressions described in this chapter, as shown in Figure 15.20.

Progression	*Procedure*	*Example*
vi–ii in major	Rule 2 (A, B, or C)	15.20a, b
V–vi in major vi–V in major	Rule 3	15.20c, d
vi–ii$_6$ in major VI–ii$^{o}_{6}$ in minor	Rule 6 (A or B)	15.20e

Fig. 15.20

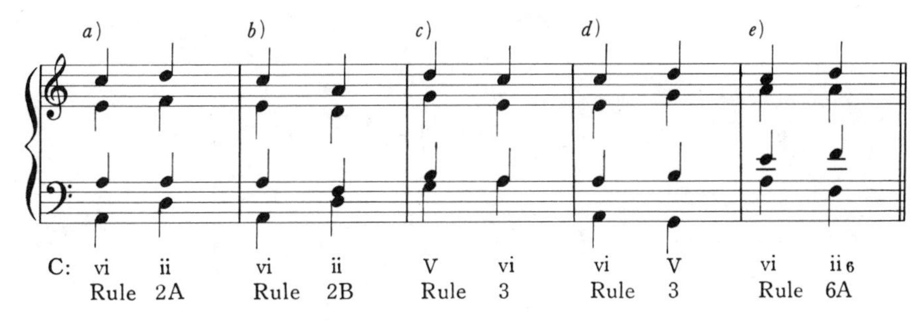

Writing Triads with Roots a Third Apart:

I–vi or i–VI; vi–IV or VI–iv; and IV–ii

Part-Writing Rule 4A. When the bass notes of two successive triads are roots of the triads and these triad roots are a third apart, hold the two common tones and move the other voice step-wise.

Fig. 15.21

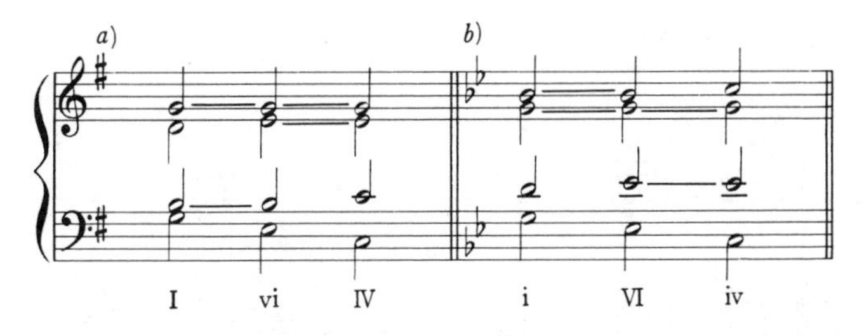

Part-Writing Rule 4B When the bass notes of two successive triads are roots of triads and these triad roots are a third apart, and when the soprano voice moves by leap, the second triad may be in either close or open position, depending on vocal range and whether fifths and octaves have been avoided.

Rule 4B applies, of course, only when it is desirable that both triads display common doubling: two roots, one third and one fifth. It will often be more desirable to double the third in one of the triads, as described under Part-Writing Rule 5 below.

Fig. 15.22 Use of Rule 4B.

Part-Writing Procedure in Unconventional Situations

Part-Writing Rule 5. When it is impossible or undesirable to follow Rules 1–4, double the third in the *second* of the two triads; however, if this third is the leading tone or any altered tone, double the third in the *first* of the two triads.

This procedure is especially helpful in writing from dominant to submediant or the reverse (V–vi, vi–V), as shown in Figure 15.23, a–e, or in other root movements a second apart, as in Figure 15.23f. Observe that the doubled note usually turns out to be one of the three primary tones of the key.

Fig. 15.23

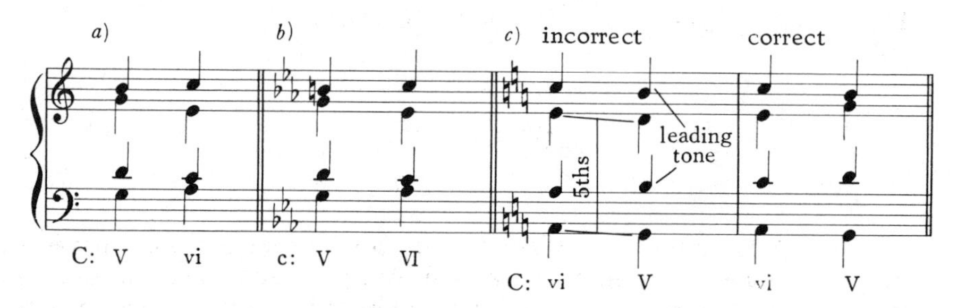

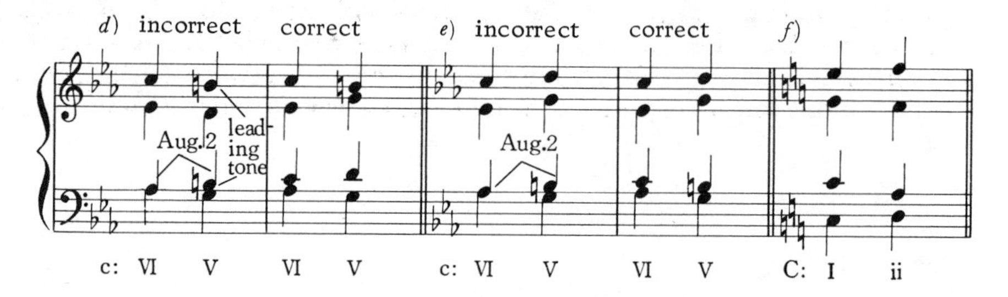

The procedure expressed by Rule 5 will be found useful in many situations in which the regular rule does not produce the best results. For example, in Figure 15.24, opening progression I–vi, Rule 4A cannot be used. Rule 4B is possible, but doubling the third in the vi triad keeps both the alto and tenor voices in better range, as is true in the other I–vi progression of this figure.

Fig. 15.24

Assignment 15.4. Part-writing. Write exercises showing various uses of the submediant triad. Fill in inner voices and make an harmonic analysis of each example.

The Mediant Triad

All progressions involving the mediant triad can be written by using part-writing procedures we have already established.

Progression	*Procedure*	*Example*
iii–vi in major III–VI in minor vi–iii in major VI–III in minor	Rule 2 (A, B, or C) (same in major or minor)	15.25a, b
iii–IV in major III–iv in minor	Rule 3 (same in major or minor)	15.25b
I–iii in major i–III in minor	Rule 4 (A or B) (same in major or minor)	15.25c

For any progression in which a doubled third is required, use Rule 5 and see Figure 15.25d.

For any progression in which one or both triads are in inversion, use Rule 6A or 6B and see Figure 15.25e.

The "mediant" triad created by the presence of a nonharmonic tone (review Figure 15.17 and accompanying discussion) is indicated by the figured bass symbol 65. The sixth above the bass is treated as a nonharmonic tone in the V triad, temporarily substituting for the fifth of the triad to which it resolves (Figure 15.25f, g).

Fig. 15.25

Assignment 15.5. Part-writing. Write exercises showing use of the mediant triad. Fill in inner voices and make an harmonic analysis of each example.

(5)
6

(6)
(7)
6 5

(8)
6 5

(9)
6 6 6 6 6

(10)
6 6 6 5

Writing Suspensions

The use of Rule 8, presented in Chapter 13 in relation to passing tones and neighboring tones, is equally applicable to the writing of suspensions. The dissonance, the suspended note, temporarily replaces a chord tone and resolves down by step to that chord tone. In each of the following examples, observe that the suspended note is so written that, at its resolution, the chord is found with its common doubling.

Suspensions are of several varieties, each being identified by the figured bass symbol usually associated with it.

1. The 4 3 suspension.

Fig. 15.26

Bach, *Du Lebensfürst, Herr Jesu Christ* (♯102)

The suspended note G in the tenor temporarily replaces the following note F♯. At the resolution, the triad has the usual doubling–two roots, one third, one fifth.

2. The 7 6 suspension.

Fig. 15.27

Bach, *Auf meinen lieben Gott* (♯304)

As its figuration indicates, the 7 6 suspension occurs in a first inversion, as in Figure 15.27, where it is found in the vii°_{6} triad. With the fifth in the soprano, the usual doubling in vii°_{6} is two fifths. Here, the suspended note temporarily replaces the root, F♯, and usual doubling is found at the point of resolution.

3. The 9 8 suspension.

Fig. 15.28

Haydn, *Missa Sanctae Caecilae*

In the 9 8 suspension, the dissonance is usually sounded simultaneously with its resolution since the note of resolution is a doubled note.

When this suspension is found in the tenor voice at an interval of a second above the bass voice, it is known as a 2 1 suspension. It is not commonly used.

Fig. 15.29

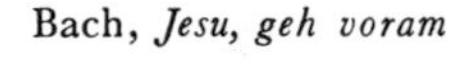
Bach, *Jesu, geh voram*

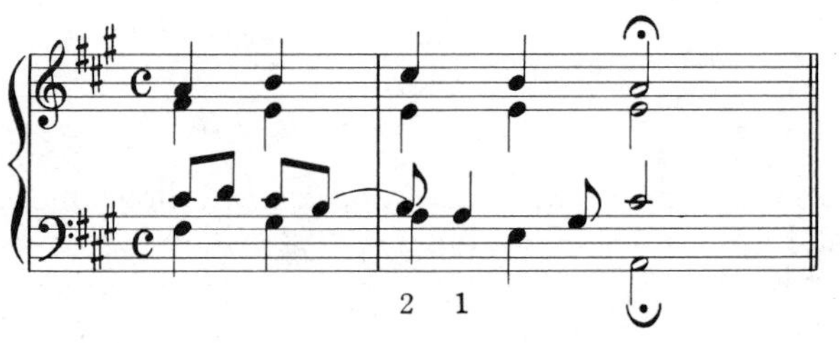

4. The $\substack{5\\2}$ suspension (also known as the 2 3 suspension).

This suspension is always found in the bass voice, the necessary figuration $\substack{5\\2}$ giving it its name. Since the suspended note in the bass temporarily replaces the third of the triad, the upper voices show the usual doubling for first inversion. The alternate name 2 3 derives from the fact that the interval of a second at the point of suspension resolves to the interval of a third.

When the interval of the second is found in its compound version, the ninth, it is still called a 2 3 suspension.

Fig. 15.30

Bach, *Aus meines Herzens Grunde* (♯1)

5. Suspensions in the tonic six-four chord. When figured above the *actual* root of the tonic triad, the 5 4 suspension of Figure 15.31 is the same as a 9 8 suspension, whereas the 7 6 suspension of Figure 15.32 is the same as a 4 3 suspension.

Fig. 15.31

Bach, *Als der gütige Gott* (#159)

Fig. 15.32

Berlioz, *La Damnation de Faust*

6. The 9, 7, and 4 suspensions.

These suspensions are identical with the 9 8, 7 6, and 4 3 suspensions, except that at the moment of resolution of the suspended note, there is a change of structure in the harmony—either another inversion of the chord, or a different chord. The 9 suspension is the most common of the three.

Change of inversion

Fig. 15.33

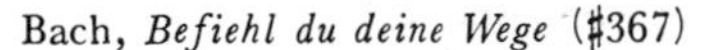

Change of Harmony

Fig. 15.34

Bach, *Meinen Jesum lass ich nicht* (#152)

7. The ornamental resolution. There are a wide variety of such resolutions, two of which are shown in Figure 15.35. The occasional upward ornamentation has already been shown in Figure 11.12.

Fig. 15.35

a) Bach, *Liebster Jesu, wir sind hier* (#328)
b) Bach, *Heilig bist du Herr, Gott Zaboath*

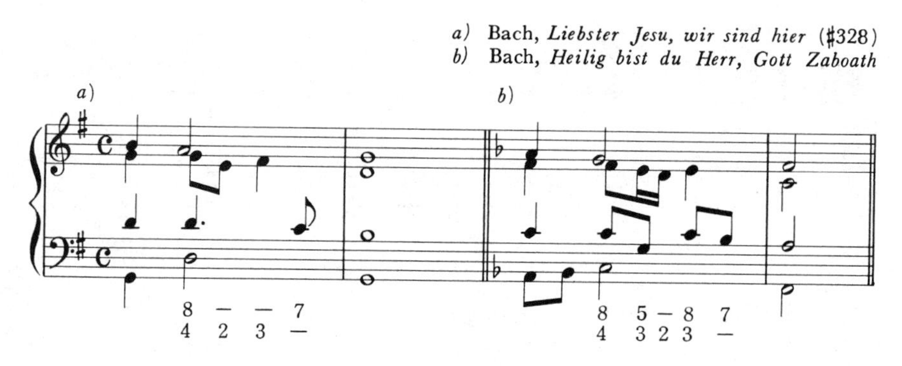

8. Chain suspensions. A chain suspension occurs when two or more suspensions follow each other in succession, the note of resolution of one suspension becoming the note of approach for the next suspension.

Fig. 15.36 Chain of 7 6 suspensions

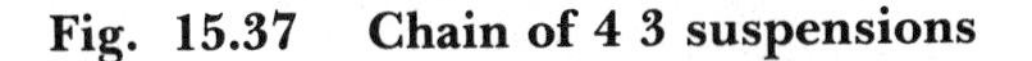

Fig. 15.37 Chain of 4 3 suspensions

Bach, *Heut ist, O Mensch, ein grösser Trauertag* (#168)

In Figure 15.38, each suspension of the chain resolves simultaneously with a change of harmony, resulting in a chain of 7 suspensions.

Fig. 15.38

Mozart, Mass in C Minor, K. 427

One more example from the vast literature of possible uses of the suspension, Figure 15.39, shows each suspension of the chain appearing on the first beat

Fig. 15.39

Schubert, Waltz, Op. 9a, No. 6

of the measure and its resolution delayed until the final note of the following measure. With the melodic line continuing between these two points, the effect is that of two separate melodies combined as one (Figure 15.39b).

The Metric Factor in Suspensions

The suspension always occurs at a point of rhythmic strength in relation to its approach and resolution. Thus, if in $\frac{4}{4}$ time the suspension resolves in quarter notes, the dissonant tone will always be on beats 1 and 3 (see Figure 15.33). If in the same meter the resolution is in eighth notes, the dissonance can be found on any beat (1, 2, 3 or 4) of the measure, since the beat itself is stronger than the half beat that follows (see Figure 15.37). Figure 15.34 includes both situations in the same measure. In triple time, the suspension dissonance, like the dissonant tonic six-four, may occur on the second beat and resolve on the third, thus leading to the following strong first beat of the measure (see Figure 15.26).

The note of approach in chorale style and similar easier styles of writing is usually the same length as or longer than the following dissonance. In instrumental styles or more complex vocal styles, the note of approach is often shorter.

Fig. 15.40

Assignment 15.6. Writing suspensions. Complete each exercise by filling in alto and tenor voices. Make an harmonic analysis. Circle each suspended note.

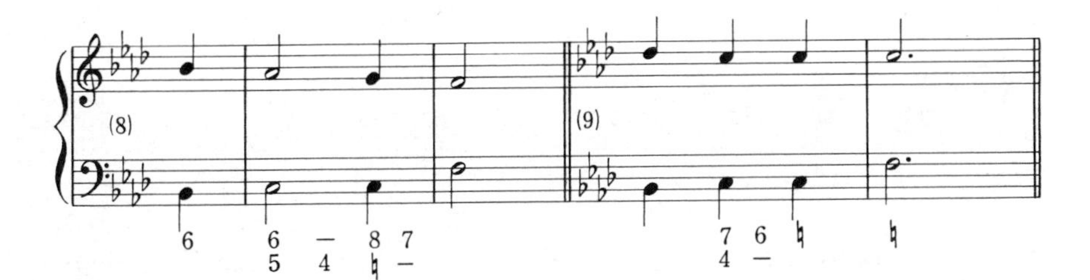

Assignment 15.7. Writing chain suspensions. Each exercise is begun for you. Continue until you reach a cadence on the tonic. Write in other keys as assigned.

Assignment 15.8. Extended exercises in part-writing. Complete each exercise by filling in the alto and tenor voices. Solve some of these exercises using open score with C clefs, as assigned. Make an harmonic analysis and identify all nonharmonic tones.

(3)
♯ ♯ 6 ♯ 6 ♯
6 ♯ 6 6 6 ♯

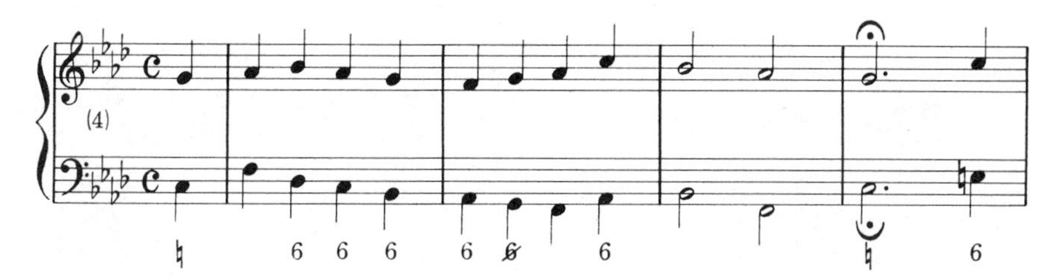
(4)
♮ 6 6 6 6 6 6 ♮ 6

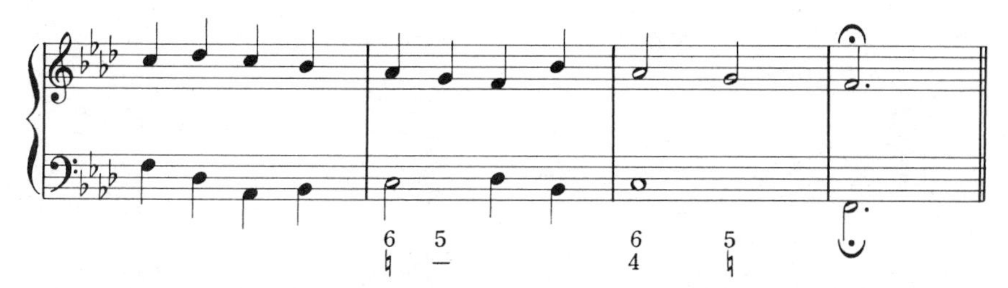
6 5
♮ —
6 5
4 ♮

(6)
7 6 8 9 8 7 4 3 ♯ 8 9 6 5 3 2 6 6 8 7
6 — 3 — 4 ♯ —

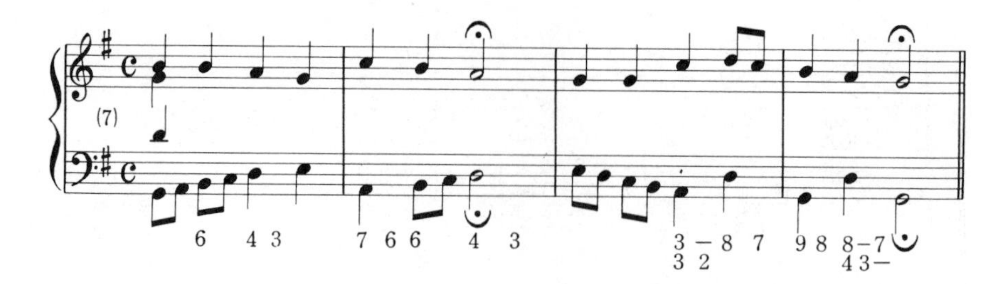
(7)
6 4 3 7 6 6 4 3 3 — 8 7 9 8 8—7
3 2 4 3—

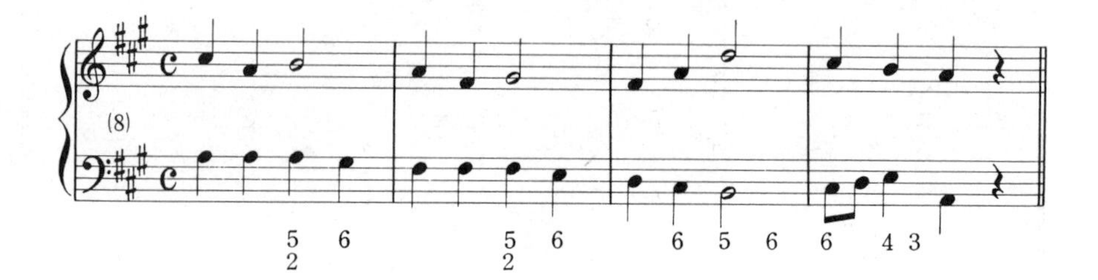
(8)
5 6 5 6 6 5 6 6 4 3
2 2

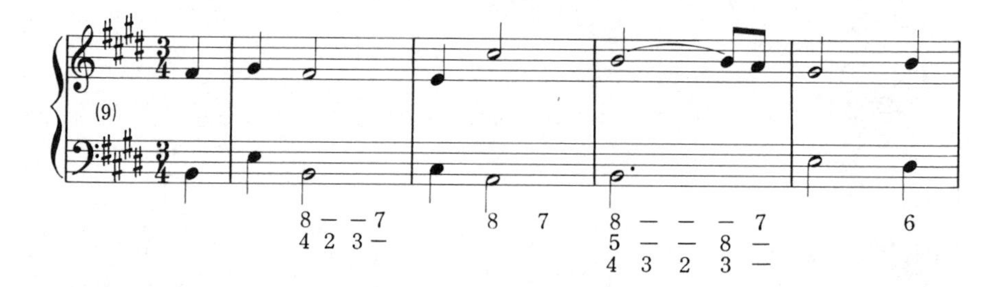
(9)
8 — — 7 8 7 8 — — — 7 6
4 2 3— 5 — — 8 —
4 3 2 3 —

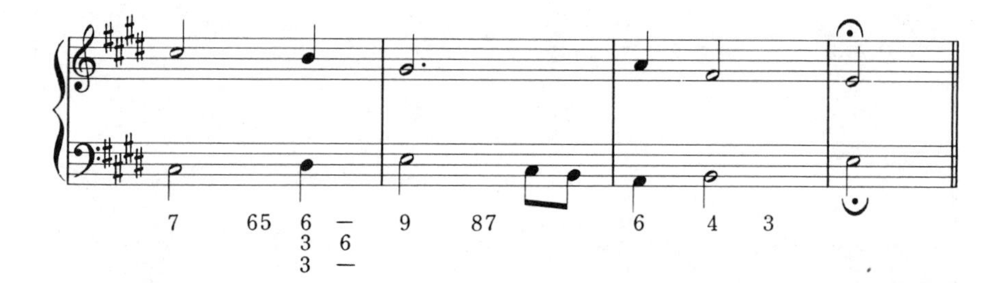
7 65 6 — 9 87 6 4 3
3 6
3 —

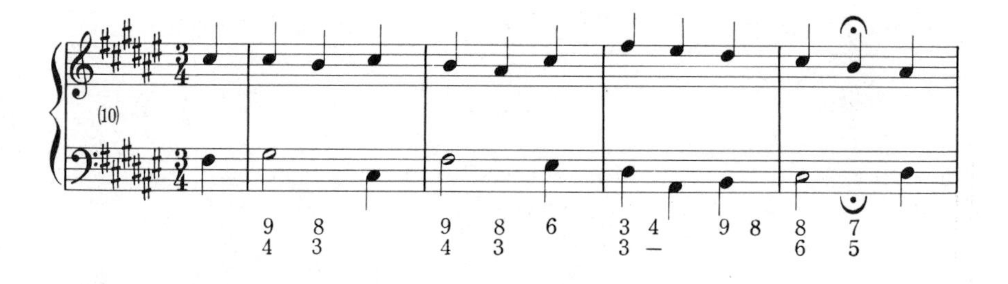
(10)
9 8 9 8 6 3 4 9 8 8 7
4 3 4 3 3 — 6 5

Ear Training

Exercise 15.1. Singing the submediant triad. Sing with letter names the tonic triad of the given key. Find the submediant note by singing a minor third below the tonic in a major key, or by singing a major third below the tonic in a minor key. Sing the submediant triad with letter names. (See Figure 15.41a, b).

Exercise 15.2. Singing the mediant triad. Follow directions given in Exercise 1.1, but find the mediant note by singing a major third above the tonic in a major key, or a minor third above the tonic in a minor key. (See Figure 15.41c, d.)

Fig. 15.41

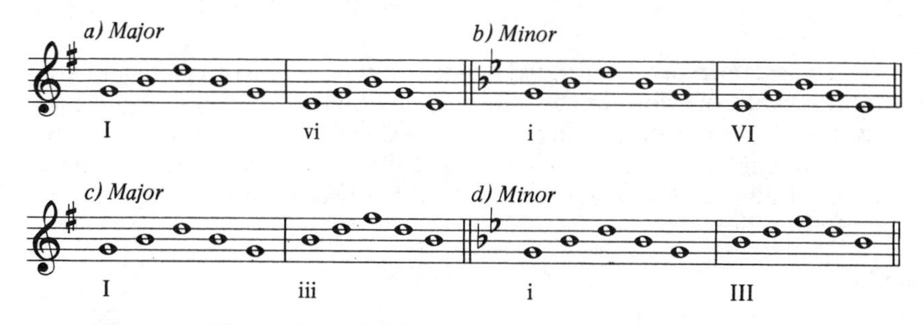

Exercise 15.3 Sing with letter names each of the following chord progressions in keys given by your instructor.

Major key:	I vi ii V I	I iii IV V I
	I vi V I	I vi iii IV V I
	I vi IV V I	I iii vi ii V I
	I V vi	
Minor key:	i VI iv V i	i III iv V i
	i VI ii° V i	i VI III iv V I
	i VI V i	i III VI ii° V i
	i V VI	

Follow the example as given in Figure 13.16.

Exercise 15.4. Harmonic dictation. Harmonic dictation will now include the submediant and mediant triads. The most common uses of these triads, and therefore the ones to be found most often in the dictation exercises, will be those in the progression in Exercise 15.3.

Keyboard Harmony

Exercise 15.5. Play the deceptive cadence in each major and minor key. In major, when the melody line between V and vi descends, use part-writing Rule 3; when melody line ascends, use Rule 5. In minor, always use Rule 5.

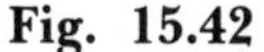

Fig. 15.42

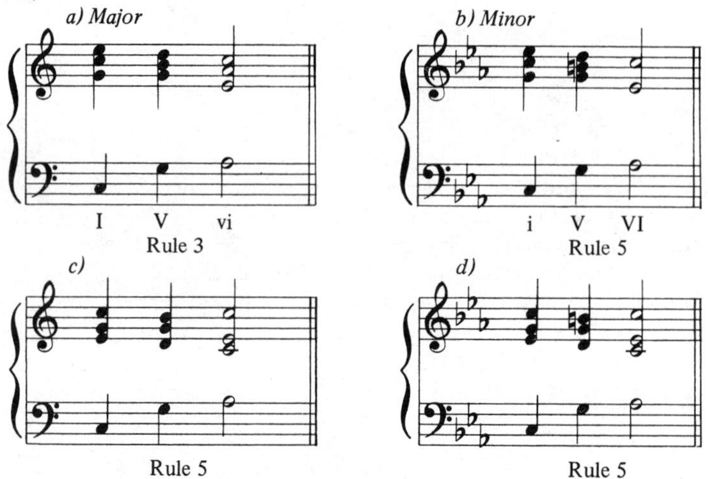

Exercise 15.6. Play chord progressions using the submediant and mediant triads. As with previous keyboard exercises, all the following progressions can be played in close position, using three notes in the right hand and one in the left, and following correct part-writing procedure from triad to triad. Although illustration of all possible progressions would consume too much space, two typical examples follow.

Fig. 15.43

a) Play the following progressions in any or all keys, as assigned.

Major keys

I vi ii V I
I vi IV V (or vii°_6) I
I vi V I
I vi ii_6 V I
I IV V vi
I ii_6 V vi

I iii IV V (or vii°_6) I
I iii vi ii V I
I iii vi IV V (or vii°_6) I
I V vi iii IV V (or vii°_6) I
(opening tonic chord with
third in soprano)

Minor keys

i VI iv V i	i III iv V i
i VI ii°$_6$ V i	i III VI iv V i
i VI V i	i III VI ii°$_6$ V i
i iv V VI	i V VI III iv V i
i ii°$_6$ V VI	(opening tonic chord with third in soprano)

b) Play part-writing exercises in Assignments 15.4 and 15.5.

Harmonizing the Scale at the Keyboard. Enough harmonic vocabulary has now been acquired to harmonize major and minor scales, both ascending and descending. More than one harmonization is possible in each case. Examples of major and minor scales, using triads with roots in the bass, are written out. Other harmoniztions are suggested by chord numbers.

Fig. 15.44 Major

*inversion necessary here

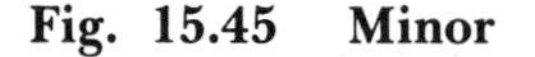
Fig. 15.45 Minor

*inversion necessary here

Major, ascending

(Scale steps)	1	2	3	4	5	6	7	8
	I	V(V$_6$)*	I	IV	I	IV	vii°$_6$	I
	I	V(V$_6$)	I	IV	I$_6$	ii	V	I

Major, descending

8	7	6	5	4	3	2	1
I	iii	IV	I	ii$_6$	I$_6$	V	I
I	V	vi	iii	IV	I$^6_4$	V	I

Minor melodic, ascending

1	2	3	4	5	6	7	8
i	V(V$_6$)	i	iv	i$_6$	IV	vii°$_6$	i
i	V(V$_6$)	i	iv	i$_6$	ii	V	i

*Triads in parentheses are alternate harmonizations for the given scale step.

Minor melodic, descending

8	7	6	5	4	3	2	1
i	III	iv	i	ii°_{6}	i_{6}	V	i
i	III	iv	V	iv_{6}	$\text{i}^{4}_{\substack{6\\4}}$	V	i

Exercise 15.7. Play harmonized major and minor scales, ascending and descending, and with various triad progressions, as assigned.

Exercise 15.8. Harmonization of melodies with lead sheet symbols. Diminished triads must be in first inversion, and supertonic triads in major will usually be more effective in first inversion. The following melodies can also be harmonized using I, IV and V only. For further practice use Mainous, *Melodies to Harmonize With,* Chapters D and E.

Exercise 15.9. Harmonize melodies by using submediant and mediant triads in addition to the triads previously studied.

Exercise 15.10. Melody Harmonization. Harmonize these melodies from sight singing books, as assigned.

Music for Sight Singing: Submediant triad: melodies 27, 44, 66, 72, 109, 137, 141, 144, 151, 173, 221, 312, 320, 326, and 343.

Mediant Triad: melodies 3, 26, 66, 72, 80, 132, 139, 307, 316, 320, and 360.

More Music for Sight Singing: Submediant triad: melodies 237, 238, 251, 252, 253, 262, 266, 267, 275, 278, 287, 289, 293, 299, 337, 397, 399, and 437.

Mediant triad: melodies 228, 239, 245, 247, 261, 263, 267, 270, 298, 300, 325, 336, 431, and 458.

CHAPTER 16

The Harmonic Sequence and Other Triadic Usages

Theory and Analysis

The Harmonic Sequence

By its name, harmonic sequence indicates a repetition of musical material at a different pitch level. For our present purposes the repetition is in root relationships or in the root movements between chords, in that the interval of a root movement is repeated one or more times at new pitch levels. The advantage of this, as of any sequence, is that it affords the opportunity to retain a feeling of repetition while avoiding the monotony of actual note-for-note repetition.

The most frequent harmonic seqeunce is that of a root movement up by the interval of a fourth and down by fifth, with the latter note ascending the fourth, followed by downward fifth, and so on.

Fig. 16.1

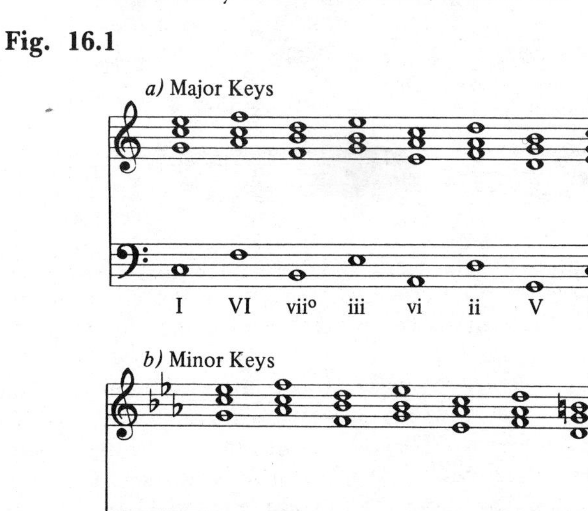

In observing sequences in this chapter, the following features should be kept in mind:

1. A minimum harmonic sequence is four chords, the given intervallic relationship, and one repetition, as in Figure 16.5.
2. The sequence need not begin or end on tonic, although it often does.
3. Root movements not common otherwise are used freely, such as vii°–iii, ii–vi, and so on.
4. Any diminished triad may be used with its root in the bass.
5. In a minor key, the use of the minor dominant triad (v) and the major subdominant triad (VII) is common. These triads will be discussed in detail later in this chapter. Their use is ordinarily required to accommodate the descending minor scale in a voice line.

Harmonic sequences can be used with chords in inversion as long as the bass line retains a sequential pattern. Figure 16.2 shows the full I–IV–vii°–iii–vi–ii–V–I sequence, with the bass line alternating between root position and first inversion.

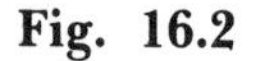
Fig. 16.2

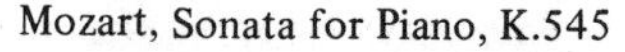
Mozart, Sonata for Piano, K.545

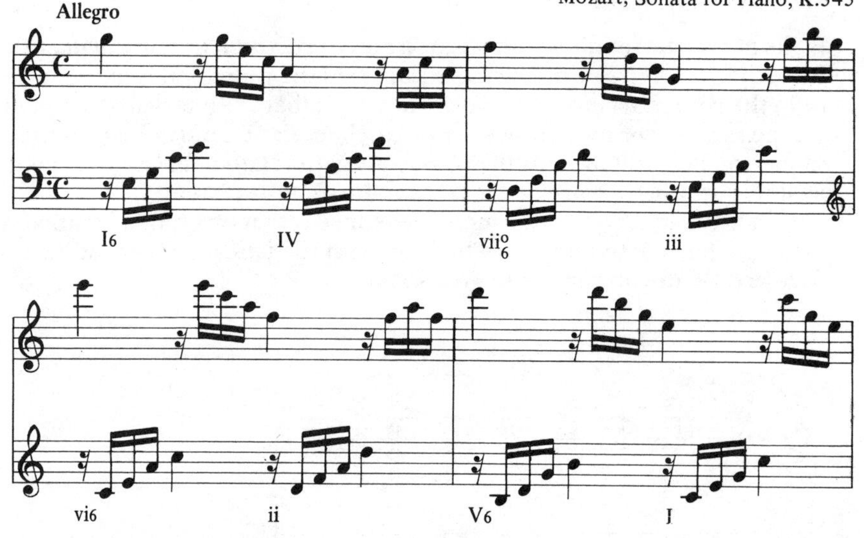

Usually, an harmonic sequence is accompanied by melodic and rhythmic sequence in the voice lines, as seen in the previous figure. Figure 16.3 shows the same harmonic sequence in full, in a minor key, with the two upper voices taking up new ideas at measure three.

Root movements in a sequence are expressed by the interval names second, third, fourth, and fifth. Sixths and sevenths are inversions of thirds and seconds, but the terms fourth and fifth must be used because both can be used in the same sequence (as seen in the previous figures). The intervals of the root movement refer only to their letter-name sizes and not to their qualities. Up a fifth from G, for example, could be D♭, D or D♯.

Fig. 16.3

Bach, *Well-Tempered Clavier,* Vol. 1,
Fugue No. 2

Here are some additional sequences, expressed in differing patterns of root movements.

1. down a fourth, up a fifth

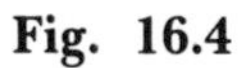

Fig. 16.4

Fig. 16.5

Schubert, Waltz

2. down a third, up a fourth

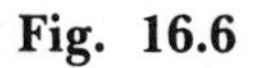

Fig. 16.6

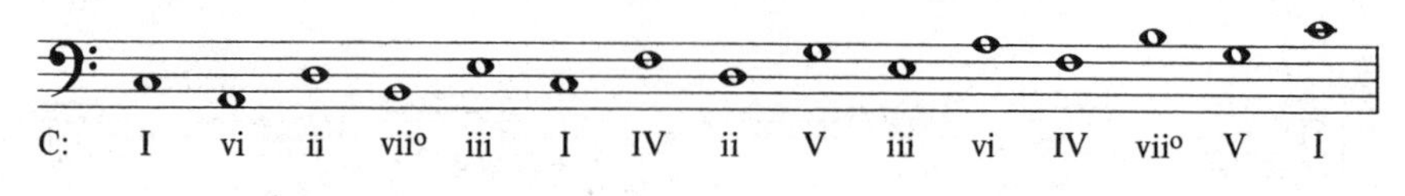

Fig. 16.7

que - sto, del - le bel - le, che a - mo il pa - dron
show you, Of the fair ones my mas - ter has
ii
vii°

mi - o; un ca - ta - lo - go e -
court - ed. Here you'll find them all
iii
I

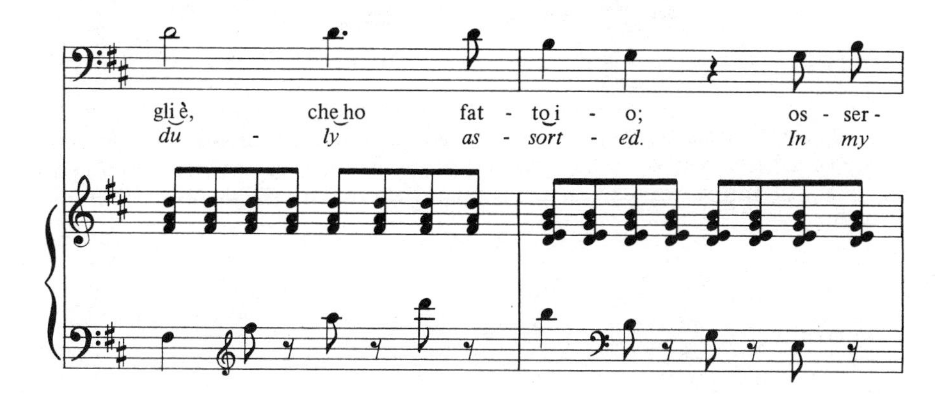
gli è, che ho fat - to i - o; os - ser -
du - ly as - sort - ed. In my

3. up a fourth, down a third

Fig. 16.8

Fig. 16.9

The use of the chromatic sixth and seventh scale steps in Figure 16.9 is of particular interest as shown in Figure 16.10. When the lower voice descends from one of these sensitive tones, and is replaced by an upper voice that ascends, both chromatic indications are necessary and the harmonic symbols change accordingly.

Fig. 16.10

The second beat of the next measure is treated similarly.

4. down a third, up a second

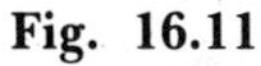
Fig. 16.11

Fig. 16.12

Fauré, Pavanne[1]

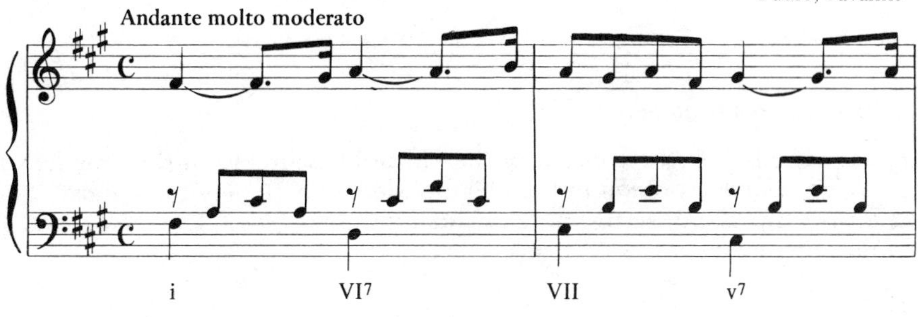

5. down a fourth, up a second

Fig. 16.13

[1]Three members of this sequence are found with added sevenths: v^7, VI^7, and iv^7. Sequences containing many sevenths, and often excluding triads, as well as ninths and altered harmonies, are very common; more so than the diatonic triadic sequences of this chapter. Extensive studies of these are included in *Advanced Harmony.*

Fig. 16.14

* N = E♭ G B♭ (in first inversion, called *Neapolitan Sixth*)

First Inversions in Series

Closely allied to the concept of the harmonic sequence is the practice of writing triads in first inversion in parallel motion. Since the intervals above the bass are always thirds and sixths, no unwanted parallels result. Obviously, no consideration of chord succession is necessary in this style.

Fig. 16.15

The Minor Dominant Triad

When, in a minor key, one of the voice lines of a composition descends stepwise from the tonic note, it passes through the lowered seventh and sixth scale steps. Placing a dominant triad at the point of the lowered melodic seventh produces a minor dominant triad (v) rather than the usual major dominant triad (V). The minor dominant triad is used *only* to accommodate the descending seventh scale step; used otherwise, with the flatted seventh ascending, it produces a sound reminiscent of a medieval mode, which in certain situations, such as a guitar accompaniment to a modal folk song, can be quite effective.

In Figure 16.16, the alto line in G minor descends from tonic to dominant. At the point of the seventh scale step, F, the chord must be D F A (v) rather than D F♯ A (V). Had D F♯ A been used, an augmented second F♯–E♭, would have occurred in the alto line. Still, this could have been avoided by following D F♯ A with VI, E♭ G B♭, which Brahms obviously did not choose to do. Figure 16.17

shows the same progression, i–v–VI, with the lowered seventh and sixth scale steps in the bass line.

Fig. 16.16

Fig. 16.17

When two voices make simultaneous use of either the sixth or seventh scale step, and each voice proceeds in a different direction, both accidentals must be used simultaneously. In most such cases, one of the two notes involved is a simple nonharmonic tone, as in Figure 16.18 where, in the V triad the F natural appoggiatura sounds at the same time as the leading tone F♯.

Fig. 16.18

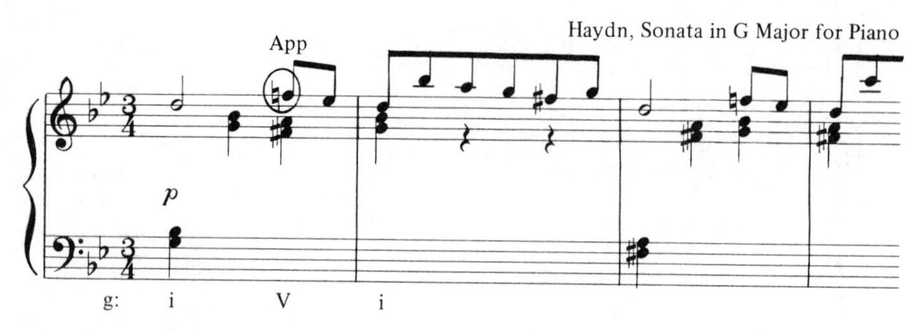

In other instances as in Figure 16.19, both notes are apparently triad tones.

Fig. 16.19

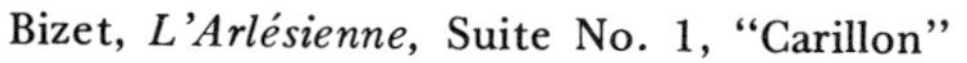

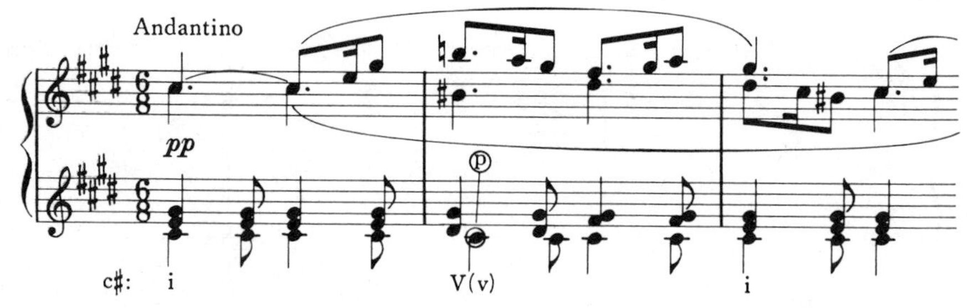

Similar passages involving the raised and lowered sixth scale steps are far less frequent. In Figure 16.20, at the asterisk, we see C natural and C♯ used simul-

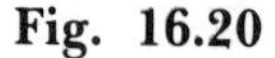

Fig. 16.20

taneously in E minor, C natural being the 9th of V^9 (B D♯ F♯ A C) and descending, whereas the C♯ is an ascending passing tone.

The Triads VII and vi° in a Minor Key

The triad built on the lowered seventh scale step in a minor key (VII; in C minor, B♭ D F) does not function by progression to the tonic as does the leading tone triad, vii°. Its aural impression is that of a major dominant harmony, in which manner it functions almost exclusively by progressing to the mediant triad (VII–III). In Figure 16.21, the VII–III progression (C E G to F A C), sounds at least temporarily like V–I in F. A chord that acts as a dominant to a chord other than tonic is known as a *secondary dominant* chord and will be discussed in full in Chapter 18.

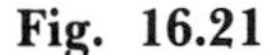
Fig. 16.21

Assignment 16.1. Spell the subtonic major triad (VII) and the minor dominant (v) in all minor keys.

The use of vi° is very limited. In Figure 16.22, it harmonzies the raised sixth scale step as part of a series of first inversions, i_6–vi°_6–vii°_6–i_6.

Fig. 16.22

Half Cadences; The Phrygian Cadence

Any diatonic triad except vii° and VII can precede the V triad to create a half cadence at an appropriate cadential point. Common are ii–V and IV–V, in both major and minor. One of these, iv$_6$–V, carries a special designation as the Phyrigian cadence. In this cadence, the soprano ascends by whole step while the bass descends by half step, a characteristic of the Phrygian mode, as seen in Figures 16.23a and 16.24. The cadence iv–V is also considered Phrygian, even though the half and whole step arrangement is reversed, as seen in Figures 16.23b and 16.25.

Fig. 16.23

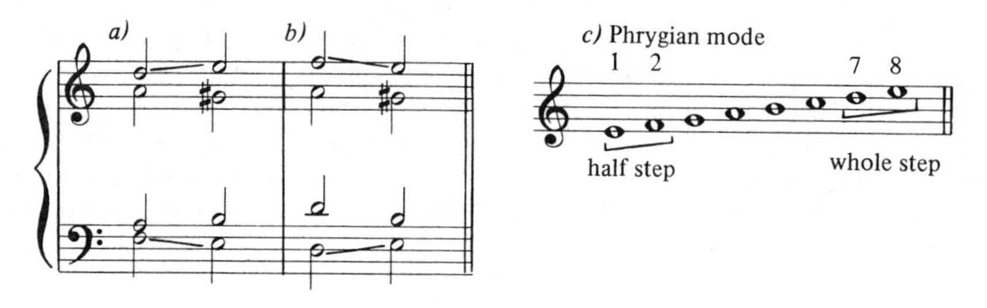

Fig. 16.24

The D F A–E G♯ B cadence seen in Figure 16.25 is the final cadence of this chorale tune in the Phrygian mode. To our ears, accustomed to major and minor, such final cadences often sound incomplete.

The Phrygian cadence exists also in a major key as ii$_6$–III. The major III triad in a major key is usually considered a secondary dominant chord (Chapter 18), but as a member of the Phrygian cadence it usually returns directly to tonic.

Fig. 16.25

Fig. 16.26

The Six-Four Chords (Triads in Second Inversion)

The *cadential six-four* chord, the most frequently used of all six-four chords, has already been studied. In its most common form, the moving voices above the bass proceed downward. But occasionally the upper voices ascend after the cadential six-four.

Fig. 16.27

The usual resolution of the cadential six-four is occasionally interrupted by another sonority whose bass note is a step above or below the bass note of the cadential six-four. An example of such an interruption ($I_{6 \atop 4}$–ii_6–V–I) can be seen in Figure 16.35.

There are three other uses of the six-four chord.

1. The Passing Six-four. This six-four chord occurs ordinarily between a triad with root in bass and its first inverison, or vice versa. Usually the three-note scale line in the bass is countered by the same three-note line, but in the opposite direction, in an upper voice, as in Figure 16.28 and in measure 2 of Figure 16.29, although at times the upper voice may display a different pattern as in Figure 16.29, measure 3.

Most common of the passing six-four chords is the passing V^6_4 found between two positions of the tonic triad.

Fig. 16.28

Fig. 16.29[2]

Passing six-four chords other than those on V and I are uncommon,[3] though theoretically any triad can be found in second inversion as a passing chord. Sometimes these passing six-four chords are found between two different chord numbers, both of which usually progress to the same chord. In Figure 16.30, the vi^6_4 is found between V^4_2 and vii^o_6, both of which usually resolve to I.

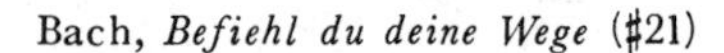

Fig. 16.30

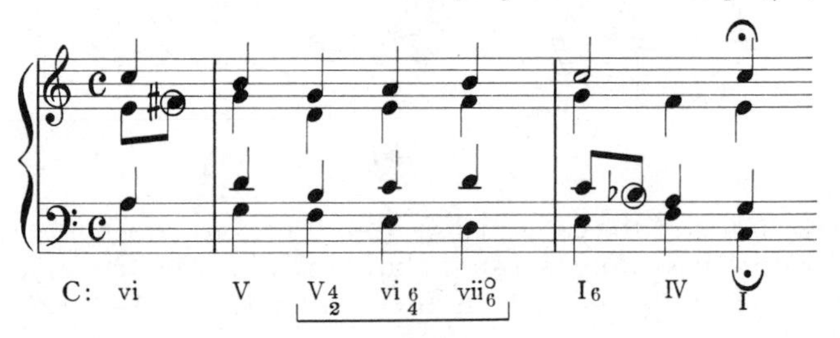

[2]The two outside voices of this excerpt form a canon.

[3]The passing I^6_4 is commonly used in the progression IV_6–I^6_4–ii^6_5 and will be considered in the study of seventh chords.

2. The Pedal Six-Four[4] Here the chord preceding the six-four has the same bass note as the six-four; the six-four usually resolves to the same triad that preceded it. The name derives from the pedal point effect in the bass. The pedal $^6_4$ is most commonly found in the pattern I–IV$^6_4$–I.

Fig. 16.31

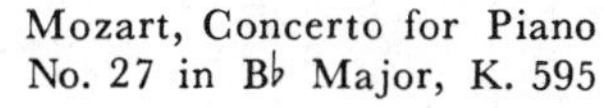

3. The Arpeggiated Six-Four. Preceding this six-four chord is the same chord with root or third in the bass. The bass line shows an arpeggio effect. This use is not common.

Fig. 16.32

Hymn: Beatitudo

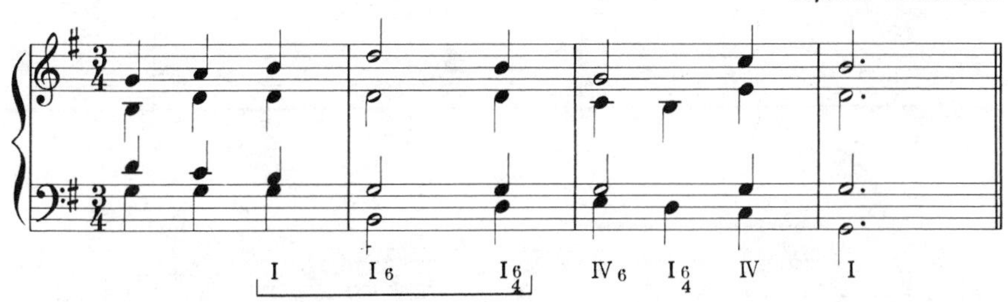

The tonic six-four chord in Figure 16.31 could be described as an arpeggiated six-four since it follows a tonic triad with root in bass; it is also a cadential six-four chord because of its location in the phrase.

Assignment 16.2. Harmonic analysis. These examples will contain a variety of the materials studied in this chapter. Make the usual harmonic analysis, and

[4]Also known as an *auxiliary six-four* or an *embellishing six-four*.

describe any compositional feature used by the composer that has been described in this chapter.

(4)
Purcell, *Adelazar,* or *The Moor's Revenge*
1st Violin
2nd Violin
Viola
Bass
(5) Andante con moto
Mendelssohn, Symphony No. 3, "Scottish"

(6) Handel, *Messiah*

(7) Schumann, *Albumblätter*, Op. 124, No. 4

(8)
Schubert, Sonata in B♭ Major for Piano
Andante sostenuto
pp

(9)
Mozart, Quartet, K.575
Allegretto
tr
p

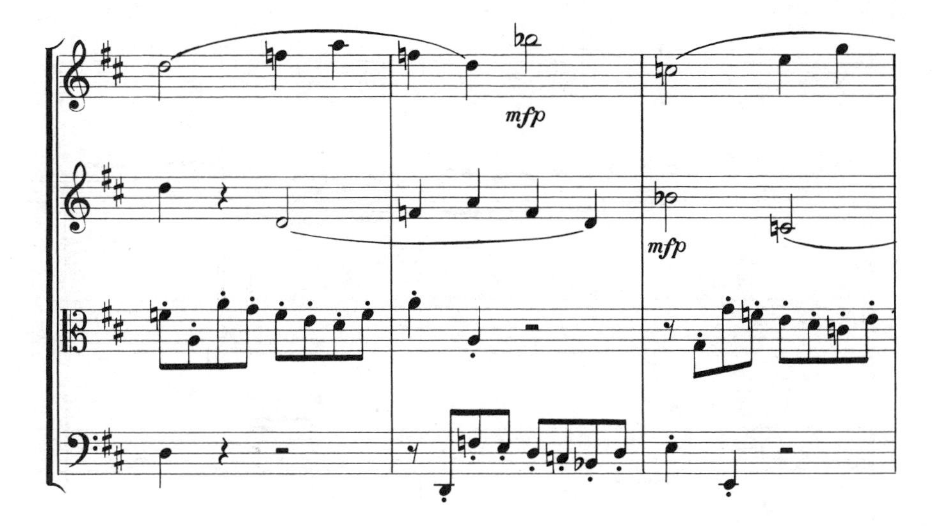
mfp
mfp

140
mfp
mfp
mfp

mfp
mfp
mfp
mfp
mf
mfp
mfp

3
tr
tr
tr
tr
f
f
f
V4/V
3

(10) **Allegro, ma non troppo** Chopin, Mazurka, Op. 68, No. 3

(11) **Vivace** Beethoven, Sonata for Piano, Op. 79

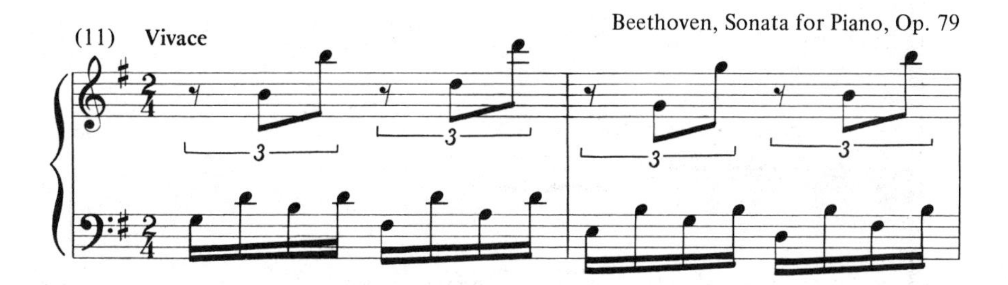

(12)
f
f
f
f

Application

Written Materials

Writing the v and VII Triads in a Minor Key

No new part-writing procedures are required for either of these triads. Each triad contains a lowered seventh scale step. In the dominant minor (v) triad, this tone must descend. In the VII triad, the lowered seventh scale degree assumes the role of root of a secondary dominant chord; therefore its properties are the same as those of the root of a dominant triad.

Fig. 16.33

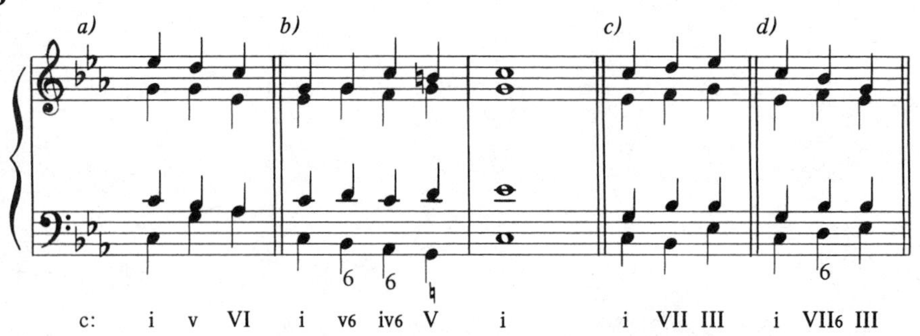

Assignment 16.3. Part-writing, v and VII triads. Fill in the alto and tenor voices. Make an harmonic analysis.

Writing the Phrygian Cadence

In the Phrygian cadence, the iv_6 triad can be written with any doubling.

Fig. 16.34

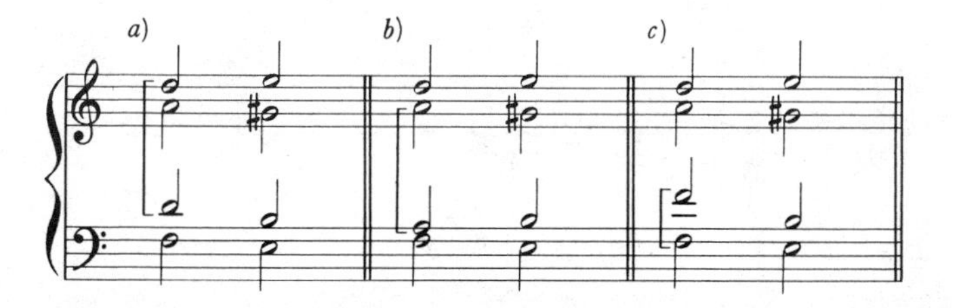

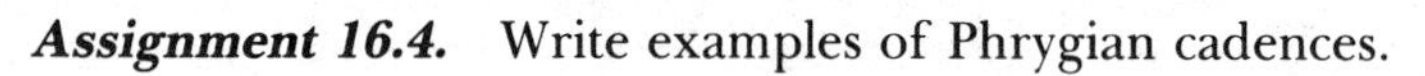

Assignment 16.4. Write examples of Phrygian cadences.

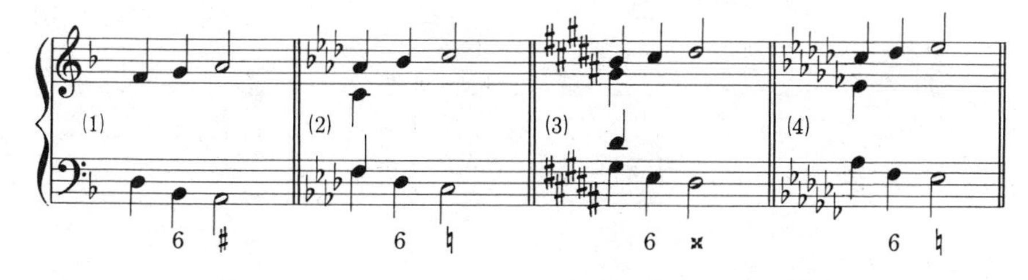

Writing Six-Four Chords

In writing any of the six-four chords, these two part-writing procedures usually apply.

1. Approach and Departure. The bass note of the six-four is preceded and followed only by

a) the same bass note;
b) a note a step above or below;
c) a skip in the *same* chord;
d) a skip from the supertonic note in the progression ii(ii^7)-I$_{\substack{6\\4}}$.

2. Doubling. The bass note, fifth of the triad, is always doubled. Use Rule 6A to approach and leave the doubled note.

Assignment 16.5. Write examples of the various uses of the six-four chord. Fill in inner voices and make an harmonic analysis. In addition, identify each six-four chord as cadential, passing, pedal, or arpeggiated.

Writing Anticipations, Escaped Tones, and Appoggiaturas

Rule 8, Writing Nonharmonic Tones, continues to be applicable in writing these three varieties of nonharmonic tones. At (1) in Figure 16.35 the appoggiatura D temporarily replaces its resolution, C. At the point of resolution, usual doubling is found.

Fig. 16.35

Bach, *Jesu, nun sei gepreiset* (#252)

There is less concern with voice distribution in writing the anticipation and escaped tone, since these usually appear on the weak part of the beat, after the chord structure has already been established.

Anticipations are fairly common, particularly when used at the cadence in the soprano or tenor voice. Use of the appoggiatura and escaped tone is minimal in four-voice texture; these two dissonances will be found more useful in instrumental style of writing.

Assignment 16.6. Part-writing. These exercises contain examples of most chord progression and part-writing procedures studied to date. Fill in inner voices and make an harmonic analysis. Solve the exercises in open score, as assigned.

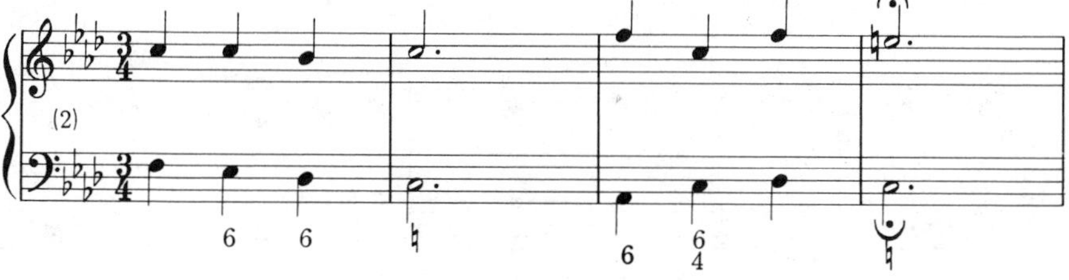

(3)

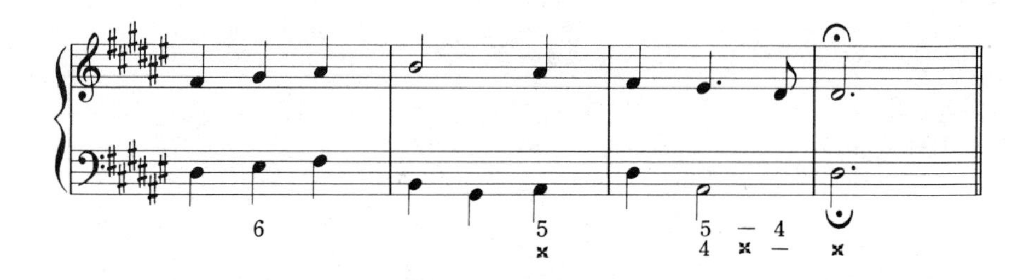

(4)

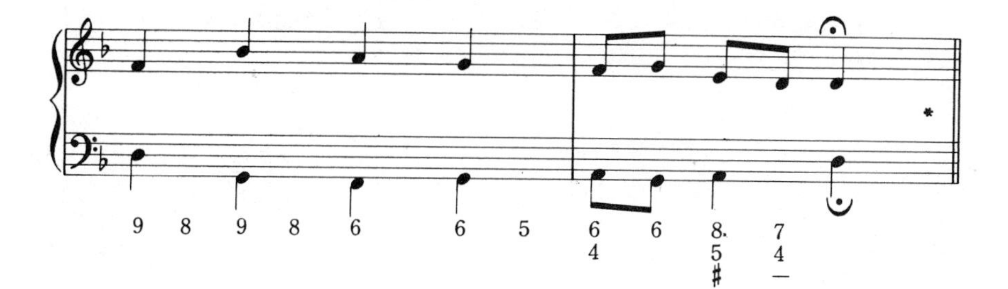

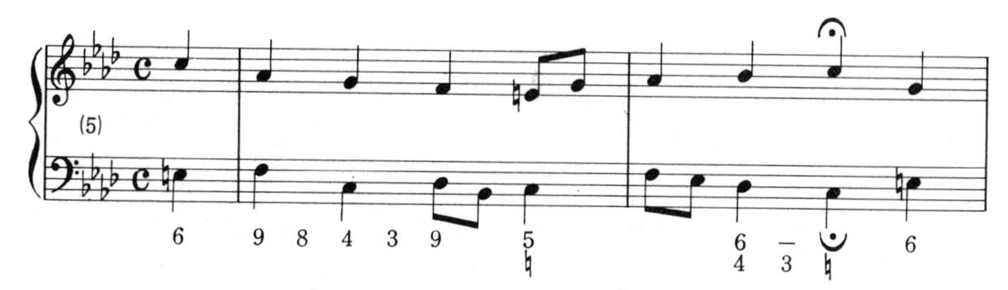

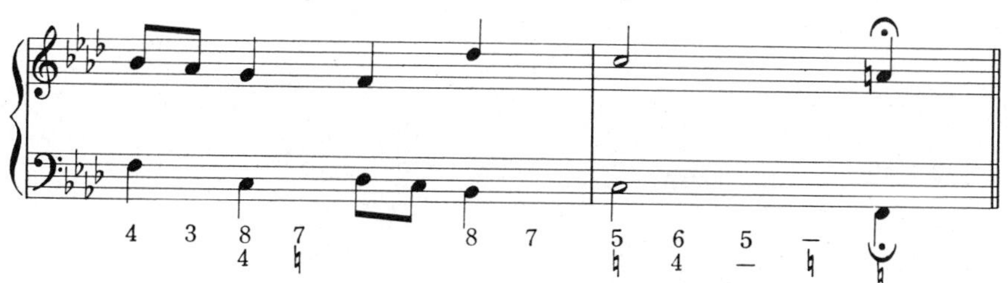

*Review Figure 11.27 and the discussion of it.

Assignment 16.7. Part-writing. The bass voice only is given. Add soprano, alto, and tenor lines. Make an harmonic analysis.

Assignment 16.8. Part-writing an unfigured bass. In this type of problem, the bass line only is given, and without figuration. It must be determined which triads are in inversion and which have the root in the bass. Many solutions are possible for each exercise, so try several and compare them with each other, finally selecting the most musical. Below are three of the possible figurations for the first two measures of the first exercise.

Fig. 16.36

Melody Harmonization

In four-part vocal style, nonharmonic tones may be used very sparingly, as in a simple church hymn where perhaps only a single passing tone is found at the final cadence. At the other extreme, they may be used to make each of the four vocal parts a truly melodic line, as in the chorales of Johann Sebastian Bach. In these chorales the use of nonharmonic tones allows almost continual melodic movement from one chord to the next, in contrast to the "block chord" effect of the usual church hymn.

The use of nonharmonic tones to create the effect of continual melodic movement can be supplemented by two other devices.

1. By changing the structure of the chord, or by changing the inversion of the chord on the weak half of the beat (for example, on the second eighth note when a quarter note receives one beat).

Fig. 16.37

Bach, *O Gott, du frommer Gott* (#337)

2. By changing chords within the beat duration.

Fig. 16.38

When harmonizing a melody line, care must be exercised not to create parallel fifths and octaves through the use of nonharmonic tones.

Fig. 16.39

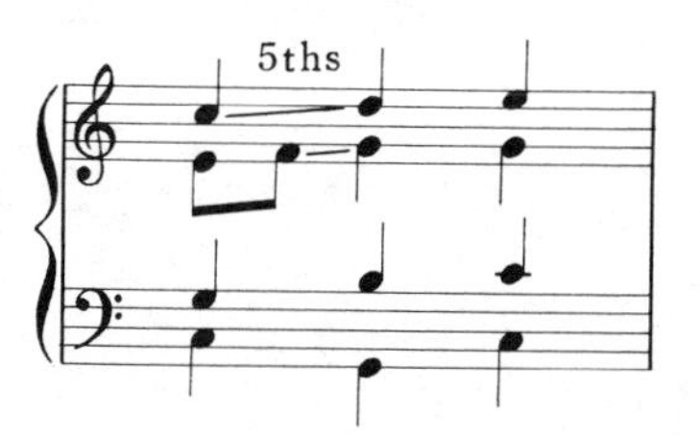

Assignment 16.9 Music examples in four voice parts are furnished. Add passing tones at appropriate places. Any given note may be placed on the weak half of the beat to make a place for an accented passing tone.

Assignment 16.10. Add suspensions and passing tones to the examples given. Given notes may be changed rhythmically to make suspensions possible.

With all the diatonic triads now available in melody harmonization, it is theoretically possible that each scale step can be a member of three different triads. Therefore, it is not enough simply to match a given triad to a given melody tone. A second and equally important consideration in chord choice is the relation of the chosen to those that immediately precede and follow it. Use Table 12.1 as a guide to this aspect of chord choice.

Assignment 16.11. Melody harmonization. Harmonize the following melodies, as assigned, from hymn, chorale, and folk sources. Review Chapter 12, "Melody Harmonization," for basic procedures. Use the submediant and mediant triads, the v and VII triads in a minor key, and any nonharmonic tones. Include harmonic analysis and tempo and dynamic markings.

When a melody begins on a tonic or dominant pickup, all four voices may carry this note, regardless of the relationship of these notes to the next chord.

Assignment 16.12. Write original exercises for voices or instruments in forms assigned by the instructor. Make an harmonic analysis. Indicate tempo and dynamics.

Writing Harmonic Sequences

Assignment 16.13. Writing harmonic sequences. In the following list, each progression of three triads is the beginning of an harmonic sequence. After reading the material following the list, continue each of these sequence patterns, concluding the exercise upon reaching the tonic triad.

Major Keys	*Minor Keys*
I IV vii°	i iv VII
I IV_6 vii°	i iv_6 VII
I_6 IV vii^{o}_{6}	i_6 iv VII_6
I V vi	i v VI
I V_6 vi	i v_6 VI
I IV ii	i iv ii°
	i VI VII
I vi ii	
I vi_6 ii	
I V ii	

The three triads in the preceding list indicate the root movement pattern. The first, I–IV–vii°, indicates roots down a fifth and up a fourth. If this sequence were started on C with the third in the soprano, Figure 16.40 would be the solution.

Fig. 16.40

Not all possible sequential patterns have been listed. When working with sequences, whether from the list above or other possibilities, it should be kept in mind that some patterns are more effective in major than minor, and vice versa, or in certain soprano positions or triad inversions. Experimentation is often necessary if a musically satisfactory sequence is to be created.

Ear Training

Exercise 16.1. *a*) Listen to the tonic note of a minor key. Sing the v triad with letter names.

b) Listen to the tonic note of a minor key. Sing the VII triad with letter names.

Exercise 16.2. *a*) Sing with letter names the progression i–v–VI–iv–V–i in each minor key.

b) Sing with letter names the progression i–VII–III–iv–V-i in each minor key.

Exercise 16.3. Harmonic dictation exercises will now include the chords and progressions studied in this chapter.

Keyboard Harmony

Exercise 16.4. Play each of the following progressions in each major and minor key.

I–V$^{6}_{4}$–I$_6$–IV–V(vii$^{o}_{6}$)–I

I–IV$^{6}_{4}$–I–V–I

i–V$^{6}_{4}$–i$_6$–iv–V(vii$^{o}_{6}$)–i

i–iv$^{6}_{4}$–i–V–i

i–v–VI–iv(ii$^{o}_{6}$)–V–i

i–v$_6$–iv$_6$–V–i

i–VII–III–iv–V(vii$^{o}_{6}$)–i

Exercise 16.5. *a*) Play this ascending minor scale;

1	2	3	4	5	6	7	8
i—	V—	i—	VII—	III—	ii—	V—	i

b) Play this descending minor scale:

8	7	6	5	4	3	2	1
i	v—	VI—	III—	iv—	i$^{6}_{4}$—	V—	i

Exercise 16.6. Playing harmonic sequences. Play the sequences listed in assignment 16.13, using three notes in the right hand and one in the left, as shown in Figure 16.1.

Exercise 16.7. Play the following seven melodies from lead sheet symbols.

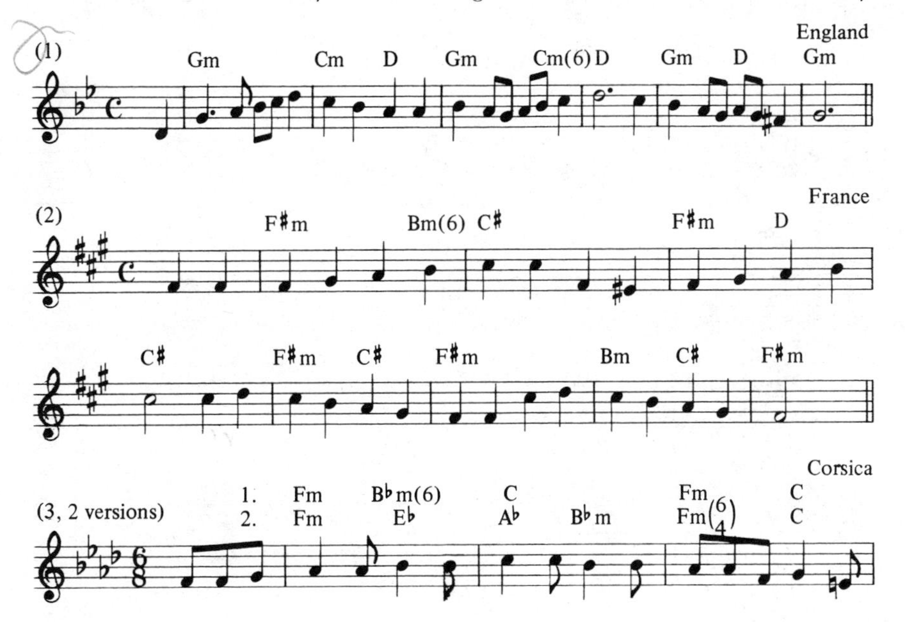

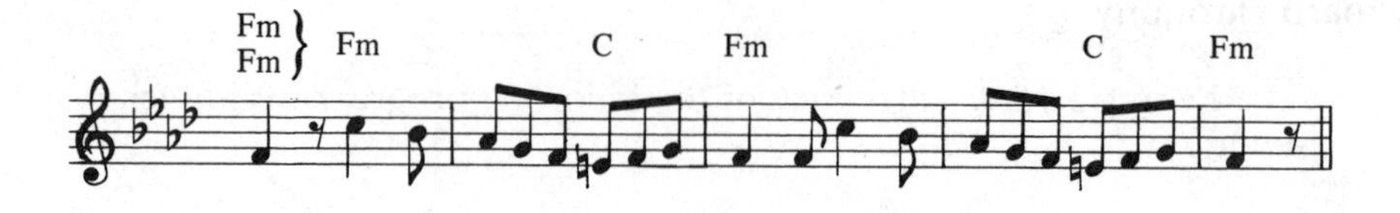

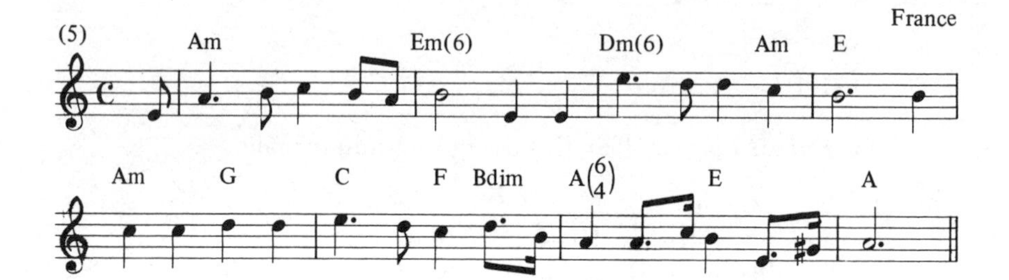

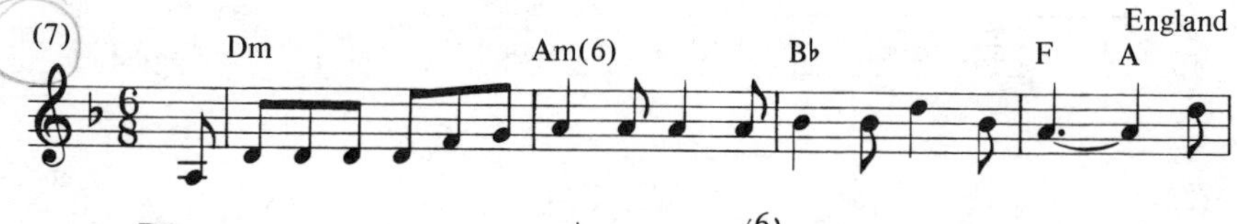

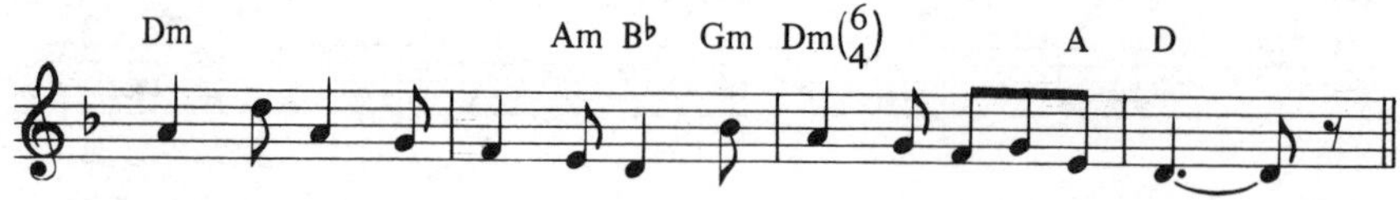

Exercise 16.8. Harmonize these melodies, using the triads v and VII, and the Phrygian cadence where musically effective.

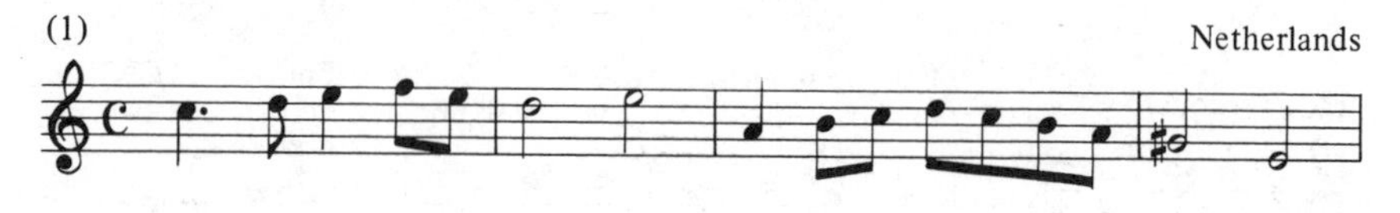

(2)
England

(3)
Netherlands
1.
2.

(4)
Russia

(5)
Denmark

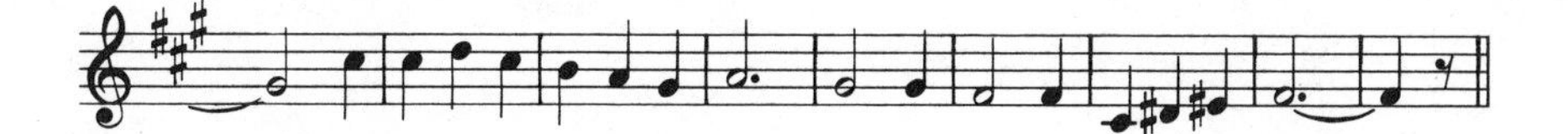

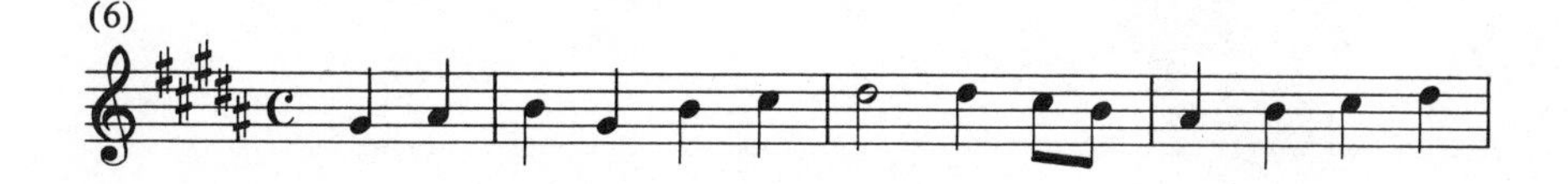
(6)

Exercise 16.9. Harmonize the melodies found in these sight singing texts. In *Music for Sight Singing:*

The Phrygian cadence: melodies 46, 47, 52, 76, 80, 88, 91, 314
The v triad: melodies 75, 125, 151, 326
The VII triad: melodies 47, 74, 75, 88

In *More Music for Sight Singing:*

The Phrygian cadence: melodies 328, 332, 333, 338
The v triad: melodies 261, 263, 337, 342
The VII triad: melodies 251, 329, 360, 361, 430

CHAPTER 17

The Dominant Seventh and Supertonic Seventh Chords

Theory and Analysis

Early Use of Dissonance

Interplay between consonance and dissonance has been one of the principal features of Western music since the development of free organum in the eleventh century. By the fourteenth century it was well established that the consonant intervals consisted of the major and minor thirds, the major and minor sixths, the perfect fifth, and the perfect octave. A vertical sonority was consonant when each of the notes in the upper voices formed a consonant interval with the lowest sounding note. Up to and throughout the sixteenth century, consonances could be used freely, but dissonance could be used only in certain well-defined situations comparable to some of the nonharmonic tone usages already described in this book. Use of any dissonance that would create what we today would call a complete seventh chord was limited to the weak part of the beat.

In Figure 17.1, at (1), the passing tone momentarily creates what appears to be an F A C E chord, though its true function as a simple passing tone is obvious in listening to the passage. A dissonance of a seventh could occur on a strong beat only as a 7–6 suspension, as at (2), where the note D is a suspension in the C E G triad rather than a part of an E G B D sonority. (Also note the simultaneous 4–3 suspension in the soprano).

Fig. 17.1

Palestrina (1525-1594), Mass *Ad Fugam*, "Kyrie"

Differentiating between a seventh chord and a 7–6 suspension is often confusing. In the 7–6 suspension, the dissonance resolves without change of chord structure, as in Figure 17.2a. The same 7–6 figure is part of a seventh chord when the sonority as a whole changes at the point of resolution, as in Figure 17.2b.

Fig. 17.2

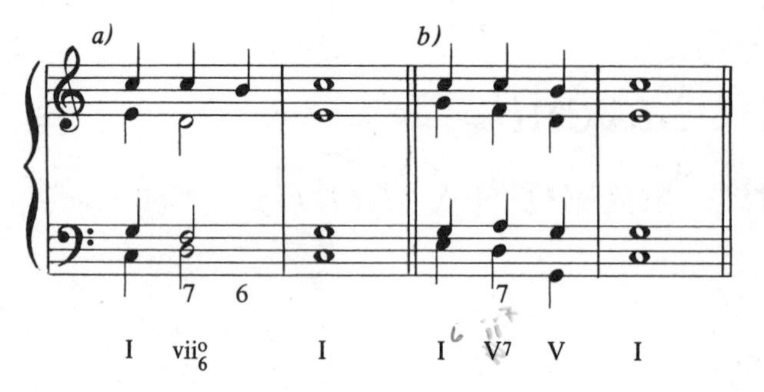

Not until the seventeenth century did the dissonant seventh appear simultaneously with a complete triad to form a complete seventh chord, although earlier rare and atypical examples can be found. An early seventeenth century example, Figure 17.3 shows the seventh sounding simultaneously with a triad to create a seventh chord structure.

Fig. 17.3

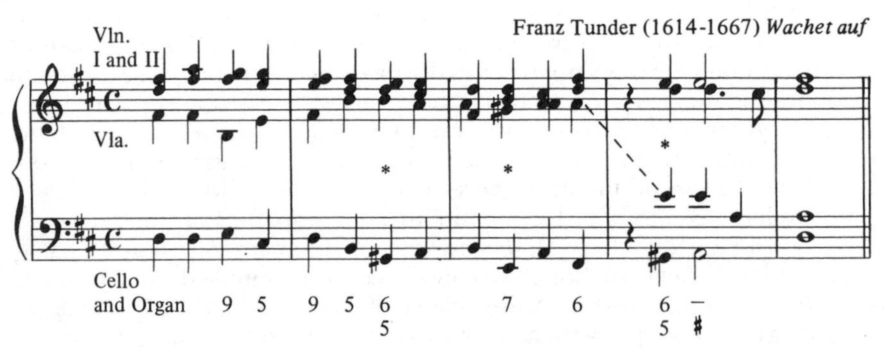

But in these four-note structures, the seventh still obeys the traditional laws of dissonance in that the seventh must be properly approached and resolved, a practice that remained standard for seventh chord usage through the late nineteenth century.

Terminology for Seventh Chords

A seventh chord, consisting of a triad plus the interval of a seventh above the root of the triad, may be built upon any scale degree. The harmonic analysis symbol for a seventh chord consists simply of the usual roman numeral for the triad with a superscript ^{7} added: V^7, ii^7, etc. A seventh chord may also be identified by the quality of its sound, describing first the quality of the triad (major, minor, diminished) and secondly the quality of the interval of the seventh, which, for purposes of this chapter, will always be a minor seventh. The chord types to be considered in this chapter are:

Major-Minor Seventh Chord: a *major* triad plus a *minor* seventh. For example, G B D F: G B D = major triad, G up to F = minor seventh; G B D F is a major-minor seventh chord, and in C major is V^7.

Minor-Minor Seventh Chord: a *minor* triad plus a *minor* seventh. For example, D F A C: D F A = minor triad, D up to C = minor seventh; D F A C is a minor-minor seventh chord. The abbreviated term *minor seventh chord* is commonly used. In C major, D F A C = ii^7.

Diminished-Minor Seventh Chord: a *diminished* triad plus a *minor* seventh. For example, D F A♭ C: D F A♭ = diminished triad, D up to C = minor seventh; D F A♭ C is a diminished minor seventh chord. The term *half diminished seventh chord* may be used, a term that differentiates this sound from the diminished-diminished (fully diminished) seventh chord (for example, D F A♭ C♭) to be studied in *Advanced Harmony*.

It is here that traditional roman numeral terminology is not consistent. The symbol ii^{07} refers to a fully diminished seventh chord—in C minor, D F A♭ C♭. The symbol $ii^{ø7}$ (slash through the ø refers to a half diminished seventh chord—in C minor, D F A♭ C.

Any seventh chord is commonly used with its root in the bass and in each of its three inversions. The list of figured bass symbols for these is illustrated in Figure 17.4 by the V^7 chord, but is applicable to any seventh chord.

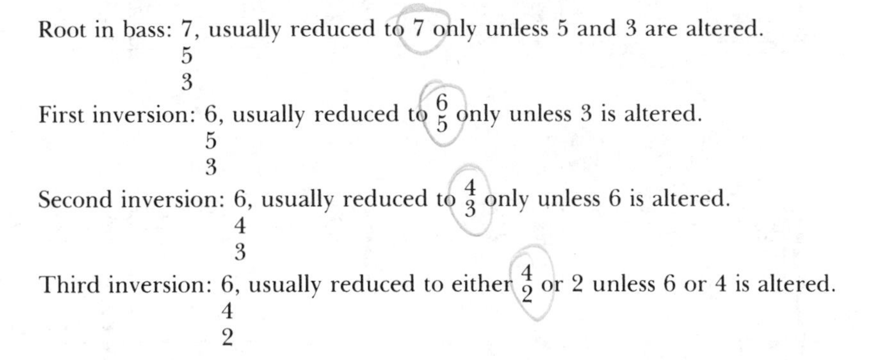

Root in bass: 7, 5, 3, usually reduced to 7 only unless 5 and 3 are altered.

First inversion: 6, 5, 3, usually reduced to $\frac{6}{5}$ only unless 3 is altered.

Second inversion: 6, 4, 3, usually reduced to $\frac{4}{3}$ only unless 6 is altered.

Third inversion: 6, 4, 2, usually reduced to either $\frac{4}{2}$ or 2 unless 6 or 4 is altered.

Fig. 17.4

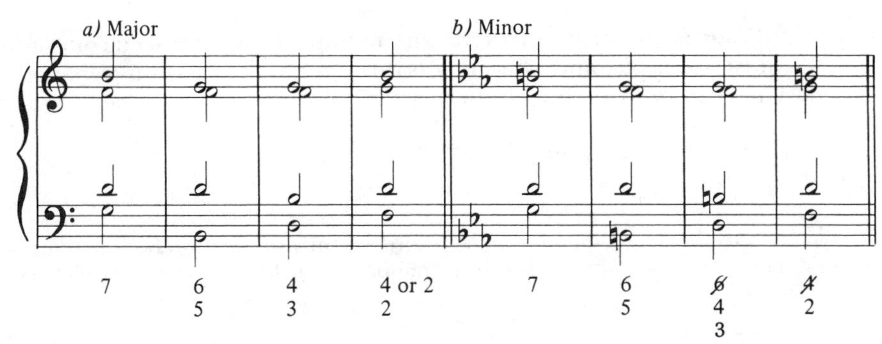

The Dominant Seventh Chord

The seventh chord built upon the dominant scale degree (V^7)[1] is by far the most commonly used of all the seventh chords, and is even more frequently used than the dominant triad. Dominant seventh chords have been common in this text, both in examples and in harmonic analysis, from the earliest chapters. As we complete our study of nonharmonic tones, it becomes possible for us to consider methods of writing this sonority.

The treatment of the seventh of the seventh chord has much in common with the treatment of the nonharmonic tone. Both are considered dissonant; both must be carefully approached and resolved. In actual seventh chord usage, the three-note figure, consisting of approach, dissonance, and resolution is similar to certain nonharmonic tone figures. In each case, the seventh resolves down by step. This principle applies not only to the V^7 chord, as shown in Figure 17.5, but to *all* other seventh chords as well.

Fig. 17.5

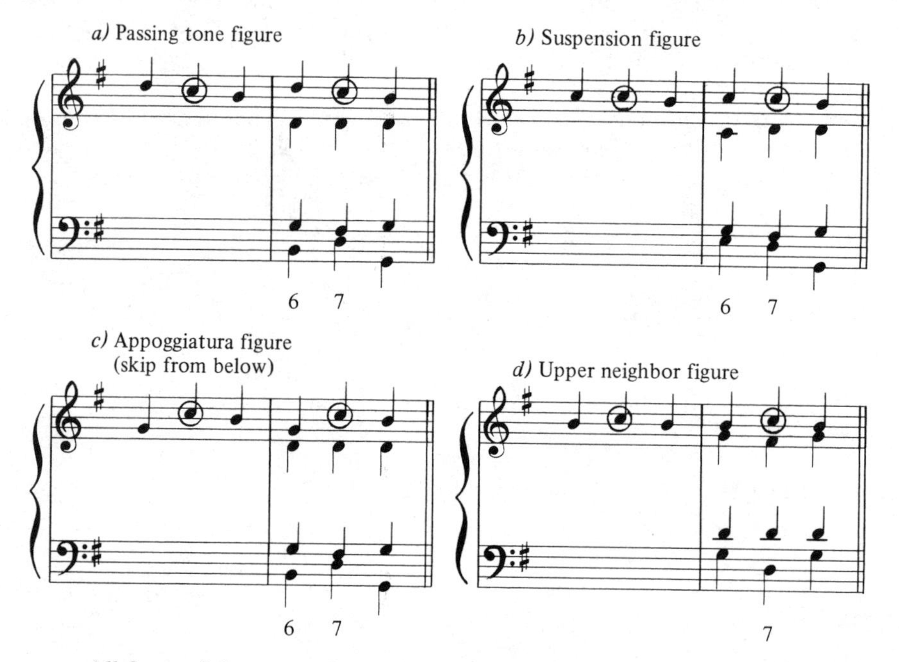

All four of the procedures shown in Figure 17.5 have been commonly used in the music examples and assignments throughout the preceding chapters of this text. They can be seen and studied at the following locations, among others:

Passing tone figure: Figures 4.8, 4.13, 9.16, 11.9

[1] V^7 refers to the major-minor seventh chord on the dominant in both major and minor keys. The v^7 (minor-minor seventh) in minor keys is little used except in harmonic sequence.

Suspension figure: Figures 3.15, 4.2, 11.7
Appoggiatura figure: Figures 3.13, 12.9; Assignment 8.4 (1), (4)
Upper neighbor figure: Figures 3.12a, 11.17.

In a chord progression, the choice of chords to precede and follow the seventh chord is limited only by the necessary approach and resolution of the dissonant seventh. Ordinarily in diatonic music, the V^7 is followed only by the tonic or the submediant.

The Supertonic Seventh Chord

The supertonic seventh chord, built on the second tone of the scale, is a minor seventh chord in a major key and a diminished minor seventh chord in a minor key. The supertonic seventh chord in minor with a raised fifth (raised sixth scale degree) is theoretically possible, but it is rarely used and will not be considered here.[2]

Fig. 17.6

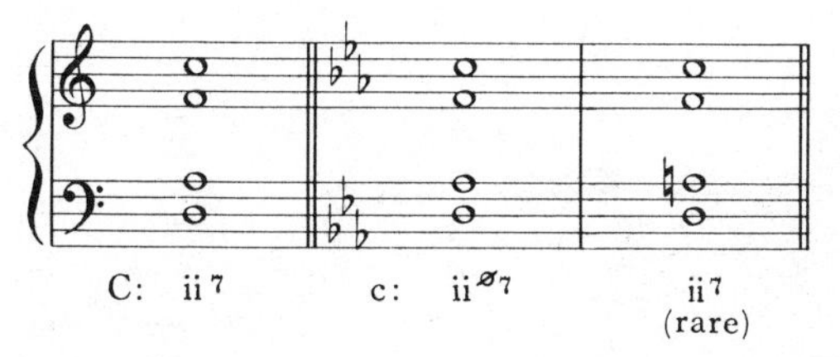

The approach to the seventh is almost always the suspension figure, simply because those chords most likely to precede the supertonic seventh, the tonic and submediant, already contain the tonic note (which, of course, is the seventh of the supertonic seventh).

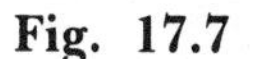

Fig. 17.7

Bach, *Herr Jesu Christ, höchstes gut* (#73)

[2]When the fifth of the chord (raised sixth scale degree) resolves upwards, and the seventh of the chord resolves downwards, both meet on the same note, resulting in a doubled leading tone.

Fig. 17.8

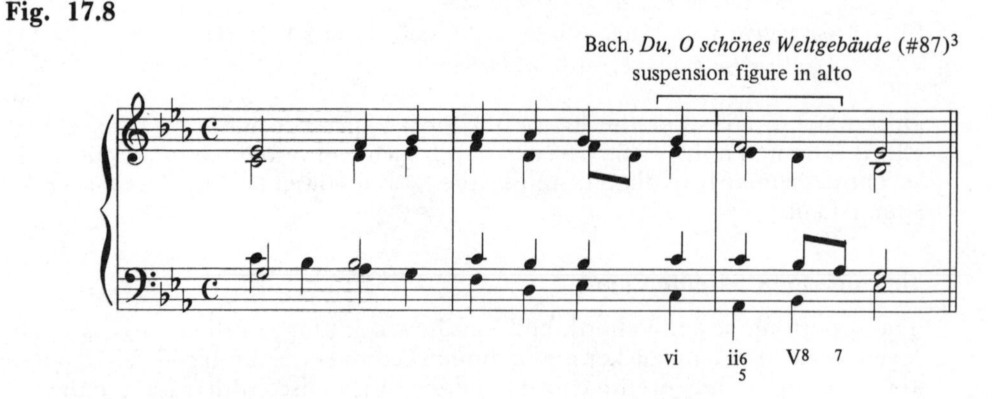

Although the supertonic seventh can appear with any one of its members in the bass, use of the chord is by far the most common in first inversion, as seen in the two preceding examples. As in the ii triad, the bass note of the first inversion is

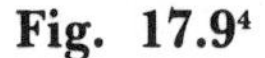

Fig. 17.9[4]

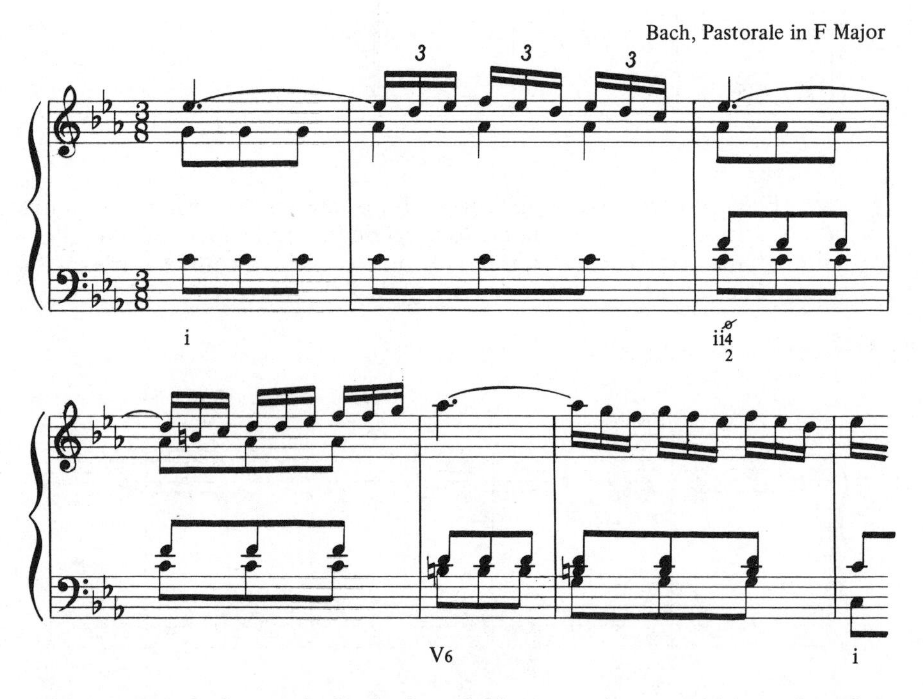

[3]The apparent six-four at the beginning of this excerpt is negated in actual performance by an instrument playing the bass line one octave lower.

[4]The A♭ in the melody in measures 4–5 is often considered the ninth of a G B D F A♭ chord. Since the A♭ resolves before a change of chord roots, we will consider it to be simply a nonharmonic tone above the G major triad, reserving the term "ninth chord" for one in which the ninth resolves with a change of harmony.

the fourth scale degree thus providing still another subdominant preparation to the dominant, and also, because of the dissonance it contains, a more satisfactory approach to the dominant than the triads IV (iv) or ii (ii°). The third inversion is particularly effective, as it can be produced merely by holding over the bass tone from the previous tonic and sounding the supertonic triad above it.

The supertonic seventh chord is also a part of the commonly used passing six-four progression, $IV_6–I_{\substack{6\\4}}–ii_{\substack{6\\5}}$ ($iv_6–i_{\substack{6\\4}}–ii^{ø}_{\substack{6\\5}}$).

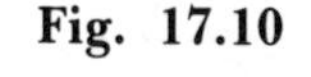

Fig. 17.10

Bach, *Du Friedefürst, Herr Jesu Christ* (#42)

Assignment 17.1. Spell the dominant seventh chord in each major and minor key. (This is a review of Assignment 4.2.)

Assignment 17.2. Spell the supertonic triad in each major and minor key.

Assignment 17.3. Harmonic analysis. Analyze these examples containing supertonic seventh chords.

D. Scarlatti, Sonata in E Major

Verdi, *Requiem*

(2)

Mozart, Sonata for Piano, K.310

(3) **Allegro maestoso**

Assignment 17.4. Harmonic analysis. Indicate chord numbers and nonharmonic tones from the following excerpts.

Beethoven, Sonata for Piano, No. 3 (Op. 2, No. 3), first movement, measures 5–8
Chopin, Mazurka No. 18 (Op. 30, No. 1), measures 5–8 (G minor)
Mendelssohn, *Songs Without Words*
No. 6 (Op. 19, No. 6), measures 28–29
No. 16 (Op. 38, No. 4), measures 4–5
No. 41 (Op. 85, No. 5), measures 6–9
No. 43 (Op. 102, No. 1), measures 25–26
Mozart, Sonata for Piano in D Major, K. 311, third movement, measures 23–26
Schumann, *Album for the Young,* Op. 68
No. 19, measures 17–20
No. 28, measures 1–4

Application

Written Materials

General Procedure for Writing Seventh Chords

In *all* seventh chords, the seventh, being a dissonance, must be treated carefully. Part-writing Rule 9 will suffice in most instances; certain exceptions to the usual resolution of the seventh will be noted as individual seventh chords are presented.

Part-Writing Rule 9. The seventh of a seventh chord, its note of approach, and its note of resolution comprise a three-note figure similar to certain nonharmonic tone figures: the passing tone figure, the suspension figure, the appoggiatura figure, and the upper neighboring figures. The resolution of the seventh is usually down by step.

Writing Seventh Chords, Root in Bass

The dominant seventh chord with its root in the bass may be found complete (all four chord tones present) or incomplete (fifth missing and root doubled). The complete V^7 is often followed by an incomplete tonic triad, the incomplete V^7 by a complete tonic triad.

Fig. 17.11 Incomplete V^7

Fig. 17.12 Complete V^7

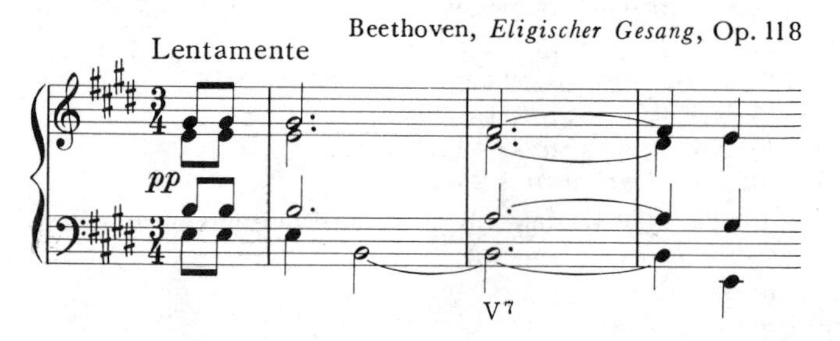

The infrequent supertonic seventh with root in bass is usually found with all four members present. When followed by V^7, the V^7 is usually incomplete, as in Figure 17.13.

Fig. 17.13

Writing Seventh Chords in Inversion

When writing any seventh chord in inversion, all four notes of the chord are usually present. The bass note should be approached by the same note, by step, or by leap from a direction opposite to its resolution. In the following figures, observe the approach and resolution both of the seventh of the chord and of the bass note.

Fig. 17.14

Hymn: Greenland

Fig. 17.15

Hymn: Dix

Assignment 17.5. Describe the approach to and the resolution from the seventh of each seventh chord in Figures 17.14 and 17.15.

Exceptional Practices

In common with any other theoretical device used in music composition, exceptions can be found in the use of the seventh chord. One such exception is unique with the V^7 chord, the *passing five four-three* (V^4_3). This chord is found between two positions of the tonic triad, similar to the passing V^6_4 (see Chapter 18). When used with an ascending bass line, the seventh of the V^7 ascends, as in Figure 17.16. The descending variety is seen in Figure 17.14.

Fig. 17.16

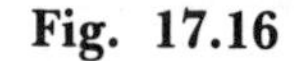

Hymn: Duke Street

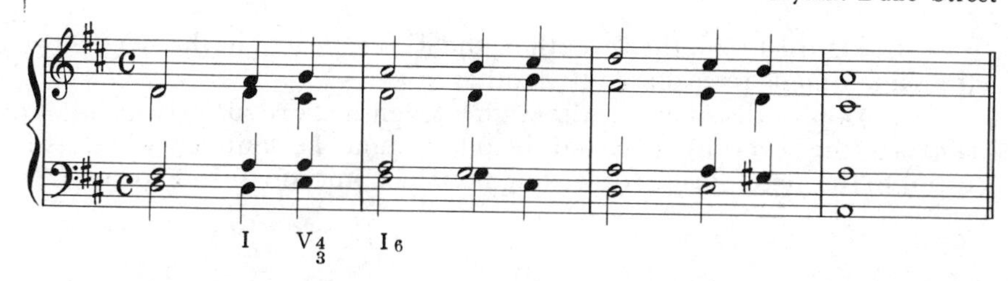

The descriptions of other exceptional practices that follow apply to both the dominant seventh and the supertonic seventh chords.

1. Transfer of seventh. The seventh chord may be repeated with the seventh occurring in a different voice part. The seventh in the last of such a series resolves normally. (See Fig. 17.17)

2. Irregular or ornamental resolutions. The seventh may be found ornamented, as in the ornamental resolution of the suspension (Figure 17.18). The resolution of the seventh may be delayed when it is held over into the next chord (Figure 17.19).

Fig. 17.17

Fig. 17.18

Fig. 17.19

In Figure 17.20, the seventh of the ii^7 is repeated in the next chord and at the same time is transferred to another voice.

3. Double dissonance. Although a seventh chord already includes one dissonance (the seventh), a second dissonance may be sounded when its use conforms to the general rule for writing nonharmonic tones. In Figure 17.21 the ac-

cented passing tone, D, temporarily replaces C♯ in the dominant seventh chord A C♯ E G. This figure also demonstrates the passing five four-three chord.

Fig. 17.20

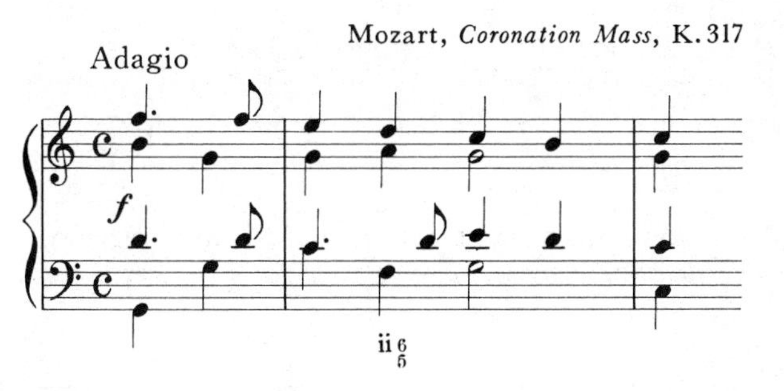

Fig. 17.21

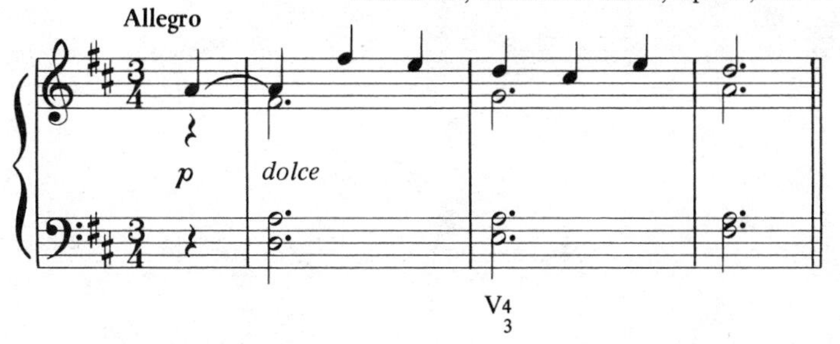

Assignment 17.6. Write dominant seventh chords with root in bass. Indicate below each example the nonharmonic tone usage represented by the seventh of the chord.

Assignment 17.7. Write dominant seventh chords in inversion. Indicate below each example the nonharmonic usage represented by the seventh of the chord.

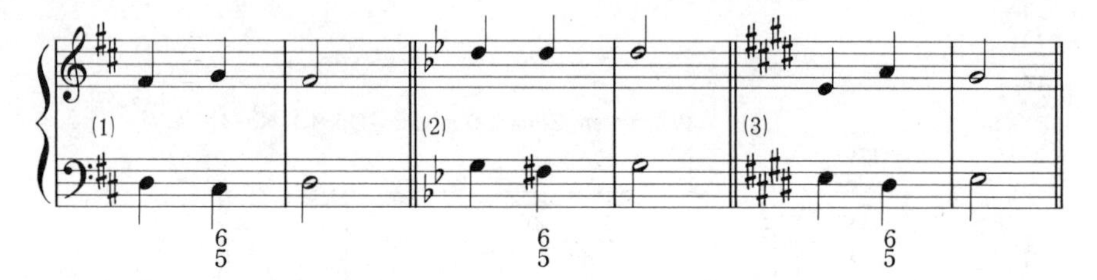

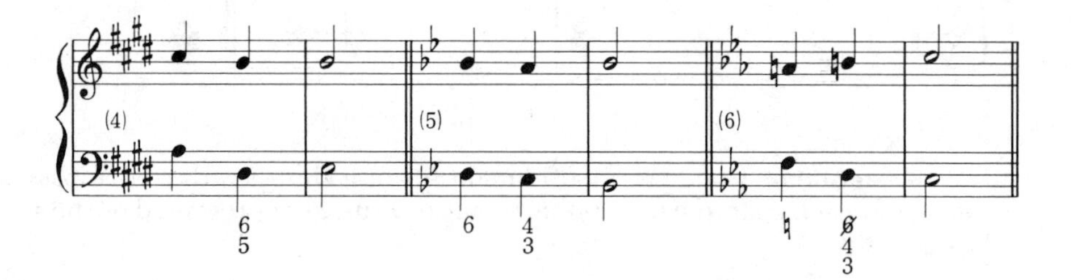

Assignment 17.8. Write examples of the supertonic seventh chord. Write an harmonic analysis below each exercise. Solve some of the exercises in open score.

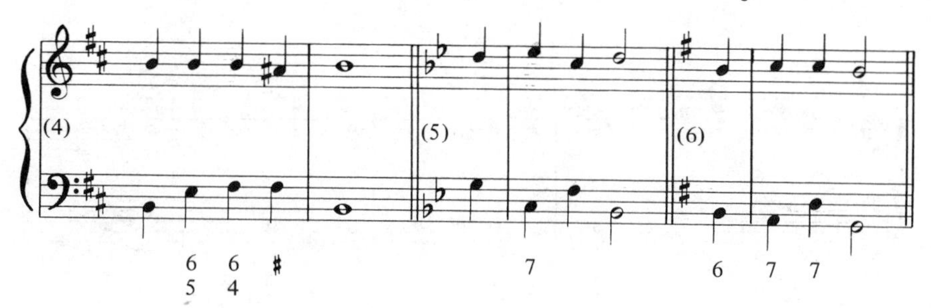

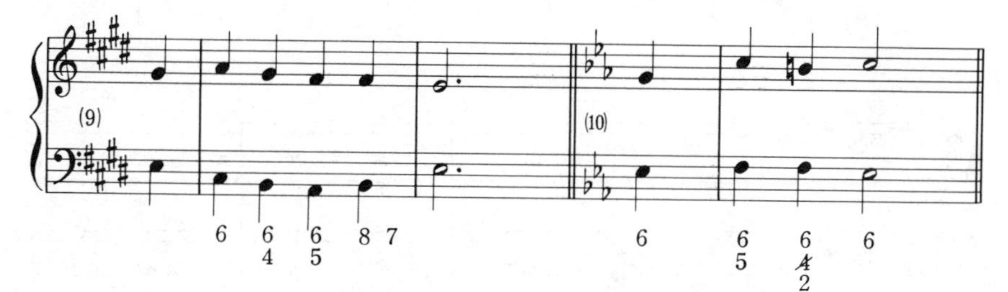

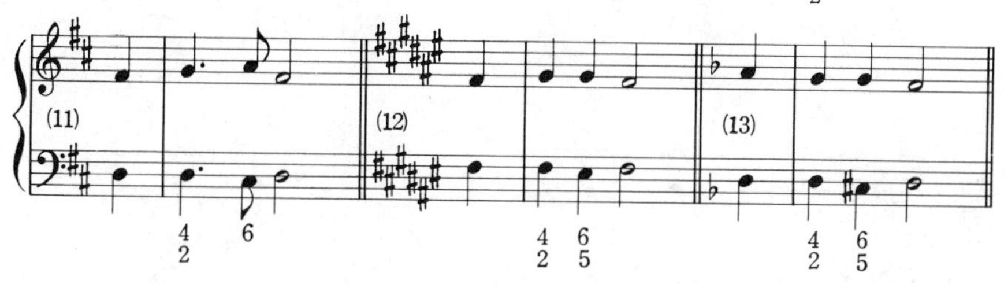

Assignment 17.9. Write extended exercises using both dominant seventh and supertonic seventh chords. Exercises 4 and 5 are unfigured. Supply a figured bass before adding alto and tenor voices. Make an harmonic analysis of all your work.

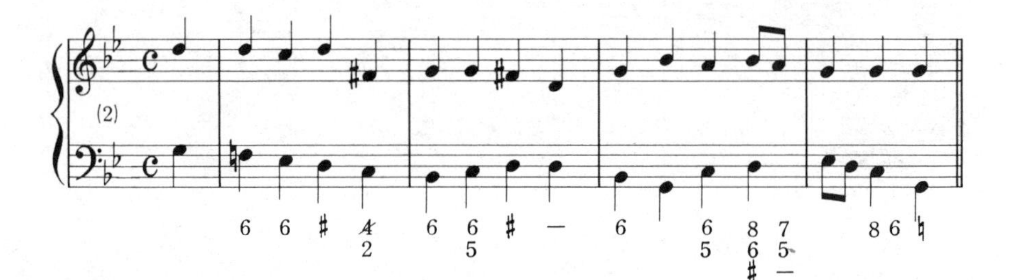

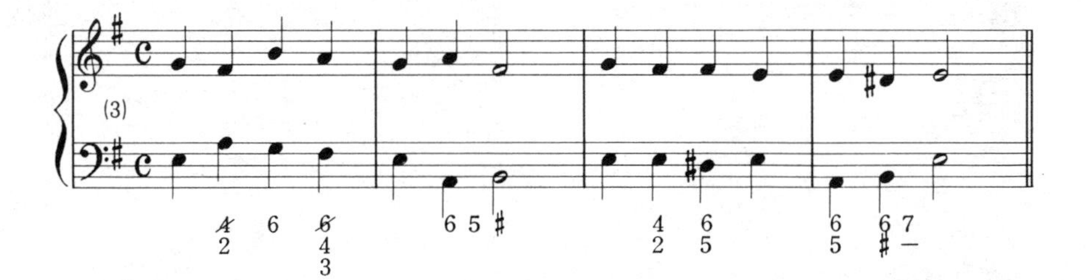

Assignment 17.10. Melody harmonization. Harmonize melodies using dominant seventh and supertonic seventh chords. Use nonharmonic tones where appropriate. Melodies from Assignment 16.11 may also be used at this time. Make an harmonic analysis of all your work.

Assignment 17.11. Write original exercises demonstrating various uses of the dominant seventh and supertonic seventh chords.

Ear Training

Exercise 17.1. Sing the progression I–ii^7–V–I in major keys and i–ii^{ø7}–V–i in minor keys, using letter names.

Exercise 17.2. Harmonic dictation will now include examples of dominant seventh and supertonic seventh chords.

Keyboard Harmony

Exercise 17.3. Play the following progressions in any major or minor key. Opening triad may be in any soprano position.

a) I–V^7–I
b) I–V^6_5–I
c) IV–V^4_2–I_6
d) I–V^4_3–I_6
e) vi–V^7–I
f) i–V^7–i
g) i–V^6_5–i
h) iv–V^4_2–i
i) i–V^4_3–I_6
j) VI–V^7–i (VI: third in soprano and doubled)

Exercise 17.4. Play the following progressions in any major or minor key. Opening triad may be in any soprano position.

a) I–ii^6_5–V–I
b) I–ii^4_3–V–I
c) I–ii^4_2–V^6_5–I
d) I–IV^6_4–I_6–ii^6_5–V–I
e) i–$ii^{ø6}_5$–V–i
f) i–$ii^{ø4}_3$–V–i
g) i–$ii^{ø4}_2$–V^6_5–i
h) i–iv^6_4–i_6–$ii^{ø6}_5$–V–i

Exercise 17.5. In many melodies, the final cadence may appear to be simply V–I, but can be harmonized alternately with ii^6_5–V–I or ii^{o6}_5–V–i.

Fig. 17.32

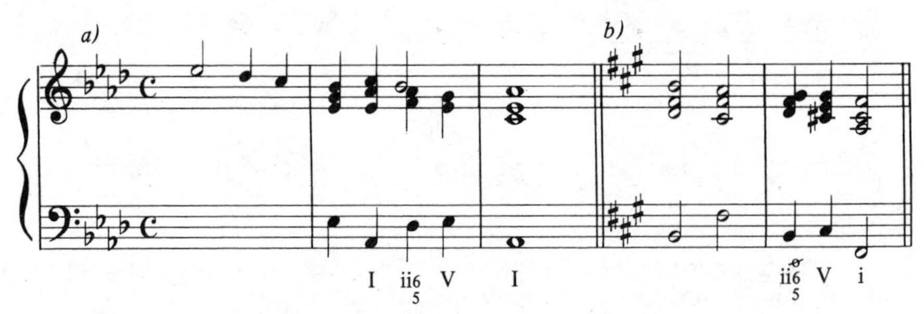

Harmonize these melodies from the sight singing texts, using a supertonic seventh chord at the cadence.

Music for Sight Singing: melodies 1, 30, 114, 134, 174, 212, 351, 367, and 373.

More Music for Sight Singing: melodies 266, 269, 295, 300, 301, 309, 311, 322, 330, 336, and 343.

CHAPTER 18

Secondary Dominant Chords; Elementary Modulation

Theory and Analysis

Extension of the Dominant Function

Right from the opening chapters of this study of harmony we have seen how the dominant-tonic (V–I) progression has been the goal for all diatonic movement, and that it is a sense of arriving at tonic through the dominant that imparts a sense of key to a succession of musical sounds. With such a principle so firmly established, it is little wonder that enterprising composers experimented very early with other chords, altering them to function as a dominant to the chords that follow them. In so doing, they established the sense of a new key, at least until the strength of the primary V–I brought the music back into its original tonality.

In the sixteenth century madrigal of Figure 18.1, note how each alteration of the melodic tone C to C♯ produces in its vertical structure a dominant pull to the following D major structure, thereby imbuing D with a temporary feeling of tonic. Each is brought back to the original tonic by a cadence in G, the final perfect authentic cadence dispelling any doubt about the location of the primary tonic.

Altering a vertical sonority other than the dominant to function temporarily as a dominant has been one of the most common processes since the seventeenth century. Simple versions of this process can clearly be seen in the folk song setting by Brahms shown as Figure 18.2.

All three examples in this song are dominants of the dominant, or as it is more simply expressed, "five of five," and symbolized as V/V. Observe the following features:

1. Measures 6–7: the bass ascends as a passing tone, altering A C E (ii) to A C♯ E (V/V). Use of the scale step number to designate the root can also be used; in this case, II = a major triad on the second scale step.

2. Measures 11–12: A C♯ E G (V^7/V) progressing to D F♯ A strongly suggests a V^7–I cadence in D until the C natural appears.

Fig. 18.1

[1]The article "Another Metrical Concept" in Chapter 6, contains an explanation of the changing meters of this composition. The original of this example was written on separate staves and without bar lines.

Fig. 18.2

German Folk Song, arr. Johannes Brahms

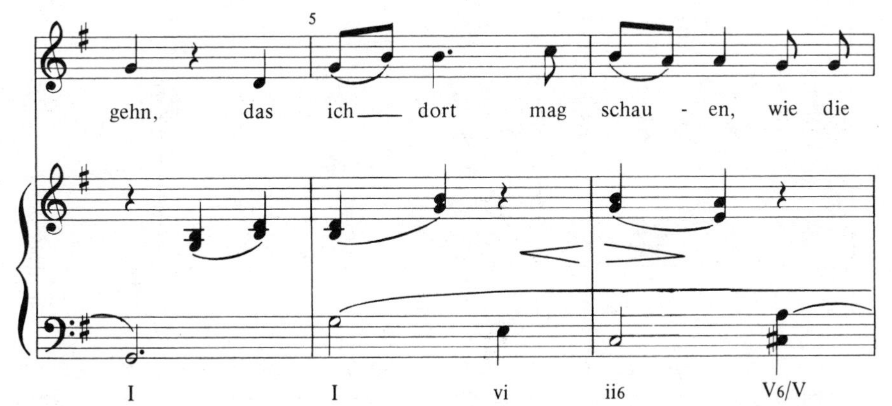

3. Measures 13–15 (a reharmonization of measures 1–3): the chromatic passing tones in the upper line of the piano score reach an F♯ as an accented passing tone at the moment the V^7/V occurs. This is accomplished in part by the *hemiola,* a metric device in which two groups of three beats (in this case, two measures of $\frac{3}{4}$) are performed as three groups of two beats each, as demonstrated in Figure 18.3a. Brahms has set this hemiola in the piano accompaniment against the regular $\frac{3}{4}$ meter in the melody line demonstrated in Figure 18.3b.

Fig. 18.3

a)

$\frac{3}{4}$ ♩ ♩ ♩ | ♩ ♩ ♩ | performed

I IV V/V

as though $\frac{3}{2}$ ♩ ♩ ♩ ♩ ♩ ♩ |

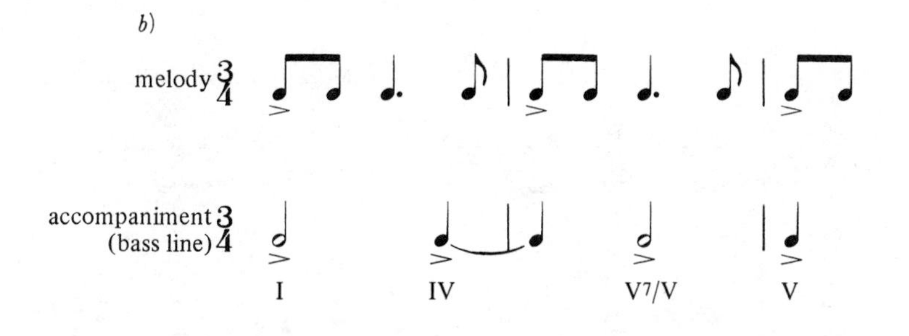

Secondary Dominant Chords

Any major or minor triad may be preceded by its secondary dominant triad or seventh chord. Since diminished and augmented triads cannot assume the function of tonic, they have no secondary dominants. Figure 18.4 shows each of the possible secondary dominant triads for diatonic triads in major and minor keys. Each can also be found as a seventh chord by adding a minor seventh above its root. In two cases the seventh will be a note not in the key signature: Major key, V^7/IV (C: C E G B♭): minor key, V^7/VI (c minor: E♭ G B♭ D♭).

Fig. 18.4

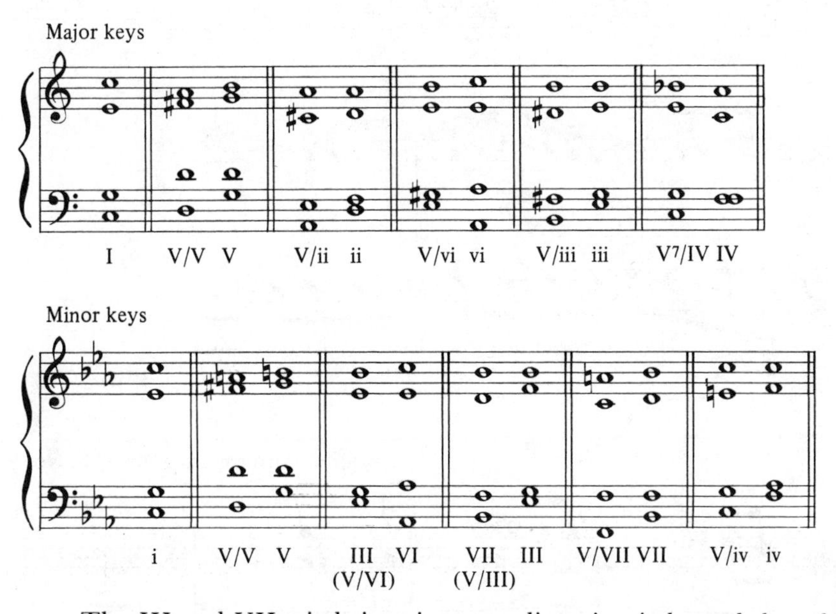

The III and VII triads in minor are diatonic triads, and though they can function as secondary dominant triads, they are often not designated by "V/" symbols. However, their seventh chords usually are designated V^7/VI and V^7/III.

The creation of a feeling of tonic in a chord by preceding it with its dominant is known as *tonicization*. Since this process is the same for all chords in Figure 18.4, a few representative examples will suffice to show typical usage of this process.

Fig. 18.5

Mozart, Sonata for Piano, K.281

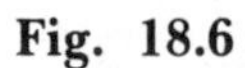
Fig. 18.6

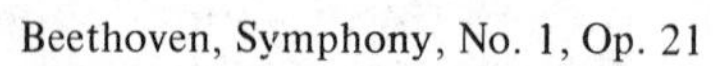
Beethoven, Symphony, No. 1, Op. 21

Fig. 18.7

Brahms, Intermezzo, Op. 116, No. 2

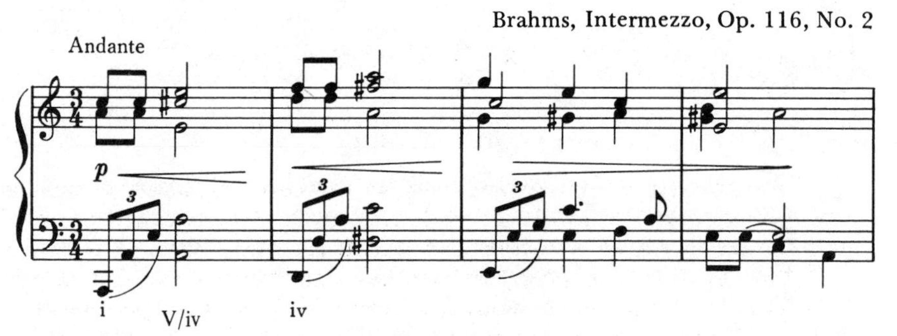

Fig. 18.8

Figure 18.5 opens the final movement with a secondary dominant, V/ii, although as far as we know it never caused the furor aroused by the opening of Beethoven's Symphony No. 1 (Figure 18.6), beginning as it does with a tonic seventh (V^7/IV) and first reaching a functioning tonic five measures later.

The Deceptive Progression

Like the deceptive progression V–vi, the root of the secondary dominant can move up stepwise in its own deceptive progression, as in Figure 18.9, where the root of V^7/vi moves up stepwise to IV. Were the root of the secondary dominant identified by its scale step number, the progression would be seen to be the common progression vi–III–iv.

Fig. 18.9

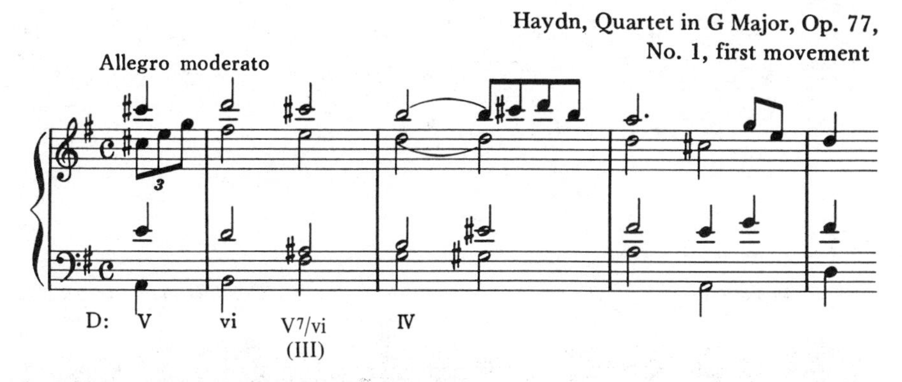

Interrupting the Common Progression

The secondary dominant is frequently found between two chords of a common progression, producing, in terms of root progressions, chord movements not listed in the Table of Commonly Used Progressions (Table 12.1). For example, IV–ii, interrupted by V/ii, becomes IV–V/ii–ii, which in root movements is IV–VI–ii, containing the uncommon progression IV–VI. This important exception to the list of common progressions can be used successfully in many situations, and many more will be added in our further study of chromatic harmony. This also applies to the use of the secondary dominant between two like chords, for example, V–V/V–V (root progression V–II–V).

Fig. 18.10

Fig. 18.11

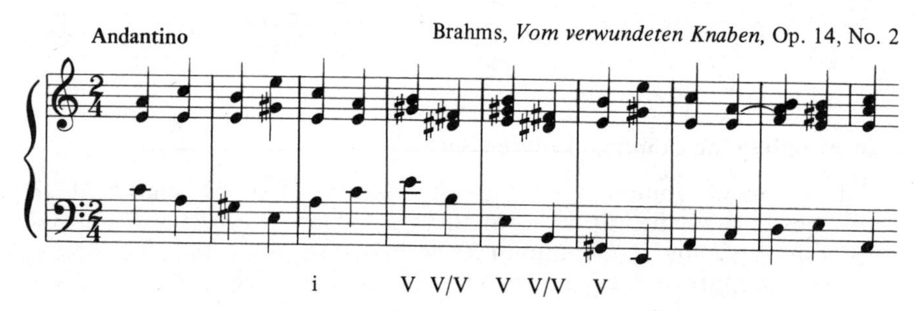

To extend this principle still further, we find two secondary dominants between the two diatonic triads. In Figure 18.12, the IV of measure 2 progresses to the V of measure 4, but preceding V is its secondary dominant V/V, in turn preceded by its secondary dominant, V/II, which adds up to IV–V/II–V/V–V. This V (first beat of measure 4) then proceeds to vi in the same manner, as shown. Using an "x" for a secondary dominant, the complete pattern can be shown as I-x-x-V-x-x-vi-ii-V-I or,

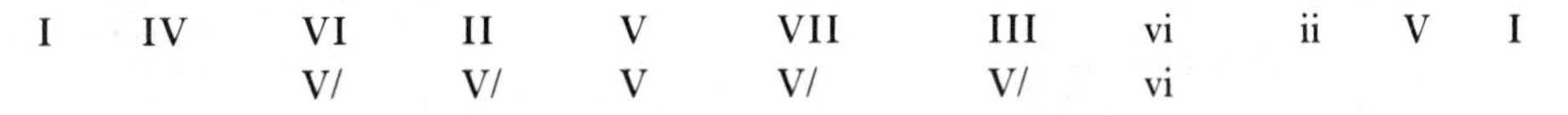

Fig. 18.12

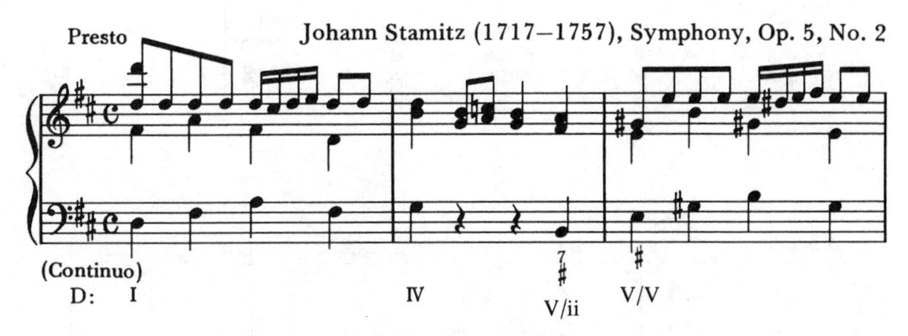

Secondary Dominant Chords in the Harmonic Sequence

The effectiveness of the familiar and much-used device of harmonic sequence is greatly enhanced through the additional possibilities for variety when using secondary dominant chords.

The common cycle of root movements by fifth could be expressed by an uninterrupted series of secondary dominant chords: I-IV-VII-III-VI-II-V-I (I-V of-V of-V of-V of-V of-V of-V-I). Although a series of such length is rare, the excerpt from Beethoven, Figure 18.13, shows such a series altered only by the absence of IV and the interpolation of vi after V/ii (E G B after E G♯ B).

Fig. 18.13

The V/V at the Cadence

In listening to the cadence at measure 12 in Figure 18.2, analyzed as V/V–V in G major, the possibility may have occurred to you that this could be a V–I cadence in D major. Listening again from measure 9, the sound of the harmonic progression could easily be heard as D: IV I_6 V^{4}_{3} V I. Should this be what you hear, you would say that there had been a *modulation* from G major to D major, the term *modulation* meaning the process of going from one key to another.

Listen to another example (Figure 18.14). Having started in A major, we arrive at a cadence in measure 8, this time preceded not only by its V, but by an even stronger I^{6}_{4}–V progression.

In both cases (Figures 18.2 and 18.14) we have arrived at a cadence with a harmonic analysis that could indicate possible arrival at a new key center. Whether or not these cadences are heard as a new tonic or as a dominant of the original key, the decision is strictly a subjective evaluation on the part of the listener. In Figure 18.2, most persons will experience no change of key, while in Figure 18.14, some will feel that the presence of the six-four helps establish E major,

Fig. 18.14

Beethoven, Symphony, No. 2, Op. 36

however temporarily. Only when it is certain that a new key center has been established is the process described as modulation. The mere presence of V/V–V at the cadence usually does not justify analysis of a new key, but the more harmonic activity there is that can be ascribed to a new key, the greater is the possibility that a new key has indeed been created.

The cadences we have just studied have been variously described by theoreticians, using terms such as "progressive cadences" or "transient modulations," indicating the degree of difficulty one has in evaluating them. In contrast, the next excerpt reaches the goal of the cadence on the dominant three successive times. Again you are asked to listen and determine for yourself: at the end of the excerpt, is the sound in the key of A major, or do those three cadences on A fail to pull away from a feeling for the key of D major? Here again, there will be no consensus, but the case for modulation, that is, for actually having reached the key of A major, is much stronger. (The analysis in Figure 18.15 assumes—for reasons that will be explained shortly—that a modulation has occurred.)

Fig. 18.15

Modulation

In the previous examples, the difficulty in determining whether or not a new key has been established stems primarily from the fact that the new key (or possible new key) is the dominant. Your work with dominant harmony has taught you to realize that the strength of the relationship of dominant to tonic makes it difficult for the dominant to establish itself as a key in its own right.

Arriving at cadences on pitch levels other than the dominant creates far fewer aural problems. In the next example, starting in F minor, we arrive in measure eight at a cadence in A♭ major. In listening, you will probably not feel the same urge to get back to tonic as you did when arriving on the dominant.

Effecting a modulation such as that shown in Figure 18.16 depends on the use of a *pivot chord,* sometimes called a *common chord,* which functions simultaneously in each of the two keys. It is usually located immediately *before* the first indication of V–I (or vii°–I, or $I_{\substack{6\\4}}$–V–I) in the new key, most often before the very first such chord, but sometimes earlier. In Figure 18.16 the first such indication is the E♭ chord of measure 6. It is preceded by the D♭ triad, which acts as IV in the new key of A♭ but at the same time functions as VI in the original key of F minor. Therefore, we have modulated from the original key of F minor to its relative key, A♭ major, through the pivot chord of D♭ F A♭, analyzed as VI = IV.

Fig. 18.16

Mozart, Sonata for Piano, K.330

To prove the location of the pivot chord, play up to and including the pivot without going further. At this point the music could still easily have continued in F minor. Figure 18.17 (not by Mozart!) starts at measure 5 and continues to a cadence in the original key.

Fig. 18.17

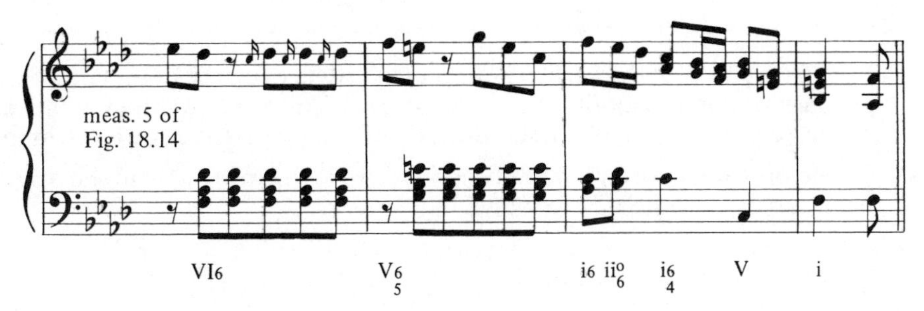

If you now play Mozart's original, beginning at measure 5, and relate this sound only to the cadence at the end of the phrase, there should be no doubt in your mind that D♭ F A♭ functions as IV in the new key.

Occasionally, a chord appearing earlier than that immediately preceding the new V–I will act as the pivot, or, each of two or more different chords immediately preceding the new V–I can assume the function of a pivot chord. In Figure 18.18, i = vi in measure 5 or iv = ii in measure 6 will serve equally as a pivot. Any choice of pivot is usually correct when the resulting harmonic progression in *both* keys is a common chord progression, as defined in Table 12.1. Measures 5 and 6 together produce in E minor the progression i–iv or in G major the progression vi–ii, both common progressions.

Fig. 18.18

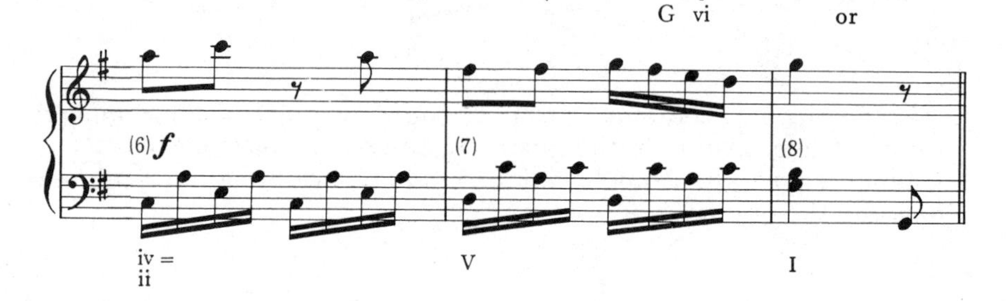

Going back to the earlier examples of cadences on the dominant, if you wish to consider these as modulations, the process is the same. In the Beethoven symphony (Figure 18.14), the first indication of A major is the I^6_4 cadence in measure 7. The previous chord pivots between the two keys, acting as vi in the original key of A and as ii in the new key of E.

Measures of Figure 18.14

	1	2	3	4	5	6	7	8	9
	A: I		I $IV_{6\atop 4}$	I	vi=				A: I
					E: ii		$I_{6\atop 4}$ V	I	

The two most commonly used modulations have been shown in previous examples: from a major key to its dominant and from a minor key to its mediant (relative major). In each case there is a choice of several pivot chords, determined by the fact that each can function simultaneously in both the old key and the new key.

For modulation from a major key to its dominant (examples in C):

C: I	= G: IV	(C E G)
iii	= vi	(E G B)
vi	= ii	(A C E)

For modulation from a minor key to its mediant (examples in C minor):

C: i	= E♭: vi	(C E♭ G)
III	= I	(E♭ G B♭)
iv	= ii	(F A♭ C)
VI	= IV	(A♭ C E♭)

Figure 18.19 shows the basic structure of each of these, each being preceded by I–IV–V–I in the original key.

Fig. 18.19

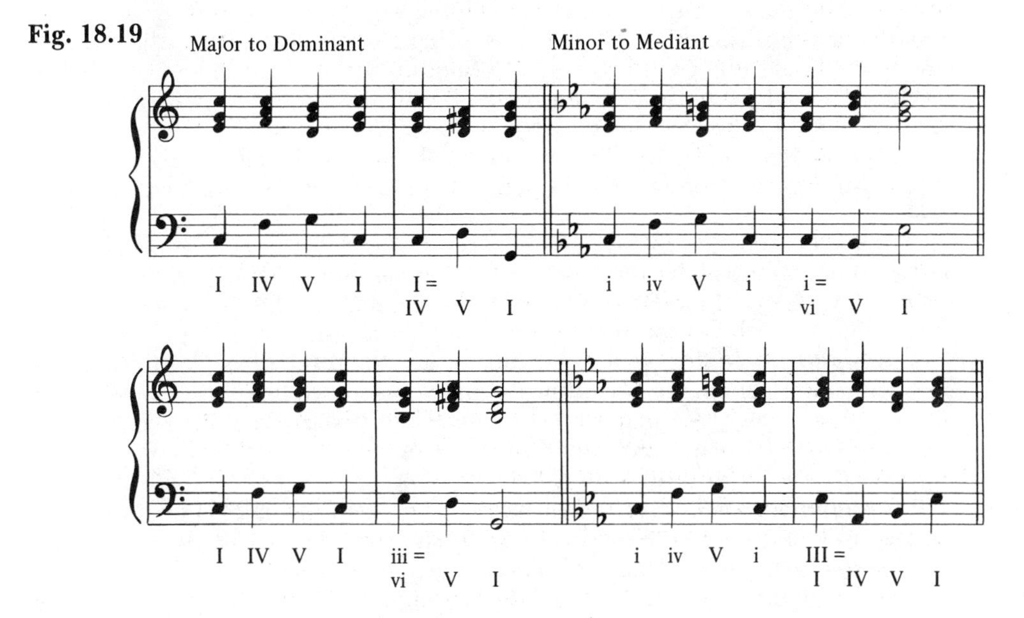

Return to the Original Tonic Key

Once a new key is achieved, there may be an immediate return to the old key—a very common occurrence—or the music may continue for a variable length of time in the new key or in other keys before making the return. For our purposes at present, we will consider only the *direct return* to the original key. After a modulation to a new key, return to the original tonic is accomplished simply by beginning the next phrase with I, V–I, or some other basic progression in the original key. In the final cadence of Figure 18.14 (modulation to the dominant), a minor seventh (D) is added to the E major triad, allowing the next phrase to begin with the tonic triad in the original key of A major.

Assignment 18.1. Spelling secondary dominant chords.

a) Spell each secondary triad listed in Figure 18.4 in each major and minor key.

b) Spell each secondary dominant seventh chord. Spell the triad as in *a* and add a minor seventh above the root to create a major minor seventh chord, e.g., G major: V/V = A C♯ E, V^7/V = A C♯ E G. Review the text preceding Figure 18.4 concerning sevenths whose spellings do not conform to the key signature.

Assignment 18.2. Spell in each major key the three pivot chords that can be used to modulate to the key of the dominant, as shown in Figure 18.19. Note: The dominant key of C♯ major is G♯ major (eight sharps), requiring an F𝄪. See the examples in C♯ major in Bach's *Well Tempered Clavier.* In some music compositions A♭ major is substituted for G♯ major.

Assignment 18.3. Spell in each minor key the four pivot chords that can be used to modulate to the mediant key, as shown in Figure 18.19.

Assignment 18.4. Harmonic analysis. Analyze each example for harmony and nonharmonic tones. Indicate any interruption of a common progression by a secondary dominant or the presence of a series of secondary dominants. Where the secondary dominant occurs at a cadence, defend a possible alternative analysis of modulation.

(5) Does this example begin on the tonic triad?

Bach, *Jesu leiden, pein und tod* (#83)

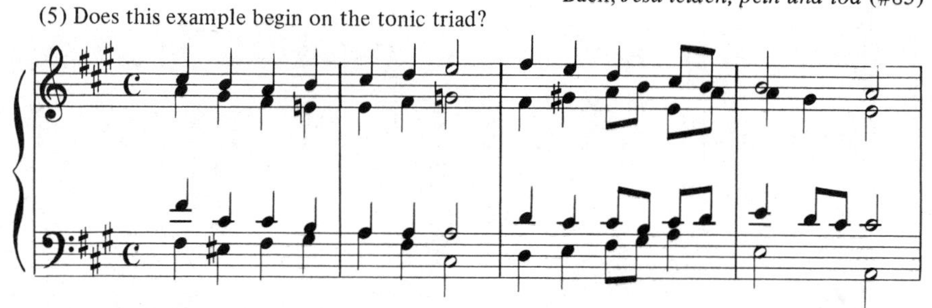

(6)

Bach, *Wo soll ich fliehen hin* (#281)

(7) Bach, *French Suite,* No. 2

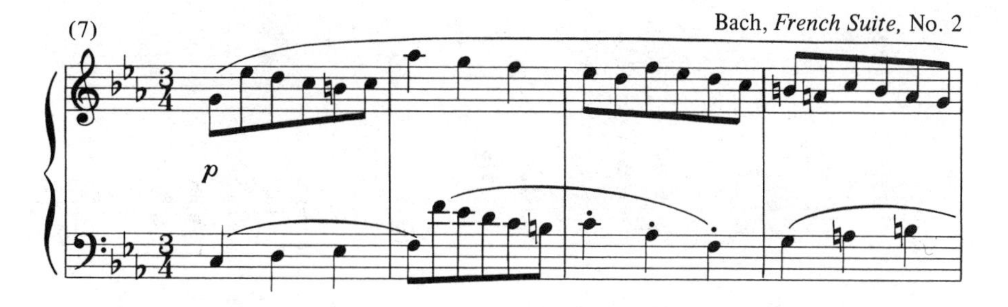

(8) Schubert, *Der Musensohn,* Op. 92, No. 1

Ziemlich Lebhaft

nach dem Mass be - we - get sich al - les an mir fort.

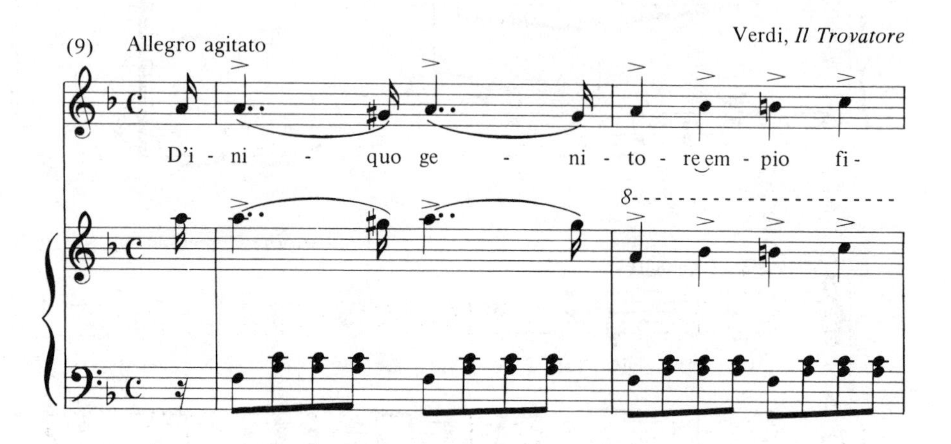
(9) Allegro agitato
Verdi, Il Trovatore
D'i - ni - quo ge - ni - to - re em - pio fi -
8-

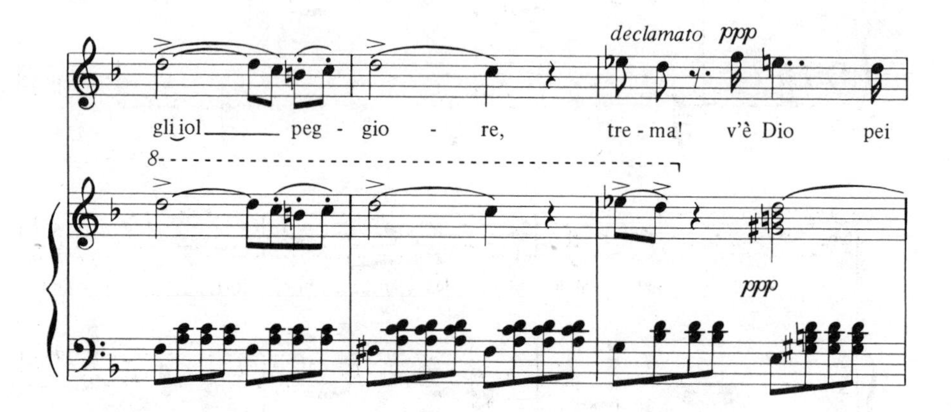
declamato ppp
gli iol peg - gio - re, tre - ma! v'è Dio pei
8-
ppp

Modulation in the Melodic Line

In a melody, a modulation becomes apparent when the implied harmony forms a cadence or a cadential progression in a new key. In Figure 18.20, measures 5 and 6, the melodic line C♯ D♯ E implies the chords IV–vii°–I, a cadential progression in the key of E major. This key is confirmed in the final cadence of the phrase.

Fig. 18.20

It is not always possible to depend upon the appearance of an accidental in the melodic line.

Fig. 18.21

Only the implied harmony here reveals the existence of the modulation. The new accidental (D♯ in this case) will appear in one of the lower voices when the harmony is written out in full.

In these short melodies, cadences on the dominant are most likely to be V/V–V. Considering them instead as short modulations provides good experience in studying the modulatory process.

Assignment 18.5. Analysis of modulation in melodic lines. Using Figures 18.20 and 18.21 as models, analyze these folk melodies. Additional material may be found in:

Music for Sight Singing: major keys, Chapter 10a; minor keys, melodies 288, 289, 290, 417, 418, 419, 422, and 429;

More Music for Sight Singing: melodies 625–630, 639–641, and 693–707

Application

Written Materials

Writing Secondary Dominant Chords

The secondary dominant contains a chromatically altered tone, an accidental not found in the key signature. Writing altered chords is covered by Part-Writing Rule 10.

Part-Writing Rule 10. Use of altered chords does not change usual part-writing procedures. Do not double any altered note unless it is the root of a chord. If unusual doubling occurs, follow Rule 6A.

The following are special considerations in writing secondary dominant chords:

1. In the secondary dominant, all members function as though the chord of resolution were actually the tonic of a key. Therefore, the third acts as a leading tone, and must be treated with the same care accorded to the actual leading tone of the key.

Fig. 18.22

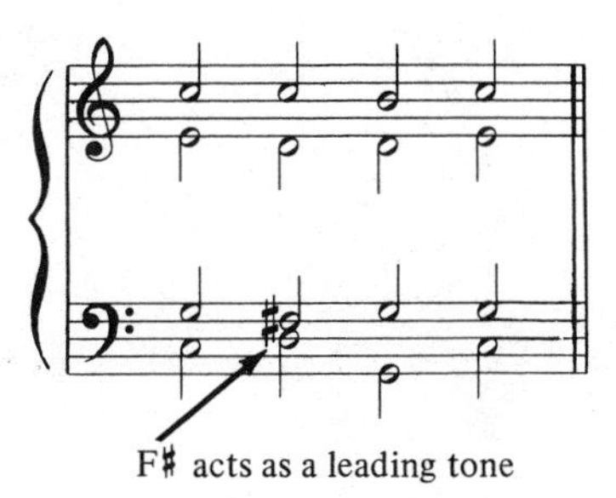

However, this secondary leading tone may descend in one particular instance: when it is followed in the same voice by a note of the same letter name but with a different chromatic sign. This will occur when the secondary dominant is followed by another major triad or major minor seventh chord whose root is a fifth below, for example, $V^7/V–V^7$,

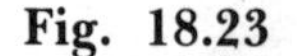
Fig. 18.23

Fig. 18.24

Mozart, Sonata in E♭ Major for Violin and Piano, K. 380, "Rondo"

Allegro

V6 5/V V4 2

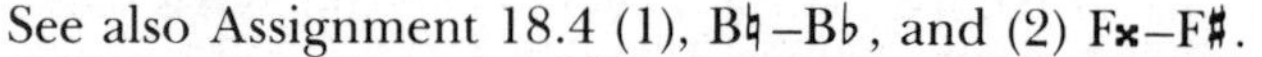
See also Assignment 18.4 (1), B♮–B♭, and (2) F𝄪–F♯.

2. In a minor key, the fifth of the V/V is the raised sixth scale step of the actual key, but in relation to its temporary tonic it actually functions as a second scale step, and therefore may descend.

Fig. 18.25

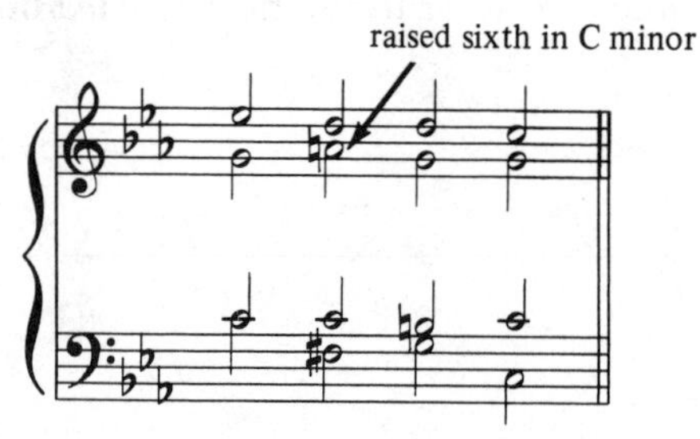

See also Assignment 18.4 (2), where in the key of C♯ minor, A♯ moves down to G♯.

3. The *cross-relation*. This occurs when a member of a chord is also found in the following chord, but in a different voice and with a different chromatic inflection. It is usually avoided because of its unpleasant sound.

Fig. 18.26

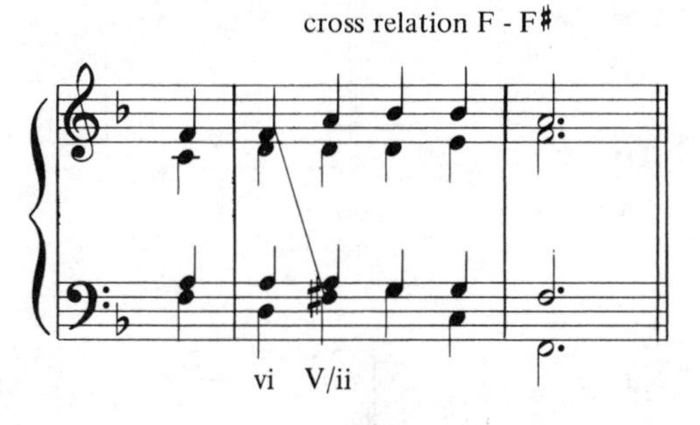

The cross-relation can be avoided by keeping the two notes in the same voice line. However, the undesirable effect of the cross relation can be eliminated simply by adding a seventh to the second of the two chords. Compare the following examples with Figure 18.26.

Fig. 18.27

Fig. 18.28

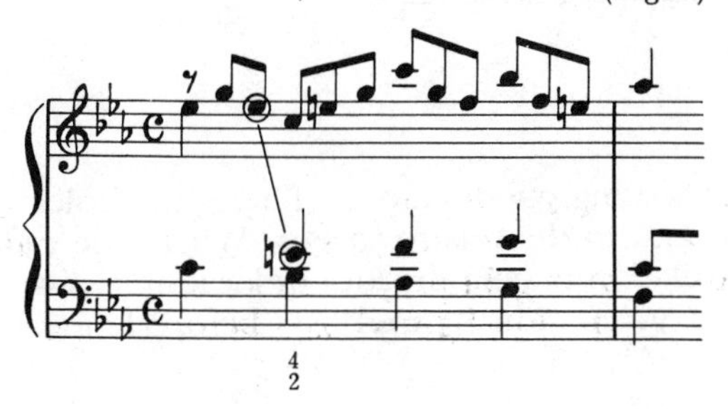

Assignment 18.6. Write examples of the V/V and V^7/V. The part-writing techniques involved can be applied to any secondary dominant triad or seventh chord.

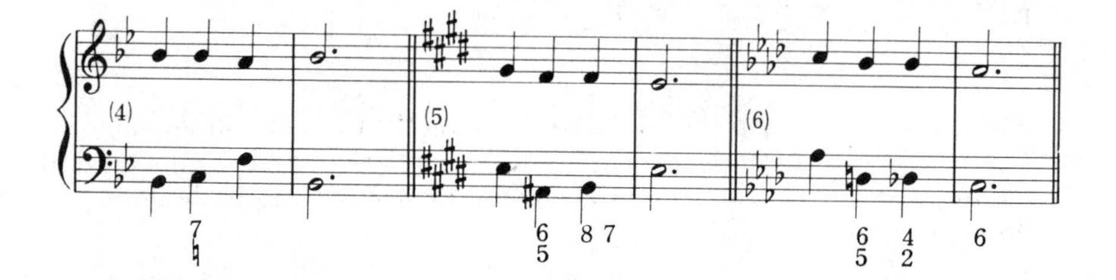

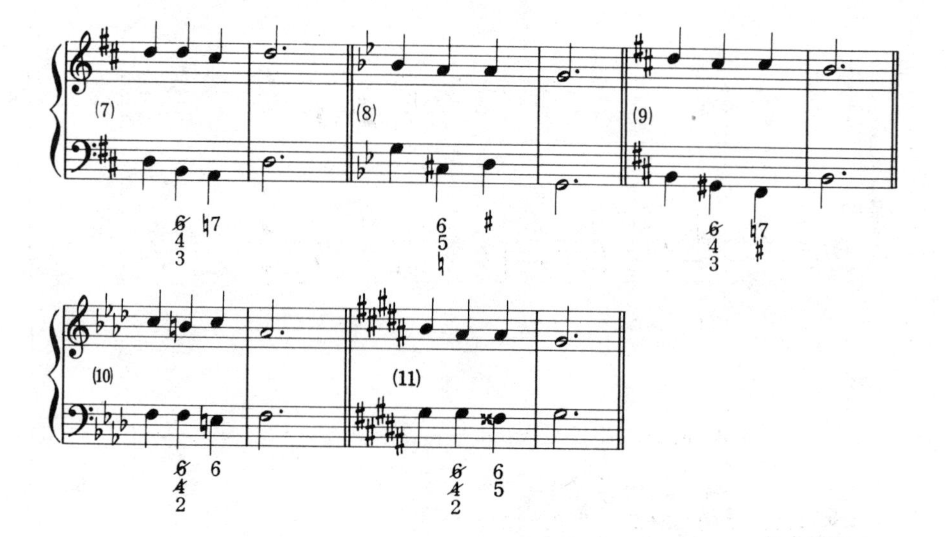

Assignment 18.7. Part-writing modulations. These examples contain modulations to the dominant and to the relative major. Where the cadence is V/V–V, analyze also as a modulation to gain practice in locating a pivot chord.

Where no figured bass is given, add figured bass before filling in inner voices.

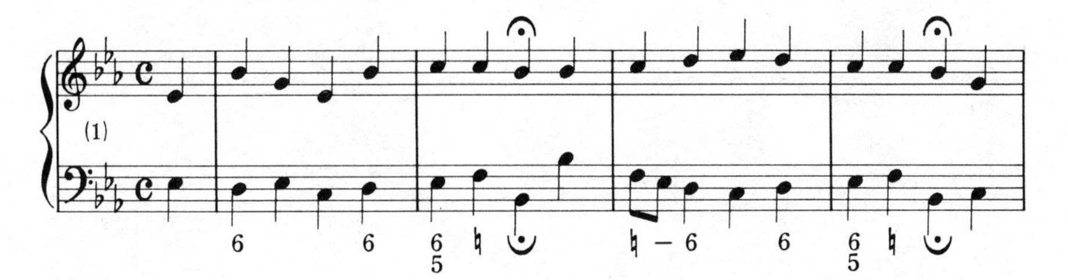
(1)

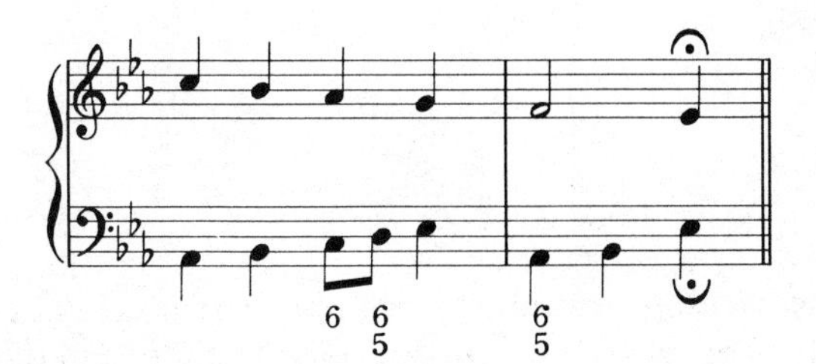

(2)

IV vi

(3)

Assignment 18.8. Part-writing secondary dominant harmony. These examples include a wide variety of secondary dominant usages other than the V/V.

Assignment 18.9. Harmonize these melodies: the first with a modulation to the dominant, and the second with a modulation to the relative major.

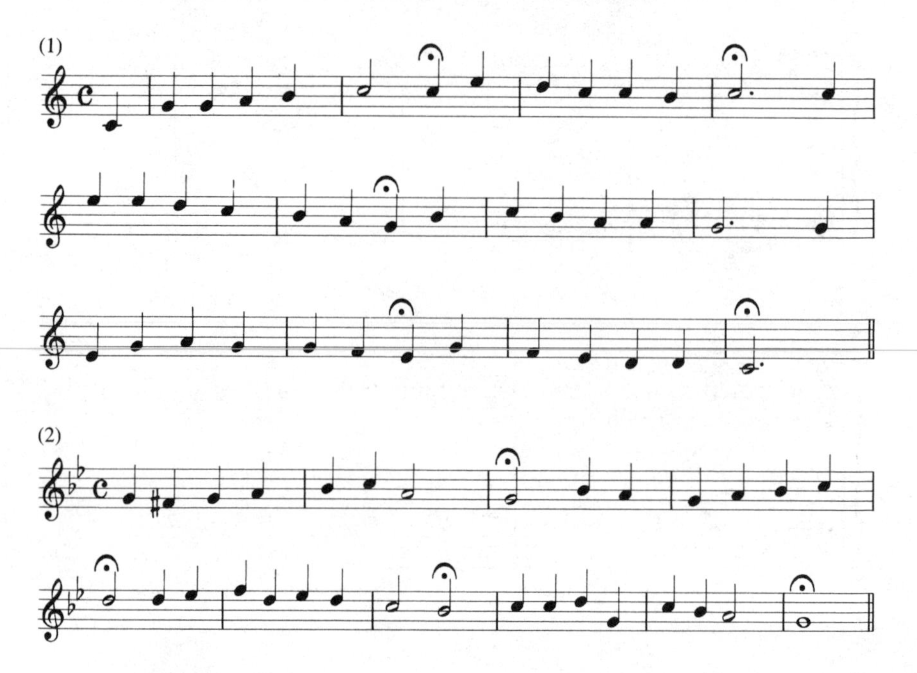

Assignment 18.10. Write, in four voices, chord progressions from Exercises 18.1 and 18.2 in keys as assigned. Use any appropriate inversions and nonharmonic tones. Also, devise other progressions using secondary dominant chords, borrowed chords, and triads not found in these exercises, as explained in Exercise 18.2.

Ear Training

Exercise 18.1. Sing each of the following progressions, using letter names, in any major key indicated by the instructor. Repeat each exercise, adding a seventh to each secondary dominant chord.

Some students may find it easier to locate the root of a secondary dominant chord by thinking in terms of the scale step number of its root. The left column uses V/ symbols and the right column uses scale step symbols.

In the right hand column, the symbol $\flat 7$ refers to the seventh of a chord requiring an accidental not in the key signature, for example, C major, I $\flat 7$ = C E G B♭.

1.	I V/V V I	I II V I
2.	I V/ii ii V I	I VI ii V I
3.	I V/ii V/V V I	I VI II V I
4.	I V/vi vi ii V I	I III vi ii V I
5.	I V/vi vi V/V V I	I III vi II V I
6.	I V/vi V/ii V/V V I	I III VI II V I
7.	I V/vi IV V I	I III IV V I
8.	I vi V/iii iii vi ii V I	I vi VII iii vi ii V I

9.	I vi V/iii iii V/ii ii V I	I vi VII iii VI ii V I
10.	I vi V/iii iii vi V/V V I	I vi VII iii vi II V I
11.	I IV V/iii V/vi V/ii V/V V I	I IV VII III VI II V I
12.	I IV V/iii iii V/ii ii V I	I IV VII iii VI ii V I
13.	I V^7/IV IV V I	I $I^{\flat 7}$ IV V I
14.	I IV V/ii ii V I	I IV VI ii V I
15.	I V^7/IV IV V/ii ii V I	I $I^{\flat 7}$ IV VI ii V I

There are many other possible combinations of secondary dominant chords and unaltered triads, which the student should devise.

Exercise 18.2. Sing each of these progressions using letter names, in any minor key indicated by the instructor.

1.	i V/V V i	i II V i
2.	i V^7/iv iv V i	i I^7 iv V i
3.	i VII III VI V/V V i	i VII III VI II V i
4.	i V/VII VII III iv V/V V i	i IV VII III iv II V i
5.	i V/V III iv V i	i II III iv V i
6.	i V/iv iv V i	i I iv V i
7.	i V VI V/V V i	i V VI II V i

Exercise 18.3. Harmonic dictation. Using the examples from Exercises 18.1 and 18.2, harmonic dictation will now include examples of secondary dominant harmonies.

Exercise 18.4. Sing with letter names the modulatory progressions from Figure 18.19, in keys indicated by the instructor. For example, sing a modulation to the dominant from E♭ major using the pivot vi = ii. Sing root names of triads only.

Fig. 18.29

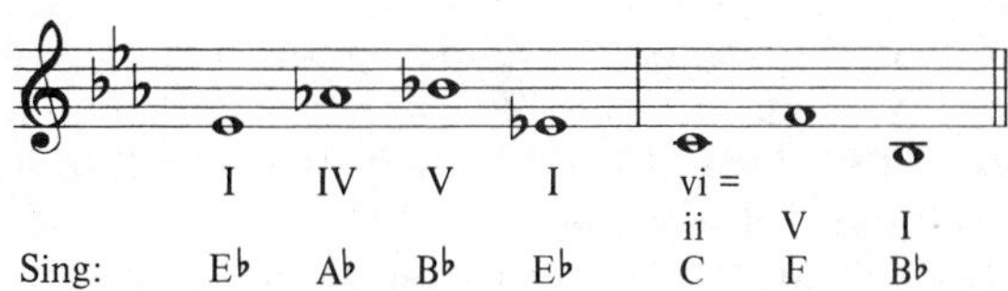

Exercise 18.5. Harmonic dictation. In taking harmonic dictation that includes modulation, it is usually not possible to hear the modulation until the pivot is passed. This is because the pivot chord functions in the old key; it sounds as a chord in the old key, and when the new key becomes apparent the pivot is no longer sounding. Follow these suggestions for listening to modulation, particularly when taking down chord numbers only (without staff notation).

a) Sing aloud or to yourself (as instructed) the tonic of the new key. Sing the tonic of the old key.

b) Compare the tonic of the new key with the tonic of the old key. The interval between the two tonic notes will indicate the location of the new key.

c) In subsequent hearings listen for a chord immediately preceding the first cadential progression in the new key—a chord that seems to function in both keys. This will be the pivot chord. For example, you have heard this phrase played:

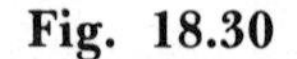

Fig. 18.30

Take down the chord numbers as usual, but when you hear a cadential progression (V–I, vii°–I) in a new key, place these numerals at a lower level, to indicate you have heard a new key:

i | i V i i_6 | V VI

vii$^{\circ}_{6}$ I | ii^{6}_{5} V I ||

Now listen for the chord just before the vii$^{\circ}_{6}$–I progression and relate it to the new tonic. It should sound like IV in the new key. Your complete solution, then, is

i | i V i i_6 | V VI =

IV vii$^{\circ}_{6}$ i | ii^{6}_{5} V I ||

Keyboard Harmony

Exercise 18.6. Play at the keyboard the chord progressions from Exercises 18.1 and 18.2, in keys indicated by the instructor.

Exercise 18.7. Play at the keyboard the modulation formulas shown in Figure 18.19, beginning in any major or minor key, as instructed. You may start any example with any soprano position of the initial tonic triad, then continue the formula using basic part-writing procedures.

Exercise 18.8. Melody harmonization at the keyboard. Secondary dominants may be used in a harmonization when the melody note is part of a secondary dominant chord and the melody note(s) following will allow a logical resolution of the secondary dominant as in these examples. These may be harmonized as follows:

Fig. 18.31

Fig. 18.32

Here are a few of the many available melodies for practice in discovering locations for secondary dominants or the two modulations studied in this chapter.

Music for Sight Singing: melodies 3, 19, 32, 33, 43, 44, 66, 68, 81, 109, 116, 196, and 261, and for modulation, Chapters 10 and 15.

More Music for Sight Singing: melodies 266, 267, 268, 269, 270, 275, 281, 282, 284, and 287, and for modulation, 693–710.

If preliminary experience in playing from lead sheet symbols is necessary, consult Mainous, *Melodies to Harmonize With,* Chapter L.

APPENDIX 1

The Essentials of Part-Writing

These essentials represent the basic procedures of part-writing. In no sense are they intended to include the countless variations in part-writing techniques that can and do exist. The reasons for the need and usefulness of this information is stated in the article "Rules? Why Rules?" found on page 97.

The Single Chord

Approximate Range of the Four Voices

Soprano:	d^1—g^2	Alto:	a—c^2
Tenor:	f—f^1	Bass:	F—c^1

Triad Position

In *open position,* the distance between the soprano and tenor is an octave or more. In *close position,* the distance between the soprano and tenor is less than an octave. The distance between adjacent voices normally does not exceed an octave, although more than an octave may appear between bass and tenor.

Usual Doubling

The tonic, subdominant, and dominant tones in a key can ordinarily be doubled freely. To go beyond this generalization, some common doubling procedures are listed here:

Diatonic Major and Minor Triads

1. Root in bass: Double the root.
2. First inversion: Double the soprano note.
3. Second inversion: Double the bass note.
4. Exception: Minor triads, root or third in bass. The third of a minor triad is often doubled, particularly when this third is the tonic, subdominant or dominant note of the key.

Diminished Triad (usually found in first inversion only): Double the third; when the fifth is in the soprano, the fifth is usually doubled.

Augmented Triad: Double the bass note.

Seventh Chord: Usually, all four voices are present. In the major-minor seventh chord, the root is often doubled and the fifth omitted.

Altered Triad: Same doubling as non-altered triads; avoid doubling the altered note unless that note is the root of a chord.

Chord Connection

The following are commonly used procedures, expressed as rules, for connecting any pair of chords. The page number reference locates the initial presentation of the procedure in the text, with its accompanying discussion, illustrations of its use, and writing assignments.

Triad Roots

When two successive triads have their roots in the bass, check the interval between these two roots, and then use one of the appropriate procedures listed below.

Rule 1 (p. 79). When roots in the bass are repeated, both triads may be written in the same position, or each may be in a different position. Triad position should be changed

a) when necessary to keep voices in correct pitch range;

b) when necessary to keep correct voice distribution (two roots, one third, and one fifth);

c) to avoid large leaps in an inner voice.

Rule 2. When roots in the bass are a fifth (fourth) apart;

2A (p. 82) retain the common tone: move the other voices stepwise;

2B (p. 83) move the three upper voices in similar motion to the nearest tones of the next triad;

2C (p. 84) move the third of the first triad up or down the interval of a fourth to the third of the second triad; hold the common tone and move the other voice by step;

2D (p. 85) at the cadence, the root of the final tonic triad may be tripled, omitting the fifth.

Rule 3 (p. 167). When roots in the bass are a second apart, the three upper voices move contrary to the bass.

Rule 4 . When roots in the bass are a third apart,

4A (p. 325) hold the two common tones; the other voice moves stepwise.

4B (p. 325) When the soprano moves by leap, the second triad may be in either close or open position, depending on vocal range and whether octaves and fifths have been avoided.

Rule 5 (p. 326). Exception to Rules 1–4: When it is impossible or undesirable to follow Rules 1–4, double the third in the *second* of the two triads; however, if this third is the leading tone or any altered tone, double the third in the *first* of the two triads.

Triads in Inversion

Rule 6. When in two successive triads one or both triads are in inversion, use the following procedures:

6A (p. 195) When one of the two triads is in inversion, first write to or from the doubled note of the triad in inversion, using oblique or contrary motion if possible, and then fill in the remaining voice.

6B (p. 196) When both triads are in inversion, each triad must have a different doubling to avoid parallel octaves, or the same doubling may appear in different pairs of voices. Avoid doubling the leading tone or any altered tone. Approach and leave each doubled tone using Rule 6A.

Position Changes

Rule 7 (p. 199). Triad position may be changed

a) at a repeated triad.

b) using Rule 2C.

c) at a triad in inversion or a triad with unusual doubling, following Rule 6A.

Nonharmonic Tones

Rule 8 (p. 283). A nonharmonic tone temporarily replaces a harmonic tone. Write the triad with normal doubling if possible and substitute the nonharmonic tone for one of the chord tones. Approach and leave the nonharmonic tone according to the definition of the nonharmonic tone being used.

Seventh Chords

Rule 9 (p. 395). The seventh of a seventh chord, its note of approach and its note of resolution comprise a three-note figure similar to certain nonharmonic tone figures: passing tone, suspension, appoggiatura, and upper neighbor. The seventh usually resolves down by step.

Altered Chords

Rule 10 (p. 427). Use of altered chords does not change part-writing procedure. Do not double altered note unless it is the root of the chord. Follow Rule 6A if unusual doubling occurs.

General Rule

Rule 11. In any part-writing situation observe the following:

a) Move each voice the shortest distance possible.

b) Move the soprano and bass in contrary or oblique motion if possible.

c) Avoid doubling the leading tone, any altered note, any nonharmonic tone, or the seventh of a seventh chord.

d) Avoid parallel fifths, parallel octaves, and the melodic interval of the augmented second.

APPENDIX 2

Instrumentation: Ranges, Clefs, Transposition

Range

The range given for each instrument is approximately that ordinarily used by the average player. Neither the lowest nor the highest note playable by the instrument is necessarily included. These ranges will be found satisfactory for purposes of this text.

Clef

Each instrument regularly uses the clef or clefs found in the musical illustrations under "Range." Exceptions or modifying statements are found under the heading "Clef."

Transposition

Unless otherwise indicated under this heading, pitches given under "Range" sound concert pitch when played. (Concert pitch: $A^1 = 440$ vibrations per second; the note A^1 on the piano keyboard is concert A). All transposing instruments sound their name when written C is played; for example, a clarinet in B♭ sounds B♭ when it plays a written C.

String Instruments

Violin

Viola

Clef. Alto clef is used almost exclusively. Treble clef is used occasionally for sustained high passages.

Violoncello ('Cello)

Clef. Bass clef is ordinarily used. Tenor clef is used for extended passages above small A. Treble clef is used for extreme upper range (not shown).

Double Bass (Bass Viol, Contrabass)

Transposition. Notes sound an octave lower than written.

Woodwind Instruments

Flute

Oboe

Clarinet: B♭ and A

Transposition.

1. Clarinet in B♭. Notes sound a major second lower than written. Use signature for the key a major second *above* concert pitch.

2. Clarinet in A. Notes sound a minor third lower than written. Use signature for the key a minor third above concert pitch.

Bassoon

Clef. Bass clef is ordinarily used. Tenor clef is used for upper range.

English Horn (Cor Anglais)

Transposition. Notes sound a perfect fifth lower than written. Use signature for the key a perfect fifth *above* concert pitch.

Horn (French Horn)

Clef. Treble clef is commonly used.

Transposition. Notes sound a perfect fifth lower than written. Key signatures are not ordinarily used. Write in all accidentals. In many published horn parts, notes written in the bass clef sound a perfect fourth higher than written. Consult with player of instrument before writing horn part in bass clef.

Horn parts are occasionally written in D, E♭, and E.

Saxophones: E♭ Alto, B♭ Tenor, and E♭ Baritone

Transposition.

1. E♭ Alto Saxophone. Notes sound a major sixth lower than written. Use signature for the key a major sixth *above* concert pitch.

2. B♭ Tenor Saxophone. Notes sound a major ninth (an octave plus a major second) lower than written. Use signature for the key a major second *above* concert pitch.

3. E♭ Baritone Saxophone. Notes sound an octave plus a major sixth lower than written. Use signature for the key a major sixth *above* concert pitch.

Brass Instruments

Trumpet or Cornet, B♭ and C

Transposition.

1. Trumpet or Cornet in B♭. Notes sound a major second lower than written. Use signature for the key a major second *above* concert pitch.

2. Trumpet or Cornet in C. Non-transposing—sounds as written.

Trombone

Clef. Both tenor and bass clefs are commonly used.

Tuba